THE FAITH ONCE DELIVERED

Ian Macpherson

THE FAITH ONCE DELIVERED

WORD PUBLISHING

Word (UK) Ltd
Milton Keynes, England

WORD AUSTRALIA
Heathmont, Victoria, Australia
SUNDAY SCHOOL CENTRE WHOLESALE
Salt River, South Africa
ALBY COMMERCIAL ENTERPRISES PTE LTD
Balmoral Road, Singapore
CONCORDE DISTRIBUTORS LTD
Havelock North, New Zealand
CROSS (HK) CO
Hong Kong

THE FAITH ONCE DELIVERED

ISBN 0-85009-141-1

Typesetting by Suripace Ltd, Milton Keynes.
Reproduced, printed and bound in Great Britain for Word (UK) Ltd by Cox and Wyman Ltd, Reading.

CONTENTS

THE FAITH ONCE DELIVERED

A Survey of Christian Doctrine

Ian Macpherson

Earnestly contend for the
faith once delivered
to the saints.
Jude 3

PREFACE

JUDE SAYS THE faith is for the saints. Some seem to think it is for scholars only. It is true that without the scholars, humanly speaking, we should not have had the faith. They have formulated, translated and transmitted to us the documents in which the faith has found historic expression. But the faith was not discovered or devised by the scholars. It was Divinely delivered to the saints. Out of that conviction this book was born.

1
THE FRIEND BEHIND PHENOMENA

The Christian Doctrine of God

In my reading of the old Greek writers, I see philosopher after philosopher falling into the unproven belief in the Friend behind phenomena.

Gilbert Murray

Is there a great Heart at the centre of the universe, or is there only a great hole?

Herbert H. Farmer

God is love. 1 John 1:8

God is Spirit. John 4:24

God is light. 1 John 1:5

God is fire. Hebrews 12:29

THERE IS A STOCK story of a student who went once to Benjamin Jowett, the famous Master of Balliol College,

Oxford, stating that he was deeply disturbed by religious doubt. "In fact," the student confided, "I regret to confess that I don't believe in God!" "You don't believe in God!" cried Jowett. "No," responded the student shamefacedly, hoping doubtless to receive from his superior some token of sympathy or at least of understanding. But no. The Master made no such gesture. On the contrary, he was furiously angry. "Believe in God by tomorrow morning," he thundered, "or leave the college!"

But *can* one thus believe in God to order? Is it possible to reach a living conviction of the reality of the Divine Being merely because one is commanded to do so? "Belief in God," wrote G.S. Lichenberg, "is as natural to a man as walking on two legs." That may be so; but, if it is, many today, like Mephibosheth, are lame on both feet. They find it very hard to accept the existence of a personal Deity.

In relation to this ultimate mystery human opinion organizes itself into five broad categories: (a) *Some believe that there is no God*; (b) *some believe that there are many gods*; (c) *some believe that it is not possible to know positively whether or not there is a God*; (d) *some believe in false gods*; (e) *some believe in the true and living God*.

Take them each in turn.

Some believe that there is no God.

They are what are called "atheists", and among them three broad types may plainly be distinguished.

One type consists of those whose atheism is naked and unashamed. To it belonged Ludwig Feuerbach, the German philosopher. He wrote: "It is clear as the sun that there is no God, and, still more, that there can be no God." Closer to our own time, Bertrand Russell subscribed to the same view, contemptuously dismissing the whole subject of theology as "Precopernican". And Julian Huxley went the length of saying: "God is no longer a useful hypothesis. A faint trace of God still broods over the world like the smile of a Cheshire cat, but psychological science will rub even that from the universe. It will soon be as impossible for an intelligent man or woman to believe in a God as it now is that the earth is flat."

Nor is this blatant atheism confined to the intelligentsia. It has filtered down into simpler minds. In his book *Peace with God* Billy Graham relates: "Two years ago a newspaper columnist died in Denver, Colorado. The mourners listened to his recorded voice at the funeral, when he said: 'This is my funeral. I am an atheist and have been for many years. I have the utmost contempt for theological nonsense. Clergymen are cowards; miracles are the product of the imagination. If any four reporters were sent to an execution and got their facts as twisted as the apostles in the Bible report, they would be fired forthwith. I want no religious songs. This is going to be a perfectly rational funeral" (*op.cit.*, New York: Doubleday & Co., Inc, 1953, p.59). Patently, for the deceased, in death as in life the Deity seemed to have no reality at all.

One finds the same sort of attitude in the fatuous observation attributed to Titov, the Russian cosmonaut, just after his historic flight into outer space: "I didn't see God up there" – a remark reminiscent of the reply of La Place, the French astronomer, to Napoleon's inquiry as to where God fitted into his scheme of things: "Sire, I had no need for that hypothesis." Both observations recall Samuel Taylor Coleridge's characterization of atheism:

an owl that,
Sailing with obscene wings across the noon,
Drops his blue-fringéd lids, and shuts them close
And hooting at the glorious sun in heaven,
Cries out: "Where is it?"

The second type of atheism is comprised of those who,

for reasons of their own, would dearly like to believe that there is no God, but are somehow haunted by the feeling that there may be a God after all. To this class belonged Edward Clodd. Of him H.G. Wells declared: "Devout atheist though he was, he looked nervously under his bed every night to make sure the Deity wasn't there, and slept with a pistol under his pillow for fear of a revelation." Yet proverbially "there are no atheists in a shipwreck", and deep in the heart of every human being, however loud his protestations to the contrary, there is an innate sense of the reality of the Divine. Says Jean Paul Sartre: "That God does not exist, I cannot deny: that my whole being cries out for God, I cannot forget." "Did I not believe," said a great man once, "that an Intelligence is at the heart of things, my life would be intolerable." Man is indigenously religious.

The third type of atheist is of a very different *genre*. He is the sort of person who would give his right hand to be able to believe there is a God; but who, after patiently sifting the evidence, has arrived at the bleak and comfortless conclusion that there are not sufficient grounds for so doing. Those in this position are not far from the Kingdom of God and are more to be pitied than blamed. Inexpressibly poignant are some of their personal confessions. George Romanes having, as he thought, disproved God's existence, had the honesty and candour to admit that, with this putative negation of God, the universe had for him lost its soul of loveliness. To the same effect was the admission of W.H. Clifford, as he spoke of his emotions on taking a final farewell of his heavenly Father: "We have seen the spring sun shine out of an empty heaven to light a soul-less earth. We have felt with utter loneliness that the Great Companion is dead." Wistful and unwilling atheism of that kind is, as I say, almost bound to be transitory and transitional. For such a person the clouds of uncertainty and dubiety are practically sure to be dissipated and to disperse, letting the sun of faith shine through.

Once only in the Greek New Testament does the term from which our word "atheist" is derived occur. It is in Ephesians 2:12, where Paul, writing of the pagans, observes that they are "without God *(atheoi)* in the world." In the Old Testament, however, there are several references to those who professed themselves unable to accept the fact of the Deity. Thus a sentence in Psalm 10:3 reads: "God is not in all his thoughts". Here the marginal rendering is most striking: "All his thoughts are 'There is no God'". Again, in Psalm 14:1 we find: "The fool hath said in his heart, There is no God" – on which an old Welsh preacher acutely commented that the text reads "The fool hath said in his heart", not that "the heart has said in the fool".

Surely the Scriptures are justified in so describing the atheist, since dogmatically to declare that the Deity does not exist demands that one should first have scoured the universe in quest of Him and failed to find Him. After all there is always the chance that God might be in some corner of the cosmos which the atheist hasn't explored. As John Foster observes: "Before any man can deny the existence of God he must have been everywhere, for in the place where he has not been God may dwell." Hence, nobody but God, who alone possesses omnipresence and omniscience, is in a position to pontificate on the matter, and He is hardly likely to deny His own existence! Moreover, as Harry Dean cogently contends, "if there is no purpose in life, there is no purpose that created the atheist's mind. Why, then, does he trust his own reason?"

Today, more than ever before, atheism has become organized and militant. In former times, it was largely philosophical: now it is aggressively political. What we are currently confronted with is not just academic, theoretical atheism, but rampant, practical atheists, shaking their feeble fists in the face of heaven. Of Julian the Apostate it is told that he hated God so bitterly that once he flung a naked dagger, point upwards, into the air, as if to stab God to death with a steel blade! He was typical of many in the modern world. Karl Marx in his famous *Manifesto* wrote: "I hate all gods. We make war against all prevailing ideas of religion and the State, of country, of patriotism. The idea of God is the keystone of a perverted civilization, which must be destroyed. The root of liberty, of equality, of culture is atheism." Following him, on the eve of the Russian revolution, Lenin said: "Every idea of God is unutterable vileness of the most dangerous kind, contagion of the most abominable sort." Not long afterwards, Lunararski, a Soviet commissar, was to exclaim: "We have done with the kings of the earth: now let us deal with the King of the sky."

At the opposite pole of speculative thinking, there were, not long ago, theologians, belonging to the notorious "Death of God" School, who were, to all intents and purposes, atheistic. They maintained that God was dead. In his best-selling book *Honest to God* John Robinson went the length of saying: "I can at least understand what those mean who urge that we should do well to give up using the word 'God' for a generation, so impregnated has it become with a way of thinking we have had to discard if the Gospel is to signify anything." Dietrich Bonhoeffer told us we must learn to live as if God did not exist. Recently a religious book was issued representing this school of thought, for which the publishers made what might well be judged a unique claim. In the blurb on the dust-jacket they actually intimated that the volume is ahead of all previous literature on the subject inasmuch as God is not named anywhere save in the title.

One way and another, therefore, W.R. Matthews does not exaggerate when, in his *Essays in Reconstruction*, he affirms: "We strive not against academic atheism or agnosticism, but against the spiritual energy which denies God with the fervour of a fanaticism."

Some believe that there are many gods.

They are known as *polytheists*. Primitive man saw gods everywhere. His religion was animistic, and he personalized and deified almost all the objects which he discovered around him. Wellnigh from start to finish, the Old Testament is a record of a conflict between God and the gods. Again and again, the primacy and ascendancy of the God of Israel is triumphantly proclaimed. To Him several times is given the title "God of gods". (Deuteronomy 10:17; Joshua 22:22; Psalm 136:2). But the gods are always in the background. Not otherwise is it in many parts of the world even today. Still "the heathen in his blindness bows down to wood and stone". Grotesque images in ancient shrines or crude fetishes in private dwellings are objects of worship for countless unenlightened multitudes. There are even yet, as Paul said of his own day, "gods many and lords many" (1 Corinthians 8:5).

Nor must we contemplate such pathetic pagan piety with contempt and disdain. For, as Alexander Mackenzie justly argues, there are worse things than superstition. To see gods everywhere is better than to see God nowhere. Polytheism is preferable to atheism. A simple savage kneeling before a heathen deity is in a way on a higher moral level than a proud, rationalistic professor who bows to nobody or nothing but Himself.

Some believe that it is not possible to know positively whether or not there is a God.

They are what are known as "agnostics". It is one of the ironies of Christian history that, while the Early Church was pestered by people calling themselves "Gnostics", that is, those who are, as we should say, "in the know", the modern Church is plagued by "Agnostics", people who profess *not* to know. The word "agnostic" was coined by T.H. Huxley to define his own intellectual position on such questions, and apparently the expression has come to stay, as a term descriptive of the mental mood of many modern men and women.

On one occasion Bertrand Russell, perhaps the most celebrated agnostic of our time, was arrested because of taking part in a public demonstration in favour of Nuclear Disarmament. At the prison-gate he had to give some account of himself to a warder. The warder asked him what was his religion. Russell answered "Agnostic". The prison-officer hadn't heard the word before. With a smile, he observed: "Ah, well, there are many religions, but I suppose that they all worship the same God!" What the prison-officer failed to realize was that the term "agnostic" is simply a confession of ignorance as to whether there is a God or not.

Nevertheless, there are many self-styled agnostics nowadays who repeat in their own lives the inconsistency of the Athenians of whom we read in Acts 17:22 – worshippers who had erected an altar inscribed TO THE UNKNOWN GOD. One of these was Sir William Watson, the noted Yorkshire poet, who penned these lonely lines:

The God on whom I never gaze,
The God I never once behold:
Beneath the clouds, above the clods –
The Unknown God, the Unknown God.

Ancient philosopher and present-day poet alike bowed before that anonymous Divinity.

What, then, is the Christian answer to the agnostic? In what way can we confute his contention that it is not possible to know whether or not there is a Divine Being?

Well, we can begin by admitting quite freely and frankly that there is a sense in which, where the study of the infinite and eternal God is concerned, we are all, to some extent, simply bound to be agnostics. Just as there is one side of the moon which we earth-dwellers can never see without the aid of technological devices, so there are, in the personality of God, heights and depths, lengths and breadths, far beyond the range and reach of our mean minds. It is that to which theologians allude when they refer to the transcendence of God. Think how majestically the Bible affirms this truth: "He humbleth Himself to behold the things that are in heaven" (Psalm 113:6); "To Him the nations are as a drop of a bucket and accounted as the small dust of the balance. Behold, He taketh up the isles as a very little thing" (Isaiah 40:15). "He sitteth upon the circle of the earth, and the inhabitants thereof are as grasshoppers" (Isaiah 40:22). Thomas Watson, the old Puritan, puts the point picturesquely thus: "We can no more search out His infinite perfections than a man on top of the highest mountain can take a star in his hand." "God, to be God," comments Rufus Jones, the American Quaker, "must transcend what is: He must be the Maker of what ought to be." To which Evelyn Underhill adds: "If the reality of God were small enough to be grasped it would not be great enough to be adored."

Moreover, as Martin Luther pointed out, there is a sense in which the God of the Bible is a hidden God. Indeed, Pascal went so far as to suggest that God actually reveals Himself by hiding Himself. There are certainly numerous passages in Holy Scripture which assert the ultimate inscrutability of the Divine Being. Here are some of them: "There shall no man see Me and live" (Exodus 33:20). "The Lord spake unto you out of the midst of the fire. Ye heard the voice of the words, but saw no similitude" (Deuterohomy 4:12). "How little a portion is heard of Him" (Job 26:14)! "Verily, Thou art a God that hidest Thyself, O God of Israel, the Saviour" (Isaiah 45:15); "No man hath seen God at any time" (John 4:12). "Ye have neither heard His voice at any time nor seen His shape" (John 5:37). "How unsearchable are His judgments, and His ways past finding out" (Romans 11:33). "The invisible God" (Colossians 1:15). "Dwelling in the light unapproachable, whom no man hath seen or can see" (1 Timothy 6:16). There is, therefore, a sense in which, where the Being of the Deity is concerned, we are all, Christians and non-Christians alike, compelled, from the nature and character of the case, to confess ourselves agnostic. If God were not too big for our minds He would be too small for our hearts. It is, however, one thing to say that God cannot be fully known and quite another to say that God cannot be known at all. In this we take issue with the agnostics.

Some believe in false gods.

These may perhaps be dubbed "pseudo-atheists". You may remember Martin Luther's saying: *"Der Mensche hatt immer Gott oder Abgott"* – "Man always has either God or an idol". What precisely are these idols which people worship today?

Think of one or two of them.

One is *Matter*. Millions of men and women in our time label themselves "Materialists", and by so doing imply that matter is the ultimate thing in the universe, that all that exists has slowly and laboriously evolved from matter and that, in the last resort, nothing matters but matter. You will perhaps remember Mr Punch's witty aphorism: "What is matter? Never mind. What is mind? No matter." Many, all the same, do mind matter, and indeed profess to find matter the only thing worth minding.

Now the Bible does not, as do some spurious religions, minimize the importance of matter or even eschew it as essentially evil. In truth, as William Temple discerningly pointed out, Christianity is the most materialistic of all religions. The Scriptures themselves declare: "The earth abideth for ever" (Ecclesiastes 1:4). And the New Testament insists on numerous occasions that "the Word was made *flesh*" (John 1:14, etc.) Although the most heavenly of Books, the Bible has about it a wholesome earthiness. To be sure, Holy Scripture provides no warrant for the proposal that man worship matter. Never can one conceive of the Bible holding up inanimate matter in whatever form, artistic or otherwise, as deserving of human devotion. How can a soul-less, inorganic substance ever be a fit focus for the faith and aspiration of an immortal spirit? Yet, some years ago, atheists *did* actually formulate a creed, one of whose articles was as follows: "I believe there is no God but matter, that matter is god and god is matter, and that it does not matter whether there is any god or no." Besides, if it be suggested that matter merits man's devotion because it is the source of his being, that assumption needs to be closely scrutinized. Giordano Bruno declared: "Matter is the universal mother, who brings forth all things as the fruit of her womb." But to this declaration Emmanuel Kant supplies a balancing corrective. "Give me matter," he exclaims, "and I will explain the formation of the world: give me nothing but matter and I cannot explain the existence of a butterfly." Matter can never produce what is above itself any more than the metal in a Ford car could have produced a Henry Ford.

Another false god is *Force*. People today are bewitched by power. Mark Twain once said that if he were erecting a statue to anything in the world of his time it would have been to Energy. In this he spoke for a large number of his contemporaries. But, in our time, by splitting the atom man has released titanic forces undreamt of before and it is not too much to claim that anyone in this period of history can hold in his hand a nuclear device containing more dynamic energy than was possessed three hundred years ago by the whole human race. Mere might is a modern Moloch to which life and health and wealth are being sacrificed nowadays on a colossal scale.

A further false god is *Evolution*, a theory which has been aptly described as "a bridge between gaps". Is it not surprising that so many today, whilst stoutly denying that they owe their being to a Person, are nevertheless rashly ready to believe that they owe it to a process? "Process" is an abstract term. No mere process, as such, can ever produce anything.

Let me put it this way. Suppose that I visit a friend in his home and find it surrounded by a large and lovely garden, in perfect order and ablaze with beauty; and suppose that I say to him, "This is a truly delightful garden. How was it made?" And suppose he answers: "Gardening." Do you think I would regard that as an adequate, satisfying and final answer? Of course, not! "Gardening!" That word merely denotes a certain mode of activity. It speaks of the application of power to purpose. Patently, gardening was involved in the production of the garden. The garden could not have come into existence without gardening. But could there have been gardening without a gardener? The process presupposes the Person. On hearing of the death of his friend John Burrows, William Quayle, the American Methodist bishop, mused: "Poor John! he loved the garden, but he never met the Gardener!" The process is inexplicable apart from the Person.

You may, if you will, extend the process by millions of years, but that does not necessarily make it productive. Personally, I could as readily believe that a monkey, entering one end of the Mersey Tunnel, could emerge as a man at the other, as that human beings, with all their marvellous aptitudes, adaptabilities and potentialities, could ever be the product of a materialistic process. Even if the Tunnel were presumed to be millions of miles long and even if it took the monkey millions of years to pass through it, the change would still be utterly incredible. Time of itself is no creator – rather the reverse! Its passing possesses no magical potency to evolve the existent out of the non-existent. One might as well expect a clock to beget a watch as expect billions of years of themselves to produce *homo sapiens*. Not even a *grandfather* clock could do that!

At one time the inhabitants of what is now known as Ghana believed that the earth was made by a Giant Spider. Even that is a more credible notion than the idea expressed in the familiar lines of William Herbert Carrugh:

A picket frozen on duty,
A mother starved for her brood;
Socrates drinking the hemlock
And Jesus on the rood;
And millions who, humble and nameless,
The same hard pathway trod:
Some call it Evolution,
And others call it God.

But God is not Evolution. Evolution is a process: God is a Person. A process of itself can produce nothing. One might as reasonably refer to the British Government as "politics".

A fourth false God is *Science*. Referring to the deference, not to say reverence, now popularly paid to the physical sciences, J.B. Phillips reports that when a well-known broadcaster proposed to give a radio talk on the failures of science, the plan was firmly, flatly and finally ruled out. No thoughtful person nowadays is unaware or unappreciative of the enormous achievements of modern science and technology and of the immeasurable contribution they have made, and are likely increasingly to make, to the wealth and well-being of mankind. It is a truism to say that science has so improved and revolutionized human social conditions that in the reign of Queen Elizabeth II the wife of an ordinary working man enjoys in her home amenities and facilities of which Queen Elizabeth I never even dreamed. Science, if properly applied and wisely controlled, can minister in a vast variety of ways to human need. It can do real good, but it is not the real god.

Yet another false god is *Humanism*. Humanism is the religion of man, the deification of the human, the idea that mankind must work out its own salvation and is capable of doing so. It is religion without God, the sort of religion which elicited from the witty Frenchman the satirical comment: *"Une religion sans Dieu! Mon Dieu! quelle religion!"*

Sometimes Humanism makes a god of the race in general, or of some part of the race, and at other times it idolizes one particular individual. Algernon Swinburne, the poet, was using it in the first way when, in his "Hymn of Man", he cried: "Glory to Man in the Highest, for man is the master of things." A more restricted meaning was assigned to it by the Editor of a Ghanian newspaper, when he wrote: "We have only one god, and that is Africa." While a still narrower significance was attached to it by a youth who, a few years back, scrawled on the door of a church in Germany: "Elvis Presley is my god." This idolization of man is one of the most popular forms of religion today. Nietszche's Superman has become the god of the godless. There are, according to Martin Luther, two forms of idolatry – one interior, the other exterior; and, as William Temple has reminded us, "A false *mental* image can lead us as far from the true God as a false *metal* image." Nevertheless, said Montaigne, "though man cannot make a worm, he will make gods by the dozen".

Such are some of the false gods commanding the allegiance of the people of our time.

Some believe in the true and living God apprehended by reason and revelation and decisively encountered in Christian experience. There are, indeed, three trunk roads along which we may travel in our quest for the Divine: (1) *The road of reason;* (2) *the road of revelation;* and (3) *the road of regeneration.*

Let us consider them one by one.

THE ROAD OF REASON – the rational approach

But is reason a reliable guide in the realm of religion? Theologians of a certain school dispute that and strenuously deny the competence of reason to operate in this domain. According to them, reason possesses no more power to convey to us a living sense of the true God than has a microscope to show us a star. It is the wrong instrument. Luther, as is well-known, described reason, in his vivid and vigorous way, as "the Devil's Whore"; and Ritschl delivered himself of the rash and risky dictum: "Without Christ, I should be an atheist." While, closer to our own time, Karl Barth, the eminent Swiss theologian, maintained that nobody can know anything at all about God apart from His biblical Self-revelation.

That, however, many feel, is taking things too far. Human reason does, of course, have limitations beyond which it is impotent to explore, far less to pronounce. As Epictetus put it: "Were I fully to describe God, I should myself *be* God, or God must cease to be what He is." The French have a neat epigram: *"Le Dieu défini est le Dieu fini"*, which may be roughly anglicized: "God defined is God destroyed." You will recall the rhetorical question asked in Job 11:7: "Canst thou by searching find out God? Canst thou find out the Almighty to perfection?"

All the same, so far as it goes, reason *is* a reliable guide on the road to religious reality, and there are seven classic theological arguments which it advances in support of the assertion that God exists.

To begin with, there is what is called the *ontological argument*, from the Greek word *ontos*, meaning reality. This approach to the subject is somewhat subtle, profound and hard to follow, and would perhaps require some special training in philosophy to understand it fully. Roughly, however, this is the line it takes: "I can think of a perfect Being. Where has that thought come from? Certainly, it cannot have come from myself, for I am not perfect. Nor can it have come from my observation of others, for they are not perfect. Nor, again, can it be an inference from the world in which I live, for it is not perfect. Whence, then, has the idea of a perfect Being come? By a process of elimination, we conclude that it can have come from no-one but the perfect Being Himself. And thus the very thought of God presupposes and postulates the fact of God.

The second classic argument for God's reality is termed *cosmological,* from the Greek *kosmos,* world. It has been sagely said that the leading arguments for the existence of God may be summed up in our language under three Cs – cause, conscience and consent. In this case the logic proceeds from effect to cause. Patently, the universe is an effect. Every effect must have an adequate cause. The universe, therefore, must have an adequate cause. That cause is God.

He is the source of all the good that is. In this connection someone has conceived a vivid and very helpful figure. He asks us to imagine a long iron chain comprised of many links, suspended perpendicularly in the air. Looking at the bottom link, we see that it is fastened to the one above it, the second to the third, the third to the fourth, and so on, upwards. But it is palpably impossible to envisage a heavy chain suspended in that manner, unless its top link is supposed to be grappled to something strong enough to bear the weight of the whole chain.

So the series of proximate and relative causes for the multifarious effects we find in the world in us and around us lead us to the great First Cause, Aristotle's Prime Mover, God the absolute Originator of every good thing. "Does the world tell us nothing of its Maker?" demands John S. Banks incredulously.

The third traditional argument for the existence of God

is termed *teleological*, from the Greek *telos*, meaning 'end'. This is the argument from design. Aristotle contended that the nature of a thing is revealed not so much in its origin as in its end. This line of logic is therefore the polar opposite of that which we have just examined. It finds evidence of the reality of the Deity not in the creation but in the consummation of the cosmos. Everywhere in nature we see signs of purpose, programme, plan – not simply in the majestic procession of the stellar heavens, but also in the most homely and familiar things in the world around us. "Every atom," it has been said, "has the look of a manufactured article." And wherever we turn in nature we discover that things have been designed with desired objectives in view – the tiny parachute that carries the seed on the wind, the leathery, air-filled float which enables the seaweed to grow up beneath the surface of the water when the tide comes in, and the fine down on the body of the bee which facilitates the process of pollenization are cases in point. Small though they are, such things are plain proof of purpose in nature. They cannot without doing violence to all the laws of logic be attributed to accident or chance any more than a glove can be explained without a hand. They are the tokens of the working of a Mastermind and point to a supreme Designer. Frankly, it is utterly incredible that they should have come about fortuitously. As James Martineau memorably expressed it: "A microscope invented in a city of the blind could hardly surprise us more."

Every informed person has heard of William Paley. In 1802 he published a book on natural theology called Paley's *Evidences of Christianity* containing an illustration which used to be the stock-in-trade of every educated preacher. Some superior people today affect to despise and disparage it and to deny its validity, but most Christians find it as cogent and compelling as when first presented. Here it is: "In crossing a heath I strike my toe against a watch. I pick it up and note that it consists of a complicated arrangement of wheels, springs, jewels and balances – all neatly combined in the case and covered with a crystal. On closer examination I discover that every tiny bit of the mechanism is performing a definite schedule, and each part is so related to every other part that the hands are moved about the dial according to a dependable and unvarying routine. Having not seen the watch made, I conclude that the watch had no maker, that out of the bowels of the earth came forth iron and gold and the elements of glass, and that they refined themselves up and started to tick. I show you the watch and tell you the story, and you tell me that I am a fool. You say that my story violates reason, that the very existence of the watch is positive proof of the pre-existence of a watchmaker and a creative mind and imagination." All of which reminds us of the quip of the German-Jewish poet Heinrich Heine: "In Frankfurt I met a watch that did not believe in the existence of watchmakers." The writer of one of the Proverbs knew better: "The Lord hath made everything for its own end" (15:4).

The fourth standard argument for the existence of God is styled *the moral argument*. On it, Emmanuel Kant, the renowned philosopher, was content to rest the whole case for the reality of the Divine Being. "There are," he wrote, "two things that fill my soul with holy reverence and evergrowing wonder – the spectacle of the starry sky that virtually annihilates us as human beings and the moral law which relates us to infinite dignity as intelligent agents." John Henry Newman likewise recognized that the existence of the Deity requires no other confirmation than the fact of conscience. Conscience witnesses to the truth that there is that within us which proves conclusively that there is One above us. "If God did not exist," declared Dostoievski, "all would be permitted." It is by no mere coincidence that a society which has turned its back upon God has come to be known as "the Permissive

Society". "That little red light in the soul," as Billy Graham describes conscience, bears compelling testimony to the reality of God. It is His voice in the human heart. Schopenhauer dismissed it as a mere social product and even detailed its constituents thus: "One fifth, fear of man; one fifth, superstition: one fifth, prejudice; one fifth, vanity; one fifth, custom." But it is impossible to see how such an assessment can be justified in view of the fact that, in the name of conscience, many have acted in a manner diametrically opposed to such popular pressures and personal factors.

The next classical argument for the existence of God may be denominated *aesthetical*. It has to do with the reality and appreciation of beauty. We all remember these sonorous lines from that monumental poetic masterpiece Gray's *Elegy in a Country Churchyard:*

Full many a gem of purest ray serene
The dark, unfathomed caves of ocean bear;
Full many a flower is born to blush unseen
And waste its sweetness on the desert air.

For whose benefit has all the loveliness of the world been created? For whose sake has been brought into being all the exquisite beauty of dawn and sunset, of flower and tree, of cloud and star? Ours? Well, there is a sense in which that is so. But it cannot have been for human beings alone, since so much of the sheer splendour of the universe never comes within the range of mortal vision. It must exist for the pleasure of someone. Mungo Park, the pioneer missionary to Nigeria, lay at the point of death in West Africa. He was lying on the bare ground, out in the open, on the sun-baked earth of a howling wilderness. Looking around he saw on the parched sod a beautiful little plant, and he suddenly realized that God was there, sustaining its life and enjoying its beauty. The thought comforted him and he began to amend. That the Lord appreciates loveliness is surely a fair inference from the fact that He has made so much of it, and beauty is itself a pointer to His reality. "He hath made everything beautiful in His time" (Ecclesiastes 3:11). The glory of Creation is but a pale reflection of the infinite glory of the Creator.

The sixth traditional argument for the existence of God may be designated *ethnological,* a term stemming from the Greek *ethnos,* signifying nation. Here the reasoning is based on the truth that religion is endemic in the human race, and that even among the most primitive and savage tribes there appear to be pathetic gropings after God, gropings which have been aptly and graphically likened to the upward striving of a wingless bird. Despite the circumstance that in our day untold millions have embraced the bleak creed of atheism, it is indisputable that, as we have seen, deep and ineradicable in the human consciousness, there is an awareness of the Divine. "The history of atheism," it has been paradoxically remarked, "is the record of a succession of gods." "If there were no God," wrote Voltaire, "it would be necessary to invent one." "The wing of the bird," it has been said, "seeks flight, the fin of the fish demands water, the instinct of the heart is for God."

An amusing illustration of the profundity and persistence of this human instinct is furnished by the following story. One wet wintry night a number of keen Christians were holding an open-air service at a street corner in a large city. Not many paid them the compliment of a hearing. Only one man listened throughout the proceedings, and he stood leaning against a lamp-post at some distance from the scene. At the close a member of the party went up to him and asked: "Well, did you enjoy the meeting?" "No," he replied bluntly, "I don't believe in all that rubbish. I'm an atheist – *thank God*!" The man was himself a living support for Henry Parry Liddon's contention: "A nation of pure atheists has yet to be discovered."

The deep religious instinct of the race is strong, standing evidence of the existence of God.

The final classic argument for the reality of the Divine Being is christened the *anthropological,* from the Greek *anthropos,* meaning man. This argues from the felt worth of human personality to the existence of a supreme Divine Personality. It used to be taken unquestioningly for granted that personality was the highest thing we know in nature. Now that axiom is being challenged. Not long ago a secularist scientist specializing in psychogenics declared that the time has come when man is making machines greater than himself, and that hence the highest thing in the visible cosmos is a machine and not a man. Is that so? Well, it is incontrovertible that man is today devising and marketing instruments and mechanisms capable of performing feats of skill far beyond his own powers. An aeroplane can fly, a man cannot; a computer can calculate with a speed and accuracy vastly transcending human capability. Nevertheless, it remains true, as we have noted, that it is man who makes the machines and that no machine can make a man. Nothing in the material order, as such, can produce personality any more than the Venus de Milo could give birth to a living baby. It takes personality to beget personality.

Now all round about us in the world we see numberless personalities. Whence have they come? Ultimately, they can only have originated in one sublime Personality. That Personality is God.

There, then, are seven milestones on this road of reason along which we may journey in our search for God. They do not take us all the way, but at least they put us on the right track. After painstakingly conducting an exhaustive scholarly investigation into the evidence for the existence of a Divine Being, Joseph Butler delivered himself of this deliberate dictum: "The balance of probability is in favour of the existence of God." That is as far as reason can go.

THE ROAD OF REVELATION

This is, of course, the Biblical approach. Now the Bible does not argue that there is a God. It assumes and asserts that fact. Majestically, in its opening sentence it proclaims it: "In the beginning God" (Genesis 1:1). Its paramount concern is not to persuade us *that* God is, but to tell us *what* God is and especially *who* God is. It introduces us to Him as Creator, Sustainer, Governor, Judge, Provider and Father.

Look for a little at each of these colossal rôles which it assigns to Him.

In the first place, it presents God as *Creator*. "To find out what really happened when the earth was created," wrote a contributor to the *Welsh Churchman*, "inquirers spent weeks gathering information, checking and rechecking it, and feeding the data into a computer. The great moment came. All was complete. Everybody gathered around. A button was pressed. The great computer spun into action. Relays operated, valves opened and closed, lights flashed and bells rang. Finally, a typed message emerged: 'See Genesis 1:1'." Many people seem to think that the only Bible reference to the creative activity of God is to be found in its first book. This is not so. That great fact is stated over and over again in Holy Scripture. It is, so to say, woven inextricably into the very texture of both the Old and the New Testament. Consider a short catena of pertinent passages: "God created man in His own image, male and female created He them" (Genesis 1:27). "The Lord made heaven and earth, the sea, and all that in them is" (Exodus 20:11). "He stretcheth out the north over the empty place, and hangeth the earth upon nothing" (Job 26:7). "The Spirit of God hath made me, and the breath of the Almighty hath given me life" (Job 33:4). "God spread out the sky, strong as a molten looking-glass" (Job 37:18). "By the Word of the Lord were the heavens made, and all the hosts of them by the breath of His mouth" (Psalm 33:6). "All the gods of the nations are idols, but the Lord made the heavens" (Psalm 90:4,5). "It is He that made us and not we ourselves" (Psalm 100:3). "By wisdom made He the heavens." (Psalm 136:7). "He made the earth, the fields, the high parts of the dust of the world" (Proverbs 8:26). "Remember now thy Creator" (Ecclesiastes 12:1). "The Lord created the heavens and stretched them out. He spread forth the earth and that which cometh out of it. He giveth breath unto the people upon it and spirit to them that walk therein" (Isaiah 42:5) "I have made the earth and created man upon it. I, even My hand, hath stretched out the heavens and all their host have I commanded" (Isaiah 45:12). "The Lord created the heavens. God Himself formed the earth and made it. He established it; He created it not in vain. He formed it to be inhabited" (Isaiah 45:18). "He hath made the earth by His power; He hath established the world by His wisdom, and hath stretched out the heavens by His discretion" (Jeremiah 10:12). "I have made the man and the beast that are upon the ground, by My great power and by My outstretched arm" (Jeremiah 27:5). "O, Lord God, behold, Thou hast made the heaven and the earth by thy great power and stretched out arm, and there is nothing too hard for Thee" (Jeremiah 32:17). "Hath not one God created us" (Malachi 2:10)? "The creation which God created" (Mark 13:19). "Without Him was not anything made that was made" (John 1:3). "God created all things by Jesus Christ" (Ephesians 3:9). "By Him were all things created, that are in heaven, that are in earth, visible and invisible" (Colossians 1:16). "God's Son by whom He made the worlds" (Hebrews 1:2). "Every house is builded by some man, but He that built all things is God" (Hebrews 3:4). "Thou hast created all things, and for Thy pleasure they are and were created" (Revelation 4:11). "He liveth for ever, and created the heavens and the things that therein are, and the sea and the things that are therein" (Revelation 4:11).

From this selective series of citations, spanning the whole Bible, it is surely compellingly clear that the doctrine of Divine creation is no monopoly of the Book of Genesis, but is in fact woven like a golden thread into the total tapestry of Holy Scripture.

Broadly speaking, there are four views as to the origin of the universe: (a) *that the universe never had a beginning*; (b) *that the cosmos was caused by an accident, a fortuitous collocation of atoms "going it blind" as a consequence of some colossal primordial explosion*; (c) *that the material order is self-creating*; and (d) *that the universe was brought into being by God*.

These are the ultimate options. Which would you prefer to be true – the view of the secular scientists, or the testimony of the infallible Word of the living God? Here is a typical statement from the former: "Three and a half billion years ago a violent celestial storm broke. Thunder, lightning and solar radiation stirred up primordial 'soup'. Out of this came amino acids, and from the brew lifeforms began to invent themselves." The Bible says: "Thus saith the Lord God, thy Redeemer and He that formed thee from the womb, I am the Lord that maketh all things, that stretcheth forth the heavens above, that spreadeth abroad the earth by Himself" (Isaiah 44:24).

Modern astronomers, probing into outer space with their gigantic new visual and audio-telescopes, favour two theories as to the origin of the universe – one is the so called "Big Bang Theory", according to which the cosmos started with a titanic explosion and as a consequence has been expanding ever since; the other is the "Continuous Creation Theory", which holds that the universe is self-creating and is constantly making itself out of nothing and falling back into nothingness again. In contrast to the first of these theories, the Bible boldly proclaims the truth that the cosmos arose not from a Bang but a Being; and, in contradiction of the second theory, it teaches that Creation is a completed work.

Belief in a beneficent, intelligent, almighty God, and that alone, makes any view of the origin of the universe credible, and existence within its parameters, not only tolerable but pleasurable. With such a Creator, nothing is too hard to be accomplished or too good to be true. When Joseph Haydn, the famous Austrian composer, had finished his great oratorio *The Creation,* he is said to have cried: "Not from me! Not from me! From above it has all come!" To God all things are possible. An old preacher once picturesquely declared that it was no harder for God to create worlds than for a small boy to blow soap-bubbles into the air from a clay-pipe.

In the second place, the Scriptures present God as *Preserver and Sustainer*. This truth is not so much underscored in Scripture as is God's Creatorhood, but it is unmistakably there all the same. As John Dow neatly notes: "As we came from His hand, we remain in His hand." Here in review are several relevant texts: "O Thou preserver of men" (Job 7:20). "He hangeth the earth upon nothing" (Job 26:7). "If He (God) gather unto Himself His Spirit and His breath, all flesh shall perish together, and man shall turn again into dust" (Job 34:14,15). "He founded the earth upon the seas and established it upon the floods" (Psalm 24:2). "He hath established the heavens for ever and ever; He hath made a decree which shall not pass" (Psalm 148:6). "O, Lord, Thou preservest man and beast" (Psalm 36:6). "God is good, and His tender mercies are over all His works. The eyes of all wait upon Thee, and Thou givest them their meat in due season. Thou openest Thy hand and satisfiest the desire of every living thing" (Psalm 145:9,15,16). "The Lord by wisdom hath founded the earth, by understanding hath He established the heavens" (Proverbs 3:19). "He left not Himself without witness, in that He did good, and gave from heaven rains and fruitful seasons, filling our hearts with food and gladness" (Acts 14:17). "By Him all things consist" (Colossians 1:17). "Upholding all things by the word of His power" (Hebrews 1:3). Yes, in the Bible God is certainly presented and represented as Sustainer and Preserver of the world. Think of a cabinet-maker producing a fine piece of furniture. Were he to die, his death would make no difference to the furniture. It would continue to exist just as it did before its maker's decease. Not so with God and His world. If He were to die, the world would fall to pieces, but He cannot die and so the universe is secure.

In the third place, Scripture depicts God as *Governor, Ruler, Potentate*. Witness these weighty words: "He is the governor among the nations" (Psalm 22:28). "He ruleth by His power for ever" (Psalm 66:7). "O, God, Thou shalt govern the nations upon earth" (Psalm 67:4). "His kingdom ruleth over all" (Psalm 103:19). "He causeth the winds to blow and the waters flow" (Psalm 147:18). "The Most High ruleth in the kingdom of men" (Daniel 4:17). "The Lord reigneth" is one of the favourite phrases of the old Hebrew poets. Despite all the apparent evidence to the contrary, they stoutly and steadfastly maintained their belief in the universal sovereignty of God. Benjamin Franklin agreed with them: "I have lived a long time, and the longer I live, the more convincing proofs I see of this truth – that God governs the affairs of men."

In the fourth place, the Bible pictures God as *Judge*. It portrays Him as Lawgiver and Minister of Justice against whose just statutes and inflexibly equitable arbitrament there can be no appeal. It describes His descent amid darkness and flame on the summit of Sinai, and His conveyance there to Moses of the Ten Commandments, affirming that human conduct is not just a matter for human dialogue: they are Divine Decalogue. It is not just a question of social desirability or personal profitability, but of the dictates of the Deity, not just the taboos of an ancient nomadic tribe, but the universal and eternal principles promulgated by God for the control and regulation of the behaviour of the human race.

Think of some of the Biblical sentences bearing directly on this issue. "Shall not the Judge of all the earth do right" (Genesis 18:25)? "God is Judge Himself" (Psalm 50:6). "Verily, He is a God that judgeth in the earth" (Psalm 58:11). "God is the Judge of the quick and the dead" (Acts 10:42). "God, the Judge of all" (Hebrews 12:13).

How ridiculous, in the light of such passages as these, are the judgments of unregenerate men, however learned along other lines, when they presume to pontificate on theological issues! A classic example is Maurice Maeterlinck's portrayal of God, seated on a sunlit hill, contemplating with amused complacency the worst crimes of His human creatures as if they were the sport of puppies playing on a hearth-rug!

Not so does the Bible represent Him. It is no mere coincidence that, alike at its beginning and at its end, it shows God as Judge. In Genesis He dons, as it were, the "Black Cap", and pronounces the death-sentence on the fallen human race, and in Revelation He is depicted as the aweful, august Moral Arbiter, from whose face the earth and the heavens flee away – the eternal Judge.

In the fifth place, the Bible reveals God as *Provider*. On the timbered facade of an ancient house in the quaint and lovely old English city of Chester, there is this inscription: "God's Providence is Mine Inheritance." According to the Scriptures, these words might well be written over the portals of the world. God is the great Provider. Is not one of His names indicative of that – "Jehovah Jireh", "The Lord will provide"? Examine these extracts from His sure Word: "While the earth remaineth, seed time and harvest shall not cease" (Genesis 8:22). "Thou visitest the earth, and waterest it. Thou prepares them corn, when Thou hast so provided for it; Thou waterest the ridges thereof abundantly; Thou settlest the furrows thereof; Thou makest it soft with showers; Thou blessest the springing thereof; Thou crownest the year with Thy goodness" (Psalm 65:9-11). "The eyes of all wait upon Thee; and Thou givest them their meat in due season; Thou openest Thine hand and satisfiest the desire of every living thing" (Psalm 145:15,16). "God having provided for us" (Hebrews 11:40). To the inquiry, "Can God furnish a table"? (Psalm 78:19), the Bible is ready with the reply: "My table Thou hast furnished" (Psalm 23:5 SMV).

Never before in human history have the civilized inhabitants of this planet been made so poignantly aware of the desperately tragic plight of so many of their fellow-creatures, who are deprived and under-privileged, as we are today. Every time the clock ticks someone somewhere dies of starvation. It is an appalling problem. But not all the famines in the world can deny the existence of food; and if there were no God, the feeding of its population would be a far greater problem than their famishing.

In the sixth place, the Bible brings before us a picture of God as *Father*. There are no fewer than six ways in which it does so. *(a) It calls Him the Father of the cosmos,* describing Him as the "Father of lights, with whom there is no variableness, neither shadow cast by turning" (James 1:17). (b) *It calls Him the Father of the human race.* "Have we not all one Father" (Malachi 2:10)? "There is one God and Father of all" (Ephesians 4:4-6). "God is the Father of the spirits of men" (James 1:17). "We ought rather to be subject to the Father of spirits" (Hebrews 12:9). (c) *It calls God the Father of Israel.* "Thou art our Father, though Abraham be ignorant of us and Israel acknowledge us not: Thou, O Lord, art our Father" (Isaiah 63:16). (d) *It calls God in a special sense the Father of the Christian believer.* "The Father of whom the whole family in heaven and in earth is named" (Ephesians 3:14,15). "Ye have received the Spirit of adoption, whereby we cry, Abba, Father" (Romans 8:15). (e) *Finally, it calls God uniquely the Father of our Lord*

Jesus Christ. "Blessed be the God and Father of our Lord Jesus Christ" (2 Corinthians 1:3). "He that hath seen Me, hath seen the Father" (John 14:9). In prayer and parable our Lord taught us thus to recognize the living paternity of God. He said: "When ye pray, say, Our Father" (Luke 11:2), and in what is probably the best-known and best-loved of His stories He gave us what is popularly known as "the Parable of the Prodigal Son", where the spotlight focuses, not so much on the prodigality of the youth's sin, as on the prodigality of the Father's love.

The Bible begins with a magnificent monotheism: "In the beginning God created the heaven and the earth" (Genesis 1:1). Perusing its pages, however, we come before long upon polytheism, the worship of a multiplicity of false deities, and from then on the spiritual background of the historical drama of Hebrew history may be described in terms of a battle between God and the gods; and not until belief in one God had been driven like a pile into the consciousness of the Jewish nation did God judge it safe, if I may so say, to disclose to mankind the sublime doctrine of the Trinity.

The term "trinity" does not itself occur in the Bible. It dates from the time of Theophilus of Antioch, round about 170 AD. Nonetheless, the roots of the term are deeply embedded in the Word of God. Some critics allege that Trinitarians read the Threefoldness of God from the threeness of things in nature back into the Bible, that they import it from without and that it constitutes no true part of the authentic Divine Self-revelation. You may recall Montesquieu's satirical comment: "If the triangles had a god, they would give him three sides" – the implication being that man has made God in his own image and that the doctrine of the Holy Trinity is an imaginative projection of the tripartite nature of man. To a Billingsgate fishwife, an unkind humorist once observed: "My good woman, you are an isosceles triangle." Naturally enough, she had not the ghost of an idea of what he was "on about", which is perhaps just as well. When, however, Christian teachers refer to God as a Trinity many modern men and women have not the slightest inkling of what they mean – and that is not at all well!

Here, again, some maintain that, from the very nature of the case, man with his finite mind cannot expect to plumb the depths of the Divine Being. "All true theologians," wrote George Smeaton, "have uniformly accepted it as their highest function simply to conserve the mystery and to leave it where they found it in its inscrutable sublimity, dark with excess of bright." To some degree we *are* compelled, as we have noted, to leave it there. Yet, whatever the limitations of human comprehension, where this high doctine is concerned, there can be no reasonable doubt that the truth of the Trinity is stitched into the very stuff of the Word of God.

As one might anticipate, the plainest statements of this truth are reserved for the New Testment, but even the Old Testament is not without adumbrations of it. Take the following sample texts: "God said, let *Us* make man" (Genesis 1:26). "Man is become as one of Us" (Genesis 3:22). "The Lord bless thee, and keep thee, the Lord make His face shine upon thee, and be gracious unto thee; the Lord lift up His countenance upon thee and give thee peace" (Numbers 6:24-26). The Trisagion, "Holy, holy, holy, is the Lord God of Hosts" (Isaish 6:3), has the same threeness about it, as has a verse further down the same chapter (v.8): "Whom shall I send? and who will go for *Us*?" If texts such as these do not explicitly and unequivocally define the plurality of the Persons in the Godhead, they most certainly do not deny it and even appear to imply it.

It is, of course, to the New Testament that we naturally turn for the clearest pronouncements on this tremendous theme. "Go to the Jordan," writes Augustine, "and you will see the Trinity." There at the baptism of Jesus the three Persons in the Godhead are simultaneously in evidence. The Father is heard speaking directly from heaven, the Son is seen being immersed in the river, and John the Baptist beholds the Spirit like a Dove descending upon the Christ.

The baptismal formula also contains a reference to the Trinity: "Go ye, therefore, and teach all nations, baptizing them in the name (note: "name", not "names"!) of the Father, and of the Son, and of the Holy Ghost" (Matthew 28:19). Jesus (the Second Person) is speaking. "How much more," He asks, "will your heavenly Father (the First Person), give the Holy Spirit (the Third Person) to them that ask Him?" (Luke 11:13). "I will pray the Father, and He shall give you another Comforter" (John 14:16). "Being by the right hand of God exalted, and having received the promise of the Father He (Christ) hath shed forth this (the Holy Spirit) which ye see and hear" (Acts 2:33). "If the Spirit of Him that raised up Jesus from the dead dwell in you, He that raised up Christ from the dead shall also quicken your mortal bodies by His Spirit that dwelleth in you" (Romans 8:11). "I beseech you by the Lord Jesus Christ, and by the love of the Spirit, in your prayers to God" (Romans 15:30). "The grace of the Lord Jesus Christ, and the love of God, and the communion of the Holy Ghost be with you all" (2 Corinthians 13:14). "The foreknowledge of God the Father, the sanctification of the Spirit, unto obedience and sprinkling of the blood of Jesus Christ" (1 Peter 1:2). And, most obviously and unambiguously of all, in a passage whose authenticity is regrettably suspect among scholars, but whose sentiments are undoubtedly those of the Early Church: "There are three that bear record in heaven, the Father, the Word and the Holy Ghost, and these Three are One" (1 John 5:7). The Trinitarian pattern also occurs like a watermark in Revelation 1:4-6.

So closely are the Persons in the Holy Trinity interrelated that it is almost impossible to speak of One without evoking thoughts of the others. "I cannot think of the

One," remarked Gregory Naziansen in his sermon on baptism, "but I am immediately surrounded by the splendour of the Three; nor can I discover the Three, but I am certainly carried back to the One." To the same effect is this saying of Ambrose: "Name one Person in the Godhead and you indicate the Three."

In his *The Creed of the Christian* Charles Gore has a helpful illustration which here comes to mind: "You are fond of climbing mountains, and you know how a surface of rock which looks flat and uniform from a distance seems broken up and complicated enough as you get near to it. So, as we got nearer to God, or rather as He came nearer to us, the distinctions in His nature began to come out. Seen from a distance, as in the Old Testament, He seems only one and single; as He came nearer to us at the Coming of the Son and the Spirit, we grew to see that the one God is manifold as well as one."

Before God could entrust His people with the knowledge of His essential Threeness, He had to propel into their minds a piercing conviction of His Oneness. The only soil in which the trefoil of the Trinity could flourish was that of monotheism. Reflect on how heavily the Old Testament underlines the truth of the unity of God: "Hear, O Israel, the Lord our God is one Lord" (Deuteronomy 6:4). "Know therefore this day, and consider it in thine heart, that the Lord is God in the heaven above and on the earth beneath: there is none else" (Deuteronomy 4:39). "The Lord He is God: there is none else" (1 Kings 8:60). "I am He: before Me there was none formed, neither shall there be after Me; I, even I, am the Lord and beside Me there is no Saviour" (Isaiah 43:10,11).

Even subsequent to the revelation of the truth of the Trinity, and concurrent with that revelation, this stress on the singularity of God was continued. The New Testament emphasizes it no less than the Old. "We know that there is no other God but one" (1 Corinthians 8:4). "To us there is but one God, the Father, of whom are all things" (1

Corinthians 8:6). "There is one God, and one Mediator between God and men, the Man Christ Jesus" (1 Timothy 2:5). "Thou believest that there is one God: thou doest well" (James 1:19).

If you had never read the Bible and were given a copy, and if you started to read it straight through from Genesis onwards, you might not find in it the doctrine of the Trinity until you arrived at the New Testament; but, once you found it there, on looking back you would discover that it had been implicit in the whole Book from the beginning.

Not far from the east coast of America there is an island which was discovered by Christopher Columbus. On first sighting it he formed a wrong opinion. He was a long way off, and all that he could see was three hills silhouetted against the sky. "Ah," he thought, "here are three islands." When, however, his ship got closer he found that they were not three islands at all, but just one island. It looked like three from a distance, but when he got near he saw that it was only one. Hence he named the island "Trinidad", Spanish for "Trinity".

It is not only, however, in isolated texts that one encounters in Scripture the doctrine of the Trinity. The very concept of a God of love, which is the underlying *motif* of the Bible, presupposes plurality in the Divine Being. A God whose nature and whose name is Love can never throughout eternity, to use Charles Hodge's graphic figure, "have been playing an endless game of solitaire". Love, to be love, must have an object. Self-love is love's opposite. Consequently, since God is eternal love, He must eternally have had objects of affection. These *foci* of His love are the eternal Son and the eternal Spirit. Thus the doctrine of the Trinity is not only theologically but logically necessary to a right understanding of the Divine Being. William Ellery Channing, a once-famous Unitarian divine, declared on one occasion: "Nature is no Trinitarian. It gives not a hint, not a glimpse, of a tripersonal

Author." Channing must have been singularly blind; for, as it has been well said, "The universe is like a great mirror reflecting the Threefoldness of the triune God". As someone has arrestingly put it: "There is a fundamental threeness in things", and of this there are countless vivid illustrations. Augustine, for example, found one in the root, trunk and branches of a tree; Patrick, in the three leaves and one stem of the shamrock; Langland, in the figure of the human hand – fist, palm and fingers. More subtle adumbrations of it have come to light as a result of the discoveries of science. Thus there are three basic elements – solids, fluids, gases; three primary colours – red, yellow, blue; three properties of light – colouring, illuminating, heating. The realm of abstract thought also has its illustrative instances – geometry with its equilateral triangle; logic with its thesis, antithesis and synthesis; psychology with its body, soul and spirit; horology, with its past, present and future, and so on. How absurd, then, the claim that there is no evidence of the Trinity in Creation!

Further, there is that in the spiritual hunger of the human heart which nothing less or other than the Trinity can fully satisfy. George Matheson speaks for us all when in these moving lines he says:

Some seek a Father in the heavens above,
Some ask a human Figure to adore,
Some crave a Spirit vast as life and love:
Within Thy mansions we have all and more.

"Batter my heart, Three-Personed God," cries John Donne; and Christopher Harvey declares:

The whole round world is not enough to fill the heart's three corners;
Only the Trinity that made it can
The vast triangled heart of man.

A poet of loftier stature than either of those states the same thing in prose. Alfred Tennyson wrote: "Though nothing is such a distress of soul to me as to hear the divinity of Christ assailed, yet I feel I must never lose the unity of the Godhead, the Three Persons being like three candles, giving together one light." God is one: yet God is three. There you have an insoluble mathematical riddle, but it is, as we have seen, a truth to which the Word of God bears repeated and emphatic witness, alike in the Old Testament and in the New, a truth adumbrated in nature, asseverated in Scripture and answering to the deepest needs of the human soul.

One – yet Three! How can that be? It is a basic problem which theology has set itself to solve. Is theology really competent to do so, or has it, to put the point colloquially, "bitten off more than it can chew", undertaken a task which, in the nature of things, cannot be accomplished? There is, as we have more than once reminded ourselves, a sense in which this is bound to be so. In his treatise *De Trinitate* Augustine half-apologizes for his polemics on the subject in these words: "We are forced by the faults of heretics and blasphemers to do that which is not lawful, to climb inaccessible heights, to speak what cannot be uttered and to trespass upon what is forbidden." Nevertheless the attempt has to be made, and the shape of the classical formulation of the doctrine of the Trinity was to some extent determined by the heresies which it opposed, exposed and sought to depose.

Glance briefly in turn at each of these heresies.

The first stressed *the Threeness of the Godhead at the expense of the Oneness*. Virtually, it taught that there were three gods, and so was tritheistic rather than trinitarian. The Jehovah's Witnesses lapse into a like error in supposing that Trinitarians conceive of God as a body with three heads. That might have been true of this ancient heresy, but it is emphatically not true of classic Trinitarianism. Of the heresy in question a survival may perhaps be found in the present-day notion of the Social Trinity, a theory which recalls the story of the Japanese gentleman who, having patiently listened uncomprehendingly to a long, involved, elaborate exposition of the doctrine of the Trinity, at last remarked brightly: "Ah, I see – a Committee!" No, God is not a committee. God is One as well as Three, and you cannot have a committee of one!

The second heresy emphasized the *Oneness of the Godhead to the detriment of the Threeness*. Historically, this notion is linked with the name of Sabellius, who flourished around AD 200. He taught that God is unipersonal, and that the other two Persons in the Trinity are merely modes or manifestations of the Being of the one God. The idea suggests the picture of a lighthouse, whose great central lamp burns fixedly and steadily, a pure white blaze, but which, as the focussing prism of coloured glass rotates around it, appears by turns white, red, green. The official theological name for this heresy is Modalism, and it was perhaps in some degree an anticipation on an infinite scale of the present-day concept of the Group Mind. However that may be, the historic faith declares that not only does God *seem* to be Three Persons, but that He *is* Three Persons.

The number three is significant and important. Carl Jung, the famous Swiss psychologist, suggested that there should be four Persons in the Godhead, while Leslie Weatherhead confessed that, for all practical purposes, two Persons would have been enough for him. But the classic creeds and confessions uniformly proclaim the existence of the Holy Three.

The third heresy, while avoiding the mistakes of the other two, falls into an error of its own – *that of confusing the One-in-Threeness,* denying the equality of the Divine Persons and dubbing some inferior to the others. Hence the heresy is known as Subordinationism. It assumed two forms. On the one hand, as in the thought of Origen, it was the First Person in the Godhead, the eternal Father, who was accorded precedence over the Son and the Spirit. On the other hand, as in the modern so-called "Jesus Only Movement", it is the Second Person, the eternal Son, who is given priority over the Father and the Spirit. Both views are erroneous. The true faith is that the Three Persons in the Blessed Trinity are co-equal. Certainly, for the purpose of human redemption, there was a measure of voluntary and temporary submission – if that is not an inadmissible mixing of categories – on the part of the Second Person to the First Person. A similar willing subordination of the Third Person to the Second Person would also appear to be involved in the statement: "the Comforter whom I will send unto you" (John 15:26). There is, however, no essential inequality between the Divine Persons. Recognition of this saves one from falling into the absurd inconsistency of the Unitarian preacher who, while denying the Deity of Christ, when administering the rite of baptism, adopted the Trinitarian formula, and thus called forth from Robert Hall the caustic comment: "Why, sir, as I understand you, you baptize in the name of an Abstraction, a Man and a Metaphor!"

To protect its members from such ludicrous vagaries the historic Church formulated in the Athanasian Creed a clear and concise statement of its own position. Here it is: "The catholic (that is, the universal) faith is this: that we worship one God in Trinity and Trinity in unity, neither confounding the Persons nor dividing the substance, for there is one Person of the Father, another of the Son and another of the Holy Ghost. But the Godhead of the Father, and of the Son, and of the Holy Ghost is all one, the glory equal, the majesty co-eternal, and in this Trinity none is afore or after other, none is greater or less than another, but the whole Persons are co-eternal together and co-equal."

Thus, stretching language almost to the breaking-point, the Christian Church has sought to capture in a cage of words this ineffable, elusive truth of the Holy Trinity. Not even that meticulously precise formulation of the doctrine, however, completely satisfied the minds of those who originally recited it as a creed. It was a safety-net to keep them from falling into error rather than a verbal net in which to trap the truth. "We talk of the Trinity," says Augustine, "not that the truth may be spoken, but that it may not be left unspoken."

This realistically modest admission of one of the most eminent of the Church fathers brings to mind a familiar story told about him. Walking one day on the shore of the Mediterranean, musing on the great theme of the Trinity about which he was then writing a book, he saw a small boy playing on the beach. The boy had dug a hole in the sand and with a tiny bucket was carrying water from the sea and emptying it into the hole he had made. "What are you doing?" queried Augustine. "I am pouring the ocean into this hole," answered the child. The great man burst out laughing. "Impossible!" he cried. Just then the Holy Spirit spoke in his heart: "Not more impossible than what *you* are trying to do with your little book on the Trinity." "The highest," it has been said, "cannot be spoken." This is supremely true of the Most High. You can no more entrap this holy mystery in a mesh of words than you could catch a Concorde in a spider's web.

But, although mentally inscrutable, the doctrine of the Trinity is spiritually illuminative. As Frederick William Faber sang:

That Thou shouldest love me as Thou dost
And be the God Thou art
Is darkness to my intellect
But sunshine to my heart.

Rabbi Lionel Blue tells of a Jew who was dying. No

representative of Judaism was at hand, but a Christian minister sought to comfort him in his last moments. He spoke of the Trinity. This incensed the sufferer. "I am dying," he said, "and you offer me a riddle!" Yet the doctrine of the Trinity is no mere theological puzzle, it is the ultimate solace of the soul. You may perhaps have heard this moving confession of Horace Bushnell: "When the preacher touches the Trinity, and when logic shatters it all to pieces, I am at the four winds. But I am glad I have a heart as well as a head. My heart wants the Father, my heart wants the Son, my heart wants the Holy Spirit. My heart says the Bible has a Trinity for me, and I mean to hold by my heart." John Henry Newman carries every orthodox Christian with him when he writes:

Firmly I believe and truly
God is Three and God is One;
And I next acknowledge duly
Manhood taken by the Son.

Adoration aye be given
With and through the angelic host,
To the God of earth and heaven,
Father, Son and Holy Ghost.

Perhaps it may be well to make as plain as possible what precisely we mean in this connection by the word "Person". As applied to God, it is essentially unsatisfactory and is employed only in default of a better. To many people it conveys the idea of "a being in a body", and this is definitely not the connotation to be assigned to it in relation to God, unless indeed the reference be to the Incarnation. Human personalities are known by their limitations. Because we recognize their boundaries, we are able to identify them and to distinguish them from others. With the Divine Personality it is not so. Since that Personality has no limitations, it defies such spatial comprehension Actually, the word "person" comes from the Latin *persona*, originally the name for masks worn by actors when playing parts on a stage. Nobody would be foolish enough to interpret the word thus when applied to the Divine Being. One might, however, invest it for oneself with a false signification by supposing it to refer to dimensions of some sort. Obviously, spirit cannot be measured as can space. When we speak of the Three Persons in the Holy Trinity, we are not, if thinking correctly, conceiving a form at all, we are conceiving of them as three independent yet interdependent centres of consciousness, each capable of thinking, feeling and willing, but all united in one basic substance which is the ground of their eternal Being.

Whatever be the nature of that ultimate essence there are certain aspects or attributes of it to which historic theology has always called attention. Those attributes are of two kinds – incommunicable and communicable. The incommunicable attributes are three in number – *omnipotence, omniscience and omnipresence*.

Just a word about each in turn.

Omnipotence! What does that mean? The long Latin term signifies all-powerful; and, patently, forasmuch as there cannot conceivably be two all-powerful beings, it is obvious that this is a predicate which applies to God alone. Is it intended to mean that God can do anything and everything? This would seem to be the case from the all-inclusiveness of the term itself. But such a notion needs qualifying. There are some things that God cannot do. He cannot do certain things because they are illogical. He cannot, for instance, make a round square or a two-sided triangle or cause four and four to add up to ten. Other things He cannot do because they are immoral. "O, mighty God, Thou canst not look on iniquity" (Habakkuk 1:12,13). "He cannot deny Himself" (2 Timothy 2:13). "God cannot lie" (Titus 1:2). "God cannot be tempted with evil" (James 1:13). What, then, *does* the concept of omnipotence imply? It implies that God can accomplish anything which it is His purpose to perform; it implies that He can never finally be baulked in any enterprise He undertakes; it implies that trying ultimately to thwart His will would be like attempting to hold back Niagara with the palm of one's hand. "Is there anything too hard for Me?" He inquires rhetorically (Jeremiah 32:27). "All power is given unto Me in heaven and in earth," He categorically asserts (Matthew 28:18). Such is His first incommunicable attribute – omnipotence.

The second is *omniscience.* "God hides Himself," as someone has succinctly and significantly said, "but He sees." Himself Invisible, He is the Observer of all that happens. Divine omniscience operates in two ways – extensively and intensively. Extensively, He is aware of all that is going on in the world without. "The eyes of the Lord run to and fro throughout the whole earth" (2 Chronicles 16:9). "Known unto God are all His works from the beginning" (Acts 15:18). "There is nothing in creation that can hide from Him" (Hebrews 14:13). Intensively, He knows everything that is going on in the world within. "O Lord, Thou hast searched me and known me; Thou knowest my downsitting and mine uprising; Thou understandest my thoughts afar off. Such knowledge is too wonderful for me" (Psalm 139:1,2,6). "Can any hide himself in secret places that I shall not see Him? saith the Lord" (Jeremiah 23:24). "All things are naked and opened unto the eyes of Him with whom we have to do" (Hebrews 4:13). So much for the second Divine incommunicable attribute.

Turn now to the third – *omnipresence*. This signifies that God's vast Being is coterminous with the universe. "Do not I fill heaven and earth? saith the Lord" (Jeremiah 23:24). There is no place where God is not except the heart that wills to exclude Him and the hell which is His absence. "God is everywhere," wrote Augustine, "and the whole of God is everywhere." Such is the mystery of the Divine Ubiquity. "God is a circle," declared Empedocles, "whose centre is everywhere and whose circumference is nowhere." You will recollect how splendidly and spaciously the Scriptures testify to this fact: "Whither shall I go from Thy Spirit, or whither shall I flee from Thy presence? If I ascend up into heaven, Thou art there; if I make my bed in hell, Thou art there. If I take the wings of the morning and dwell in the uttermost parts of the sea, even there shall Thy hand lead me, and Thy right hand shall hold me" (Psalm 139:7-10). "Thus saith the High and Lofty One that inhabiteth eternity" (Isaiah 57:15). "He filleth all in all" (Ephesians 1:23).

Moving on now, let me mention what are known as the communicable attributes of God, those qualities of His Divine nature, which, although superlatively exemplified in Himself, He can and does, on certain conditions, extend to and express through His human creatures. These moral qualities may be listed as follows: (a) *holiness*; (b) *goodness*; (c) *wisdom*; (d) *truth* and (e) *love*.

Let us pass them rapidly in review

(a) *Holiness*. Those who come into direct, challenging proximity to the Divine are inevitably overwhelmed by a sense of God's moral majesty. With cases of this the Bible is replete. Consider the following: "I have heard of Thee with the hearing of the ear, but now mine eye seeth Thee; wherefore I abhor myself and repent in dust and ashes" (Job 42:5,6). "I saw also the Lord, sitting upon a throne, high and lifted up, and His train filled the temple. Then said I, Woe is me, for I am undone, because I am a man of unclean lips, and I dwell in the midst of a people of unclean lips, for mine eyes have seen the King, the Lord of

Hosts" (Isaiah 6:1-5). "Depart from me, for I am a sinful man, O Lord" (Luke 5:8). "Be ye holy; for I am holy" (1 Peter 1:16). Holiness is God's first communicable attribute.

(b) *Goodness*, a passion for righteousness. To those who accept Him, God is gracious: to those who reject Him, He is just. These are the two ways in which His goodness manifests itself. "Some people," as James Denney used to say, "have an irreligious solicitude for God." They seem half-afraid that He will fall short of His own moral standards. About that they need have no apprehension. One might as sensibly expect time to turn back in its flight, or the earth to reverse its revolutions round the sun, as that God could justly be impugned for moral imperfection of any kind. "Shall not the Judge of all the earth do right?" (Genesis 18:25). "Justice and judgment are the habitation of His throne" (Psalm 89:14). Zephaniah speaks of "the just Lord" (3:5). And in the Book of Revelation we have the beautiful ascription: "Just and true are Thy ways, Thou King of saints" (15:3).

(c) *Wisdom.* Wisdom and knowledge are sometimes confused with one another. Knowledge, in its intellectual sense, is the mental acquisition of facts: wisdom is the constructive use of those facts. The Bible assures us that God possesses both in infinitude. "God is a God of knowledge" (1 Samuel 2:3). "O, Lord, how manifold are Thy works. In wisdom hast Thou made them all" (Psalm 104:20). "To God only wise be glory through Jesus Christ for ever" (Romans 16:27). "The only wise God" (1 Timothy 1:17).

(d) *Truth.* To God we not only apply the adjective "true" but the noun "truth". In Deuteronomy 13:4 He is referred to as a "God of truth" and in 1 Thessalonians 1:9 Paul describes Him as "the true and living God". This means that He is *real* in contradistinction to the *false* gods and that

He is *right* in opposition to the *wrong* ones; that is to say, God is not only true in Himself, but true also to all for which He stands. He is truth personified.

(e) *Love*. Four pregnant epigrams in the Bible sum up its teaching about the being, nature and attributes of the Deity: (i) "God is a Spirit" (John 4:24); (ii) "God is light" (1 John 1:5); (iii) "God is fire" (Hebrews 12:39); (iv) "God is love" (1 John 4:8). John and Paul are like two men climbing a conical mountain from opposite sides. On reaching the top they arrive at the same point. Thus the apex of John's revelation is the sublime aphorism: "God is love": while that of Paul is contained in 1 Corinthians 13:13: "The greatest is love." To state that God is love is not, of course, to deny that there is such a thing as what the apostle called "the terror of the Lord" (2 Corinthians 5:11) or what the seer in Revelation speaks of as "the wrath of the Lamb" (6:16). Yet, whatever the anger of the Almighty may mean, and there can be no doubt that it does mean something unimaginably awful, it can never contradict or annul His love. Have you perhaps read how, in one of his sermons, Jonathan Edwards broke out with this horrendous outburst: "You cannot face an infuriated tiger? How, then, will you stand when God rushes upon you in His wrath?" That was certainly a terrifying inquiry. We must ever remind ourselves, however, that God's anger is not blind fury. It is not the ferocity of the tiger, but the wrath of the Lamb. R.W. Dale once publicly lamented: "There is something wrong with our land today. Nobody is frightened of God." Yet proper fear of the Lord is not trepidation but reverence, not fear to enrage Him but fear to offend Him, not cringing, craven pusillanimity but the adoring prostration of the soul before the Highest. Thomas Browne's enigmatic saying brings out well the difference between the two emotions: "I fear God, yet I am not afraid of Him." Human language cannot get closer to the Divine reality than in the sublime utterance of Augustine: "God the Father is the Lover, God the Son is the Beloved, God the Spirit is the Love." And the wonder of it is that this love is transmissible, that it can be conveyed from God to us, that because "God so loved us, we ought also to love one another" (1 John 4:11) and that this love can be "shed abroad in our hearts by the Holy Ghost which is given unto us" (Romans 5:5).

And so we reach the end of the second road along which we may hopefully fare in our search for God – *the road of revelation.*

THE ROAD OF REGENERATION – this is the road of Christian experience

No truth in the whole gamut of Christian theology is, by many who ought to know better, so played down, or, indeed, totally ignored, as the great doctrine of regeneration. Nevertheless it is absolutely crucial to a comprehension of the things of God. What birth is to natural life, the New Birth is to spiritual life – the initial miracle upon which everything else depends.

Let me try to put the point in a picture. Imagine, say, one hundred expectant mothers in the last stages of pregnancy assembled at a clinic in a maternity hospital. They are all thinking of the babies about to be born to them and each resolves to do the best she can for her prospective offspring.

A gynaecologist, who is also an expert educationist, we will suppose, attends them and points out the vital necessity of beginning early with the training of the malleable minds of their little ones. "In fact," we will imagine him saying, "it is advisable to start with the foetus." This surprises the women, but they bow to his professional expertise, and arrange to go together to a university for ante-natal instruction. They duly present themselves. A class is formed and a number of distinguished academics consent to give the unborn babies the benefit of their hoarded learning. A professor of astronomy lectures on the starry heavens, a botanist on the structure, colouration and growth of plants and flowers, a physiologist, on the wonders of the human body.

What would be the point of such an exercise? The knowledge would be true, the information conveyed would be correct, but of what profit could it possibly be to the foetuses? Although brilliantly illuminative to the minds of men and women, the lessons would be utterly and totally beyond the comprehension of the unborn. Birth would be the basic prerequisite to understanding.

No less essential to the assimilation of spiritual truth, the realities of the unseen world and of a personal God, is the New Birth. Many who profess and call themselves Christians have not the foggiest idea what it means. If they *do* use the term regeneration at all it is in connection with a magical rite administered to unconscious infants. Adult regeneration, that is, the sort of regeneration spoken of in the New Testament, is to them a sealed book. They have no more conception of it than the unborn babies in our illustration would have of the learned disquisitions of the professors. To talk to such persons about God is like trying to describe to a foetus its father's face.

Of this the classic New Testament illustration is, of course, the story of our Lord's encounter with Nicodemus. Nicodemus was the leading religious scholar in the Israel of his time, yet he had not the slightest notion what the Master was speaking about when He said: "Ye must be born again" (John 3:7). He could not understand this curious yet imperious demand. He thought it meant some strange regression into the natal cave, and this appeared to him, as indeed it is, anatomically impossible. For the learned Rabbi religion was not enough, he needed regeneration. Without that there could be no real knowledge of spiritual things. Paul makes the same point powerfully in 1 Corinthians 2:14: "But the natural man receiveth not the things of the Spirit of God: for they are foolishness unto him: neither can he know them, because they are spiritually discerned."

The best way to get to know there is a living God is to be born again, indeed it is the only way. A theological education can present you with possibilities and probabilities, conjectures and speculations. Only regeneration can put you in saving contact with the Divine Being Himself. We shall have more to say about this later. For the present let it suffice to note that none but a twiceborn soul can really solve the riddle of the universe, no-one but such as he is able to make his own John Kelman's moving confession: "I believe that there is Someone beyond the material, that that Someone is a Friend, and that Jesus is the incarnate Friendliness of God."

2
THE QUARREL OF THE UNIVERSE

The Christian Doctrine of Moral Evil

O, leave the wise to wrangle, and with me
The quarrel of the universe let be. Omar Khayyam

"I accept the universe," said Margaret Fuller. "Gad, she'd better!" snorted Thomas Carlyle.

God saw everything that He had made, and, behold, it was very good. Genesis 1:31

He hath made everything beautiful. Ecclesiastes 3:11

The earth was without form and void; and darkness was upon the face of the deep. Genesis 1:2

The foundations of the earth are out of course. Psalm 82:5

All things are double, one against another. Ecclesiasticus 42:24

The whole creation groaneth and travaileth in pain together until now. Romans 8:22

An enemy hath done this. Matthew 13:28

His hand hath formed the crooked serpent. Job 26:13

Now the serpent was more subtil than any beast of the field which the Lord God had made. Genesis 3:1

I beheld Satan as lightning fall from heaven. Luke 10:18

For this purpose the Son of God was manifested, that He might destroy the works of the Devil. *1 John 3:8*

That old serpent, called the Devil, and Satan, was cast out into the earth, and his angels were cast out with him. Revelation 12:9

I saw an angel come down from heaven, having the key of the bottomless pit, and a great chain in his hand. And he laid hold on the dragon, which is the Devil, and Satan, and bound him a thousand years. Revelation 20:1ff.

The Devil was cast into the lake of fire and brimstone, and shall be tormented day and night for ever and ever. Revelation 20:10

TWO OLD WELSH preachers were talking once about their pulpit and pastoral work. One was in the throes of literary composition. "I am writing a sixpenny pamphlet," he said, "to explain how evil came into the universe." With typically Celtic wit, the other replied: "Better make it a shilling pamphlet and tell us how to get evil out of the universe!"

That story may well furnish us with a fitting frontispiece for our study of the Christian doctrine of moral evil. Such a study is bound to be based on the Bible, for there is not, and cannot possibly be, any other authentic and reliable source of information on the subject; and when we search the Scriptures with that inquiry in mind we discover that four key-words may well summarize its theodicean teaching.

Those four words are: (1) *Creator*; (2) *conspirator*; (3) *collaborator*; and (4) *Consummator*. To explain: the Creator is, of course, God; the conspirator is Satan; the collaborator is man; and the Consummator is Christ.

Consider them in that order.

CREATOR

The universe is there – palpably there – an effect, and an effect, as we have earlier noted, presupposes a cause. There are those who, in the name of a false philosophy, profess to disbelieve in its objective reality, but Samuel Johnson's method of invalidating that theory by stubbing his toes on a stone could hardly be bettered. Yes, the universe is there, a self-evident fact, and its existence has somehow to be accounted for.

How is that to be done?

Six answers may be given to that query.

(a) *It was never made.* According to this theory, matter is eternal and, as a consequence, the universe never had a beginning. What are we to say to this? Well, it must be admitted that there is at least one text in the Bible which appears to support it: "The earth abideth for ever" (Ecclesiastes 1:4). Obviously, however, the Hebrew word there rendered "for ever" must be construed in the total context of biblical revelation. Scripture must be compared with Scripture. Moreover, the very concept of creation connotes commencement. "The world," as someone has said, "has the look of a manufactured article." Most certainly, it has; and a manufactured article presupposes a manufacturer.

Think, too, of the appalling implications of this theory.

If it be true, then, as D.M. Baillie has pointed out, we are driven irresistibly to the comfortless conclusion that the material order is Godless, and dust and ashes all that is. Any notion leading to this dreary deduction surely contains within itself its own refutation.

(2) *It made itself.* Modern materialistic astronomers who maintain this theory are divisible into two main groups. We shall have occasion in subsequent chapters to go into this in greater detail. Here it must suffice to note the fact. One propounds what it calls "the Big Bang Theory", the theory that the cosmos commenced with a gigantic explosion; the other holds that the universe is explicable in terms of what it describes as "the Continuous Creation Theory", the notion that the cosmos was self-originating and that even now whole new galaxies are in process of formation.

(3) *It was made by chance or accident.* A present-day scientist has spoken of the universe as "one colossal coincidence consequent upon an infinite succession of flukes"! Anyone who accepts that as true would as readily believe that Sir Christopher Wren is a fictitious character and that St Paul's Cathedral simply rose of itself out of a slagheap! "What can be more foolish," says Jeremy Taylor, "than to think that all this rare fabric of heaven and earth could come by chance, when all the skill of science is not able to make an oyster?"

There is a familiar story of how Robert Ingersoll, a notorious agnostic, called once at the home of the eminent American preacher Phillips Brooks, though I can find no reference to the incident in Brooks' definitive biography. Brooks had in his home, it seems, a fine model of the globe, designed to illustrate its movements in relation to the other planets. Ingersoll was fascinated by the model and kept turning the pasteboard globe round with the tips of his fingers. "That is just what I want," he at length remarked. "It's splendid. Who made it?" Recalling Ingersoll's elaborate arguments against the Divine creation of the world, Brooks replied with a sly smile: "Who made it? Why nobody! It just happened!" Ingersoll, as we say, "got the message".

(4) *It was made by some malign power.* This was the position adopted by Bertrand Russell. In one of his earlier works he wrote: "If there be any purpose in the universe, it must be the purpose of a Fiend." To say such a thing was, however, to visualize the Devil in an entirely uncharacteristic, not to say impossible, rôle. Satan is not a creator: he is a destroyer. He could no more bring cosmos into being than a cyclone could construct a city. In my personal copy of the volume by Bertrand Russell just mentioned, an unconsciously inspired compositor had inadvertently inserted an "r" after the first letter of the final word and it had escaped the proof-reader's eye. So that, as it stands in this edition of the book, it reads: "If there be any purpose in the universe, it must be the purpose of a *Friend.*" Sometimes it seems an error can express the truth.

(5) *It was made by two opposing forces.* I think that, had I not been a Christian, I might have been strongly attracted to Dualism. Like the ancient Parsees, I should have believed in two gods – a Deity and a Demiurge – in continual conflict for the mastery of the world. Nature would certainly appear to suggest that. It is so ambiguous. It speaks with two voices and seems to indicate the existence of a great line of moral cleavage running right through the universe. Illustrations of this strange dichotomy abound. Can the milk in a mother's breast and the venom in a snake's fang come from the same hand? Can the sunshine which ripens the golden grain and the storm which lays it flat hail from the same source? Can the violet and the volcano, the wheat germ and the cholera germ, be

products of the same Intelligence and the same intention? It certainly does not look as if that were so. You will remember William Blake's tremendous lines entitled "The Tiger" contained in his *Songs of Experience* in which he raises this very issue:

Tiger! Tiger! burning bright,
In the forests of the night,
What immortal hand or eye
Could frame thy fearful symmetry?
Did He who made the lamb make thee?

That appears highly improbable. There is in nature much to *appeal*: much also to *appal*. It looks as if it were the work not of one only but of two artificers.

(6) *It was made by a good and loving God.* The most daring thing that can be said about the apparently ambiguous cosmos is that it is the product of a God of love. There is much in the world as we know it which positively shrieks against that comfortable creed. Yet it is the teaching of the Bible. Here are a few confirmatory quotations: "In the beginning God created the heavens and the earth" (Genesis 1:1). "Let all the inhabitants of the world stand in awe of Him, for He spake and it was done, He commanded and it stood fast" (Psalm 33:8,9). "Of old hast thou laid the foundations of the earth: and the heavens are the work of Thine hands" (Psalm 102:25). "He hath made the earth by His power, He hath established the world by His wisdom, and hath stretched out the heavens by His discretion. When He uttereth His voice, there is a multitude of waters in the heavens, and He causeth the vapours to ascend from the ends of the earth: He maketh lightnings with rain, and bringeth forth the wind out of His treasures" (Jeremiah 10:12,13). "All things were made by Him, and without Him was not anything made that was made" (John 1:3). "Every house is builded by some man; but He

that built all things is God" (Hebrews 3:4). "Thou hast created all things, and for Thy pleasure they are and were created" (Revelation 4:11).

According to the Bible, God is the only Creator. Other beings can make things out of pre-existing material; but, strictly speaking, none but God can create. And when He had completed the colossal undertaking, He pronounced the product "very good" (Genesis 1:31).

From the Talmud comes a story of close relevance here. A sceptic once approached Rabbi Joshua and said to him: "You believe that God knows the future?" "Yes," replied the Rabbi. "Then," went on the interlocutor, "why is it written, 'The Lord God said, I will destroy everything which I have made, because it repenteth Me that I have made them'? Did not the Lord foresee that man would be corrupt?" The Rabbi answered: "Do you have children?" "Yes," was the answer. "When a child is born, what do you do?" "I make great rejoicing!" "What cause have you to rejoice? Don't you know that children must die?" "Yes, that is true. But in the time of the enjoyment I do not think of the future." "So it is with God," said Rabbi Joshua. "He knew that men would sin. Still, that knowledge did not prevent the executing of His benevolent purpose to create them."

Some impious and foolish persons have presumptuously fancied that they could improve on God's creative work. "If I had been present at the Creation," observed Alfonso of Castille (1221-84), "I would have given some useful hints for the better arrangement of the universe." In the Book of Job, however, the Lord counters man's unbounded arrogance and self-conceit by loftily inquiring: "Where wast thou when I laid the foundations of the earth? Declare, if thou hast understanding" (38:4).

A wiser attitude was advocated by James Edward Le Rossinquol when, commenting of the story of the Creation in Genesis, he remarked: "When we speak of the Creation, it behoves us to be humble, for we must remember that none of us was present on that occasion."

To hear some secular scientists expatiating on the subject, one would think they had been there! In their view the initiating energy in the universe was "mostly hydrogen": the Bible says it was the Most High.

According to the Scriptures, then, God, is the sole Maker of the universe. But precisely *how* did He make it?

Various possibilities present themselves.

(1) *He made it out of pre-existent matter.* But if matter antedated the cosmos, it must either have been eternal or else created by God in some primordial era.

(2) *He made it out of His own Being,* as an emanation from His own substance, an extension of His own existence. D.M. Baillie demolishes that theory in his great book *God was in Christ*. Discussing this notion, he writes: "That would make God directly responsible for all the evil in the universe, and not merely indirectly responsible for it, we must go further and say that all the evil is *in* God – an intolerable suggestion." Not in this manner did God make the world.

(3) *He made it "out of nothing"*. This is the orthodox theological position. Nothingness is the presupposition and precondition of Divine creativity. Human beings can make something of something, but we cannot make something of nothing. Only the Creator can do that, and that is exactly what He *has done* in bringing this vast material order into existence.

Over the entrance to the Geology Hall in Redpath Museum, which forms part of the McGill University, Montreal, Canada, I read a quotation from the Psalms, which a former principal, Sir William Dawson, had had incised in the stone portal. It read: "O, Lord, how manifold are Thy works! In wisdom hast Thou made them all:

the earth is full of Thy riches" (104:24). It is a good thing when geology goes hand in hand with theology.

But that raises a relevant question. Many years ago I crossed the Nullabor Plain in Australia by train in the company of a Professor of Geology. We conferred on matters of mutual interest, especially on those to the study of which we had respectively given our lives. At the close of the conversation, he observed: "But, then, *geological* time is not the same as *theological* time, is it?"

The Genesis account of the origin of the universe and of human life would seem plainly to intimate that the world and all that it inhabit were brought into being in six literal days. That appears to be ruled out, however, by the narrative itself. George Bernard Shaw, in that impish way of his, used to poke fun at a twenty-four-hour interpretation by asking how there could possibly be "days" (Genesis 1:5,8,13) before there were "lights in the firmament" (Genesis 1:14). But, as Peter reminds us, we must not lose sight of the fact that "one day is with the Lord as a thousand years, and a thousand years as one day" (2 Peter 3:8); and since modern methods of computing prehistory seem to demand prodigious periods of time before the appearance of the human race, many conservative scholars have felt compelled to assign to the word "day" in this context a connotation other than that commonly ascribed to it, conceiving of it on a time-scale of undefined duration. When a simple-minded but devout lad was told that the world was made by God in six days, he remarked: "I wonder why it took Him so long!" God *could* have made it more quickly, but apparently He didn't!

Attempts are sometimes made to account for the disparity between geological and theological time by envisaging the occurrence of some cosmic disaster between Genesis 1:1 and Genesis 1:2. John Henry Newman in his *Apologia pro Vita Sua* observes that "the human race was implicated in some terrible aboriginal catastrophe." And, in his definitive study *Satan* Lewis Spencer Chafer speaks of "that dateless period between the perfect creation of the heavens and the earth (Genesis 1:1), and the desolating judgment which ended that period, when the earth became waste and empty (Genesis 1:2, Isaiah 24:1; Jeremiah 4:23-6). One passage (Ezekiel 28: 11-19) deals at length with Satan, and his relation to that age".

"In the beginning God created the heavens and the earth." And the earth was what? Paradise? A world of order, beauty, peace, joy? No. "The earth was without form and void." Not so does God create. Of this more anon.

When we state that God created the world, we must, then, be wisely mindful to add the phrase "out of nothing", although the words are really redundant, since the concept of creation implies them. Equally we must avoid the error of saying that God created it "out of Himself" or that He fashioned it out of pre-existent matter. The orthodox Christian position is that He created it "out of nothing", and nothingness is, as we have seen, the precondition of creativity.

"In the beginning God created the heavens and the earth" (Genesis 1:1). "And the earth was without form and void" (Genesis 1:2). Obviously between what is described in verse 1 and what is depicted in verse 2 some colossal cosmic catastrophe must have occurred. "Without form and void." That is not how God creates. "God Himself formed the earth and made it; He hath established it. He created it not in vain, He formed it to be inhabited" (Isaiah 45:18).

What *was* that appalling primordial tragedy? To this inquiry we now turn.

CONSPIRATOR

It was the introduction into the universe of moral evil. Its presence is unmistakable, its occurrence to a large extent inscrutable. What *is* moral evil and whence does it come?

In other words, what are its origins and nature?

As to its origin there are several classic theories.

(1) *Some say that moral evil is an illusion.* They look upon it as having no objective reality, but as merely a morbid fantasy of the human mind; not something in and of itself, but rather as the absence of something. This was how Augustine construed it – as an entity too negative to have had an origin. Robert Herrick, the poet, was of the same mind. He wrote:

Evil no nature hath: the loss of good
Is that which gives to sin a livelihood.

To the same effect Robert Browning cried:

Evil is null, is nought,
Is silence implying sound.

Some oriental religions and philosophies have denied the reality of evil and in modern times the literature of Christian Science, where it refers to evil at all, encloses the word, either literally or metaphorically, in inverted commas. In her standard work *Science and Health with Key to the Scriptures* Mary Baker Eddy categorically declares: "Evil has no reality. It is neither person, place, nor thing, but is simply a belief, an illusion without real basis. If sin, sickness or death were understood as nothingness, they would soon disappear." Some say moral evil is an illusion.

(2) *Some say it is an impenetrable mystery,* a problem too profound for finite minds to fathom. There is room, we are told, in all religious thinking for a reverent agnosticism, certain "no-go areas" into which we are forbidden to pry. You may recall this view of it by the American Quaker poet, John Greenleaf Whittier:

Not mine to look where cherubim
And seraphs may not see;
But nothing can be good in Him
Which evil is in me.

When finite beings presume to probe into the will and ways of an infinite Being there are bound to be esoteric secrets which the finite cannot comprehend. Some say that moral evil is an inscrutable mystery.

(3) *Some say it is good in the making.* It is true that, by the marvellous alchemy of Divine grace, God can bring good out of evil, but this does not mean that He deliberately *wills* the evil in order that good may result. That would implicate Him in the slimy slander slung at the apostle Paul, which he rebuts so vehemently: "Let us do evil that good may come" (Romans 3:8). Alexander Pope's sentiments expressed in his *An Essay on Man* are nothing more than baseless optimism:

All nature is but art unknown to thee,
All chance direction which thou canst not see;
All discord harmony not understood,
All partial evil universal good;
And, spite of pride, in erring reason's spite,
One truth is clear – whatever is, is right.

The Scriptures never subscribe to such a shallow and superficial view of the problem of moral evil.

"Science has now discovered anti-matter, and some scientists postulate an anti-world. Perhaps in this anti-world time might run backwards. (In fact some claim it must to keep symmetry). It might be that, going faster than the speed of light, would take one into a world where time ran 'anti' too" (James Reid, *God, the Atom and the Universe;* Grand Rapids, Zondervan, 1968, p.66).

What, then, is moral evil? It is the working of a malign

will in the universe in a manner completely counter to the good, wise and loving purpose of God. Such is its essential nature.

But how did it originate? How are we able to describe this vast scheme of things as a *uni*verse, the expression of a single purpose, when it seems to contain so many conflicting and contradictory elements – the mushroom and the toadstool, the first pearly tooth of a baby and the terrible tusk of a wild boar, the song of a nightingale and the wail of a wolf? Where did evil come from?

There are four views.

The first is that moral evil originated in nothingness. It is a startling fact that the same Hebrew word *bara*, to create, is used in Genesis 1:1: "God created the heaven and the earth", and in Isaiah 45:7: "I create evil." Karl Barth, reputed to be the greatest theologian of the twentieth century, informs us in his massive *Dogmatik* that "evil came from nothingness" – a patently difficult concept which only a close and clever student of the works of that profound Christian thinker can be expected to comprehend.

The second view is that evil comes from matter. We earlier quoted Mr Punch's classic conundrum: "What is mind? No matter. What is matter? Never mind." But there are thinkers who trace the origin of evil to that which is essentially *amoral*, namely, matter. Yet the implications of such an identification make it untenable; for, if it were true, that would mean that the Incarnation would be impossible, since a holy God could not unite organically with what is essentially evil. No Incarnation, no salvation, and so the Christian faith can never accept as true the notion that evil originates in matter.

The third view is that moral evil stems from God. W.N.

Carter actually goes the length of saying: "The existence of evil demands the existence of God." How are we to reply to that? Well, we must begin by admitting that, since God is the ultimate Author of all that is, He is inevitably responsible for everything in the universe, although He is not, and never can be, chargeable with anything incompatible with the righteousness and holiness of His own nature. "His angels He charged with folly" (Job 4:18); "The heavens are not clean in His sight" (Job 15:15); He is "of purer eyes than to behold evil, and cannot look on iniquity" (Habakkuk 1:13). How, then, can He be justly said to originate evil? As we shall see later, in the person of Christ He accepted at the Cross responsibility for the introduction of evil to the cosmos, and died to expel it. But, from the very nature of the case, there is no conceivable way in which He could be criminally implicated in it.

Let me put it this way. To will a benevolent effect does not necessarily imply willing a consequent cause. Suppose a surgeon performs a delicate operation on a blind man and totally restores his sight. Nobody in his senses would regard that as other than a benevolent act. But suppose that, while the man has been blind another man, taking advantage of the sightless man's disability, has raped the poor fellow's wife; and, as soon as the sightless man's vision is restored, the first thing he does with his eyesight is to pick up a revolver and shoot the rapist through the heart. Is the surgeon to be blamed for the murder? Certainly, in one sense, he *is* responsible, because had he not performed the ophthalmic operation on the blind man, the latter would not have been able to take up the pistol and kill the rapist. Surely, however, the surgeon was not guilty of culpable homicide! He did not *will* the murder. He willed good and nothing but good, but his will was twisted by his patient to a deed which was no part of his intention.

Just so with God. Though there are texts, such as

Proverbs 16:4, "The Lord hath made all things for Himself: yea, even the wicked for the day of evil," yet His purpose in creation was entirely good, wise, loving, but it has been temporarily baulked, thwarted, frustrated by the action of an evil will.

The fourth view – that sanctioned and substantiated by the Bible – *is that moral evil was fathered by the Devil.* But is there a Devil? Many nowadays think not. "Since the eighteenth century," writes Theo Preiss in his *Life of Christ*, "we have reduced the religious drama to two partners – God and Man. With a superior smile, we have eliminated the rôles of Satan and his acolytes." In his book *The Inward Light* Fielding Hall states, "Good and evil are both from God, and there is no Devil – only another face of God." "The theory that there is in the universe a power or principle, personal or otherwise," remarks George Galloway, "in eternal opposition to God, is generally discarded by the modern mind." Rabbi Lionel Blue does not believe in a personal Devil: he holds that the Devil is the personifacation of that part of our nature which we cannot love. "The Devil," declares Josef Barton, "is an ancient way to symbolize the existence of evils of social unrest and political instability."

Years ago the *New York Independent* printed these lines by Alfred H. Hough:

Men don't believe in a Devil now, as their fathers used to do;
They forced the door of the broadest creed to let His Majesty through;
There isn't a print of his cloven hoof, or a fiery dart from his bow
To be found in earth or air today, for the world has voted so.

But who is mixing the fatal draught that palsies heart and brain,
And loads the bier of each passing year with ten hundred thousand slain?

Who blights the bloom of the land today with the fiery breath of hell,
If the Devil isn't and never was, won't somebody rise and tell?

Who dogs the steps of the toiling saint and digs the pit for his feet?
Who sows the tares in the field of time wherever God sows His wheat?
The Devil is voted not to be, and of course the thing is true;
But who is doing the kind of work the Devil alone should do?

Won't somebody step to the front forthwith and make their bow and show
How the frauds and crimes of a single day spring up? We want to know.
The Devil was voted fairly out, and of course the Devil's gone:
But simple people would like to know who carries his business on.

All this is in line with satanic strategy. The Devil is an expert at the disappearing act. As someone has written: "Probably Satan's most skilful accomplishment has been the vanishing trick performed successfully in full view of the Christian Church." "The Devil's best ruse," observes Beaudelaire, "is to persuade us that he does not exist." On which Denis de Rougemont makes this inspired comment: "God says 'I am that I am', but the Devil, who delights in imitating the truth that he may distort it, says 'I am not.'"

It is noteworthy that so many of the modern cults do not believe in a personal Devil. "There is no personal Devil," declares Theosophy. "There is no Devil," says Spiritism. "The Devil is not a personal supernatural agent of evil," asserts Christadelphianism, "and in fact there is no such being in existence."

An unsigned article, entitled "Giving the Devil His Due", which appeared in *Newsweek* on August 30, 1982 emphasizes this point. "Over the last two centuries," the author states, "the Devil has been debunked by rationalists, exorcised by psychotherapists, and demythologized by theologians." As Bezzel argues: "The world is bedevilled in the same proportion as it appears to be dedevilled by the theological intellect."

There is point and pertinence in the story of how Joseph Parker, a famous London pulpit figure of a former day, was told by a ministerial friend, Newman Hall, that he intended delivering a popular lecture on "Satan" and invited Parker to come and hear him. The invitation was decisively declined. "Satan!" cried Parker. "I don't need to go to a lecture to hear more about Satan: I know too much about him already!"

Still, the fact is that, however people today may be disposed to deny or ignore his existence, the Devil has been believed in from time immemorial. Great philosophers have credited his reality. Although far from being an orthodox Christian, John Stuart Mill is said to have held that it is not unreasonable to suppose that the universe is the work of a beneficent Being, whose designs were hindered and thwarted by a malignant spirit.

Poets, too, have expended their genius on the portrayal of this evil personality. One thinks of Dante with his *Divine Comedy*, of Milton with his *Paradise Lost*, of Goethe with his *Faust*.

One thing is certain. The Bible recognizes Satan's reality. To Holy Scripture he is no moral myth, not a phantom of the mind, but a grim and terrible personality, the arch-enemy of God and man. We may perhaps sum up its teaching on the subject in three rhyming words: (1) Satan's *perfection*; (2) *Satan's defection*; (3) *Satan's ejection*.

Take them one by one.

(1) *Satan's perfection.* It is not natural for us to associate that quality with such a personality. All we know of him makes us think of him as ugly, sinister, repulsive. Yet, coming from the creative hands of God and before his Fall, he must have been a being of surpassing beauty. I have read of three little French boys who were asked: "Who created the Devil?" Rènè answered that it was quite impossible that God created the Devil, since He made nothing but what was good. Guy did not venture to reply, for it seemed to him that the question was put only to give them a lesson. Finally, Henri, the most sedate and rational of the three, responded after some reflection: "God created him an angel, but he made Himself a Devil by his sin." In fact, as someone has credibly argued, Lucifer was probably the loveliest creature God ever made.

Two eloquent paragraphs in the Old Testament thus portray him under the figures respectively of the King of Babylon and the Prince of Tyre: "How art thou fallen from heaven, O Lucifer, Son of the Morning! How art thou cut down to the ground that did weaken the nations! For thou hast said in thine heart, I will ascend into heaven, I will exalt my throne above the stars of God: I will sit also upon the mount of the congregation in the sides of the north; I will ascend above the heights of the clouds; I will be like the Most High" (Isaiah 14:12-15). "Thou art the anointed cherub that covereth; and I have set thee so; thou hast been upon the holy mountain of God; thou hast walked up and down in the midst of the stones of fire. Thou wast perfect in thy ways from the day that thou wast created, till iniquity was found in thee" (Ezekiel 28:14,15).

Liberal theologians tell us that these two passages refer, not to Satan, but to Ithobal II. But surely the language is such as could not be predicated of any earthly monarch! What human being was perfect from his creation or aspired to set his throne above the stars of God or walked on the stones of fire? The law of double reference operates here. The paragraphs may have had, in certain of their aspects, allusions to some oriental potentate, but their application goes far beyond that and extends to the Prince of Darkness himself.

(2) *Satan's defection.* "Of the original cause of sin," wrote Reader Harris, "we shall probably never know more than our Lord tells us in the Parable of the Tares, when He says: 'An enemy hath done this'." But manifestly more is revealed than that. Not everything our curiosity would like to pry into is disclosed, but enough is unfolded to solve for us the otherwise inscrutable mystery as to how moral evil got into God's good universe.

The Bible informs us that the Fall took place at that point in Lucifer's career where *aspiration* became *ambition*, where in him a laudable desire to *resemble* God became a rebellious resolve to *supplant* Him. Swedenborg, founder of the so-called "New Church", emphatically denied that Satan had ever been an angel of light and had fallen from his first estate. But the Scriptures plainly state that this was so. "It was when Lucifer first congratulated himself upon his angelic behaviour," declared Dag Hammerskjold, "that he became the tool of evil." Pride was the primary sin. Evil entered the cosmos when, on the part of Lucifer, a praiseworthy longing to be *like* God became an arrogant craving to be *as* God.

Disrespect for the Devil is not a Christian virtue. To dub him satirically "His Satanic Majesty" (John Brown of Haddington); "Old Smutty Face" (Billy Bray); or "Our Father Below" (C.S. Lewis) is to run a grave risk of underestimating our mortal enemy. "Satan," as F.P. Harton declared, "is not a second God." Brook Fosse Westcott put the position well when he pointed out that, despite the apparent Dualism in the world, it is "not a war between rival powers, but a rebellion of a subject against his Lord."

All the same it is never wise or politic to minimize or

under-rate your enemy. One of the basic prerequisites of effective military strategy is a true measurement of the opposing force. It is reported that, during World War II, General Montgomery, as he then was, used to display in a prominent position in his field-office a portrait of his archfoe – Rommel. So with the Christian and Satan. We must keep him in our thoughts, and yet not be obsessed by him. We must not focus too much on the foe, for that would be bad for morale: equally, we must not forget him, as that will be bad for morals!

Always we must remember that he is a fallen foe, fighting a losing battle. Oscar Cullmann's classic illustration is apposite here. We are living, he has told us, between D-day and V-day, and so is the Devil! The decisive encounter is over, but there remain extensive mopping-up operations. Satan is still violently active and aggressive. John Trapp spoke of him as "the Great Peripatetic" – always "on the go"! Charles Lamb called him "Sabbathless Satan" because the Evil One never has a holiday, never takes time off. As Peter says, "Your adversary the Devil, as a roaring lion, walketh about, seeking whom he may devour" (1 Peter 5:8).

(3) *Satan's ejection.*

The Devil is on the way down. He fell from heaven to the heavenlies. "I beheld Satan as lightning fall from heaven" (Luke 10:18). He will fall from the heavenlies to the earth. "The Devil was cast out into the earth, and his angels were cast out with him" (Revelation 12:9). And he will fall at last from earth into hell. "The Devil was cast into the lake of fire" (Revelation 20:10). His fall is irreversible. In the sonorous syllables of Shakespeare's Cardinal Wolsey: "When he falls, he falls as Lucifer, never to hope again."

Nor did he fall alone. Jude speaks of "the angels which kept not their *principality*" (6 AV margin), and they have become the "principalities and powers" to which Paul refers in Ephesians 6:12: "For we wrestle not against flesh and blood, but against principalities, against powers, against the rulers of the darkness of this world, against spiritual wickedness in *heavenly* places"; and these are the demons that wage unremitting war on the saints and constantly stir up trouble in the world.

COLLABORATOR

Nor was the Fall limited to the Devil and his angels: man, too, was, and is, implicated. Man is the collaborator. His life is set at the tension of worlds; he is continually confronted by moral choices which will eventuate in eternal consequences – good and evil, right and wrong, truth and error. Just as at Shechem Joshua, on an historic occasion, faced the tribes of Israel, together with their heads, elders, judges and officers, with the stern, ineluctable demand, "Choose you this day whom you will serve" (Joshua 24:5), so God constantly places before mankind inescapable ethical options. Profoundly upset by the aspect of things around him, a young man is said to have asked petulantly: "Why did God make such a world?" To which came the wise reply: "That is exactly the reason why God put you into this world – to make it better! Now get busy and do so." In other words, become a collaborator with God.

CONSUMMATOR

The Consummator is, of course, Christ. At the Incarnation He entered the arena of history as moral Champion of the human race, challenged the Devil and all his hosts to mortal combat at Calvary and there routed them decisively and irreversibly. "For this purpose the Son of God was manifested, that He might destroy" – *what*? "The Devil?" No. "The works of the Devil" (1 John 3:8). Satan is not yet to be consigned to his fate. He still roams the world on his nefarious activities. God wills it so. It suits His present purpose to have him around. As someone has said: "The world is all the better for having a Devil in it, so long as our foot is on his neck!" In his *A Textbook of Apologetics* Charles Harris lists some of the advantages accruing to us from having a Satan. "The hypothesis of a personal Devil has many advantages," he writes. "It explains the whole of the facts; it avoids the postulation of two First Causes; it vindicates the moral perfection of the Deity; and it allows the optimistic hope to be entertained that in the end good will triumph over evil." Satan is not to be annihilated: he is first to be incarcerated, and finally consigned without trial or appeal to everlasting punishment. About this we shall have more to say in our final chapter. Meantime, let us comfort ourselves with the reflection that, although Satan *roars*, Jesus *reigns*.

3
THE BELOVED REBEL

The Christian Doctrine of Man

We are not just aliens: we are rebels taken with the weapons in our hands. Peter Taylor Forsyth

If the Eternal Father were to say to me, "I am your Friend", I would put up my fists to Him. Benito Mussolini

Absalom, in his relations with King David, his father, is perhaps the closest Biblical parallel to the unregenerate man's relationship with God. Anon

Sinful man is not just an imperfect creature who needs improvement: he is a rebel who must lay down his arms. C.S. Lewis

The death of Jesus was the most cowardly murder of an Ambassador, the foulest outrage that rebels at any time committed against the kind Father of their fatherland.
Quoted by Erich Sauer in *The Triumph of the Crucified*

If Jesus is God, and we fail to worship Him, we are the worst rebels of all.
Stuart Olyott

He maketh the rebel
A priest and a king
Arthur T. Pierson

ON JULY 23, 1969, Edwin R. Aldrin – "Buzz" to his intimates – one of the first men to set foot on the moon, was coasting earthwards at colossal speed on the Apollo 11 spacecraft. From it he broadcast a message to the world. During the historic flight, he said, his mind had been much taken up with a text in the Bible. That text was this: "When I consider the heavens, the work of Thy fingers, the moon and the stars which Thou hast ordained, what is man?"

What is man? That question will be relevant as long as there is a human race. Significantly, the Bible poses it in three distinct contexts – Psalm 8:4; Job 7:17 and 15:4 – but the inquiry will continue to be made till the end of time.

Before examining the Biblical doctrine of man in some detail, let us pause for a moment to reflect that replies popularly returned to this query commonly range themselves into one or other of two categories.

Some seek to *magnify man*. In this connection one thinks of the German philosopher Nietszche with his notion of the superman. "As against the background of a slave morality," he wrote, "there is at the same time gradually defining itself, at present dimly seen, a master-caste of free, adventurous spirits. They prepare the way for a superman. He is not yet here. The succeeding ages, even at their highest, are but the forerunners of the supermen of the future." One thinks, too, of Shakespeare, and in particular of a familiar passage in *Hamlet:*

What is a man,
If his chief good and market of his time
Be but to feed and sleep? A beast, no more!

Sure, He that made us with such large discourse,
Looking before and after, gave us not that capability
And God-like reason to fust in us unused?

One thinks, moreover, of the blasphemous outburst of Swinburne in his *Hymn of Man:*

Glory to Man in the highest! For man is the master of things.

Yes, some certainly do seek to magnify man.

Others try to *minify man.* They endeavour to detract from his importance and to diminish his stature. Their design is to disparage him. To this end they stress three things about him:

(1) *His physical insignificance in comparison with the vastness of the universe.* Man is no more than a microbe in the context of the cosmos. Let Alexander Clark stretch our imaginations in this regard with his vivid word-picture of the awesome amplitude of the material order we inhabit. "Make a dot on a piece of paper. It will probably measure one-fiftieth of an inch. Suppose the world to be that size. The distance to the sun will then be nineteen and a half feet, to the nearest star a thousand miles and to the farthest photographed galaxy nearly eighty-two thousand million miles." Nothing so reduces man to size as does the sight of himself in that phenomenally vast setting.

(2) Another way in which man's physical insignificance is emphasized is *reflection on the brevity of his life.* As Chaim Potok puts it in his book *The Chosen*: "We live less than the time it takes to blink an eye, if we measure our lives against eternity. I learned a long time ago that a blink of an eye in itself is nothing. But the I that blinks – that is something. The span of life is nothing, but the man who

lives that span, he is something. He can fill that tiny span with meaning, so its quality is immeasurable though its quantity may be insignificant."

(3) Yet another way in which man's littleness is stressed is by pointing to *the frailty of his frame.* Writing in his *Philosophy for our Time,* C.E.M. Joad thus listed man's material constituents: "Man's body contains enough water to fill a ten-gallon barrel; enough fat for seven bars of soap; carbon for seven thousand lead pencils; phosphorus for two thousand two hundred match-heads; iron for a medium-sized nail; lime enough to whitewash a hencoop; and small quantities of magnesium and sulphur." A creature compounded of such common chemical substances can hardly be of much consequence. So once again the question thrusts itself upon our consideration: "What is man?"

Some seek to magnify man: some try to minimize man. Who are right? What appraisal of human values corresponds the more closely to reality? Is man great or is he small?

The fact is, both are right. Man is both magnificent and mean; sublime and sordid; of the sky and of the sty. The third view of his personal worth is a mixture of the other two. "Man," said Augustine, "is a good thing spoiled." "Man," declared Disraeli, "is an archangel slightly damaged." Who can forget the famous satirical outburst of Blaise Pascal: "What a chimera is man! What a novelty! What a monster! What a chaos! What a contradiction! What a prodigy! Judge of all things, feeble worm of the earth, depository of truth, sink of uncertainty and error, the glory and the scandal of the universe!"

Before proceeding further with our study of the Biblical doctrine of man, let us note that there are four false views of man in widespread currency today.

The first view is that *man is an accident*. He is no more than a bubble which has blown up on the surface of some oozy primordial "soup" and is destined to burst into oblivion. His existence was neither planned nor foreseen. It was the unexpected outcome of unintelligent forces unconsciously co-operating in the production of an organism whose emergence was neither envisaged nor designed.

The second view sees man *as an animal*. Is he? Well, a glance at the physical basis of his being makes it patent that he has much in common with the lower orders of creation. Who has not heard the classic story of Plato and Diogenes? Plato having described man as "a two-legged animal without feathers", Diogenes plucked a cock and, bringing it into the academy, exclaimed: "Here's Plato's man!"

Thinkers in all ages have spoken of man as an animal, but they have usually sought to soften the blow by intimating, while so doing, how greatly man differs from the brutes. "Man," said Edmund Burke, "is an animal that cooks his victuals." "Man," asserted Benjamin Franklin, "is a tool-using animal." "Man," affirmed Adam Smith, "is an animal that makes bargains." "Man," stated Aristotle, "is a political animal." "Man," averred Baruch Spinoza, "is a social animal." And so on. Yes, the physical resemblance between man and beast is obviously there, but surely Ralph Waldo Emerson spoke for us all when he cried: "God defend me from ever looking at a man as an animal."

Yet that brilliant Jewish doctor Jonathan Miller can actually bring himself to say: "Some ancient ape that stood and learned to talk gave rise to a new species, perhaps at first in Africa, and then across the planet, the first creature to contemplate his own origins – man himself!"

One day some years ago I was in Glasgow Cathedral. It was a hot afternoon in summer. The doors were open to admit the fresh air and warm sunshine. In ambled a small dog. It paid no attenton whatever to the architecture, showed no interest at all in the stained-glass windows, passed without notice the imposing mural monuments. Its sole concern was with the musty corners of the old edifice. In these it sniffed with manifest delight. That was a perfectly normal little dog, behaving in a perfectly normal way; but one could not help, while observing it, thinking not so much of the similarity between man and animal, as of the categorical difference between them. That difference was neatly defined by Imogen Fry when she epigramized: "The difference between man and the animals is that man is, or should be, aware that there is more to life than begin, beget and begone."

A further false view of man visualizes him *as a machine*. Some people in our time look upon mankind as what Lord Coggan calls "a race of robots". One writer tells of seeing prominently displayed on the wall of a city office a sign which read: "Look smart! You may be replaced by a button!" The great demagogue of today is not Stalin, "the Man of Steel", but robot, "the Steel Man".

In the heyday of the industrial revolution Henry Ward Beecher cried: "He that makes a machine emancipates me." There was obvious truth in the remark; but if he were to come back today he might have to confess: "He that makes a machine either enslaves man or replaces him." "Man," wrote Robert G. Ingersoll, in *The Gods*, "is a machine into which we put what we call food and produce what we call thought." "Made in God's image," says Francis Schaeffer, "man was made to be great, he was made to be beautiful, and he was made to be creative in life and art. But his rebellion has led him into making himself nothing but a machine."

The absurd lengths to which this mechanization of mankind is likely to go was indicated lately by Barbara Crane. "A machine has been invented," she reports, "to stand at the side of a baby's cot. Whenever the infant wakes and starts to coo or whimper, a plastic head moves towards him, emitting sounds similar to those made by a parent talking to a baby. This invention was probably inspired by someone who had heard of research which revealed that, during the first few months of life, a baby responds happily to any face-like object, even an ugly mask which would frighten it later." Unmistakably, the machine is now donning the aspect of that ugly mask.

A fourth false view of man regards him *as simply a statistic.* Nowadays we live in the Book of Numbers. No wonder that, when someone was asked not long ago for a reference to Joshua in the Book of Numbers, he immediately dialled Directory Enquiries! Yes, we are currently in a state of statistics!

In her racy and readable book *Here and Now* Rita Snowden relates that a friend of hers, Bill Topliss, stepped one day from a busy street into a building in the centre of London to keep an appointment with the dentist. As soon as the receptionist spotted him, she raised her voice to announce his arrival. "Here's the 10:30," she exclaimed. Bill felt depersonalized. "It seemed," he afterwards commented, "as if I was puffing into Euston Station." The Age of the Computer is threatening to turn human beings into numerals. "Men," according to Napoleon, "are like ciphers: they acquire their value merely from their position." "What is the number of your children?" the mother of a large family was asked by a census canvasser. "None of them's got a number," she replied indignantly. "They've all got names!"

With these things said, let us turn to the Word of God and see what it says about the origin, nature and destiny of man.

Five pegs may supply places on which to hang our

thinking-caps. We shall think of man (1) *Formed;* (2) *Deformed;* (3) *Informed;* (4) *Conformed;* and (5) *Transformed.*

Consider the headings in that order.

MAN FORMED

According to Dr John Lightfoot, an eminent scholar of the seventeenth century, man was created at a quarter to nine on Saturday morning, October 23, 4004 BC. The timing is so precise that one might be pardoned for supposing that the good doctor had been present on the occasion. It goes without saying that he was not, and a point often missed in discussions of human origins is that, from the very nature of the case, we are bound to be totally dependent for any reliable information on the subject upon one Person – the Person who was there. We have really no option but to depend solely on the Word of God. Of this the Lord reminded Job when He addressed him out of the whirlwind: "Where wast thou when I laid the foundations of the earth? Declare, if thou hast understanding" (Job 38:4).

Others who speak with what is almost tantamount to the authority of eye-witnesses about human origins are the evolutionists. They talk with the glibness of those who have inside information, referring not to a Fall but to a Rise.

> *And age by age since time began*
> *We mark the steady rise of man.*

But Man is not by nature an ape on the way up: he is an angel on the way down.

It is only the mumbo jumbo of anthropology, its long Greek names for the ages which it believes geology demands, its mesmerizing multiplication of periods of time, and so on, which blinds ordinary minds into supine acceptance of its supposed credibility and prevents them from seeing that it is the ultimate lunacy. As W.E. Orchard cogently contends: "To believe that God created everything out of nothing may be difficult, but it is simplicity itself in comparison with the only alternative – that everything was created by nothing out of nothing!" *The Origin of Species by means of Natural Selection* was the title of the epoch-making book published in 1859 by Charles Darwin. But as we have earlier noted, a mere process never produced anything. One might as well say that gardening produced a garden. That is a half-truth. Certainly gardening produced the garden, but only because there was a gardener. So-called *Christian* evolutionary theory could possibly be true, but non-Christian evolutionary theories are a nonsense.

Besides, if evolution were indeed true, one would expect the progress from stage to stage in human development to be gradual, phase overlapping phase. This is not so. Hybrids like the centaur and the mermaid are purely fictitious creatures. Two things in this regard impress me profoundly – the individual integrity of the forty thousand columns of basaltic rock in the Giant's Causeway, said to result from a prehistoric volcanic eruption on the Antrim Coast in Northern Ireland, and the sharply defined differentiation of the species in creation, each after its kind.

Many years ago, when I lived in Australia, the aborigines were popularly regarded as just about the most backward race on the face of the earth. Not without good reason. They had not so much as learnt the art of fire-making; they fed on worms, grubs, snails and insects of all kinds; they practised the most bestial and barbaric rites. Some civilized people doubted if they were really human. But human they most certainly were; and, in the thirty or so years since, those aborigines have made great strides. More and more of them are accepting Christ as Saviour, as a result of missionary enterprise in the Australian outback, and, with the help of education and culture, they are being radically changed as a race.

Now at the same time there were tribes of anthropoids in central Africa. Superficially, they did not then seem all that different from the aborigines. In some activities – such as climbing trees – the anthropoids may even have excelled the aborigines. Nevertheless there was a categorical distinction between them. No amount of culture and education could have turned those monkeys into men. Between anthropoid and anthropos there is a great gulf fixed.

Yet some anthropologists today speak almost with the authority of eye-witnesses about human origins. "Man's story begins somewhere between ten and twenty thousand million years ago, when all the matter of the universe was somehow contained within less than a pinpoint from which it all exploded outwards in something called the 'Big Bang'. One million years after the Big Bang the universe became transparent. Simple atoms – hydrogen and helium – expanded in the void until gravitation sucked them into massive concentrations, regions where the galaxies condensed, and stars lit up – giant radioactive furnaces that cooked the matter of the universe; and some, dying, seeded the universe with their heavier elements. About four and a half million years ago, our own sun's nuclear reactor switched on, and our earth grew fatter under a storm of rock and ice. And yet, on this precarious platform in space some three billion years ago life was established. On the mystery of its origin, Charles Darwin wrote to a friend: 'But if – and, O, what a big 'if!' – we could imagine it, some warm little pond, with all sorts of ammonia and phosphoric salts, light, heat and electricity present, a protein compound was chemically formed, ready to undergo some more complex changes, then, in the absence of predators, the first living organism would emerge'" (BBC 2 18:3:86).

But no. Man has not emerged from a primordial period. He is not just a developed and differentiated full-stop. Nor is he merely a superior anthropoid. He is made in the image of the Almighty, not in that of the ape. He is not a beast on the way up: he is a fallen creature on the way down. He is not simply a monkey with a high IQ: he is, as Disraeli put it, "an archangel slightly damaged". The only Author who can write truthfully about the Origin of Species is the One who originated the species – the Creator Himself.

In this connection a memorable anecdote is recorded in the *Life* of a minor Scottish poet, James Beattie. At the time of the incident his son was a small boy of six. Anxious to teach him a basic lesson about life, the father went out into the garden at the rear of their home and, smoothing the surface of the soil in a patch which no one could fail to see, he traced with his finger in the soft earth the letters of the child's Christian name, sowed in the rills thus made the seeds of cresses, covered them over with earth and went his way without saying a word to the child. Time passed, and one day when the child went out to play in the garden he made an exciting discovery. The green was beginning to show above the ground. Greatly astonished, the boy ran to find his father and, when he at last discovered him, he shouted excitedly: "Daddy! Daddy! Somebody's written my name in the garden." "Nonsense," said his father. "You must be mistaken. Nobody has been in the garden, far less written your name in the soil." But the boy insisted that it was so. "Come and see," he cried. "It's quite true. Somebody *has* written my name in the garden!" Hastily, the lad conducted his Dad to the patch. "There," he said, "I told you so. Somebody *has* written my name in the garden!" "O," suggested his father, "I expect it just happened. The name has come there just by chance." But the little fellow would not have it. "No," he insisted, "*somebody* has written my name there."

And then the father let him into the secret, told him about the plot behind the plot, and taught him that, whenever he thought of himself and the wonderful way in which he was made, he ought always to remember that

that great Somebody whom we call "God" was responsible for his existence. It was a salutary lesson which the boy never forgot.

Nor should we. For the Bible tells us that it was so. In passage after passage it proclaims the truth that man owes his being to the creative power of God. In his massive manual on the subject of human origins, *Evolution: a Theory of Crisis,* Michael Dunton pontificates: "The origin of life is still as much a mystery as it was before Darwin wrote."

Not so. Hear the Word of God on the issue: "God created man in His own image, in the image of God created He him" (Genesis 1:27). "The Lord God formed man out of the dust of the ground, and breathed into his nostrils the breath of life; and man became a living soul" (Genesis 2:7). "In the day that God created man, in the likeness of God made He him; male and female created He them; and blessed them, and called their name Adam, in the day when they were created" (Genesis 5:1,2). "Ask now of the days that are past, which were before thee, since the day that God created man upon the earth, and ask from the one side of heaven unto the other, whether there hath been any such thing as this great thing is, or hath been heard like it" (Deuteronomy 4:32). "Is not the Lord your Father, your Creator, who made you and formed you?" (Deuteronomy 32:6 NIV). "Thine hands have made me and fashioned me together round about" (Job 10:8). "Thou hast clothed me with skin and flesh, and hast fenced me with bones and sinews. Thou hast granted me life and favour, and Thy visitation hath preserved my spirit" (Job 10:11,12). "I also am formed out of the clay" (Job 33:6). "O come, let us worship and bow down: let us kneel before the Lord our Maker" (Psalm 95:6). "It is He that hath made us, and not we ourselves" (Psalm 100:3). "Thy hands have made me and fashioned me" (Psalm 119:73). "I have made the earth, and created man upon it" (Isaiah 45:12). "The souls which I have made" (Isaiah

57:16). "Now, O Lord, Thou art our Father; we are the clay, and Thou art our Potter; and we are the work of Thy hand" (Isaiah 64:8). "I have made the earth, and man and the beast that are upon the ground, by My great power and by My stretched out arm, and have given it unto whom it seemed meet unto Me" (Jeremiah 27:5). "The Lord stretcheth forth the heavens and layeth the foundation of the earth, and formeth the spirit of man within him" (Zechariah 12:1). "Have we not all one Father? Hath not one God created us?" (Malachi 2:10). "He that made them at the beginning made them male and female" (Matthew 19:4). "He giveth to all life, and breath, and all things, and hath made of one blood all nations of men for to dwell on the face of the earth" (Acts 17:25,26). "Man is the image and glory of God" (1 Corinthians 11:7). "Put on the new man, which is renewed in knowledge after the image of Him that created him" (Colossians 3:10). "Men are made after the similitude of God" (James 3:9).

The references extend to the Apocrypha, which although not of equal inspiration and authority with the accepted canon of Holy Scripture, does nevertheless endorse the Biblical records. "Thou gavest unto Adam a body without soul, which was the workmanship of Thine hands, and didst breathe into him the breath of life, and he was made living before Thee" (2 Esdras 3:5). "God created man to be immortal, and made him to be an image of His own eternity" (Wisdom 2:23). "The Lord created men of the earth, and made them according to His image" (Ecclesiasticus 17:1-3).

With these things said about human origins, let us pass on now to look at human nature. One of the disputed issues of anthropology is the question as to whether man is a dichotomy or a trichotomy, whether he is a bipartite or a tripartite being, whether he is body, *soul* and spirit, or just body and spirit. The Bible teaches that he is tripartite: "I pray God your whole spirit, soul and body be preserved blameless unto the Coming of our Lord Jesus Christ" (1

Thessalonians 5:23). According to the New Testament, man is a house comprised of three floors. The body is the basement, containing the animal quarters; the soul is the ground floor, from which a door leads straight out into the world of natural beauty and human society; the spirit is the upper room through whose windows glorious prospects of the heavenly world may be obtained. God is a Trinity: so, in his measure, is man.

MAN DEFORMED

What God has formed, sin has deformed. That is the tragic doctrine of the Fall. With that in mind, we naturally turn to the Genesis narrative. Is it moral myth or historic fact? About that theological opinion is sharply divided. Some would subscribe to the sentiments expressed by Robert Louis Stevenson, when he spoke of "the luminous Hebrew myth of the Fall, one of the biggest things ever done". But is that what the story really is – a mere improving fable? Not if the Word of God is to be believed. "For the New Testament writers," states H.C.G. Moule, "beyond doubt Adam was as real a person as Christ." To be truthful, some of Christianity's most savage critics have in this connection exhibited more penetrative insight than many of its salaried representatives. "No Adam, no Fall," wrote Robert Blatchford, "no Fall, no Saviour." "If there is no Fall," wrote H.G. Wells, "the historic fabric of Christianity collapses like a house of cards."

Not all Christian commentators were as obtuse as some. "The Fall of man was the fault of man," writes Harold F.G. Cole. "The Fall of the First Adam was the end of the beginning," observes S.W. Duffield: "the Rise of the Second Adam was the beginning of the End." And you may recall Alexander King's witty aphorism: "Newton *saw* an apple fall, and thus discovered the Law of Gravity: Eve *made* an apple fall and discovered the gravity of law."

The Fall is no fiction. It is a grim and awful fact. "Each

one of us," asserts the Apocalypse of Baruch, "hath been the Adam of his own soul"; and, by the same token, every life has its private Fall. In his personal copy of his own autobiography George Tyrrell drew a thick black line across one of its pages. Tyrrell himself explained why. It marked his first Fall. "And so here," he says, "I drew a black line to mark my departed innocence and separate it from the period when I began to tamper with and spoil the self which God had given me." The racial Fall was as real as is the personal.

Paradoxically, however, the doctrine of the Fall is one of the most flattering of all to mankind. As Benjamin Fosse Westcott arrestingly expresses it: "No view of the human state is so inexpressibly sad as that which leaves out the Fall. The existence of evil in so many forms, as self-will and suffering and vice and crime, cannot be gainsaid; and, if this evil belongs to the essence of man as created, then there can be no prospect of relief here or hereafter." It is the infinite worth of man that makes his sin so terrible. A crack in an old tea-cup is no great matter, but a crack in a piece of the best china is a domestic disaster.

Let me put the point in a picture. Suppose that I see a young man struggling along a street on crutches, pausing every now and then to "get his breath", as we say, and obviously proceeding with considerable pain. And suppose you come up to me, and say: "That man is a world champion runner, an Olympic gold-medallist. He is the fastest man alive!" I burst out laughing. "You must be joking," I reply. "Why, that fellow can hardly drag one leg after another. Don't try to persuade me that he's an athlete." "Yes," you reply, "he certainly is. His present crippled condition is due to the fact that he has recently sustained a bad fall, but he is a swift racer all the same!" The Fall both flattens and flatters us, pointing at one and the same time to both our depravity and our dignity.

MAN INFORMED

It is the express desire of the Last Adam that all the members of the race founded by the First Adam should be told that, as there has been a Fall, there has also been a Rise. The two Adams are the federal heads respectively of the old and the new humanity. "As by one man sin entered into the world, so much more the grace of God, by one Man, Jesus Christ, hath abounded unto many" (Romans 5:12,15). "Since by man came death, by Man came also the resurrection of the dead" (1 Corinthians 15:21). "As in Adam all die, even so in Christ shall all be made alive" (1 Corinthians 15:22). "If ye then be risen with Christ, seek those things which are above, where Christ sitteth on the right hand of God" (Colossians 3:1). Yes, if there has been a Fall, there has also been a Rise; and it is the Last Adam's dynamic directive that every descendant of the First Adam should be apprised that this is so. "*All* power is given unto Me in heaven and in earth. Go ye therefore, and teach *all* nations, baptizing them in the name of the Father, and of the Son, and of the Holy Ghost: teaching them to observe *all* things whatsoever I have commanded you: and, lo, I am with you *alway*, even unto the end of the world" (Matthew 28:19,20). Note the four "all's" in that passage. They speak of universality – the universality of *power*; the universality of the *peoples*; the universality of *proclamation*; the universality of the *Person*. As we shall be dealing extensively with these matters in subsequent chapters, they must await later treatment.

MAN CONFORMED

"Whom He did foreknow, He also did predestinate to be conformed to the image of His Son" (Romans 8:29). In the original Greek that word *summorphos* means literally having the same form. And what form is that? It is the form of Jesus Christ, and what form does *He* bear? Let Paul tell us in his Letter to the Philippians: "Who, being in the *form* of God, thought it not robbery to be equal with God: but made Himself of no reputation, and took upon Him the *form* of a servant, and was made in the likeness of men, and was found in fashion as a Man" (2:6-8).

It is to that image, Divine and human, that God has predestinated us to be conformed. Just as the First Adam "begat a son in his own likeness and after his image" (Genesis 5:3), so the Last Adam is throughout this age of grace producing a progeny bearing a moral resemblance to Himself. The Fall has marred God's image in man and the whole purpose of the Rise is to restore it.

Let me illustrate. Picture a young man who has an extraordinarily handsome father of whose appearance he is justifiably proud and whom he closely resembles. Nothing delights the lad more than to be told that he is like his dad. But then suppose that a tragedy occurs. The son is involved in a terrible motoring accident, trapped in a blazing car, and horribly disfigured by facial burns. He is rushed to hospital. There a prolonged process of plastic surgery begins. An eminent surgeon performs the operations and his patient makes one request of him. It is that, while his face is being reconstructed, the surgeon should have near him in the operating theatre a photograph of the casualty's father, to which he can have recourse from time to time as he remoulds the disfigured face.

That is a picture of what the Holy Spirit is doing to fallen but repentant human beings who put their faith in Christ. He is restoring the Divine image. Of this we shall have more to say later on. Suffice it for the moment to quote the classic text on the subject: "We all, with open face beholding as in a glass the glory of the Lord, are changed into the same image from glory to glory, even as by the Spirit of the Lord" (2 Corinthians 3:18).

MAN TRANSFORMED

"Behold, I show you a mystery. We shall not all sleep, but we shall all be changed, in a moment, in the twinkling of an eye, at the last trump: for the trumpet shall sound, and the dead shall be raised incorruptible, and we shall be changed. For this corruptible must put on incorruption, and this mortal must put on immortality. So this corruptible shall put on incorruption, and this mortal shall put on immortality" (1 Corinthians 15:51-54). "The Lord Jesus Christ shall change our lowly body, that it may be fashioned like unto His glorious body, according to the working whereby He is able even to subdue all things unto Himself" (Philippians 3:21). "It doth not yet appear what we shall be: but we know that, when He shall appear, we shall be like Him; for we shall see Him as He is" (1 John 3:2).

Some years ago Her Majesty the Queen commissioned two official portraits of herself, which were duly executed within a short space of time of one another. One was by Annigoni, the celebrated Italian artist: the other was by the world-famous photographer Karsh of Ottawa. They were both beautiful portraits, but there was a very marked difference between them, and that was in the way they were produced. For Annigoni's portrait numerous sittings had to be arranged at the Palace. Her Majesty posed for the artist who stood there before her with his canvas, his palette and his brushes and pigments. Touch by touch of paint was transferred by the hand of the artistic genius from the palette to the canvas and gradually the royal image emerged.

What a contrast was presented by Karsh. All he had to do was to press a button on his highly-sophisticated camera, and, hey presto! he had the exact likeness of the Queen on celluloid!

The former process is analogous to what is technically known as "sanctification" – a method whereby redeemed man is gradually restored to the image of his Maker: the latter will transpire at that dramatic moment when the trumpet will sound and he will be transformed in a flash into the likeness of his Lord. We shall deal with this in greater detail in our last chapter, noting how at the Parousia in every true Christian who has borne the image of the First Adam the likeness of the Last Adam will be instantly reproduced.

4
THE INFINITE INFANT

The Christian Doctrine of The Incarnation

The Babe of Bethlehem is the infinite Infant. Charles Haddon Spurgeon

In the beginning was the Word, and the Word was with God, and the Word was God. John 1:1

No man hath seen God at any time; the only-begotten Son, which is in the bosom of the Father, He hath declared Him. John 1:18

He that hath seen Me hath seen the Father. John 14:9

Who, being in the form of God, thought it not robbery to be equal with God. Philippians 2:6

Unto the Son He saith, Thy throne, O God, is for ever and ever. Hebrews 1:8

Behold, a virgin shall conceive and bear a son. Isaiah 7:14

Before they came together, she was found with Child of the Holy Ghost. Matthew 1:18

The Word was made flesh and dwelt among us. John 1:14

Unto you is born this day, in the city of David, a Saviour, which is Christ the Lord. Luke 2:11

Unto us a Child is born, unto us a Son is given. Isaiah 9:6

God so loved the world that He gave His unique Son. John 3:16 NASB margin

Great is the mystery of godliness: God was manifest in the flesh. 1 Timothy 3:16

PHILLIPS BROOKS, THE prince of American preachers, had a pleasant pastoral practice. When visiting the homes of members of his Boston congregaton, where there had been a recent addition to the family, he was wont to gaze admiringly at the tiny occupant of the cradle for a few moments, and to exclaim within the hearing of the doting parents: "Now that *is* a baby!"

With all reverence be it spoken, when in pious fancy we stand in that star-crowned stable at Bethlehem, peering into the little pink face of the Mite in the manger, we can say, as we can of no other in human history: "Now that *is* a Baby!"

Contemplating that Child, we can take upon our lips the lordly language of William Shakespeare:

Who is this
That rises like the issue of a king
And wears upon His Baby brow the round
And top of sovereignty?

Who indeed? None other than He whom a mediaeval poet christened "Great Little One" and of whom Charles

Haddon Spurgeon spoke as "the Infinite Infant".

On the brink of our discussion of the Christian Doctrine of the Incarnation, it may be for our profit to reflect that four key-words provide clues as to the route along which our thoughts should travel: (1) *eternity*; (2) *prophecy*; (3) *history*; and (4) *theology*.

Take them in that order.

ETERNITY

It has been arrestingly pointed out that the Lord Jesus is the only person who ever lived before He was born. As George Sweeting neatly notes: "He *had* no beginning: He *was* the Beginning." About that the Bible leaves us in no doubt. Not only does it *affirm*, it *assumes* Christ's preexistence.

Consider some representative quotations: "Who hath established all the ends of the earth? What is His name, and what is His Son's name, if thou canst tell?" (Proverbs 30:4). "His goings forth have been from of old, from the days of eternity" (Micah 5:2 margin). "I am from above" (John 8:23). "Before Abraham was, I am" (John 8:58). "The glory which I had with Thee before the world was" (John 17:5). "Thou lovedst Me before the foundation of the world" (John 17:24). "The Second Man is the Lord from heaven" (1 Corinthians 15:47). "Who, being in the form of God, thought it not robbery to be equal with God: but made Himself of no reputation and took upon Himself the form of a servant, and was made in the likeness of men" (Philippians 2:6,7). "He is the firstborn of every creature" (Colossians 1:15). "God hath spoken unto us by His Son, whom He hath appointed heir of all things, by whom also He made the worlds: the brightness of His glory and the express image of His Person, upholding all things by the Word of His power" (Hebrews 1:1-3). "Thou art My Son, this day have I begotten Thee" (Hebrews 1:5) "Thou hast created all things" (Revelation 4:11). "The Lamb slain from the foundation of the world" (Revelation 13:8). Truly, as Bishop John Pearson expressed it: "Christ was in the form of God before He was in the form of a servant."

Christ's nativity was, in a sense, a regeneration. It was Origen who first used of Christ the classic phrase "eternal generation". Our Lord Himself refers to it in the stupendous sentence: "I proceeded forth and came from God" (John 8:42).

It is noteworthy that the New Testament nowhere says that the Father *created* the Son: what it does say is that He *begot* Him. There is a radical distinction here. C.S. Lewis makes the point memorably in his *Mere Christianity*: "When you beget, you beget something of the same kind as yourself. What God begets is God: what God creates is not God." How significant, then, that in the Christian Scriptures Jesus should be referred to no fewer than six times as "only-begotten". The Bible tells of other miraculous births – that of Isaac, of Samson, of John the Baptist, but none like this one. This is unique. Everyone who has ever lived on this planet has originated on this planet. Each has commenced his existence here. His being has begun on this spinning speck in space. Not so Jesus of Nazareth. He did not start in Bethlehem. He was in the bosom of His heavenly Father for untold ages before He lay on the breast of His earthly mother. His *conception*, if we may say so, was not His *inception*. Certainly in BC 10 there was no such person as the human Jesus, but there never was a time when the Christ who became Jesus was not.

The following moving words of Teilhard de Chardin ring with the eloquence of profound conviction: "The prodigious expanses of time which preceded the first Christmas were not empty of Christ: they were imbued with the influx of His power. When Christ first appeared in the arms of Mary, He had already stirred up the world." G.H. Morrison is our mouthpiece when he confesses: "To me the Bible is an unmeaning riddle if Jesus began to be when He was born." Those slim memoirs which we call the Gospels do not comprise a complete Life of Christ. Nobody could ever write a complete Life of Christ. The apostle John does not exaggerate when he asserts: "There are also many other things which Jesus did, the which if they had been written every one, I suppose that even the world itself could not contain the books that should be written" (21:25). That is not hyperbole: it is simple fact. Eternity – that is the first word.

PROPHECY

That is the second. Besides being unique in having lived before He was born, our Lord is likewise unique in having had the most minute particulars of His personal life predicted centuries before He came into the world. His advent as Messiah was first announced in Hannah's Magnificat: "The Lord shall judge the ends of the earth, and He shall give strength unto His King, and exalt the horn of His Messiah" (1 Samuel 2:10). The fact of His birth is plainly predicted. He was to come of Eve, not Adam (Genesis 3:15); of Abraham, not of Lot; of Isaac, not of Ishmael; of Jacob, not of Esau; of Judah, not of Levi; of David, not of Saul. "David shall never want a man to sit upon the throne of the house of Israel. If you can break My covenant of the day, and My covenant of the night, and that there should not be day and night in their season; then may also My covenant be broken with David My servant, that he should not have a son to reign upon his throne" (Jeremiah 33: 17-21).

The place of His birth was actually pointed out on the map. "But thou, Bethlehem Ephratah, though thou be little among the thousands of Judah, yet out of thee shall He come forth unto Me that is to be the ruler in Israel" (Micah 5:2).

The time of His birth was also intimated. His advent was divinely dated between two calendar events. "Know therefore and understand that, from the going forth of the commandment to restore and to build Jerusalem unto the Messiah, the Prince, there shall be seven weeks and three score and two weeks, and after three score and two weeks shall Messiah be cut off, but not for Himself; and the people of the prince that shall come shall destroy the city and the sanctuary" (Daniel 9:25,26). This means that Christ was to be born some time between 445 BC and AD 70 – between, that is, Artaxerxes and Titus.

The nature of His birth was further foreshown: "Behold, a virgin shall conceive and bear a Son, and shall call His name Immanuel" (Isaiah 7:14). The character of the nativity is surely implied, too, in the language of Micah 5:2: "Out of thee, Bethlehem, shall He *come forth* unto Me, whose *goings forth* have been from of old, from everlasting", and in Isaiah 9:6: "Unto us a Child is born" – there you see Mary, "burdened with blessing", bringing forth her Baby in patient pain; "unto us a Son is given" – there you see God the Father, holding out in His arms, as it were, for our acceptance His beloved Son. "To me," wrote Blaise Pascal, "the strongest proof of the Deity of Jesus is to be found in the fact that, centuries before He appeared, it was foretold by the prophets of the Old Testament."

No fewer than three hundred and thirty two distinct Old Testament predictions were literally fulfilled in the person of Christ. The mathematical probability of all these predictions being fulfilled in one Man is one in eighty-four with seventy-three nothings after it! Of many of these forecasts we shall have occasion to speak later. Meantime let it suffice to note the astounding fact.

HISTORY

Looking for Christ in the Old Testament is rather like looking for someone by the name of Jones in a Welsh telephone directory. His is everywhere. This brings us to the vexed question of the Virgin Birth, or *parthenogenesis*, to give it its technical term – the point at which eternity and time, the Divine and the human, the heavenly and the earthly intersect and converge. The visitor to Israel finds it deeply moving to stand in the crypt of the Church of the Nativity in Bethlehem – even though he may have strong suspicions that it is *not* the authentic place! – contemplating the multi-pointed silver star and reading the Latin inscription: "Here Jesus Christ was born of the Virgin Mary." That is the focus of the Church's faith – "God and Man in oneness blending". "The Incarnation," as one has well said, "is a dateable piece of history" – the date 753 on the Roman calendar.

How strange that the pure Son of heaven, when He came to earth, should have had a somewhat morally sullied pedigree! Yet it was so. In His ancestry are to be found names which, to put it mildly, seem oddly out of character with the genealogy of the Lord of Glory. There were Judah and Tamar (Genesis 38); David and Bathsheba (2 Samuel 11:12); Ahaz, Manasseh and Amon (2 Chronicles 28 and 33); and, of course, there was, of all possible progenitors, Rahab the Harlot, of whom a poet has written:

And Rahab the Harlot,
Her sins were as scarlet,
As red as the thread which she hung from the door;
Yet alone of her nation
She came to salvation
And lived to be mother of Boaz of yore;
And he married Ruth,
A Gentile uncouth,
In a manner quite counter to Biblical lore.

Nevertheless, there is an unmistakable watermark of royalty in the Lord's lineage. In the Hebrew language each of the letters had a certain numerical value, and the name "David", in consonantal Hebrew – DVD – adds up to fourteen (D=4; V=6; D=4: =14). Note how this number – 14 – recurs in Matthew's genealogy of Jesus: "So all the generations from Abraham to David are fourteen generations; and from David unto the carrying away into Babylon are fourteen generations; and from the carrying away into Babylon unto Christ are fourteen generations" (Matthew 1:17). Thus "David, David, David" is stamped on the pedigree of Jesus.

Despite that the birth of the Saviour, when it happened, seems to have been, as we say, "pretty-low-key". On reading the birth narratives one is impressed by their extraordinary reticence. It is true that angels burst into sight among the hills of Bethlehem, but it was, after all, a very localized celebration. As the poet says:

When came in flesh the Incarnate Word,
The heedless world slept on,
And only simple shepherds heard
That God had sent His Son.

At this point it is perhaps pertinent to inquire: Was there no other way in which God could have displayed His love for a fallen race than by sending His Son thus, no other method whereby He could have accomplished His redemptive purpose? Was it absolutely necessary for God to become flesh? The Chaldean soothsayers, summoned by Nebuchadnezzar to interpret his forgotten dream, found the idea incredible. They spoke of "the gods whose dwelling is not with flesh" (Daniel 2:11). Even King Solomon greeted the possibility with blank astonishment: "But will God in very deed dwell with men on the earth? Behold, heaven and the heaven of heavens cannot contain Thee" (2 Chronicles 6:18). Was Incarnation imperative if God was to reveal Himself and to redeem the world? If there had been no Fall, would God have become a Man? Some say No. Others, with a deeper insight, remembering the Divine desire to have fellowship with His human creature, say Yes.

Look at it like this. Suppose that, instead of encapsulating Himself in human form, God had simply shouted His message of love from the skies after the manner of a lunarnaut, would that have sufficed? Not at all. In point of fact, the New Testament does record that, during our Lord's earthly lifetime, God thrice spoke thus from the heavens: once, above the Jordan River when Jesus was being baptized; once on Hermon's glittering height at the Transfiguration; and once in the Temple Court. But the *bath qol* made no converts. Doubtless it did confirm the disciples' faith in our Lord's Deity, but it was, in itself, powerless to redeem. Incarnation was essential. "Not in cheap words He owned mankind His kin."

Of Huber, the famous Swiss naturalist, it is told that as a boy he stood one day with his mother near an anthill, watching the tiny creatures scurrying to and fro in frantic agitation. To his mother he said: "They are afraid of me!" "Yes," she replied, "but you wouldn't hurt them. You are so fond of them." "Certainly," agreed the boy, "but how can I let the ants know that I am so fond of them except by becoming an ant?"

That is an almost perfect illustration in miniature of the great truth of the Incarnation. From all eternity God had loved us as only God can love, but how could He – the Almighty, invisible God – tell us – poor, puny mortals – that He loved us, unless, as John Hadham has expressed it, He became "God-in-a-Human-Being", or to be more exact, God–as–a-Human-Being. That is precisely what He did.

Let the New Testament tell us how it happened: "Now the birth of Jesus Christ was on this wise: when as His mother Mary was espoused to Joseph, before they came together, she was found with Child of the Holy Ghost" (Matthew 1:18). "Jesus was born in Bethlehem of Judaea" (Matthew 2:1). "The angel Gabriel was sent from God unto a city of Galilee, named Nazareth, to a virgin espoused to a man whose name was Joseph, and the virgin's name was Mary. And the angel said, Behold, thou shalt conceive in thy womb, and bring forth a Son, and shalt call His name Jesus. The Holy Ghost shall come upon thee, and the power of the Highest shall overshadow thee. Therefore, also, that Holy Thing which shall be born of thee, shall be called the Son of God. Joseph went to Bethlehem with Mary, his espoused wife, being great with Child, and so it was that, while they were there, the days were accomplished that she should be delivered and she brought forth her firstborn Son; and she wrapped Him in swaddling clothes and laid Him in a manger" (Luke 1:26,27,31,35; 2:46). As Billy Graham observes: "No other man in all history could say that his mother was a virgin." Full discussion of this issue must be deferred until later: now it must suffice to state the stupendous fact.

With something approaching genius, a recent writer has described the inn at Bethlehem as a "one-star hotel". Spartan enough accommodation at best was provided in that inn, but for a woman in the last stages of pregnancy who had just travelled some eighty miles on the back of a jogging donkey, it must nevertheless have been a most welcome sight. Even that humble habitation was, however, to be denied them. "There was no room for them in the inn" (Luke 2:7). To be sure, the word "them" in that sentence is to be underlined. Had Joseph not been a poor carpenter, had he been able to dangle a bag of silver shekels before the inn-keeper's eyes, things might have been very different for the travel-stained strangers. Better hospitality might, in that case, have been quickly forthcoming. As it was, the only shelter offered them was a sort of annexe to the khan, a cave used as a stable, where the beasts fretted, fed and foamed; and there in circumstances of abject poverty the God-Man was born. As an old Welsh preacher picturesquely phrased it: "Though He was a King, there were no tapestries around His cradle, but the webs spun by the spiders on the walls of the stable."

To say even that is not enough. We must go further. For He who was the *pleroma,* the fulness, of God experienced a *kenosis* or self-emptying more astounding still. Someone has strikingly said that we all start life the size of a fullstop. That is just how Jesus began. Think of it. He who is the crowned Lord of thirty trillion galaxies and constellations became no bigger than the dot on an i that He might really enter and save our human race. After Bethlehem there is one Old Testament text which could never be rewritten. It is this: "God is not a man" (Numbers 23:19), for "He was found in fashion as a Man" (Philippians 2:8). An early critic of Christianity protested that "a Child of two or three months old cannot be called God". The fact is far more staggering. "That Holy Thing", no bigger than a pinhead, can and must be called God, or our salvation is impossible. G.K. Chesterton, with his gift for striking prose, put it thus: "God, who had been the circumference, was seen as a centre, and a centre is infinitely small."

In Los Angeles, California, at Christmas 1965, I saw a brilliantly painted poster displayed on a billboard outside a suburban church. It simply said: "It's a Boy!" But everybody knew what it meant.

> *Unto us a Boy is born,*
> *King of all creation,*
> *Came He to a world forlorn,*
> *Lord of every nation.*

THEOLOGY

In this section of our study it is important to reflect that there are two major matters to be considered: first, the historical development of the doctrine of the Person of Christ and, second, the question of the Virgin Birth.

Take them in that order.

The theology of the Incarnation commences in the New Testament with the comments of the inspired writers on the colossal facts. The term "incarnation" itself is derived from the Latin *in carnis,* that is, "in flesh". Note how the Christian Scriptures insist on this – not only that He became *Man* but that He became *flesh.* "The Word was made flesh and dwelt among us" (John 1:14). "God sending His own Son in the likeness of sinful flesh" (Romans 8:3). "The fathers, of whom as concerning the flesh, Christ came" (Romans 9:5). "We have known Christ after the flesh" (2 Corinthians 5:16). "God was manifest in the flesh" (1 Timothy 3:16). "Jesus Christ is come in the flesh" (1 John 4:31; 2 John 7).

After the closure of the sacred canon, belief in Jesus as the God-Man continued to be the official faith of the Church. Bit by bit, however, heresies kept cropping up and creeping in. Surveying the Christological literature of the centuries, it is possible to distinguish no fewer than twelve views on the subject, eleven of which are heresies, ancient or modern, and the twelfth the historic orthodox faith. It may assist our understanding of the matter if we pass them rapidly in review.

The first says that *Christ had only one parent.* This is a modern error stemming from Mary Baker Eddy, founder of Christian Science, whose ideas on the issue differ by a whole diameter from those of her namesake, Mary of Nazareth! Mrs Eddy wrote: "The virgin mother conceived the idea of God, and gave her ideal the name of Jesus. Jesus is the offspring of Mary's self-conscious communion with God." According to this theory, through much mental conceiving of Messiah, Mary came physically to conceive Him.

The second heresy is that *Christ had three parents.* Here we have the view of another modern cult – Mormonism. Just as Christian Science, so–called, accords to Christ one parent too few, so Mormonism gives Him one parent too many. It represents Christ as the Son of God, Adam and

Mary.

The third false theory is that *Jesus was God but not Man.* This is the Gnostic or Docetic heresy – "Gnostic" from the Greek *gnosis,* knowledge, and "Docetic" from the Greek *dokeein,* "to appear". Those subscribing to this theory professed to be in possession of some esoteric information concerning Christ, not available to ordinary mortals. They regarded our Lord's humanity as a mere apparition. Holding that matter is essentially evil, they judged an incarnation to be a moral impossibility. Of this a variant view was Apollinarianism, which taught that Christ was fully God but not fully Man. Nevertheless, as Henry Parry Liddon pointed out, "If Jesus be not truly Man, the chasm between heaven and earth has not been bridged, and God – as before the Incarnation – is still remote and inaccessible." But, as G. Bromley Oxnam says: "In the Incarnation the Ultimate became the Intimate."

The fourth theory is that *Jesus was Man but not God.* Patently, this is the precise opposite of the one which we have just examined. It is not *every* man who needs to have his humanity insisted upon! The humanity of most of us is all too evident! Even the greatest religious teachers have emphasized their human identity and fallibility. "I am only a man like yourselves," Muhammad told his followers. "I am an ordinary man," confessed Gandhi, "I have blundered and committed mistakes." Jesus Christ made no such disclaimer. Constantly, during His earthly life, He was transcending merely human categories and constraining observers to account for Him in terms of a supernatural dimension. There were, all the same, those who failed or refused to recognize in Him anything that could not be subsumed under a purely human classification. They saw Him as Man but not God.

The fifth theory is that *Jesus was God and Man in confused intermixture.* This is an old heresy dating back to Eutyches, who is known in history as "the theologian who confused the Divine Persons", declaring that "in our Lord the

Manhood was lost in the Godhead like a drop of wine in the ocean". Hence he denied both the true Deity and essential humanity of Christ, and presented him as a sort of amorphous amalgam of both. As D.M. Baillie pawkily comments, however, "Eutych*es* is dead, and he is not likely to be as fortunate as Eutych*us* in finding an apostle to revive him!"

The sixth heresy is the view that *the Man Jesus, so to say, graduated into Godhead by virtue of His moral perfection*. Here, again, we have an ancient theological deviation known as "Adoptionism". Between the Creator and the creature there is an infinite categorical difference; and, if Jesus had become as a mere man, He could never by any expedient have exceeded humanity. In the same way as it is impossible by educating a woman to the highest degree to turn her into a man, so it is beyond man's capacities to rise into Godhood by dint of his moral attainments. "The Eternal Son," says Plummer, "was not united with Jesus *after* Jesus was born of Mary, He *came* in the flesh: He *became* flesh."

The seventh heresy held that *Jesus possessed a human body and soul but not a human spirit*. This likewise is a very old misconception of the Person of Christ. It was propounded by Apollinarius, a fourth century Bishop of Laodicea, who believed that in Jesus the human spirit was displaced and replaced by the Logos. From the Gospel records, however, it is plain that our Lord possessed a human spirit as well as a Divine Spirit. He was close on thirty years of age when the Paraclete descended like a Dove upon Him in the River Jordan, but quite clearly He had a human spirit before that! Moreover, as He hung upon the Cross, He commended His spirit to the Father. It was not the Holy Spirit – the Third Person in the Trinity – that He thus resigned: it was His human spirit. Analogously, when the apostles and others were filled with the Holy Spirit on the Day of Pentecost, the Comforter did not extinguish or absorb their human spirits, but, on the contrary, not only co-existed with them in their respective personalities, but confirmed and reinforced their personalities. "The Spirit Himself beareth witness with our spirit" (Romans 8:16). As in the believer, the Spirit of God indwells but not expels the spirit of man, so in the personality of Christ: He had a human spirit as well as a Divine.

A like error – the eighth in our list – asserts that *Christ assumed human nature without assuming human personality.* R.C. Moberley deals a death-blow to this heresy when he argues that "human nature which is not personal is not human nature". Our Lord could no more have taken the one upon Himself without *ipso facto* taking upon Himself the other, than He could have become fire without at the same time becoming light.

The ninth false notion of the Person of Christ took the view that *He was a god not the God.* The most modern proponents and exponents of this theory are the selfstyled Jehovah's Witnesses, who declare that Jesus was *a* god with a small "g". Their denominational version of the New Testament, entitled the *New World Translation,* renders John 1:1 thus: "In the beginning was the God, and the Word was a god." It need hardly be said that this reading and rendering of the text is patently propagandist and arbitrary. The Greek tongue can scarcely be supposed to support it since it has no indefinite article!

The tenth fallacious theory of the Person of Christ is that which affirms that *Jesus became Man for a bare three and thirty years.* This heresy cuts the ground from under its own feet, forasmuch as, on the one hand, it professes to accept the Deity of our Lord, and, on the other, ascribes to Him a conjunction of being terminable in time. Obviously, God cannot be other than God for thirty three years! Whatever He does, He does eternally. The great God of the Ages did not take manhood into Himself for a mere three decades: He took manhood into His own being for ever.

The eleventh and final heresy in our catalogue is closely similar to that which we have just examined. It maintains that *in Jesus God changed into a Man.* Here is another error which blurs the infinite categorical distinction between the Creator and the creature. God can never change into anything without ceasing to be what He is. To say that He is capable of any alteration or modification is to impugn His perfection, since, if He were to change for the worse, He could not then be perfect, and if He were to change for the better, He could not before have been perfect. In this connection consider these weighty words of William Temple: "The Virgin Birth was not effected by the conversion of Godhead into flesh, but by the taking of Manhood into God."

We come, then, by a process of elimination, to the one remaining view in our survey – the official, historic, orthodox faith. It may be succinctly expressed as follows: *Jesus is perfect God and perfect Man perfectly united.* Think this through. Jesus is perfect God. Not only do I deprecate, I absolutely abhor, all those miserable subterfuges by which some theologians and preachers today try to disguise the fact that they do not believe in the true and full Deity of Jesus. To say that He is *like* God, that God is *like* Jesus, that Jesus possesses for us the religious value of God, that Jesus is *a* Son or even *the* Son of God, may all sound very pious and reverential. All too often, however, it is simply verbal camouflage designed to conceal a defective Christology. Jesus is perfect God: He is also perfect Man. He is not just a Divine Idea, a Christ-myth, a religious fictional character. He is a genuine human being. While on earth, He was God walking in sandals on the dusty roads of Israel and before long He is coming back just as He went away to walk this world once more. Jesus is perfect God and perfect Man in perfect unison. As Stanley E. Ellison strikingly phrases it: "He is the unhyphenated GodMan". "Jesus," observes John Eddison, "was not a sort of hybrid or amphibian, like a centaur or a merman. He was perfect and complete God and, at the same time, perfect and complete Man." As a certain Dr Pope once put it with pointed precision: "Christ is truly God, perfectly Man, unconfusedly in two natures, indivisibly in one Person." To much the same effect is something written by Marcus Loane: "It was not as if Christ's Godhead were humanized, nor as though His Manhood were deified, for both natures were linked in a perfect union in a unique Person."

It was almost as much to combat heresy as to define faith that the great Creeds and Confessions were drawn up. The so-called Apostles' Creed begins very simply: "I believe in Jesus Christ, God's only Son, our Lord, who was conceived by the Holy Ghost, born of the Virgin Mary." In the interests of clarity and exactitude the Nicene Creed embellished that statement quite considerably. Here is what it says: "Jesus Christ, the only-begotten Son of God, was begotten of the Father before all worlds, God of God, Light of Light, very God of very God, begotten, not made, being of one substance with the Father, by whom all things were made: for us men and for our salvation, He came down from heaven and was incarnate by the Holy Ghost of the Virgin Mary, and was made Man." Further amplification and clarification came in the Athanasian Creed. This strenuous statement runs as follows: "Our Lord Jesus Christ, the Son of God, is God and Man: God, of the substance of the Father, begotten before the worlds, and Man of the substance of His mother, born in the world, perfect God and perfect Man, of a reasonable soul and flesh subsisting, equal to the Father as touching His Godhead, and inferior to the Father as touching His Manhood. Who, although He be God and Man, is not two but one Christ, one altogether, not by confusion of substance, but by unity of Person. For as the reasonable soul and flesh is one Man, so God and Man is one Christ."

Broadly speaking, there are four views of the nature of Christ. Some deny His historicity altogether; some look upon Him as Divine but not wholly human; some look upon Him as human but not essentially Divine. The true view is that which regards Him as for ever fully God and fully Man.

In the eleventh Christian century a classic work on the subject appeared. It was called *Cur Deus Homo (Why God became Man)* and was from the pen of Anselm, an Archbishop of Canterbury. In it the whole theme of the Incarnation is thoroughly threshed out. The author penetratively observes that there are four ways in which God has made man: (1) by the ordinary biological process; (2) by direct creative act as He made Adam; (3) by indirect creative act as He made Eve; and (4) by direct creative incarnation as He made the body of Christ.

Our Lord could not have been made Man by the first method, for then God and Man could not have been united in His personality. Nor could He have become man in the manner requisite to His redemptive purpose by the second mode, as in that case He would not really have entered the human race at all. Nor, again, could He have become Man by the third process, for in that event He would have been wedded merely to a part of man. The only way, therefore, by which God and Man could be savingly united was that actually adopted by God, namely, Incarnation.

So much, then, for the first division of this section of our study – that of the development of the doctrine of the Person of Christ.

Turn now to the second – that which has to do specifically with the Virgin Birth. But *was* Jesus born of a virgin? If we are to believe the so-called *First Gospel of the Infancy of Christ,* an early apocryphal document, the matter is placed beyond controversy. In it our Lord is reported as having, even in the cradle, said to His mother: "Mary, I am Jesus, the Son of God, that Word which thou didst bring forth, according to the declaration of the angel Gabriel to thee, and My Father hath sent Me for the salvation of the world" (op.cit.1:1-30). But the issue is not quite so clear as that.

Look at some of the views held concerning it.

Some deny it outright. Among them are not a few famous names. Harry Emerson Fosdick, leading American liberal preacher of our age, confessed in the pulpit: "I am a liberal in theology. Of course, I do not believe in the Virgin Birth." With that sentiment, Leslie D. Weatherhead – Fosdick's opposite number in Great Britain – entirely concurred. "The claim that Jesus was virgin-born," he wrote, "does not stir me emotionally in the least." Lord Soper is of similar mind. "Personally," he admits, "I do not believe in the Virgin Birth. The reality of Christianity for me is that Jesus began as I began. He does not come to me as a supernatural being from another sphere."

Years ago in a Belfast bookshop I picked up a volume purporting to contain modern sayings of Jesus alleged to be communicated from the spirit world by a spiritistic medium. I was naturally eager to know what such putative communications were like. With excited interest, I turned to a passage in which Christ was supposed to have made a statement about His own birth. "My real father was Joseph," He is reported to have said, "and the story of the Virgin Birth is a hoax and a fraud." Naturally, the Devil does not want us to believe in the Virgin Birth since it is the essential precondition of belief in Christ's Deity.

Rèné Pache, the well-known Swiss professor who died recently, relates: "I was hearing not long ago about a theological student, who was asked to go to preach in a certain parish left without a pastor. He was supposed to go on Christmas Day, and he said: 'What am I to tell them? I cannot preach about a myth!'"

In January, 1970, there was a great furore in theological circles in Scotland. Under the banner headline VIRGIN BIRTH SHOCKER, an article appeared in the *Daily Express* reporting the doctrinal opinions of Alestair Bennett, a Church of Scotland clergyman, who had just made public his views on the Virgin Birth of Christ. They outraged the feelings and convictions of the faithful. Speaking of the

Virgin Birth, he wrote: "This is a belief which causes great disbelief. It is built upon the flimsiest of evidence. It should be publicly dropped, and its end officially announced." More recently, when Professor Jenkins was installed as Bishop of Durham in York Minster, the ancient fabric was struck by lightning. Among the credulous this was supposed to indicate Divine displeasure at his appointment to the See after having lately expressed on television views denying the Virgin Birth of Christ.

Others *suspend judgment on the matter.* "The historical evidence for the Virgin Birth is inconclusive," says Hugh Burnaby, "it is equally impossible to prove the tradition true or to prove it false. We must shelve the question indefinitely." "You can believe the Gospel without believing in the Virgin Birth," declares G.C. Caird. "We can believe that Jesus is the Son of God, whether He had one parent or two. Personally, I am quite content to leave the question in the balance." "I am not concerned with arguing the pros and cons of the Virgin Birth," states Mervyn Stockwood, "whether you regard it as factually true or as a meaningful myth seems to me to be comparatively unimportant."

Before consulting the Bible on the point, it may be well to pause here for a moment to inquire: Is the Virgin Birth biologically possible? There are those who insist that it is not. According to them, parthenogenesis just does not happen, and so could not possibly have happened in the case of Christ. That, however, is not so. Some time ago the *Lancet*, official organ of the British Medical Association, contained an article by a distinguished professor of genetics, proving that virgin birth could not be scientifically ruled out. In these days of cloning, genetic engineering, who is to say what can and cannot be accomplished in this field? And if man is capable of such miracles of human production, how dare we limit almighty God? Louis Cassels has every right to be dogmatic on the point. "It is simply absurd in my opinion," he writes, "to argue that the Author of the universe, the Creator Spirit, who invented the whole process of procreation, cannot set it aside and bring a human life into being by other means any time He chooses to do so."

The fact is incontestable that, since its very beginning, the Christian Church, when true to its tenets, has boldly proclaimed its faith in the Virgin Birth of Christ. What is the Biblical basis for this profound conviction? There are texts which declare it unequivocally, and texts from which it may reasonably be inferred. Among the former are these: "Behold, a virgin shall conceive, and bear a Son, and shall call His name Immanuel" (Isaiah 7:14). "The angel Gabriel was sent from God unto a city of Galilee, named Nazareth, to a virgin, espoused to a man whose name was Joseph; and the virgin's name was Mary" (Luke 1:27). "Now the birth of Jesus Christ was on this wise: when as his mother Mary was espoused to Joseph, before they came together, she was found with child of the Holy Ghost" (Matthew 1:18). Other texts confirm, or at least do not contradict, these asseverations. "The Lord hath created a new thing in the earth. A woman shall compass a man" (Jeremiah 31:22). "Many good interpreters understand this 'new thing' to be the incarnation of Christ," comments Matthew Henry, "a woman, the Virgin Mary, enclosed in her womb the Mighty One." "When the fulness of the time was come, God sent forth His Son, made of a woman" (Galatians 4:4). One of the apocryphal Gospels actually records that a midwife, in attendance on Mary at her sublime confinement, afterwards provided surgical evidence that Mary was a virgin at the time of the birth. The hymen is the seal of purity. That Mary's was unbroken when Christ tenanted her womb is an indispensable part of the Christian faith. The hallmark of unsullied chastity was on His mother.

We may accept as valid the criticism of John Mackintosh Shaw and others that we should more properly speak of a virgin conception than of a virgin birth. It was the conception of Jesus alone that was supernatural: the birth was perfectly natural. The Virgin carried the Baby under her heart for the normal nine months' gestation period, and the delivery seems to have happened, in spite of reports to the contrary by apocryphal writers, in the usual prolonged and painful manner. It was the conception that was miraculous: the actual birth was not. And yet, although the correction is valid, everybody knows what is meant by the phrase "Virgin Birth".

A virgin birth? As we have seen, it is not biologically impossible and it is Biblically unmistakable. Is it theologically necessary? Was there not some non-miraculous manner in which the Divine and the human could have been united in one Person? Did there have to be a supernatural nativity? Had God no other option? No. We can state quite emphatically and unequivocally that He had no alternative. Why?

To that interrogation various replies may be given.

In the first place, *Jesus had to be born of a virgin in order to be the unique Person He was and is.* The Latin version of the Apostles' Creed has the word *unicus* for "only" as a description of God's Son. From *unicus* we get our English term "unique", and that is exactly what the Lord Jesus is – God's *unique* Son. And surely if we acknowledge the truth of the pre-existence of Christ – a truth woven inextricably into the fabric of Holy Scripture – this is a reason not for disbelieving but for believing in the Virgin Birth! In the instance of our Lord the presuppositions are all in favour of such a supernatural nativity. Had such a thing been reported of Herod, we should have rejected it out of hand as palpably incredible. But with Jesus it was different. "Only a pronounced pantheist," comments Benjamin B. Warfield, "could so confound things that differ as to imagine that, for bringing a supernatural Being into the world, those causes may be thought to suffice by which commonly mere men are produced."

In the second place, *Jesus had to be born of a virgin in order* to become the federal Head of a new humanity. Middleton Murry dubbed Him a "metabiological Man", the first of a new evolutionary species. But it is not on that mundane level that we are to seek for our Lord's significance. Tertullian was nearer the mark when he affirmed: "It was meet that He who was to introduce here on earth a New Birth should Himself be born by a new mode. It was not fit that the Son of God should be born of the seed of man, for then He would have been entirely a Son of man: He would not have been the Son of God at all. The Divine Germ had to be substituted for the human seed."

In the third place, *Jesus had to be born of a virgin in order to be born pure*. This raises an absolutely vital issue. That issue is this: Was it of unfallen nature that Christ partook in the Incarnation, or was it of fallen human nature? James S. McEwan holds the former: "Jesus Christ is not a Child of the *fallen* race," he argues. Edward Irving in a former day, and Karl Barth in our own, have felt obliged to say that it *was* fallen nature which Christ assumed. But the orthodox faith of the Church is that it was *unfallen* human nature. Well, if it was unfallen nature He assumed, how did it come to be unfallen when communicated to Him?

To that query three answers may be returned.

One is that *the nature Christ assumed was unfallen because of the exclusion of the male parent*. But surely that is shallow thinking! For was not original sin as likely to be conveyed through Mary herself as through any union she might have with Joseph? Unless sex itself is to be regarded as impure, it is hard to see how the barring of the human father could have ensured the sinlessness of the nature of Christ.

Another answer is that *the nature Christ assumed was unfallen because Mary herself was immaculate*. This is, of course, the position officially adopted in Roman Catholic dogma. We can watch it taking shape quite early in the history of the Church. It started innocently enough. "She was a virgin," said Ambrose, "not only of body, but of spirit, humble of heart, serious in speech, prudent in thought, of few words, zealous in reading. She harmed no one but desired the good of all." The romanticizing process is patent in this saying of Augustine: "She who had been worthy to conceive and bear Him who was without sin has received a greater grace to conquer sin completely." Bernard of Clairvaux went even further. "The mother of our Lord," he maintained, "was certainly sanctified before her birth." With this Thomas Aquinas was in full agreement. "Mary contracted original sin, but was cleansed of it before birth," he pontificated, though it is hard to see how in that case she could truly be said to have contracted it at all! In 1661 Pope Alexander VII made the Papist position plain: "Mary's soul, in the first instant of its creation, and infusion into the body, by special grace and in consideration of the merits of Christ, was preserved immune from all stain of original sin." And so it went on. Mary came to be described as *theotokos*, "the Mother of God", "the Queen of Heaven"; "the Mediatrix of all the Graces", and so on, until in our own day a papal encyclical has enjoined upon the faithful belief in her bodily assumption to heaven.

What are we to say about all this? Well, we must frankly admit that the character of Mary – her chastity, her humility, her submissiveness, her obedience – did have something to do with her selection as the human instrument of the Incarnation. To put it at its crudest, it is unthinkable that the Divine choice should have fallen on a harlot! Yet, to the embarrassment of those who insist on the dogma of her alleged Immaculate Conception, Mary persists in acknowledging that she was a sinner. This is surely implied in the Magnificat where she sings: "My soul doth magnify the Lord, and my spirit hath rejoiced in God my Saviour" (Luke 1:46.47).

Nonetheless, despite this candid confession, Catholic theologians actually *personalize* the Immaculate Conception. With almost brutal bluntness, Benjamin B. Warfield tilts thus at this daft dogmatic development: "It is not God who rules at Lourdes so much as that incoherent goddess, who has announced herself to her worshippers with as fine a disregard of the ordinary laws of grammar and intelligible speech as the fundamental principles of Christianity, in the remarkable words: 'I am the Immaculate Conception', as if one should say, 'I am the Procession of the Equinoxes' or 'I am the Middle of Next Week!'"

No, it is not by some putative immaculate conception of the Virgin that the sinlessness of the nature Christ assumed is guaranteed. There must be another reason.

There is. In searching for it we turn the spotlight on one word in the New Testament, the word "therefore", *dia* in the Greek, as it occurs in Luke 1:35 "The Holy Ghost shall come upon thee, and the power of the Highest shall overshadow thee, therefore also that Holy Thing which shall be born of thee shall be called the Son of God." That "therefore" or "wherefore" (dia) is the clue to the mystery. It was not by the exclusion of the male parent in Christ's begetting, nor by the alleged immaculate conception of His mother that He inherited an unfallen nature. It was by a direct Divine intervention in Mary's life.

To this there is an arresting and impressive analogy in what is popularly known as "Deep-Ray Therapy". Just as the cancer in the patient is destroyed by the cauter, burnt out by the searing beam, so in Mary, for the purpose of the Incarnation, the Holy Spirit effected a temporary moral sterilization, thus enabling her to transmit to her Divine Son a sinless nature, and ensuring that He was made in all points like unto His brethren, sin excepted.

As a footnote to this study, may I put in a plea for a rational approach to the concept of the Christ-Child in the cradle? The idea of the Manager of the universe in a manger is surely grotesquely incongruous? With Charles Wesley we marvel at the thought of

Our God contracted to a span,
Incomprehensibly made Man,

and with the poet we cry:

O, wonder of wonders, which none can unfold,
The Ancient of Days is an hour or two old,

but any notion of the Baby Jesus running the cosmos from His cradle is surely crazy. Nestorius, Archbishop of Constantinople, caused a scandal in his day by publicly intimating that "he could not regard a three or four month old Baby as God". Certainly, the Infant is God, but He is God expressing Himself through a tiny Baby, not a Baby acting as God. Some well-meaning attempts to safeguard the Deity of the Christ-Child effectively rob Him of His real human Boyhood. Take A.B. Davidson's sombre portrait of Him: "Did it ever strike you that Christ never was a child? You do not fancy Him a child like your children, gay and free of concern: He was grave, retired and sad. He moved about with a weight upon Him. It is nowhere recorded of Him that He smiled. You can hardly fancy that He ever looked young." That, assuredly, is a caricature, not a true picture. Luther limns a closer likeness. "There in a stable," he writes, "lay the Creator of all the worlds. There was the maid of fifteen years, bringing forth her Firstborn, without water, fire, light or pan – a sight for tears. What Mary and Joseph did next nobody knows. The scholars say they adored. They must have marvelled that this Child was the Son of God. He was also a real Human Being. Those who say that Mary was not a real mother lose all joy. He was a true Baby, with flesh, blood, hands and legs; He slept, cried and did everything else that a baby does, only without sin." God is to be found in the little as well as in the great, in the Infant and in the Infinite. As an old Scottish poet, William Robertson, wrote:

A little Child the Saviour came,
The Mighty God is still His name;
And angels worshipped as He lay,
A seeming Infant of a day.

5
THE PERFECT SPECIMEN

The Christian Doctrine of the Earthly Life of Christ

Unto the Son, He saith, Thy throne, O God, is for ever and ever. Hebrews 1:8

The Word was made flesh and dwelt among us. John 1:14

God was manifest in the flesh. 1 Timothy 3:16

The Man Christ Jesus 1 Timothy 2:5

Jesus of Nazareth, a Man approved of God among you. Acts 2:22

After three days they found Jesus in the Temple, sitting in the midst of the doctors, both hearing them, and asking them questions. Luke 2:46

He went down with them, and came to Nazareth, and was subject unto them; and increased in wisdom and stature, and in favour with God and man. Luke 2:51,52

Jesus being baptized, and praying, the heaven was opened.
Luke 3:21

Jesus Himself began to be about thirty years of age. Luke 3:23

God anointed Jesus of Nazareth with the Holy Ghost and with power: who went about doing good, and healing all that were oppressed of the Devil; for God was with Him. Acts 10:38

Never Man spake like this Man. John 7:46

Christ also suffered for us, leaving us an example, that ye should follow His steps. 1 Peter 2:21

IN HIS VERBAL portrait of our Lord entitled *Jesus* Geoffrey Grogan tells of a conversation he once had with a famous Scottish artist. The artist confided to him how, many years before, he had first come to feel the urge to paint. It happened when he was taken as a boy to the Art Galleries in Glasgow. Passing from room to room of the spacious and beautiful building, he paused briefly to examine and admire each exhibit. Not until he stood before Rembrandt's masterpiece "Man in Armour", however, was he absolutely, as we say, "bowled over". Riveted to the spot, he was overwhelmed by a sense of awe. "I felt," he said afterwards, "this was not the portrait of the man, but the man himself" –

> *As when a painter, poring on a face,*
> *Divinely, through all hindrance, finds the man*
> *Behind it, and so paints him that his face,*
> *The shape and colour of a mind and life,*
> *Lives for his children, ever at its best*
> *And fullest.*

That is precisely what is meant to take place when we open those slim memoirs which we call the Gospels. They are not just records of the life of Jesus: they are repositories of His Person. Once in Philadelphia, U.S.A., I saw a poster dated July 4, 1776 in which the Declaration of Independence had been cleverly printed in such a way that the type presented a portrait of George Washington. It was possible, if one were not very quick in the uptake, to read the text without seeing the portrait, but that was an impoverishment, since it was the man who made the Declaration possible. So in the reading of the New Testament. It is the Person behind the page that mostly matters.

This was just the charge that Jesus brought against the Jews of His day: "Ye search the Scriptures; for in them ye think ye have eternal life: and they are they which testify of Me. And ye will not come unto Me, that ye might have life" (John 5:39,40).

To some the Gospels are but literature: to others they are life. We must not stop at the manuscripts: we must pass through them to the Man; we must not halt at the page: we must proceed to the Person; we must not stay at the Book: we must advance into the presence of the sublime Being of which the Book is the biography – the Perfect Specimen. With Mary A. Lathbury we must pray:

Beyond the sacred page
I seek Thee, Lord.

In this chapter we are to be concerned with just that – the earthly life of the Perfect Specimen. To help get our kaleidoscopic subject into focus, we may perhaps profitably divide our study into seven sections: (1) *Boy and Youth*; (2) *Apprentice and Craftsman*; (3) *Catechumen and Ascetic*; (4) *Pattern and Example*; (5) *Preacher and Teacher*; (6) *Doctor and Deliverer*; (7) *Messiah and Prophet*.

BOY AND YOUTH

Although born in Bethlehem, our Lord was brought up in Nazareth, a busy, bustling, smelly, typically oriental town, nestling in a saucer of hills flanking the northern border of the Plain of Esdraelon, some twenty miles east of the Mediterranean, about fifteen miles south of the Sea of Galilee and some 1,300 feet above sea level. Nazareth has one spring from which the inhabitants derive their water supply.

Quite literally, our Lord put Nazareth on the map. It is not even mentioned in Hebrew literature until it became associated with Him. It seems to have been held in evil odour in other parts of Israel. "Can there any good thing come out of Nazareth?" asked Nathanael with wholly uncharacteristic cynicism (John 1:49). To which has been given the inspired answer: "Yes, the best thing in the world has come out of Nazareth!"

Jerome, who once lived in Nazareth, reports that over the door of Joseph's workshop hung a sign: "Our Yokes are Easy."

Papist piety, in its ingenious concern to safeguard its dogma of the alleged perpetual virginity of Mary, has turned Joseph into an almost comic figure. He is always depicted as, in biblical phrase, "well stricken in years" – a concept hardly compatible with carrying on the strenuous trade of a carpenter! – and he is said to have sought to decline the favour of marital alliance with Mary with the remark: "I have sons, and I am an old man, and she is a girl. I shall become a laughing-stock to the people of Israel."

That is legend. The fact is that both Joseph and his contemporaries evidently thought him virile enough to father a supposedly illegitimate child, and he was minded to put her away.

Besides, is there not something bordering on obscenity in conferring on an old man custody of a chaste girl? Why not put her in the charge of an old woman?

In any case, the fact that Jesus is twice called "firstborn"

(*Gk prototokos*) places the matter beyond dispute. Telling the truth is so simple compared to fabricating falsehood. There is no need to speculate that those described in the Gospels as Jesus' brothers and sisters were cousins or stepbrothers and step-sisters or anything other than just that – actual brothers and sisters.

In this family of nine, then, the Boy Jesus grew up. We can picture Him playing in the shavings on the carpentry floor, fetching timber for Joseph's trade, trying His hand at the use of the tools of joinery. Here, occasionally, doubtless His grandparents – Anna and Joachim – would pay a visit, and there would be romps on the hills and excursions with a pitcher for water to the well. "He was subject unto His parents," we are told, "and increased in wisdom and stature, and in favour with God and man" (Luke 2:51,52). "The one boy that really knew more than His 'father' and mother," wrote A.T. Robertson, "was a model of obedience." How strange that the only child who ever existed that knew infinitely more than His parents should have been subject to them! No wonder "He grew, and waxed strong in spirit, filled with wisdom: and the grace of God was upon Him" (Luke 2:40).

In sharpest contrast to all this are the pictures of His boyhood drawn by the authors of the apocryphal gospels. The so-called *Gospel of Thomas* depicts Him as a sort of Dennis the Menace. Thwart Him and you pay for it: cross Him and your number is up! "A child bumps into Him and is killed for His pains. Those who complain at His excessive reaction are blinded. The son of Annas, the scribe, is 'withered' for daring to cross Him. A teacher is cursed for striking Him. The dyer Salem finds that his white cloths have all been dipped in a cauldron full of indigo. Children who hide from the Boy are turned into goats. "And no one after that dared to provoke Him, lest He should curse him and he should be maimed" (David Day, *This Jesus*, p.39).

We may be certain that the best Boy who ever lived was not in the least like that. How different from such bizarre narratives are the homespun stories in the New Testament!

At the age of six Jesus would be enrolled as a pupil at the local primary school. There he would be taught by the *chazzan*, or minister, who received whatever increment he got from the congregation of the synagogue rather than from the parents of the children, as such. Imagine Him there, slate in hand, waiting for the first lesson. That slate has been smeared with honey and inscribed on it are the words of Psalm 119:103: "How sweet are Thy words unto my taste! Yea, sweeter than honey to my mouth!" The Boy is instructed to lick the honey from the slate and thus He is psychologically conditioned for a lifetime to associate sweetness with the Word of God. It was to be a long time before another Jew, Sigmund Freud, was to say so much about the "association of ideas", but the ancient Rabbis had already got the idea.

Here a happy little story comes to mind. It is about a lady who once took a small Hindu orphan boy to live in her home and taught him about Jesus. One night she suggested to the six-year-old that he should offer a prayer of his own. He did; and this is what he said: "Dear Jesus, make me like You were when You were six years old!" – a story which reminds us of a gentle couplet from the pen of Francis Thompson:

> *Little Jesus, wert Thou shy*
> *Once, and just as small as I?*

Apart from the hours spent in innocent sports and pastimes, not to speak of household chores and joinery tasks, the major part of the life of the Boy Jesus must have been passed between the *shool* (synagogue) and school – very probably in the same building. If tradition is to be trusted, the synagogue in which He worshipped was hardly more than a hundred yards from His home. Until recently, the *shool* was a dark, bare, dusty chamber, but it has now been at least partially furnished and decorated and is much more presentable. Here it was that our Lord learned to pray and later to preach. It is recorded: "He came to Nazareth, where He had been brought up: and, as His custom was, He went into the synagogue on the Sabbath day" (Luke 4:16). No doubt the holy habit was formed in early life. Little did the local Rabbi know, as he went about his sacred duties, that among his congregants was the incarnate God! "How strange," exclaims James Stalker wonderingly, "to think of His being preached at Sabbath after Sabbath for so long!"

Nazareth then would not be all that different from what it is now, with its narrow, crooked, cobbled streets, those on the slope leading to His home having a sort of spinal culvert running down them, forming an open sewer for the disposal of domestic and commercial waste; its squat, dusty, open-fronted shops – fruit-vendors, woodworkers, blacksmiths, bakers, grocers, and the rest, and picturesque stalls with their multi-coloured cotton, calico and leather goods on show in the sunshine. One can picture in one's mind's eye a tall, sun-bronzed, auburnhaired Lad, making His way periodically through the bustle of the mart to and from the town's only internal well, an earthen pitcher on His head, fetching water for the family's needs. Thomas Maynard paints the portrait unforgettably:

For in that quiet town of Nazareth
Where heaven was conscious in a growing Boy,
Walked its white streets and drew of human breath
E'er Golgotha made an end of Mary's joy.

(Somehow one gets the irresistible impression that Thomas Maynard had never been in Nazareth; but, after all, there *is* such a thing as poetic licence!)

Roughly half way up the narrow, stone-flagged, bazaar-fringed street on the north west side of the town, the traditional site of the home of the Boy Jesus is located. One hopes, for His sake, it was not as sordid then as it is today. Fancy exchanging heaven for a hovel like that! G.K. Chesterton called Christ "the Caveman", and Chesterton was right. Jesus was born in a cave and buried in a cave and, if tradition is to be trusted, seems to have spent the larger part of His brief earthly life in a cave. The home would be part of the carpentry, simply equipped with homemade furniture, and providing sparse accommodation for domestic animals as well as for its human occupents. Our Lord's parabolic reference to the woman lighting a taper and searching in the dark corners of the house for a lost coin is doubtless based on personal recollection.

Fastened to the doorpost of the crude dwelling would be a *Mezuzah*, which the Boy Jesus would see every time He went out or came in. What *is* a *Mezuzah*? It is a tiny filigree metal cylinder with the Hebrew word *Shin*, the first letter of the term in that language translated into English by the word "Almighty". Within the cylinder would be a scrap of Scripture comprised of Deuteronomy 6:4-9 and 11:13-21. With these words of divine command, promise and warning so much in mind, all from the same Old Testament book, it is no wonder our Lord came to make Deuteronomy His favourite Old Testament reading.

The immediate family of the Boy Jesus consisted of at least nine persons – Mary and Joseph, James, Joses, Simon and Judas, and at least two anonymous sisters. Reputedly, Mary was by trade a hairdresser, a circumstance which may have given rise to the report that, due to her possession of such digital dexterity, to her was given the privileged task of spinning the true purple and scarlet for the veil of the Temple.

Joseph, the Boy's foster-father, was a carpenter, employed in the construction and repair of properties, the manufacture of agricultural implements and of articles of household furniture.

The highlight in the religious life of a Jewish boy occurs when, at the age of thirteen, he undergoes his *barmitzvah*, and so becomes a "Son of the Law". Some scholars believe that this practice was not introduced until after the Fall of Jerusalem and that for this reason our Lord's recorded visit to the Temple at the age of twelve is not to be so interpreted. However that may be, the fact that Jesus *did* pay a visit to the Holy City, accompanied by His parents, is vouched for by Luke. He writes: "Now His parents went to Jerusalem every year at the feast of the Passover. And when He was twelve years old, they went up to Jerusalem after the custom of the feast. And when they had fulfilled the days, as they returned, the Child Jesus tarried behind in Jerusalem: and Joseph and His mother knew not of it. And when they found Him not, they turned back again to Jerusalem, seeking Him. And it came to pass that after three days they found Him in the Temple, sitting in the midst of the doctors, both hearing them and asking them questions. And all that heard Him were astonished at His understanding and answers" (2:41-47).

How differently the authors of the apocryphal gospels would have depicted this scene! They would have pictured the Boy Jesus instructing the Rabbis, giving profound lessons in theology to the learned doctors of the Law, and probably displaying His supernatural powers in their presence. Instead how simply and naturally the New Testament writer actually does record it. "Hearing them and asking them questions" (v.46). That is how Luke describes Jesus' attitude and activity in the company of those theological experts. Modesty and teachability were both highly becoming in the juvenile Jesus.

The sequel shows, however, how already the realization of His unique identity and destiny was dawning on His consciousness. When Mary, His mother, expostulated with Him for getting lost by staying behind in Jerusalem, with the words: "Thy father and I have sought Thee sorrowing", His answer contained a mild reminder and remonstrance: "Did you not know that I must be in My Father's House" (Luke 2:48,49)? "*Thy* 'father' – in inverted commas – Joseph," she had said. "*My* Father – Jehovah," He had replied.

APPRENTICE AND CRAFTSMAN

"He who does not teach his son a trade," declares the Talmud, "teaches him to be a thief." On this principle the Jews proceeded in the education of their children. Thus Hillel was a wood-cutter, Paul a tent-maker, and Jesus a carpenter.

Like all good craftsmen, He began as an apprentice. He was "the carpenter's Son" (Matthew 13:55) before He was "the Carpenter" (Mark 6:3).

Richard Pyke actually suggests that He may not have been very good at His trade. "Whether Jesus was a good Carpenter, as some loyal but rather unimaginative people have affirmed," he writes, "I cannot say. I remember it is said of Alexander Whyte that, though he was a shoemaker as a lad, he was a very poor shoemaker – his heart was not in his boots!" One thing may be taken as certain – the Maker of all things was not a poor cabinet-maker. The Creator in human form can never have been a bad Carpenter. Jesus the Joiner would be famous for the excellent quality of His work. "Everyone," it has been said, "we may be sure admired His woodwork. His doors and chests and yokes were without a flaw."

High above Nazareth, on a rocky ridge to the north east of the town, stands the stately Church of Jesus the Adolescent. Above the altar there is a charming statue, executed in white stone, of the juvenile Jesus. It looks as if artificially illuminated. One is certain there is a floodlight or spotlight somewhere, but on investigating one finds that it is natural light which throws the figure into such bright relief.

Underneath the church is the chapel of a French school for boys, in an adjunct of which one may see them at benches learning the craft of carpentry.

From the fact that Jesus is first called "the carpenter's Son" (Matthew 13:55) and later "the Carpenter" (Mark 6:3), it is assumed that round about this time Joseph died and Jesus, as the eldest Son in a large family, took over responsibility for the affairs of the household. It is difficult, if not impossible, to think of death invading the home where dwelt the One who is the Resurrection and the Life. But certain it is that, as from this point in the narrative, Jesus became Himself the Carpenter, either in partnership with Joseph or in replacement of him. Joseph is the classic example of one who plays the second fiddle well. He is, and from the nature of the case, always will be, overshadowed by his wife. This the poet Gilbert Thomas has noted and in this graceful lyric has sung the praises of Jesus' foster-father:

Who has not carolled Mary
And who her praise would dim?
But what of humble Joseph –
Is there no song for him?

If Joseph had not driven
Straight nails through honest wood;
If Joseph had not cherished
His Mary as he should;

If Joseph had not proved him
A sire both kind and wise,
Would he have drawn with favour
The Child's all-probing eyes?

Would Christ have prayed "Our Father",
Or cried that name in death,
Unless He first had honoured
Joseph of Nazareth?

And so the "Hidden Years" passed in the early life of our

Lord – not even, by some dreadful omission, so much as mentioned in the Apostles' Creed – and Jesus, in Leonard Small's graphic phrase, was "chewed into the machinery of circumstance", until one day He took off His leathern apron for the last time, and laid His axe and hammer by, swept up the crisp shavings from the carpentry floor, bade His family farewell and set off on the colossal mission which His heavenly Father had assigned to Him.

At this point in the narrative a modern biographer would undoubtedly interpolate a portrait of his subject in his prime. Nor is it idle to deny that in the life of every true lover of the Lord there are moments when he wishes that Jesus had sat for Michelangelo or deferred His Advent till after the invention of the camera, the film, television. If only we could have a classic oil painting of Him from a supreme old master! If only we could see Him on the screen! But no. We do not even have a verbal portrait of Him. The New Testament does not gratify our very natural desire for such a pictorial likeness. It does not provide us with a single touch of personal portraiture. We know more about the physical appearance of King David from the Bible than we know about King David's greater Son.

This has led to a great deal of speculation as to His appearance. Some, taking their cue from Isaiah 53:2, have conceived of Him as physically ill-favoured. Flavius Josephus, the Jewish historian, who had other reasons for seeking to discredit Him, presents us with a picture of Him which is far from flattering: "He was a small, bent, homely figure, only four feet nine inches in height, and hunch-backed, the face and nose long, the eyebrows meeting in the middle." A dwarf of that size could hardly have driven the money-changers out of the Temple with a whip of small cords!

At the opposite pole is a word-picture of Jesus which began to be circulated in the twelfth century but claims to be contemporary with Christ Himself. Here it is: "There appeared in our times a Man of tall stature, beautiful, with a venerable countenance, which they who look upon can both love and fear. His hair is waving and crisp, somewhat wine-coloured, and glittering as it flows down over His shoulders, with a parting in the middle after the manner of the Nazarenes. His brow is smooth and most serene: His face is without spot or wrinkle and glows with a delightful flush; His nose and His mouth are of faultless contour; His beard is abundant and hazel-coloured like His hair – not long, but forked. His eyes are prominent, brilliant and change their colour. His hands and limbs are lovely to look upon; and He is fair among the children of men."

That is a delectable portrait, but it is amazing how, by some unerring instinct, we know when a thing is false. The fact is, we have no authentic physical delineament of Jesus. The terrific posthumous impact He has made upon the world is totally spiritual.

CATECHUMEN AND ASCETIC

Read imaginatively, the account of the baptism of Jesus is one of the most moving episodes in the Gospel records. Jesus walked not a few miles over rough and hilly terrain to Bethabara beyond Jordan where John the Baptist was baptizing. (Incidentally, it is pretty obvious that the Scriptural mode of baptism is immersion. Had sprinkling been the method, there was enough water in the Pool of Siloam to "baptize" the whole population of Jerusalem! But more of this anon!) Picture, then, the thirty-year-old Jesus joining the crowds amid the tall reeds on the east bank of the muddy River Jordan. It would have been so natural for Him to take His stand alongside the Baptist, saying: "Come on, John, let Me help you to immerse these sordid sinners!" But no. He does not. With touching humility, He takes His stance among the sinners. "Then cometh Jesus from Galilee to Jordan unto John, to be baptized of him. But John forbad Him, saying, I have need to be baptized of Thee, and comest Thou to me? And Jesus answering said unto him, Suffer it to be so now: for thus it becometh us to fulfil all righteousness" (Matthew 3:13-15).

Notice that personal pronoun *"us"*. It implies complete identification of the Saviour with sinners, sin only excepted. Contrast it with the *"Us"* in our Lord's great high-priestly prayer: "That they may be one in *Us*" (John 17:21).

"Go to the Jordan," said Augustine, "and you will find the Trinity." As Jesus rose, praying, from the river, the Father broke the silence of the heavens to cry: "This is My beloved Son, in whom I am well pleased" (Matthew 3:17) – as if to say to the assembled multitude: "You may think because My Son is identifying Himself with sinners that He is Himself a sinner. That is not so. He is My beloved Son in whom there is no evil." That was the voice of the First Person of the Trinity. Jesus standing dripping in the waters of the Jordan. That was the Second Person. And then there was the Dove, symbolic of the Holy Spirit – the Third Person – whom John saw descending upon the Christ. "Jesus, when He was baptized, went up straightway out of the water: and, lo, the heavens were opened unto Him, and He saw the Spirit of God descending like a Dove, and lighting upon Him" (Matthew 3:16,17). This was in line with Messianic prophecy: "The Spirit of the Lord shall rest upon Him" (Isaiah 11:1). No one has ever seen that Dove fly back.

Immediately after His baptism, our Lord, being filled with the Holy Spirit, was led by the Spirit into the barren wilderness of Judaea to be tempted of the Devil. As quaint old John Trapp comments: "No sooner was Christ out of the water of baptism, than He is thrust into the fire of temptation." Some liberal scholars treat the story of the Temptation in the Wilderness as the dramatic objectification of a conflict in our Lord's mind. They do not believe that our Lord actually *saw* Satan. One writer belonging to this school of thought quotes Hebrews 4:15, "He was tempted in all points like as we are," adding: "No black bogey tempts us." The argument is fallacious. Notice exactly what the writer to the Hebrews says and what he does not say. He says: "He was tempted in all points *like as we are*": he does not say: "We are tempted in all points like as He *was*." We are mercifully spared the pain and peril of moral combat with a *seen* Satan. Our antagonist is invisible. But, after all, as A.T. Robertson contends: "It is no more difficult to think of the Devil making a visible manifestation of himself to Jesus than to believe in the existence of a Devil at all."

In your study of the Scriptures you must have noticed that the Devil's favourite word is "if". That comes out clearly in Luke's account of the Temptation: "*If* Thou be the Son of God" (4:3); "*If* Thou be the Son of God, cast Thyself down" (4:9). We may term the Temptations respectively: (1) *The Temptation of the Stones.* "Turn these *stones into scones*" (James Moffatt). (2) *The Temptation of the Stoop.* "If Thou wilt bow down". And (3) *The Temptation of the Stunt.* He sought to make the Master a mountebank. "Cast Thyself down." These represent three ways of attaining the messiahship which Jesus knew to be His royal role – to give the people bread, to submit to Satan and to dazzle the populace with some supernatural feat. Our Lord rejected all three – although it cannot have been easy, even for Him, to do so. "I used to think," writes Michael Green, "that because Jesus never sinned, it must somehow have been easier for Him. I now appreciate that whereas I never get the full blast of temptation – I fall before it gets that far – He did face that without yielding, and He did so, time after time" (*I Believe in Satan's Downfall*, p. 62).

PATTERN AND EXAMPLE

Having triumphantly passed Satan's testing, Jesus embarks upon His public career. Winning His spiritual spurs on the battlefield of good and evil, He was now the one Person in history fit to be the moral model and exemplar of mankind.

His perfect character, as portrayed in the Gospels, is a combination of apparent contraries: He was (1) *tough yet tender;* (2) *a solitary yet a socialite;* (3) *meek yet masterful;* (4) *sinless yet sin-bearer;* (5) *restful yet ever working.*

Take them one by one.

(1) *Tough yet tender.* It was William James, the American psychologist, who was responsible for this somewhat simplistic classification of the human race into the tough and the tender. In Jesus these seemingly incompatible personal qualifies are fused in moral perfection. He is not just man with a small "m" but Man with a capital "M", exemplifying in His peerless personality the finest attributes of both male and female. He is both tough *and* tender.

To take only one instance. Reflect how for forty days and forty nights He resolutely resisted the clamant demands of physical hunger in the midst of a hot and howling wilderness. He had to be tough to bear that. But recall, too, how in Matthew 15:23 He is recorded to have said: "I have compassion on the multitude, because they continue with Me now three days, *and have nothing to eat*: and I will not send them away fasting, lest they faint by the way" – tough yet tender.

(2) *A Solitary yet a Socialite.* He was the Great Solitary. "And when He had sent the multitudes away, He went up into a mountain apart to pray; and when the evening was come He was there alone" (Matthew 14:23). "And in the morning, rising up a great while before day, He went out, and departed into a solitary place, and there prayed" (Mark 1:35). Yet the Master was no monk. He did not retire within the high walls of a monastery, cultivating a pale and cloistered piety. "He was not a Dreamer among shadows but a Man among men." He was in fact what we

would today describe as a "socialite". He let people get close to Him, loved to have them around Him, permitted them to observe Him at close quarters. His moral perfection was not an illusion created and maintained by isolationism. It was open for all to see.

Most moralists have tended to put bad people into quarantine, to segregate them, if not actually to ostracize them, for fear of moral infection. Even the great and good Socrates, the best of the pagans, advocated this policy. "Never consort with wicked men," he said, "live only with the virtuous." That is, of course, good counsel, a salutary caution against contamination. The Lord Jesus ignored it. By fraternizing with the riff-raff of contemporary society. He deliberately exposed Himself to misunderstanding. The religious leaders were outraged by such flagrantly unconventional conduct on the part of an ethical teacher. "Behold, a Friend of publicans and sinners" (Matthew 11:19). "This Man, if He were a prophet, would have known what manner of woman this is that toucheth Him: for she is a sinner" (Luke 7:39). "Then drew near all the publicans and sinners for to hear Him. And the Pharisees and scribes murmured, saying, This Man receiveth sinners, and eateth with them" (Luke 15:1,2). – solitary yet socialite.

(3) *Meek yet masterful.* Could any one person be both of these? Are not the attributes and attitudes mutually exclusive? For everyone else they would be, but not for Jesus. He was meek. He said Himself that He was meek. "Take My yoke upon you, and learn of Me; for I am meek and lowly in heart: and ye shall find rest unto your souls" (Matthew 11:29). Paul speaks of "the meekness and gentleness of Christ" (2 Corinthians 10:1). The spirit of meekness is the Spirit of Christ. And yet Jesus was also masterful. "Ye call Me Master and Lord: and ye say well; for so I am" (John 13:13). The word there translated "master" is in the Greek not *despotes* but *didaskalos*. Nevertheless the thought of authority is there. Jesus is called

"Master" by five different words in the New Testament, four Greek and one Hebrew. Not only is He meek, He is masterful.

(4) *Sinless yet sin-bearer*. Strikingly, James Denney stated: "Jesus is not only separate from sinners, He is distinct from the saints." At the Jordan when He was baptized, we noted that the Father broke in to make it transparently plain that, although His Son was aligning Himself with sinners, He was not one of them. "This is My beloved Son," He cried, "in whom I am well pleased" (Matthew 3:17). On Mount Hermon, at the Transfiguration, we witness another Divine intervention. This time it is to distinguish Jesus from the saints. Here is Mark's crisp account of it: "After six days Jesus taketh with Him Peter, and James, and John, and leadeth them up into a high mountain apart by themselves: and He was transfigured before them. And His raiment became shining, exceeding white as snow; so as no fuller on earth can white them. And there appeared unto them Elias with Moses: and they were talking with Jesus. And Peter answered and said to Jesus, Master, it is good for us to be here: and let us make three tabernacles; one for Thee, and one for Moses and one for Elias. For he wist not what to say; for he was sore afraid. And there was a cloud that overshadowed them: and a voice came out of the cloud, saying, This is My beloved Son: hear Him" (9:2-7). The New Testament taxes the resources of language in its efforts to convince us of the absolute impeccability of Jesus. It says that "He knew no sin" (2 Corinthians 5:21); "He did no sin" (1 Peter 2:22); "In Him is no sin" (1 John 3:5). And it declares that, although tempted in all points like as we are, He was "yet without sin" (Hebrews 4:15).

In spite of that He was from the beginning of His ministry marked out as the *Sin-bearer*. Notice how John the Baptist introduced Him to a waiting world. "Behold the Lamb of God, which taketh away the sin of the world" (John 1:29). Observe the tense of the verb. "Taketh." Even at the start of His public work He was already bearing the sins of the world. Sinless yet sin-bearer.

(5) *Restful yet ever working.* The life of the Lord Jesus had about it a delightful tranquillity and serenity, the calmness, composure and collectedness of conscious power. He was never thrown into a "flat spin" by anything that happened. Even in Pilate's judgment hall He was more relaxed than His judge. And yet He was always busily engaged in His great task. "I work," He declared (John 5:17). The Carpenter was never unemployed, nor will He ever be while the world stands. "My meat is to finish His work" (John 4:34). "I must work the works of Him that sent Me" (John 9:4). The Lord was a Labourer. His rest was not that of idleness but of adequate resources and perfect adjustment to the demands of duty.

Our Lord has thus drawn for us in flesh and blood a model of the true life. Indeed, we can go further and say with Clement of Alexandria: "He *is* the Model of the true life." In the oft-quoted words of William E. Lecky: "It was reserved for Christianity to present to the world an ideal character, which through all the changes of the centuries, has inspired the hearts of men with an impassioned love; has shown itself capable of acting on all ages, nations, temperaments and conditions; has been not only the highest pattern of virtue, but the strongest incentive to its practice."

PREACHER AND TEACHER

Jesus made His debut on the stage of world history as a preacher. "He hath anointed Me to preach" (Luke 4:18); "I must preach" (Luke 4:43); "Jesus began to preach" (Matthew 4:17); "Jesus went about preaching" (Matthew 4:23). That was His distinctive mission, His all-absorbing task. Above everything He was a preacher. Our Lord was a Layman. He was not a product of the schools. The appellation "Rabbi" when applied to Him was a courtesy title. He was not a graduate of the University of Jerusalem, as was Paul. Yet He had a licence to preach such as no college can confer. Not only was He the minister: He was the message. He came not merely to preach the Gospel but to *be* the Gospel. "Philip preached unto the eunuch *Jesus*" (Acts 8:35). "Ye have not so learned *Christ*" (Ephesians 4:20). If He preached on the Kingdom of God, *He* was the King; if He preached on the forgiveness of sins, *He* was the pardoner; if He preached on the gift of eternal life, *He* was the Divine donor. He was not only *kerugma*: He was *Logos*. Everything was in Him. As one has well said, "Christ knew no higher duty than to point men to Himself."

Not only was He *kerux*, however, He was also *didaskalos* – Teacher as well as Preacher. He needed no university chair from which to address His pupils. A boat would do. He delivered His Beatitudes on a mountainside; He taught by the seaside; He gave His great Olivet Discourse in a cave on the side of that hill. He *did* teach in synagogues, however, and even in Herod's magnificent Temple. He had stature without status, tutorial rank without the warrant of any college senatus. James A. Francis carries us all with him when in this glowingly eloquent passage He celebrates the greatness of Jesus: "He was an itinerant Teacher. He never wrote a book. He never held an office. He never owned a home. He never had a family. He never went to college. He never did one of the things that usually accompany greatness. Well-nigh twenty wide centuries have come and gone. Today He is the Centrepiece of the human race and the Leader of the column of progress. I am within the mark when I say that all the armies that ever marched, and all the navies that ever were built, and all the parliaments that ever sat, and all the kings that ever reigned, put together, have not affected the life of man upon this earth as powerfully as has that one solitary life."

DOCTOR AND DELIVERER

It often surprises me that the term "doctor" is not more frequently applied to our Lord, for if there is one profession, other than that of the Christian ministry itself, to which Christ patently belonged, it was the medical profession. Many people divide physical healing into two distinct categories – natural healing and supernatural healing. The first, they say, is human; the second, divine. Medicine is man's method; miracle is God's. They are wrong. Ultimately, there is only one Healer, and He is Christ. As Benjamin Franklin pawkily put it: "God healed me, the doctor took the fee." Gratefully acknowledging, as we do, all that medical and surgical science can do for the alleviation and removal of human suffering, we are bound to recognize that behind all man's therapeutic ministries, there is the great Divine Healer Himself.

He is our physician. He Himself has said so. "They that be whole need not a physician, but they that are sick" (Matthew 9:12). "Ye will surely say unto Me this proverb, Physician, heal Thyself" (Luke 4:23). In the stuff of which our planet is made He has stored the chemicals which man employs medicinally. As the writer of Ecclesiasticus had the insight to perceive: "From the Most High cometh healing: the Lord created medicines out of the earth; and He gave men skill that He might be glorified in His marvellous works" (38:2,4,6).

Not otherwise is it with surgery. No doctor would dare insert a scalpel in a human body if God did not heal. Introducing Himself to His people Israel and, through them, to the world, He said: "I am the Lord that healeth thee" (Exodus 15:26). Or, as Luther finely translates it in his vigorous German version: *"Ich bin der Herr, dein Artz"* ("I am the Lord, your Doctor").

As John Bunyan expresses this truth in his *Jerusalem Sinner*: "Christ Jesus, as you may perceive, has put Himself under the term of a physician: and you know that applause and a fame, is the thing that physicians much desire. That is it that helps them to patients, and that also that will help their patients to commit themselves to their skill for cure, with more confidence and repose of spirit.

And the best way for a doctor or physician to get himself a name is, in the first place, to take in hand and cure some such as all others have given off for lost and dead." Such is precisely the fame Christ has. His specialty is raising the dead!

As a good Doctor, Jesus went regularly on His "rounds" in the Israel of His day. His was a peripatetic, ambulatory ministry. He sought His patients out and healed them where they were. Of Him Peter said that "He went about doing good, and healing all that were oppressed of the Devil" (Acts 10:38). An American poetess has written:

I read
In a Book
That a Man called
Christ
Went about doing good.

It was very disconcerting to me
That I am so easily
Satisfied
With just
Going about.

The life of the Great Galilean is a challenge to us all.

But more. Not only was He Doctor, He was Deliverer. He exercised a miraculous ministry. If His words were oracles, His deeds were miracles. But *do* miracles happen? About that there are broadly three views. Some, like Matthew Arnold, say bluntly: "Miracles do not happen." Others, like Walt Whitman, declare: "Everything is a miracle. I myself am a miracle. A mouse is miracle enough to stagger sextillions of infidels." Others still, taking their stand on the New Testament, affirm: "It is irrational to profess to believe in the existence of an omnipotent Deity and at the same time to deny the possibility of miracle." For, as G.K. Chesterton perceptively pointed out: "A miracle is only the liberty of God."

Every attempt to desupernaturalize the New Testament only succeeds in irrationalizing it. Barclay's suggestion that Jesus did not really still the storm on Galilee but only the storm in the disciples' hearts; Weatherhead's submission that our Lord did not in fact feed the five thousand, but simply induced others to emulate the example of the generous boy with the five loaves and two fishes, and so there was enough to go round; Soper's supposition that the Master did not really walk on the water, but was just paddling in the shallows – all such naive simplifications make nonsense of the narratives. With Alexander Maclaren we are therefore fain to confess: "I would rather believe in the miraculous than in the ridiculous."

The world of our time is rightly impressed with the rigid reign of law. It is not stunned, as were the credulous ancients, into stupid awe by some stupendous occurrence: rather is it stimulated to inquire by the operation of what law it took place. In former days men believed in God because they believed in miracles: today they believe in miracles, if they do at all, because they believe in God. W.E. Orchard was entirely typical of his time when he once rather flippantly remarked: "If I saw someone walking on the sea, I should not say: 'This is Divine'; I should say: 'Excuse me, do you mind doing that again? I did not see how you did it.'"

Now it is all to the good that there should be this respect, this reverence, for law. Without law nature would be a nightmare – completely unpredictable, utterly unreliable. One day the application of heat would make water boil, the next day freeze it. Today if you place your foot on the surface of the earth, it will bear your weight: tomorrow if you attempt the same thing it will give way beneath you and you will drop into the womb of the world. Now you eat a certain type of food and it pleases your palate and nourishes your body. Later if you were to appropriate it, it would operate on you as a deadly poison. No, we couldn't live in a universe like that. There must be law and law must be respected.

Yet – and this is the point I am concerned to make – there must also be the possibility, when some beneficent objective demands it, of the supercession of law.

Perhaps I can best get the point over by means of a homely illustration. Many years ago I found myself one day at the centre of a great Scottish city. It was rush-hour and the thoroughfares were jammed with pedestrians and vehicles. At one busy intersection there was a long line of cars waiting for the changing of the traffic-lights. Now, the drivers of those vehicles knew their *Highway Code*. They had learned to recognize and to respect the signals. They knew that it was obligatory upon them as motorists to obey the rule of the road. So they waited for the green light to show. Just then, however, there was the wail of a siren and the roar of a huge red machine. A fireengine was hurtling along the wrong side of the street and, although the signals were still against it and it ran a dreadful risk of catastrophic collision, it thundered across the intersection and sped on its way.

That familiar incident illustrates the nature of miracle. It was well that those traffic-lights were there. It was well also that their presence was recognized and respected. But it was likewise well that, when the need arose, it should, for altruistic and humanitarian reasons, be temporarily set aside.

Just so the miracles of Jesus. They were not arbitrary and erratic interferences with the operation of the laws of nature, still less were they mere acts of spectacular magic. They were deeds of mercy. They were works of love. They were charitable performances expressive of the tender care and concern of Christ for those whose condition gave them a special claim upon Him.

MESSIAH AND PROPHET

Of these two aspects of our Lord's ministry we shall have much to say later on. All that is necessary now is to call attention to them. The fact that He was the Messiah must have been present to the mind of Jesus from the time when He reached the age of discretion. Perhaps even before that His mother may have confided to Him the secrets concerning His identity and destiny which she usually kept locked in her heart. Certainly through His reading of the Hebrew Scriptures He was sure to know that in them the advent of Messiah was predicted. "In the Old Testament," writes Josh McDowell, "there are sixty major Messianic prophecies and approximately two hundred and seventy ramifications that were fulfilled in one Person – Jesus Christ" (*More than a Carpenter*, p.102).

Later, during His earthly life, certain discerning persons recognized Him as Messiah. Nathanael, for instance. "Rabbi," he cried, "Thou art the Son of God; Thou art the Messiah" (John 1:49) and the thief on the cross: "Lord, remember me when Thou comest into Thy kingdom" (Luke 23:42). And there were others, it appears, to whom our Lord revealed Himself in that royal role. The woman of Samaria, while talking to Him, had piously observed: "I know that Messias cometh, which is called Christ", and to her He gave the decisive answer: "I that speak unto thee am He" (John 4:25,26).

But more. Jesus was also a prophet. A large part of His recorded ministry is prophetic in character. Think of some of the things He predicted, some already literally fulfilled, some awaiting fulfilment. He foretold His own death, His resurrection on the third day, the pouring out of the Holy Spirit, the founding and future of the Church, the destruction of Jerusalem, His Second Coming, the Judgment of the Living Nations, the Millennial Reign, the dissolution of heaven and earth, the Great Assize, the Eternal State. All this will be our special concern in the closing chapter of this book.

So, in some thirty years, there was lived out the most wonderful life that ever graced this world. W.E.H. Lecky did not exaggerate when in these now almost hackneyed words he bore eloquent tribute to the Lord Jesus: "The character of Jesus has not only been the highest pattern of virtue, but the strongest incentive to its practice, and has exerted so deep an influence that it may be truly said that the simple record of His three short years of active life has done more to regenerate and soften mankind than all the disquisitions of philosophers and the exhortations of moralists." At the same time we do well to remind ourselves of the sentiments expressed by Lillias Trotter: "The world's salvation was not wrought out by the thirty years in which Christ went about doing good, but in the three hours in which He hung, stripped and nailed, in uttermost exhaustion of spirit, soul and body, till His heart broke."

To that tremendous theme we now turn.

6 THE CRUCIAL CROSS

The Christian Doctrine of the Atonement

Time has nothing worse, yet nothing better, to show than the Cross. John S. Whale

The Cross is the best compendium of the Gospel history. T. Zahn

Jesus was not crucified in a cathedral between two candles, but on a Cross between two thieves. George F. Macleod

There is no comma after Cross: the Cross is a continuous affair. Evert F. Ellis

They shouted once to a Man on a Cross: "If Thou art the Son of God, come down. Force Thyself upon us and we will believe! But, as General William Booth said, 'We believe because He stayed up!'" John Foster

The Lamb slain from the foundation of the world. Revelation 13:8

*The prophets testified beforehand the sufferings of Christ.*1 Peter 1:10

There they crucified Him. Luke 23:33

If any man will come after Me, let him deny himself, and take up his cross daily, and follow Me. Luke 9:23

ANATOLE FRANCE, the brilliant French man of letters, has a strangely fascinating story, told with all the skill of consummate literary art, entitled *Judaeus Procurator*. It is about Pontius Pilate, and it seeks to indicate the place occupied by Jesus in the consciousness of a contemporary Roman. The central character in the tale is one Titus Aelius Lamia, who in youth had been entertained in Palestine by Pilate and who, meeting him forty years later, at Baiae in Italy, inquires about a certain young lay-preacher and miracle-worker, well-known in Israel in those distant days. "You remember Him, of course," says Lamia. "No," answers Pilate. "His name was 'Jesus', I think," adds Lamia. "He was from Nazareth." "I don't remember Him," Pilate repeats. "You were obliged to have Him crucified," prompts Lamia. "Jesus?" muses Pilate. "From Nazareth? No! I have no recollection of it."

That shocks us. We find it frankly unbelievable. To us it is incredible that one so intimately implicated in the blackest crime of human history could ever have forgotten all about it. "Crucified under Pontius Pilate" – so runs the clause in the Apostles' Creed, thus tethering the death of Jesus to a point in time between AD 26 and 36, when Pilate was Prefect of the turbulent province of Judaea, restive under Roman rule and liable at any moment to rise in open revolt. Is it conceivable that the man who, for two thousand years, has by millions of Christians been credally connected with the judicial murder of the Son of God, could ever have let it slip from his mind? No. That is impossible. Much likelier to be true is the tradition that

Pilate – disgraced, deposed and exiled by a cruel and capricious emperor – was banished to Vienna in Gaul, where at last he lost his reason and spent his ebbing hours after the fashion of Lady Macbeth in the play, ineffectually washing his hands and finally committing suicide. According to legend, his body lies buried somewhere at the base of Mount Pilatus, the seven thousand feet peak in Switzerland, which bears his name.

In the course of his professional career as governor of Judaea, Pilate must have sent thousands to the cross. Why should the crucifixion of this particular young Jew have burnt itself so indelibly into his brain that forty years afterwards it troubled him so much that he took his own life?

Why indeed?

For two reasons: First, *because of the phenomenal increase in the numbers of the followers of the Nazarene.* On the Day of Pentecost itself three thousand were converted, soon another five thousand were added, and as the disciples "went everywhere preaching the Word" (Acts 8:4), the Church mushroomed into such a multitude that no man in public life in that part of the world could possibly have been unaware of its existence. "A hundred years after the Crucifixion," wrote John Roach Straton, "it is estimated that there were two hundred thousand Christians in the world. Three hundred years later there were about eight million, one fifteenth of the Roman population." Pilate cannot but have known of this extraordinary expansion of Christianity, and every time he was reminded of it he must have recalled with a shudder his own shameful involvement in the trial and death of its Founder.

Second, *the Procurator must always have remembered the Cross of Christ because of the personality of his noble and notable Prisoner.* From the narratives it is patent that our Lord made a profound impression on Pilate. Between them there seems to have been a great deal of mutual respect. Pilate was convinced of Christ's innocence of the charges laid against Him – the more so after receiving the admonitory note from Procula, his wife – and the Roman could not but be deeply moved by the silent self-command of this august Jew in face of the palpably false allegations being made by the religious authorities and the people baying for His blood. Indeed, as the apostle Peter afterwards publicly stated: "Pilate was determined to let Him go" (Acts 3:13). And if, at last, the Governor *did* yield to popular clamour and sentence Him to death, it was not until he had performed the rather fatuous ritual act of washing his hands before them as a disclaimer of responsibility for his so flagrant miscarriage of justice.

No. It is psychologically certain that, to the end of his dreary days, Pilate never forgot Jesus of Nazareth. If, however, the procurator could have penetrated to the meaning of the Cross of Christ, he would have had infinitely greater reason to remember it.

Not far from where I live Snowdon, the tallest mountain in Wales, thrusts its shaggy shoulders towards the sky. It is a spectacular sight. Procure a picture-postcard, and you will be greatly taken with its symmetrical shape and colourful beauty. Turn the card round, though, and look at the back. What do you see? Nothing but plain, blank, white cardboard with a few printed words and lines. Even the scene depicted on the coloured side is, of course, flatly two-dimensional. It lacks depth, variety, completeness. Only a small part of the huge mountain mass does it show. But now go to Snowdon itself. Motor round its great girth. View it from various angles. Thus you will be subject to far fewer visual limitations. To be sure, Snowdon will look very different when contemplated from Beaumaris than when surveyed from Capel Curig; the view of it from Rhyl will vary greatly from that obtained at Llandudno. Yet the mighty mountain itself will be the same.

Just so with the Cross of Christ. It is not merely twodimensional: it is multi-dimensional. To see it aright you must study it in various perspectives.

There are several viewpoints and vantagepoints from which the Cross may be contemplated. Four call for special mention. The Cross is kaleidoscopic. It may be regarded in the following four aspects: (1) *the Cosmic Cross*; (2) *the Prophetic Cross*; (3) *the Historic Cross* and (4) the *Symbolic Cross*.

Look at them in that order.

THE COSMIC CROSS

"The Lamb slain from the foundation of the world" (Revelation 13:8). "I beheld, and, lo, in the midst of the throne, a Lamb as it had been (newly) slain" (Revelation 5:6). We do not rightly read the Cross until we see it in a cosmic and eternal context. The crucifixion of Christ was no private affair conducted clandestinely in an obscure corner of a peripheral province in the ancient Roman Empire. It spans all space and transcends all time. Before it was an *act* in history, it was a *fact* in eternity. "The cosmos," as Brian A. Greet neatly notes, "is cruciform."

In a previous chapter we reminded ourselves that God can never properly be spoken of as the Author of evil. This would seem a self-evident proposition. Since God is the All-good, how can there be any badness in Him at all?

Nevertheless the Bible, with its customary candour, contains passages which almost appear to charge God with ultimate responsibility for the introduction of evil into the universe. Take, for instance, the following texts: "I am the Lord, and there is none else; I form the light and create darkness; I make peace and create evil" (Isaiah 45:6,7). "Out of the mouth of the Most High proceedeth not evil?" (Lamentations 3:38). "Shall there be evil in a city and the Lord hath not done it?" (Amos 3:6). Well, whatever such sentences may imply, they cannot possibly mean that God is the source of moral evil.

How, then, are we to explain the introduction of iniquity into the world? Christ's own account of it, as we have noted, is clear, succinct, unequivocal: "An enemy hath done this" (Matthew 13:28). And, further down the same chapter, our Lord identifies the foe: "The enemy that sowed them (that is, the tares) is the Devil" (v.39).

But, if God is not the author of evil, if it is monstrously wrong even to suggest it, He certainly *did* will the conditions in which evil became a tragic possibility. In bringing the worlds into being He knew what He was doing. As George Canty contends: "When God made all things, He knew what it would mean. To make trees meant the Cross; to make iron meant nails; to make man meant Judas." Contemplating a glorious sunset, the Elizabethan poet Christopher Marlowe cried: "See where Christ's blood streams in the firmament." That was, of course, poetic rhapsody, the romantic concept of a sublime imagination. But it was more. It was the utterance of a tremendous truth. The Cross of Christ, as it has been graphically put, casts its shadow on the cosmos. According to the Bible the first page and the last in the book of human history are splashed with the blood of the Lamb.

Tintoretto, the sixteenth century Venetian artistic genius, is said not to have signed any of his pictures until he painted his celebrated "Crucifixion". Then for the first time he signed his work. And so, as Colin Bell has somewhat daringly declared: "God has set His signature to the universe as an illiterate man signs his name – with a Cross."

At Calvary Christ, as God, accepted responsibility for the introduction of moral evil into the cosmos. As we have earlier stated, He was not, and never could be, directly and personally liable for that colossal mystery and tragedy. Yet, by creating the universe and endowing His creatures with the dangerous gift of freewill, He brought into existence the cosmic conditions in which evil became a possibility. Evil was not His purpose. It never could have been. But evil became possible within the parameters of

His purpose. "Without Him was not anything made that was made" (John 1:3). So far as we can see – which, in this connection, it must be admitted, is not very far – there was absolutely no reason outside of His own holy will, why He should have created anything at all. A little Sunday School pupil recently stumped her teacher by asking: "Please, miss, why did God make anything anyway?" Obviously, God *has* made the world, and He has made it despite His foreknowledge of all the sin and misery which, contrary to His will, would ensue from that act. He must, therefore, have foreseen that in the end greater glory to Himself and higher good to humanity would result from the making of the material order and its inhabitants than from allowing them to remain uncreated. Thus, and thus alone, He became accountable for the entry of moral evil into the cosmos and at the Cross He accepted responsibility for it, handling the colossal issues with masterly strategy and out of the wreck which sin had wrought bringing about not only the redemption of mankind but that of the whole universe.

Often we short-sightedly assume that the supreme crisis in the passion of our Lord took place in Gethsemane, where, as the poet, unforgettably put it, "God fought with God, and all the lights of heaven were afraid", and where in His hour of deepest woe there was wrung from the soul of our Saviour the submissive cry: "Not My will, but Thine be done" (Luke 22:42). Nor would we wish to derogate in the slightest degree from the cruciality of that act of filial self-surrender. Still, Gethsemane was anticipated and, so to say, antedated in eternity past and will be recollected and post-dated in the ages to come.

The Cross was in the heart of God aeons before it stood stark on the crest of the hill of Calvary. "The Lamb was slain from the foundation of the world" (Revelation 13:8). And it will be in the heart of God when time shall be no more. "I beheld, and, lo in the midst of the throne a Lamb as it had been slain" (Revelation 5:6). Yes, according to the

Bible, the first page and the last of human history are daubed with the blood of the Lamb. "As the flash of a volcano discloses for a few hours the elemental fires at the earth's centre," writes Dinsmore in his *Atonement in Literature and Life* (page 232), "so the light on Calvary was the bursting forth through historical conditions of the very nature of the Everlasting. There was a Cross in the heart of God before there was one planted on the green hill outside Jerusalem."

The finest illustration I know of this fact comes from the nimble pen of Leslie Weatherhead. He says: "I remember one night in the Mediterranean we passed quite close to Stromboli, the famous island volcano, which rises sheer out of the sea. It was after dinner and almost dark. Suddenly there was a great burst of flame from the crater at the summit. Huge tongues of fire shot up hundreds of feet into the sky, lighting up the ocean for miles around. Tons of molten rock were thrown into the air. Through our glasses it was possible to distinguish redhot boulders racing down the mountainside, and gradually a stream of lava forced its way almost to the sea. For many hours – when our vessel had slipped westwards towards the last lingering light of sunset, which lay upon the horizon, when the bold outline of Stromboli was lost in the gathering shadows of night – that redhot stream of lava, like some awful open wound gashed the darkness. What did it mean? It meant that for a few hours there had been revealed those great fires which had been burning in the mountain's heart since the foundation of the world."

I sometimes think about the Cross,
And shut my eyes and try to see
The cruel nails and crown of thorns,
And Jesus crucified for me.

But even could I see Him die,
I could but see a little part

Of that great love which, like a fire,
Is always *burning in His heart.*

THE PROPHETIC CROSS

"The prophets testified beforehand the sufferings of Christ" (1 Peter 1:10,11). To be sure, they did! That is the second facet of the kaleidoscopic Cross. And what a sheer, shouting wonder it is! "According to the law of compound probabilities," says Herman Neumark, "the likelihood of the Old Testament prophecies concerning Christ's death coming true by chance is one in 5,537,000,000."

Yet they did – to the letter!

It is a curious fact that the most intimately poignant picture we get in the Scriptures of the sufferings of Christ is found not, as one might have expected, in the Gospels or in the Epistles, but in the twenty-second Psalm. The evangelists and the apostles depict the death of the Redeemer from the objective standpoint; they report it from without: but the writer of this Psalm records it from the subjective standpoint; he reports it from within. He had, if we may so say, "inside information" about it, entering in spirit proleptically into the sufferings of the Saviour. In this he is typical of the Old Testament prophets as a whole. With what a wealth of foresight and of feeling do they describe in advance the agonies and death of the Son of God! In this regard the Old and New Testaments stand related to one another like voice and echo. The former forecasts and the latter records the fulfilment. Look at some of these prophetic corroborative correspondences. Consider in each case first the prediction and then how it came literally to pass.

1) "They weighed for My price thirty pieces of silver" (Zechariah 11:12). "Then one of the twelve called Judas Iscariot went unto the chief priests, and said unto them, What will ye give me, and I will deliver Him unto you? And they covenanted with him for thirty pieces of

silver" (Matthew 26:14,15).

2) "It was not an enemy that reproached Me; then I could have borne it; neither was it he that hated Me that did magnify himself against Me; then I would have hid Myself from him: but it was thou, Mine acquaintance" (Psalm 55:12,13). "Yea, Mine own familiar friend, in whom I trusted, which did eat of My bread, hath lifted up his heel against Me" (Psalm 41:9). "Judas, one of the Twelve, came and with him a great multitude with swords and staves from the chief priests and elders of the people. Then came they and laid hands on Jesus and took Him" (Matthew 26:47,50).
3) "Cast it unto the potter" (Zechariah 11:13).
   "They took counsel and bought with them the potter's field, to bury strangers in" (Matthew 27:7).
4) "Smite the shepherd and the sheep shall be scattered" (Zechariah 13:7). "All the disciples forsook Him and fled" (Matthew 26:56).
5) "False witnesses did rise up; they laid to My charge things I knew not" (Psalm 35:11).
   "Now the chief priests and elders sought false witnesses against Jesus to put Him to death" (Matthew 26:59).
6) "They shall smite the Judge of Israel with a rod upon the cheek" (Micah 5:1)
   "They smote Him with the rods (palms) of their hands" (Matthew 26:67).
7) "I hid not my face from spitting" (Isaiah 50:6).
   "They did spit in His face" (Matthew 26:67).
8) "I gave my back to the smiters" (Isaiah 50:6).
   "Then Pilate took Jesus and scourged Him" (John 19:1).
9) "Many were astonished at Thee; His visage was so marred more than any man" (Isaiah 52:14).
   "They buffeted Him" (Matthew 26:67). "They struck Him on the face" (Luke 22:64).
10) "As a sheep before her shearers is dumb, so He openeth not His mouth" (Isaiah 53:7).

"He answered nothing... He answered him to never a word, insomuch that the governor marvelled greatly" (Matthew 27:12,14).

11) "He was wounded for our transgressions; He was bruised for our iniquities" (Isaiah 53:5).
"One of the soldiers, with a spear pierced His side" (John 19:34).
12) "What are those wounds in Thine hands?" (Zechariah 13:6).
"They crucified Him" (Luke 23:33).
13) "They pierced My hands and My feet" (Psalm 22:16).
"Reach hither thy finger, and behold My hands" (John 20:27).
14) "He was numbered with the transgressors" (Isaiah 53:12). "With Him they crucified two thieves" (Mark 15:27).
15) "He made intercession for the transgressors" (Isaiah 53:12)
"Father, forgive them" (Luke 23:34).
16) "When they looked upon Me, they shaked their heads" (Psalm 109:25).
"They that passed by reviled Him, wagging their heads" (Matthew 27:39).
17) "All they that see Me, laugh Me to scorn" (Psalm 22:7).
"The chief priests mocked Him, with the scribes and elders" (Matthew 27:41).
18) "They open the lip, saying, He trusted on the Lord that He would deliver Him" (Psalm 22:8).
"He trusted in God: let Him deliver Him now, if He will have Him" (Matthew 27:43).
19) "They parted My garments among them, and cast lots upon My vesture" (Psalm 22:18).
"Then the soldiers took His garments, and made four parts, to every soldier a part; and also His coat. They said, Let us cast lots for it" (John 19:23,24).
20) "My God, My God, why hast Thou forsaken Me? (Psalm 22:1).

"Jesus cried with a loud voice, My God, My God, why hast Thou forsaken Me?" (Matthew 27:46).

21) "I am weary of My crying; My throat is dry. In My thirst they gave Me vinegar" (Psalm 69:1).
"Jesus saith, I thirst. Now there was set a vessel full of vinegar: and they filled a sponge with vinegar, and put it to His mouth" (John 19:28,29).

22) "They gave Me also gall" (Psalm 69:21).
"They gave Him to drink gall" (Matthew 27:34).

23) "Into Thy hand I commit My Spirit" (Psalm 31:9).
"Jesus cried with a loud voice, Father, into Thy hands I commend My Spirit" (Luke 23:46).

24) "He was cut off out of the land of the living" (Isaiah 53:8).
"After three score and two weeks shall Messiah be cut off" (Daniel 9:26).
"He bowed His head and gave up the ghost" (John 19:30).

25) "My lovers and friends stand aloof, and My kinsmen are afar off" (Psalm 38:11).
"All His acquaintance stood afar off, beholding these things" (Luke 23:49).

26) "He keepeth all His bones; not one of them is broken" (Psalm 34:20).
"They brake not His legs" (John 19:33).

27) "My heart is like wax: it is melted" (Psalm 22:14).
"One of the soldiers with a spear pierced His side, and forthwith came there out blood and water" (John 19:34).

28) "It shall come to pass in that day, saith the Lord God, that I will cause the sun to go down at noon, and I will darken the earth in the clear day" (Amos 8:9).
"Now from the sixth hour there was darkness over all the land unto the ninth hour" (Matthew 27:45).

29) "This is the Lord's doing" (Psalm 22:31 NEB) "He has performed it" (NASB) "It is finished" (John 19:30 AV).

Such are some of the prophetic forecasts of the sufferings and death of the Redeemer. With what a wealth of minute detail do they predict them! "It has been noted," remarks Charles G. Trumbull, "that there are no fewer than twenty-nine Old Testament prophecies bearing on the betrayal, trial, death and burial of the Lord Jesus Christ, uttered by many different voices, during five centuries from the year BC 1,000 to 500 BC, which were all literally fulfilled within twenty-four hours at the time of the Crucifixion." Surely an immensely impressive forecast of events then in the far future. Were the New Testament to be irrecoverably lost – in some unenvisageable tragedy – it would almost be possible to reconstruct the closing scenes in the drama of the life of Christ from the relevant prophetic passages of the Old Testament. Indeed, Blaise Pascal, the Einstein of his day, declared that he would be content to rest the whole case for the Deity of Christ on the fact that so many details of His arrest, trial, crucifixion and burial were predicted with such precision in the Hebrew Scriptures hundreds of years before they happened. Many of the searchlights of biblical prophecy converge on the Cross and come to brilliant focus on the Crucified. Such forecasts were not inspired guesses or informed conjectures: they were divine predictions. None but God could have foreknown and foretold what was to transpire that dark day on Golgotha.

THE HISTORIC CROSS

"There they crucified Him" (Luke 23:33).
Thus in one brief sentence with a miserly minimum of language the New Testament records the mightiest event of all time. Think what a modern imaginative writer would have made of it. Yet the verbal economy of Holy Scripture is infinitely more moving and more telling than any attempt at literary sensationalism. The biblical account of the Crucifixion is as stark as the Cross itself.

The most awful word ever uttered by human lips was spoken by elders at the trial of Jesus. It was *staurotheto*, "Let Him be crucified" (Matthew 27:22). The stem of the term is *stauros* (Greek for Cross), and to be condemned to it was the worst fate that could befall a man.

Accustomed as we are to conceive of the Cross in the shape commonly assigned to it by Christian tradition, it comes to us as something of a shock to realize that originally *stauros* did not have quite that meaning. It simply meant a wooden post pointed like a pencil at one end. A stake of that kind has often been used as an instrument of public execution. Sometimes it was set up in a market-place, the hapless victim being roped to it, faggots piled high around him and lit from a flaming torch and, as the raucous rabble looked on in morbid wonderment, heavenward sped "the pale martyr in his shirt of fire". On other occasions it was erected on the seashore, full in the path of the flowing tide, the martyr tied to it as the swelling waters gradually crept up to his lips and at last drowned him. And, at yet other times, the person under sentence of death would be laid spread-eagled on his back upon some patch of soft earth, the sharp pointed part being driven through his body at some part where no vital organ was located, and he was thus pinned down in excruciating agony until death mercifully released him.

Bit by bit, however, in ancient Roman usage, the cross began to assume the form of the two beams, transfixed upon one another, with which we are now so familiar – the upright post and the horizontal bar. There were in fact three types of such crosses. One was shaped like the capital letter T, another like the capital X, and the third in accordance with the traditional pattern.

On which of these was the Lord Jesus nailed? The sacred narrative makes it clear: "*Over His head* His accusation written, This is Jesus the King of the Jews" (Matthew 27:37). That superscription could not have been fixed there unless the gibbet had been constructed in the familiar fashion, composed, that is, of cross-beam and shaft, transom and vertical plank. "Crucifixion was a diabolical method of administering the death-penalty, invented, it seems, by some twisted mind in ancient Persia or Phoenicia and imported from thence, first by the Carthaginians and then by the Romans. So brutal and humiliating was it that it was reserved for the worst class of criminals. Of it Cicero said: 'It is the most shameful and cruel of all punishments. Let it never come near the body of a Roman citizen, nay, not even near his thoughts, eyes or ears.'" Joy Davidman depicts it thus with graphic realism:

A crucified slave beside the Roman road
Screamed until his voice died,
And then hung – a filthy, festering clot of flies
Sometimes for days, a living man,
Whose hands and feet were swollen masses of gangrenous meat

It was not the practice of the Romans to remove the corpse from the cross. Usually they left it hanging there, as farmers are wont to suspend shot marauding birds to posts in fields to frighten others off, left it there until it rotted away and fell to pieces or until the bones were picked bare by the beaks of vultures. This was the sort of death assigned to the Son of God. His blessed hands and feet were "nailed to the cedar". Elevated there between earth and heaven, He hung naked, limp and bleeding, a public spectacle on a bald knoll outside the city wall. The story of His sufferings and death is no sentimental tale, spun on the loom of pious fancy. It is hard reality. As R. Leonard Small comments, "It has about it the solid feel of history", providing the scenario for the colossal cosmic drama of redemption: "There they crucified Him" (Luke 23:33).

Modern theologians often speak of the miracle of the Resurrection of Christ. They are properly impressed with the supernatural character of His rising from the dead. To the older theologians, however, our Lord's death seemed even more marvellous than His resurrection. That the Resurrection Himself should die was to them as unthinkable as that the sun should be swallowed up by universal dark. As Ronald A. Knox forcibly expressed it: "Every second during which He stayed dead, on Good Friday and Holy Saturday and Easter Sunday morning, was a kind of miracle, a much more remarkable miracle really than His Resurrection."

So much for the fact of the Cross. Now what of its meaning? It is not just history; it is a very special sort of history, unique history, redemptive history, the history of human salvation. It is true that, as George Jackson used to point out, we are saved by the fact of the Atonement and not by any theory about it. Yet the development of theological theories concerning the Cross was one of history's inevitabilities.

Myself when young did eagerly frequent the works of the great theological writers on the subject. In process of time the knowledge thus acquired bred in me a certain sense of confidence and competence when preaching on the death of Jesus. Having studied in some depth the classical theories of the Atonement – Augustine's Commercial Contract theory, Anselm's Satisfaction Theory, Hastings Rashdall's Vicarious Obedience Theory, MacLeod Campbell's Vicarious Penitence Theory, R.J. Campbell's Moral Influence Theory, I thought I knew a thing or two about the tremendous theme. Then one day, pushing past such profound and pious lucubrations, I stood face to face with the stark fact of the Cross itself, and as I dwelt on the truth that the crowned Lord of thirty trillion galaxies and constellations came down to earth to bleed and die for me and for my sins, I was utterly broken down and could no more theorize about it than I could "botanize on my mother's grave". It is the fact that saves.

Nevertheless, theory matters, theology matters, and matters profoundly. It is true, as we have noted, that we are saved by the Cross and not by an attempted interpretation of it. It is also true, as August Sabatier has somewhere reminded us, that no historic creed compels those subscribing to it to accept in relation to the Atonement any specific theological position. Yet the Bible itself spurs us to reverent speculation as to the meaning of the Cross, picturing it in various lights and presenting it in different perspectives; and perhaps, in the final analysis, it is best for every individual Christian, with the New Testament open in his hand and whatever scholarly aids of which he can avail himself, with the help of the Holy Spirit, to hammer out his own doctrine of the Atonement.

After long brooding on the sacred mystery it seems to me that the ultimate truth about the Cross, as it impinges upon Christian experience, can be summarized in three terse and simple sentences: (a) *it is the price of loving; (b) it is the prize of living; and (c) it is the principle of learning.*

(a) *It is the price of loving*

Love always has to pay a price. A love that costs nothing counts for nothing. In this the love of God was no exception. As we have already observed, God could have signalled His affection for us from the skies, after the fashion of an astronaut addressing mankind from outer space. But, if He had, we could not have given credence to the communication. "If some bright angel had come down from heaven with the message that God is love," wrote Charles Gore, "we could not have believed it. We should have said: 'These are fine words, but we know the facts, and the facts of experience contradict this fine message.'" None but the Man of Sorrows could possibly have convinced us that it is true.

Why did Christ die? To that pointed inquiry the New Testament provides three clear and clean-cut replies. (1) It says: *He died for our sins* (1 Corinthians 15:3); (2) it says: *He died for us* (Romans 5:8); and (3) it says: *He died that He might be Lord* (Romans 14:9). The death of Jesus was not due to natural causes; it was not a tragic accident; it was not merely a cruel crime; it was not just a gross miscarriage of justice; it was not simply a heroic martyrdom. It was a deliberate act of self-sacrifice, motivated by pure affection for a fallen and apostate and rebellious race. Such was the high cost of loving. "He loved me, and gave Himself for me" (Galatians 2:20). "No man taketh it (that is, My life) from Me, but I lay it down of Myself. I have power to lay it down and I have power to take it again" (John 10:18). And the witness of the Word is that He did lay it down for sheer love of us. "Christ died for us," quoted H.G. Wells, "do we care?" "Christ died for me," exclaimed Charles Haddon Spurgeon, "that is the root of every satisfaction I have." "When God gave His Son," said Harrington Evans, "He gave an infinite proof of infinite love." That is the first facet of the meaning of the Cross.

(b) *It is the prize of living.*
"God forbid that I should glory," cried Paul, "save in the Cross of our Lord Jesus Christ" (Galatians 6:14). A famous French writer has said: "When Christ came into the world He only asked for one thing, and that was a Cross on which to die. All else He borrowed." You may remember the following artless yet haunting lines:

They borrowed a bed
To lay His head,
When Christ the Lord came down;
They borrowed an ass
In the mountain-pass,
For Him to ride to town:
But the crown that He wore
And the Cross that He bore
Were His own.

He borrowed the bread
When the crowd He fed
On the grassy mountainside;
He borrowed the dish
Of broken fish
With which He satisfied:
But the crown that He wore
And the Cross that He bore
Were His own.

He borrowed the ship
In which to sit
To teach the multitude;
He borrowed a nest
In which to rest;
He had never a home so rude:
But the crown that He wore
And the Cross that He bore
Were His own.

He borrowed a room
On His way to the tomb,
The Passover lamb to eat;
They borrowed a cave,
For Him a grave,
They borrowed a winding-sheet:
But the crown that He wore
And the Cross that He bore
Were His own.

The author of these lines has scorned to blot his work with a name, but we do know his initials – L.M.N. They illustrate Christ's evaluation of the Cross. The Cross was the only thing in the world He thought really worth having; and when He came to die it was quite literally all He had – and it was all He wanted.

A man is a Christian to the extent to which he shares

Christ's estimate of the Cross. What *is* the Cross? Ask a carpenter. "It is only two lengths of timber," he will tell you, "a couple of beams, two-by-fours." What is the Cross? Ask a botanist. "It is wood," he will inform you, "from the trunk of an oak, cedar, sycamore, or the like." What is the Cross? Ask a jurist. "It is an instrument of capital punishment," he will reply, "now happily discarded by our modern, more civilized, humanitarian society." What is the Cross? Ask the Christian. "It is the most wonderful thing in the world," he will answer, "for there will come a day when everything else that one possesses will have to be left behind, and the Cross will then, as now, be the sole bridge from time to eternity, from earth to heaven. It is life's supreme prize."

Paul had that outlook upon the Cross. "God forbid," he cried, "that I should glory save in the Cross of our Lord Jesus Christ" (Galatians 6:14) – sentiments which Sir John Bowring has enshrined in imperishable verse:

In the Cross of Christ I glory,
Towering o'er the wrecks of time;
All the light of sacred story
Gathers round its head sublime.

When we acquire that attitude to the Cross and that evaluation of it, we have penetrated deeply into its mystic meaning.

(c) *It is the principle of learning*

"When Christ had called the people unto Him, with the disciples also, He said unto them, Whosoever will come after Me, let him deny himself, and take up his cross, and follow Me" (Mark 8:34). Notice the phrase "When He had called the people unto Him". This was no esoteric secret to be divulged clandestinely to a small group of initiates. It was a condition of discipleship which He made no effort to conceal. Summoning the crowds, He told them bluntly that, if they decided to be His followers, they were, as we colloquially say, "in for it". Sternly, ineluctably, He confronted them with a Cross.

This leads us, by a natural transition, to the last main section of our study.

THE SYMBOLIC CROSS

"If any man will come after Me, let him deny himself, and take up his cross daily and follow Me" (Luke 9:23). "I am crucified with Christ" (Galatians 2:20). Manifestly these texts do not refer to an actual, literal, physical crucifixion. The word "cross" is here being used as a figure, a metaphor, a symbol. There were no holes in Paul's hands and feet, although he could quite justifiably claim to have been crucified with Christ. This he himself plainly implies when he asks the rhetorical question: "Was Paul crucified for you?" (1 Corinthians 1:13).

There have indeed been occasions when Christians have been threatened with literal crucifixion. A moving story tells of a small Japanese boy, converted to Christianity through the preaching of evangelical missionaries, whose faith was put to a terrible test by foreign soldiers. One of the soldiers said: "If you do not spit on the cross, we will crucify you." "Man," answered the brave boy, "do you think I should be a Christian if I was afraid to be crucified?"

We may not, in the good providence of God, be called upon to face so fierce a test as that; but, if we are to be true followers of the Lord Jesus, crucified we shall be in one way or another. Our Lord Himself forewarned us that it would be so: "If any man will come after Me, let him deny himself, and take up his cross, and follow Me" (Matthew 16:24).

Take up the Cross, and learn to die
Into the life of God thereby;

Take up the Cross, and learn to do
For others what He did for you,
For only by its woes
The life of fulness grows.

Nevertheless, although actual bodily impalement may not be involved, this symbolical crucifixion does represent something very real. The cross which our Lord bids us take up for His sake is an instrument of death, entailing the crossing out of self, not just one dramatic gesture of selfabnegation, but a continuous protracted series of such acts. "I die daily," says Paul (1 Corinthians 15:31). A modern philosopher epitomized the Christian ethic in the phrase: "Die to live." He was right.

I wonder what eventually happened to the wood of Christ's Cross. After they had lifted down the limp form from its rough arms, what did they do with it? Was it just flung out to rot? Or was it, as some maintain, mysteriously and magically preserved, so that its pieces might be displayed to the credulous piety of succeeding generations? Nobody knows. Indubitably, however, Martin Luther was right when he said: "The true Cross of Christendom is that Cross of Christ which is divided throughout the whole world, not in particles of wood, but that Cross which comes to each as his own portion of life."

The Cross, as I have said, is no cushioned gibbet. "No man," wrote Samuel Rutherford, "hath a velvet cross, but the Cross is made of that which God will have it." "When Christ calls a man," declared Dietrich Bonhoeffer, hanged in a Nazi concentration camp, "He bids him come and die." Frederick L. Knowles has written:

Our crosses are hewn from different trees,
But we all must ascend our calvaries;
Each climbs the height from a different side,
But we all go up to be crucified.
As we scale the heights another may share

The heavy burden our shoulders bear;
But the costliest sorrow is still our own –
For on that bleak summit we bleed alone.

Years ago a wealthy American and his wife went to Oberammergau in Bavaria to see the Passion Play. At the time the famous Anton Lang was the Christus. After a performance at which they were present he placed the cross he had been carrying against a wall of the stage. The American had a high-powered camera and, seeing Lang laying the cross down, he thought it would be a capital idea to have a photograph taken of himself bearing it. Handing the camera to his wife, he climbed on to the stage and went over to where the cross was lying and tried to pick it up. The cross was too heavy for him to carry. Approaching Lang, he remarked: "I did not know that the cross was so heavy." Drawing himself up to his full stature, the actor replied with dignity: "Sir, if I did not feel the weight of His Cross, I could not play His part!" In W.H. Auden's withering words: "Only the unscarred and overfed enjoy Calvary as a verbal event."

Yes, the Christian *must* feel the weight of Christ's Cross if he is to play His part. And yet – here is the miracle of it! – the person who voluntarily bears that Cross, finds in time that the Cross is bearing him and that it is indeed, as the old saint said, "No greater burden than sails are to a ship or wings to a bird." Anyone who, for Christ's sake, undertakes some uncongenial task, some act or activity that goes against the grain and calls for a measure, greater or less, of self-sacrifice and self-commitment – work among drug addicts and alcoholics, or consistent Sunday School teaching, or costly evangelism, or responsible financial stewardship, or prophetic denunciation of social wrongs – discovers often to his relief, and indeed to his delight, that there is another Shoulder beneath the Cross as well as his own, the shoulder of the Crucified; for, after all, as B.D. Johns has done well to remind us: "He who has been *on* the Cross *for* us, has promised to be *under* the Cross *with* us." And He is able to lift not the Cross alone, but us with it and on it by His superlative supporting power.

There, then, are the four crosses, which are essentially one – the Cosmic Cross, the Prophetic Cross, the Historic Cross and the Symbolic Cross are all organically related. Viewing it from various angles, we get different perspectives of it, and yet all come to blazing focus in the Figure on the central Cross of Calvary.

7
THE COSMIC COMEBACK

The Christian Doctrine of the Resurrection of Christ

The miracles of reversal all belong to the new creation. It is a miracle of reversal when the dead are raised. Old nature knows nothing of this process. It involves playing backward a film which we have always seen played forwards. The one or two instances of it in the Gospels are early flowers – what we call spring flowers, because they are prophetic, although they really bloom while it is still winter.

C.S. Lewis

"Paint Christ," cried Tommasco Campenella, to the Italian artists of his day, "not dead, but risen, with His foot set in scorn on the split rock with which they sought to hold Him down. Paint Him the Conqueror of death, the irresistible Victor who, tested to the uttermost, has proved Himself in very deed mighty to save."

Arthur John Gossip

Creation is the victory of Omnipotence over nothingness: the Resurrection is the victory of the same power over death, which is the thing most like to nothingness that is known to us.

M. Gode

The Resurrection is a showdown between the power of death to destroy and the power of God to reverse the work of death.

Carroll E. Simcox

I am the Resurrection and the Life.

John 11:25

God raised Him from the dead and gave Him glory.

1 Peter 1:25

The Lord is risen indeed.

Luke 24:34

God hath given proof to all men in that He hath raised Him from the dead.

Acts 17:31

Because I live, ye shall live also.

John 14:19

IN THE ARCHAEOLOGICAL department of the British Museum, London, there is a particularly grim and grisly exhibit known as "the Galilee Man", so called because his remains were disinterred in that part of Israel. One is always immensely grateful that those macabre relics of prehistoric *homo sapiens* are not the mortal remains of the Man of Galilee!

There are those, of course, who do believe that our blessed Lord is indeed dead and buried. "We may freely say," states Professor Gregor Smith, "that the bones of Jesus lie somewhere in Palestine." "I quite expect the bones of Jesus will be dug up one day," declares Dr Harry Emerson Fosdick. "I have not the slightest interest in a conjuring trick with bones," observes Bishop David Jenkins.

The late Bishop John Robinson concurred. He maintained that it was possible to be a Christian although denying the physical resurrection of Christ. "The resurrection of the body of Christ," he wrote, "is no essential belief for Christian people, and it would make no difference to their faith if the Lord's body had been flung into the Valley of Hinnom, like those of the malefactors, to disintegrate among the rotting corpses." Such stark and startling statements are in flat and flagrant contradiction of Paul's explicit affirmation in Romans 10:9, where he defines the "word of faith": "If thou shalt confess with thy mouth the Lord Jesus, and shalt believe in thine heart, that God hath raised Him from the dead, thou shalt be saved." In that verse the apostle makes it patent that acceptance of the factuality of Christ's physical rising from the dead is a basic precondition of being a Christian.

But we had better begin by defining our term.

What do we mean by "resurrection"?

Let us start by stating quite definitely what we do *not* mean.

In the first place, by the resurrection of Christ *we do not just mean His spiritual survival.* The New Testament goes to great lengths to leave us in no doubt that the body of our Lord which rose from the tomb was identically the same as that which was nailed to the Cross. True, it did possess additional powers, properties and faculties, but the continuity of its identity is not open to question. The inquiry as to whether or not, prior to Calvary, it possessed those powers, properties and faculties is a purely speculative one which need not detain us here. Quite possibly, had it then exhibited such supernatural traits, its historical reality might have been in some doubt. Passing through solid walls and doors and appearing and disappearing at will, are not attributes and activities which we normally associate with a human body. The body of Jesus was a real human body and it had to be seen to be a real human body before it could be prudent to reveal those supernatural potentialities. Eric Sauer somewhere makes the illuminating point that, just as our Lord's body was capable of *transfiguration* without losing its identity, so it was capable of *disfiguration* without losing its identity. It was not just the spiritual part of Jesus which persisted beyond the tomb: it was the total Christ.

In the second place, by the resurrection of Christ *we do not merely mean resuscitation*. Resuscitation implies a return to the former life and likewise liability to death again. Altogether the Bible records no fewer than nine such resuscitations, but none of them can properly be included in the same category as the resurrection of Christ. Every other was a *raising*: this was a *rising*. Certainly, it was God who "raised Christ from the dead" (Ephesians 2:20), but equally of His own life Christ could say "I have power to take it again" (John 10:18). The Lord Jesus was the only man in history who had the power to take up His own life: others had the power to take their own life: He only had the power to take it *up*. He did not simply resume the former mode of living: He arose to a new dimension of being. He did not live to die again: He lived to die no more. "Christ, being raised from the dead, dieth no more" (Romans 6:9). Resurrection must be distinguished from resuscitation.

Matthew Henry, "the Shakespeare of Commentators", made the point tellingly: "When Lazarus rose from the dead, he took his grave-clothes with him, because he was going to need them again. But when Christ rose from the dead, He left His grave-clothes behind because He had finished with them for ever."

In the third place, by the resurrection of Christ *we do not simply mean reincarnation*. The idea of reincarnation pervades the religions of the East, and even in the West there are those, such as the Theosophists, who find it attractive. Nevertheless, the resurrection of Christ was not a reincarnation. Admittedly, Paul does speak of Christ as "the

Firstborn from the dead" (Colossians 1:18), but that must not be taken to signify anything in the nature of a repetition of the Incarnation. Indubitably, our Redeemer came from a virgin womb and He rose from a virgin tomb, but the body that emerged from the sepulchre was not fashioned in the sepulchre, as was the body of the infant Christ within Mary. It was the same body as before.

Not long before his death, Napoleon Bonaparte boasted: "When I am gone, my spirit will return to France to throb with ceaseless life in new revolutions." But it didn't! Speaking of the Lord Jesus, however, in his *Emperor and Galilean*, Henrik Ibsen puts into the lips of Julian the Apostate these glowing words: "Where is He now? Has He been at work elsewhere since that happened at Golgotha? Where is He now? What if that at Golgotha, near Jerusalem, was but a wayside matter, a thing done, as it were, in passing! What if He goes on and on, and suffers and dies and conquers, again and again, from world to world?" In other words, what if His posthumous existence is simply an extended series of reincarnations? But no. Resurrection is not reincarnation.

In the fourth place, by the resurrection of Christ *we do not only mean that after His death our Lord lived merely in the recollection of others.* It must be acknowledged that some people are so vibrantly vital that one finds it hard to think of them as dead even after one has attended their funeral! Of such our omnipotent Redeemer is the supreme example. When we refer to His resurrection, however, we are not just saying that He survives in our memories. According to the hackneyed aphorism, "To live in the minds and hearts of those we love and leave behind is not to die", but we get buried all the same! Emphatically, recollection is not resurrection.

In the fifth place, by the resurrection of Christ *we do not merely mean that after death He lived influentually.* No one has ever exerted any comparable posthumous influence to that of our blessed Master. Since His death He has done infinitely more for humanity than any living person could possibly accomplish. "Influence," it has been neatly said, "is the effluence of affluence"; and who could be more morally and spiritually affluent than He of whom it is written: "In Him dwelleth all the fulness of the Godhead bodily" (Colossians 2:9)? Etymologically, influence is that property belonging to one person which flows into others. No one has so poured Himself into the lives and hearts of men as has the Lord Jesus Christ. To millions His influence has meant affluence. Nevertheless, when we speak of the Resurrection, we are not just thinking of His social influence.

Of what, then, *are* we thinking? Having indicated in some detail what the Resurrection is *not*, let us now inquire what it *is*. And here, before proceeding further, let me state the evangelical position on the Resurrection of Christ as forcibly as I can. We believe that the Resurrection is history, that this thing really happened, that the body which was reverently laid in that cool grave among the lilies on the evening of Friday April 3, A.D.33 (the latest date assigned to it by the chronological experts), literally vacated that grave before six o'clock on the following Sunday morning (April 5). For us it is all as literal and as factual as that. This, nothing less and nothing else, is what we mean by the Resurrection of Christ.

It may help our thought if we divide the remainder of our study into six parts: (1) *the Problem;* (2) *the Promise;* (3) *the Proofs;* (4) *the Presence;* (5) *the Power;* and (6) *the Prospect.*

THE PROBLEM

Three proposed solutions of the problem of the Resurrection are popularly propounded. Some say that *Jesus did not die on the Cross at all;* some say that *He died but did not rise;* some say, with Paul, that *He died and rose and revived* (Romans 14:9).

Some say that Jesus did not die on the Cross at all. Those holding this view subscribe to what is known as "the Swoon Theory". It is a notion first advanced in the early nineteenth century by a rationalist named Venturini. The theory assumes two forms. One maintains that on the Cross the Redeemer merely fainted – surely a not unreasonable supposition in view of the brutal treatment to which He had been exposed during the preceding more than twelve hours. Long before man discovered anaesthetics, nature possessed its own. When pain becomes intolerable, the victim mercifully lapses into unconsciousness. This, we are told, is what took place at the Crucifixion. Think how much Jesus had suffered – the awful anguish of Gethsemane, the indignities and injuries inflicted on Him in the Jewish court, the mocking and flogging at the hands of the Romans, the crowning with thorns and the long drag along the Via Dolorosa, bearing the heavy Cross, the nerve-shattering hammering at Calvary, all took a terrible toll of the Saviour's strength. So weak and exhausted was He by sheer fatigue and copious loss of blood, this theory suggests, that on the gibbet He sank into a deep coma from which He only returned to consciousness after the Deposition when He was borne to the rockhewn tomb and His body was laid in the chilly atmosphere. The night air, it is said, and the aromatic spices stung Him back to consciousness.

The other form which this theory takes is referred to by Dr Hugh I Schonfield in his book *The Passover Plot*. The idea here is that when our Lord cried on the Cross, "I thirst" (John 19:28), drugged wine was given Him, a palliative for His pain, which induced in Him a stupor so deep that it was mistaken for death itself. Or, so we are asked to believe, He did not really die: He only swooned.

First to present this theory was Professor K.F. Bahrdt. He taught that the whole thing was a secret plot, conjured up by an esoteric sect called the Essenes, a sect which we know from the writings of the Jewish historian Flavius

Josephus and others and from modern archaeological discoveries, to have existed in Israel at the time of Christ. Our Lord is supposed to have been Himself a member of this ancient society and to have been party to the plot in which He was to play a leading rôle. According to the theory, not long before the Crucifixion a band of conspirators belonging to this sect foregathered in a cave close to Jerusalem. Our Lord is alleged to have joined them and to have been subjected by them to a type of treatment, by means of what would now be described as psychedelic drugs, or a primitive sort of Yoga, which made Him able to endure extreme agony, to survive a protracted period of unconsciousness and to return to complete normality. When, later on, He *did come back* to consciousness, He convinced His credulous followers that He had risen from the dead. Such is this theory.

How are we to answer it? Several replies may be given.

For one thing, we can remind ourselves that the New Testament narratives of the Crucifixion provide surgical evidence that our Lord really did die. "One of the soldiers with a spear pierced His side, and forthwith came there out blood and water" (John 19:34). The *pericardium* was punctured and the colourless fluid flowing from the wound proves that life was extinct.

For another thing, we can remind ourselves that it was no convalescent Christ whom the disciples encountered on the first Easter Day. Such a pathetic and powerless Figure could never have persuaded them that He had conquered death and was alive for evermore. Even the destructive critic David S. Strauss was shrewd enough to see that and candid enough to confess it. "It is impossible," he wrote, "that a Being who had stolen half-dead out of the sepulchre, who crept about weak and ill, wanting medical treatment, who required bandaging, strengthening and indulgence, and who still at last yielded to His sufferings, could have given to the disciples the impression that He was a conqueror over death and the grave, the Prince of Life, an impression which lay at the bottom of their future ministry."

We may, then, dismiss as utterly incredible the Swoon Theory. So much for those who deny that Christ died on the Cross.

Some say that He died but did not rise. Ernest Renan is debited with the dictum: "I would not believe that Jesus rose even if I saw it." In this he is typical of many today. A number of years ago I lodged in the home of friends of Aneurin Bevan, and they told me that, on the occasion of his Methodist mother's funeral, someone said to him: "Do you believe in the resurrection of the body?" Aneurin looked at his questioner silently for a moment or two, and then replied: "My *heart* would like to believe it, but my *head* won't let me." To accommodate such doubts eight explanations are offered in an effort to dispense with the Resurrection.

What *are* those suggested alternatives?

Let us review them rapidly each in turn.

(1) *The Twin Theory.* This notion is that Jesus had an identical twin who at times "stood in" for Him in public although for the most part he kept in the background, and that one of the occasions on which he deputized for his Brother was when he acted His part on the third day after the Crucifixion. His Brother having died on the Cross, the hypothetical twin then appeared before the populace, and people mistook him for his Brother. What arrant nonsense! For such a view there is not the slightest shred of evidence in the New Testament. Describing the theory, Dr Paul Maier writes: "Jesus had an exact twin brother, who substituted for Him on occasion, but generally stayed out of sight. When Jesus truly died on Calvary, the twin emerged triumphantly from seclusion on Sunday and people beheld the Risen Lord." Thomas was certainly called "Didymus", which means "Twin", but Jesus was

never called Twin and indeed the very conception is repugnant to anyone who believes in the Incarnation. Mary brought forth her firstborn Son – *not twins!*

Someone has ingeniously suggested that Thomas's scepticism concerning the Resurrection appearances may have stemmed from the fact that he was a twin, and thus being perhaps often mistaken for his brother – assuming that his twin *was* a brother! – might have been preconditioned to believe that it was not Jesus Himself, but some look-alike of His, who had manifested himself to the disciples. For this reason, he demanded the proof of the prints – and he got it! And thus his doubts help our faith. And so, before long, he became the first, so far as the records go, to ascribe to our Lord absolute Deity: "My Lord *and my God*!" Liberal preachers and teachers who regard this outburst as blasphemy do not deserve a hearing. This was the cry of a soul recognizing Jehovah in Jesus.

(2) *The Gas Theory*. This spurious assumption was sponsored by among others Leslie D. Weatherhead. In that compendium of his theology to which, significantly, he gave the title *The Christian Agnostic* – though it is hard to see how that adjective can logically qualify that noun! – he states: "I am in no doubt in my own mind that Jesus finished in the tomb with the matter which composed His earthly body by means of a metamorphosis which we cannot as yet understand, a change in the matter from the flesh and bones of a body into gas, which would easily escape through the crevices of the cave-tomb, or indeed into nothingness or some invisible form of energy" (*op. cit.*, pp. 80, 81). Well, certainly, if Jesus *did* survive solely in the form of a gas, Thomas was demanding the impossible. No one ever saw a gash in a gas or nailprints in a vapour!

C.S. Lewis deals a death-blow to the Gas Theory when he points out that the Greek word for Resurrection is *anastasis,* which means "a making to stand up", on the basis of which Lewis cogently contends for the corporeality of the risen Christ by inquiring: "In what position would a soul or spirit be, if it stood up?"

(3) *The Removal Theory.* This is the oldest of them all, dating back beyond the day of the Resurrection itself. It was Mary Magdalene's own quite understandable surmise on first seeing the empty grave. Even prior to that the chief priests and Pharisees had approached Pilate, warning him that some such scheme might be put into effect by our Lord's followers, to fake a fulfilment of His forecasts that on the third day He would rise from the dead. "Sir," they said, "we remember that that Deceiver said while He was yet alive, After three days I will rise again. Command therefore that the sepulchre be made sure until the third day, lest His disciples come by night, and steal Him away, and say unto the people, He is risen from the dead" (Matthew 27:63,64). To guard against such a contingency sentries were posted at the sepulchre on those nervous nights and the imperial seal affixed to the tomb. But the angel of the Lord came down and at his descent the earth shook. Rolling back the barricading boulder, he sat upon it, and at sight of him the sentinels were frozen with fear and became as dead men. Later, hasting back to the city, they reported to the religious authorities what had happened and were paid hush-money to say nothing about it. Money! For love of it Christ was sold and for money the report of His resurrection was almost smothered in its cradle. "They gave large money unto the soldiers, saying, Say ye, His disciples came by night and stole Him away, while we slept" (Matthew 28:13). That is the New Testament's account of the origin of the Removal Theory.

Imaginative use has been made of it in a book published at the turn of the twentieth century under the title *When it was Dark.* Its author was Guy Thorne, and its name is a quotation from John 21:1. The book is a work of fiction with an ingenious plot. The plot is much too complicated to be gone into here in any detail, but the idea behind it is the discovery of a tomb in which, it is alleged, Joseph of Arimathaea deposited the remains of Jesus in order to spare the disciples the pain of the tragic dénouement to the career of Christ. The whole thing is, of course, a forgery, but for a while the bogus inscription on the tomb fools the world into believing that the report of the Resurrection is a fraud. That inscription reads as follows: "I, Joseph of Arimathaea, took the body of Jesus, the Nazarene, from the tomb where it was first laid and laid it in this place" (*op. cit.*, London: Greening & Co., Ltd., 1905, p.197). The remainder of the work is taken up with describing what happened throughout human society when it seemed to have been demonstrated beyond doubt that Jesus had not risen from the dead, and of how the diabolical fraud was at last detected and exposed.

"Say ye, His disciples came by night, and stole Him away, while we slept" (Matthew 28:13). "How utterly ludicrous!" comments Dr Paul E. Little. "That story is so obviously false that Matthew doesn't even bother to refute it! What judge would listen to you if you said that while you were asleep your neighbour came into your house and stole your television set? Who knows what goes on while he's asleep? Testimony like this would be laughed at in any court" (*Know why you Believe*, p.64).

A modern variant of the Removal Theory is contained in the doctrinal manual of the Jehovah's Witnesses, entitled *The Truth shall Make you Free:* "Jehovah-God disposed of the body of Jesus just as He disposed of the body of Moses." Charles Taze Russell, founder of the cult, has an echo of this in his *Studies in the Scriptures*. "Our Lord's human body", he says, "was supernaturally removed from the tomb." But, as Matthew Henry points out, the precise opposite is the fact: "When Moses was dead, God buried him: when Christ was dead, God raised Him."

(4) *The Fraud Theory*. Analogous to the Removal Theory is the Fraud Theory, which presupposes not only that the followers of Jesus surreptitiously spirited Christ's body away, but also that they fraudulently proclaimed that He had risen from the dead, thus involving themselves in a double imposture. What are we to say to it?

Well, we can point out that the disciples – weak, dispirited and disorganized, as they were – had not a ghostly chance of burglarizing that "close-sealed, sentinelled sepulchre". They were no match for the Temple Guard.

More convincing still is the argument that it would have been completely foreign to their characters to do so, since those characters had been moulded by the teaching and example of the Master Himself. Knowing them, as we do, from their verbal portraits in the New Testament, we cannot conceive of their perpetrating so heartless a hoax. Downright duplicity of this kind was utterly alien to them. Besides, is it really credible that such marvellous benefits could have accrued from Christianity to mankind, as actually did accrue to it, had the report of the Resurrection been a baseless rumour? The question has but to be asked to be answered.

(5) *The Theft Theory*. Patently, there are points of correspondence with those which we have just examined. The Removal Theory presupposes that it was the friends and followers of Jesus, or indeed the Almighty Himself, who opened the tomb and took away the body: the Theft Theory says it was His foes who rifled the sepulchre, sealed with the waxen cord to prevent unauthorized entry and to protect the sacred corpse from molestation. Did His enemies in fact steal the body?

Patently, had that been the case, the body-snatching must have been the work of either the Romans or the Jews. But would either have done so? The Romans would not have stooped to anything so furtive and clandestine.

After all, they were the masters. They did what they liked with cavalier indifference to public opinion. As for the Jews – they had a vested interest in keeping the body in the tomb or at any rate in pretending it was there. Moreover, not long afterwards, when rumours of the Resurrection were being blown about the Holy City, why did not the Jews silence them at once by displaying the body, supposing them to have had custody of it?

As William Paley, of *Evidences* fame, reasonably remarks: "If we admit, upon the concurrent testimony of all the histories, in the very place in which He had been buried, and a few days after He had been buried, His Resurrection, it is evident that, if His body could have been found, the Jews would have produced it, as the shortest and completest answer possible to the whole story. The attempt of the apostles could not have survived this refutation for a moment."

Picture Peter preaching in Jerusalem at Pentecost within a few hundred yards of the sepulchre, and claiming: "This Jesus did God raise up" (Acts 2:32), when suddenly on the skirts of the crowd there is a scuffle. Annas and Caiaphas, with others, appear carrying the embalmed body of Christ, which they had stolen some six weeks before. For how much longer would the apostolic preaching of the Resurrection have been publicly credible? Writing in the *Church Times*, J.B. Phillips, the wellknown translator of the Bible, had this to say: "Quite honestly, had I been Caiaphas and found an empty tomb, I would have produced a body – any body! – rather than let them get away with it and cause more havoc." Truly, as Andrew Fairbairn put it: "The silence of the Jews in relation to the resurrection of Christ is as striking as the voice of the disciples."

The son of a friend of mine, a soldier in the British Army in Palestine at the time of the British Mandate, told me that one of his most hazardous and nerve-wracking assignments, while serving there, was that of driving in an open truck through the packed streets of Jerusalem, holding up to public view the blood-bespattered corpse of a Jewish terrorist, as a deterrent to similar patriotic acts of promiscuous violence. The scribes and Pharisees could have done something like that. Why didn't they? The presumption is that they *did* not because they *could* not. The corpse was not in their custody.

(6) *The Earthquake Theory*. Matthew mentions, as we have noted, that at the rising of Jesus from the dead, there was a mighty seismic disturbance: "Behold, there was a great earthquake; for the angel of the Lord descended from heaven, and came and rolled back the stone from the door, and sat upon it" (Matthew 28:2). Dorothy L. Sayers dramatically accounts for that tremor thus: "The molecular rearrangement required by the physical resurrection gave rise to electrical disturbances felt as an earthquake." However that may be, the Gospel narrative does inform us that there was an earthquake, and R.S.T. Haslehurst suggests that there may be a connection between this seismic tremor and the report of the Resurrection. "That there was an earthquake of considerable magnitude," he says, "is borne out by Matthew 27:51–53. In this it may be permissible to see a disinterment of corpses in the local cemeteries, and consequent hasty reinterment during the Feast, magnified into a tradition that these corpses were vivified. The earthquake may have caused the fissure into which our Lord's body disappeared, the tomb subsequently recovering its previous shape, more or less, and the stone rolling away. The guards, unlike the sentinel at Pompeii, scrambled away and one or two persons who happened to be on the spot said something to the hysterical and overwrought women which led them to think that an angel had told them He had risen."

Truly, a sensible-seeming theory and one which might be thought to have greater antecedent probability than some others! But surely if the earthquake had split the tomb open the body would not have disappeared "without trace", when the disciples later searched the sepulchre as thoroughly as we know they would. And what about the grave-clothes? Are they just part of a legendary embroidery? And the angel, the two angels? Are they just fictional figures, figments of the excited women's fancy? And what about the young man? If, as is fairly generally believed, he was in fact John Mark, there can be no rational spiritualizing of his historical reality. Moreover, what about the rest of the impressive circumstantial evidence? Is that too to be airily swept aside as unworthy of credence? We cannot think so.

(7) *The Ghost Theory*. To this we have already incidentally alluded when arguing that resurrection does not merely mean spiritual survival. It is a theory which, in one form or another, has gained wide currency in our time when so many are disinclined to credit the bodily resurrection of Christ. One thinks of the extraordinary utterance of Dr Harry Emerson Fosdick: "I should not be at all surprised if archaeologists, excavating in the Middle East, were to unearth the remains of Jesus of Nazareth." One thinks, too, of a recent observation of Professor John Macquarrie who said on television: "The resurrection of Christ is not an event in the same category as His Crucifixion. His body is still in the grave." Patently, people who speak like that, while affecting to believe in the living Lord, whether they realize or deliberately intend it or not, subscribe to some sort of Ghost Theory.

But the New Testament insists on the tangible corporeality of the Risen Redeemer. When He suddenly burst into visibility in the Upper Room on the evening of the day of the Resurrection, not unnaturally, the disciples were startled, indeed terrified, "They thought they were seeing a ghost" (Luke 24:37 NEB). Jesus, however, soon allayed their fears and disabused their minds of that erroneous idea. "Touch Me and see," He challenged, "no ghost has flesh and bone as you can see that I have" (v.39 NEB). On the authority of our blessed Lord Himself, therefore, we flatly and firmly reject the Ghost Theory.

(8) *The Hallucination Theory.* In this notion we have the subjective counterpart of the theory we have just been reviewing. It alleges that those who profess to have seen Christ after He died on the Cross were the victims of illusion. Sincerely enough, they really thought they were seeing again the Master they so dearly loved, but they were deluded. It was only a vision. What they actually saw was an image projected on to the screen of their highly sensitive and credulous minds by their own excited expectations. Was that so? No honest and intelligent student of the New Testament could possibly concur. Several weighty considerations militate against such a conclusion. One is the emptiness of the tomb. At least five persons saw it vacant on the first Easter Day, and the empty tomb is a powerful part of the evidence for the Resurrection. Next, there is the mental make-up of the disciples and the psychological state in which they happened to be at the time. It would not have been surprising if the disciples had been joyously anticipating a return of the Lord Jesus from the dead. Three times during His earthly life He had explicitly and in set terms predicted His own death and rising again. The fact is, however, that the truth of the Resurrection had not dawned on them. So often the Master had spoken to them parabolically, that perhaps they thought these forecasts were metaphorical and meant to be spiritualized. In any case, they had no idea whatever that He intended the words to be taken literally. Once more, the disciples were not fanatical, gullible, impressionable. On the contrary, they were balanced and sane and even disposed to disbelief. Nobody is likely to suspect of hallucination those who dismiss reports of resurrection as "idle tales" (Luke 24:11). The Vulgate, or Latin version of the Scriptures, renders the original Greek *leros* by the Latin *deliramentum*, from which

we derive our English word "delirium".

Of Keim, who held a spiritistic view of the Resurrection, maintaining that it was only Christ's *Spirit* which survived the grave, someone has wittily commented: "Queer fellow! He believed in any kind of ghost but the Holy Ghost!" Nevertheless, Dr Wade, in his *New Testament History*, espouses and retails Keim's theory. "Our Lord," he writes, "having passed into the spiritual sphere, acted upon the senses of His disciples from within, the brain-cells being stimulated in such a way as to create the same impression as would have been caused if a figure had been presented to the sensory organs from without." The New Testament records no fewer than twelve appearances of the Risen Lord to individuals, besides those to Stephen, Paul and John, not to mention His self-manifestation to the five hundred on the hill in Galilee. Is it likely that all these were the victims of some strange illusion? Were they merely delirious? Was the impression they received merely the result of over-heated brains? "No," says Matthew Henry, "the witnesses of Christ's Resurrection, who attested it to the world, and pawned their lives upon it, were not easy, credulous men, but cautious enough, and who suspended belief of it till they saw the utmost evidence of what they could desire." The idiot who fancies himself Napoleon Bonaparte, frets and fumes because others do not recognize his celebrated identity. Hallucinations are highly subjective and individual. Not so with the Risen Christ. As many as five hundred persons saw Him at once, most of whom were still convinced of the reality of what they had seen after a lapse of many years. Moreover, hallucinations commonly affect only one, or at the most two, of the senses concurrently – sight, hearing, touch – but the first followers of Jesus had visual, audible and tactual proofs of His risen reality. Furthermore, it may be asked, Why did the alleged hallucinations cease abruptly only about a month and a half after they began? "Nobody ever claimed that they happened after the Great

Forty Days," says Paul E. Little. "It is immeasurably more difficult to believe that the Resurrection was a delusion than to believe that it was a Divine fact," declares Brook Fosse Westcott. This theory cannot be entertained for one moment. It is palpably false.

(9) *The Mistake Theory*. Kirsopp Lake initiated this idea. His suggestion was that in the grey of that April dawn Mary Magdalene went to the wrong grave and, finding it open and empty, concluded that her Master had risen. What dunces and dupes those people seem to think the primitive disciples were! With whimsical satire J.H. Withers pokes fun deliciously at this ridiculous notion. "An Eastern cemetery," he writes, "was laid out in higgledly-piggledly fashion and the disciples must have gone to the wrong tomb. It is just as if Joseph of Arimathaea had taken a plot No D.26410 and subsequently lost the identity ticket!" In point of fact, as C.G. Killick has reminded us, "our Lord was not buried in a public graveyard but in a private garden, belonging to Joseph of Arimathaea. The probability is that there was no other tomb in the garden." Certainly, the tomb would have been readily identifiable with the Roman imperial seal upon it and, even had it been possible to mistake it in the dusk, it would soon have been discoverable as the dawn broke and on subsequent visits to the tomb by the disciples. "It is inconceivable that a man should rise from the dead," says Renan, "but not that witnesses may be mistaken." Were they? The New Testament expressly informs us that the women present at the entombment of our Lord "beheld (*etheoroun GK* "to take a long close look") where He was laid" (Mark 15:48). They were not in the least likely therefore later to err in knowing which it was.

Such, then, in brief outline, are the nine alternative explanations of the phenomenon we are considering. We have noted that not one of them is tenable. For the solution of the problem we must look elsewhere.

(10) *The Historic Fact.*
That is the evangelical position. All we shall have to say afterward in this chapter will only serve to confirm us in our conviction that it is the right one.

THE PROMISE

Did our Lord definitely promise to rise from the dead? Undoubtedly He did. There are no fewer than nine such pledges recorded in the New Testament although some of them are patently duplicates, and these promises of the Lord Jesus are themselves echoes of Old Testament prophecies to the same effect. Here, for example, are three from the ancient Hebrew Scriptures: "I know that my Redeemer liveth" (Job 19:25); "He will swallow up death in victory" (Isaiah 25:8); "Thou wilt not suffer Thine Holy One to see corruption" (Psalm 16:1). Our Lord's own personal pledges to rise from the grave are as follows: "As Jonas was three days and three nights in the whale's belly, so shall the Son of Man be three days and three nights in the heart of the earth" (Matthew 12:40); "Jesus began to show unto His disciples how He must be killed, and be raised again the third day" (Matthew 17:16,21); "The Son of Man shall be betrayed into the hands of men, and they shall kill Him, and the third day He shall be raised again" (Matthew 17:22,23) "The Son of Man shall be betrayed unto the chief priests and unto the scribes, and they shall condemn Him to death, and shall deliver Him to the Gentiles to mock, and to scourge, and to crucify Him, and the third day He shall rise again" (Matthew 20:18,19); "Jesus began to teach them that the Son of Man must suffer many things, and be rejected of the elders, and of the chief priests and scribes, and be killed, and after three days rise again" (Mark 8:31); "Jesus taught His disciples, and said unto them, The Son of Man is delivered into the hands of men, and they shall kill Him; and after He is killed He shall rise the third day" (Mark 9:31); "The Son of

Man shall be delivered unto the chief priests and unto the scribes; and they shall condemn Him to the Gentiles; and they shall mock Him and shall scourge Him and shall spit upon Him and shall kill Him: and the third day He shall rise again" (Mark 10:33,34); "The Son of Man must suffer many things, and be rejected of the elders and chief priests and scribes, and be slain and be raised the third day" (Luke 9:22); "It behoved Christ to suffer and to rise from the dead the third day" (Luke 24:26); "Jesus said, Destroy this temple, and in three days I will raise it up. He spake of the temple of His body" (John 2:19,21); "I lay down My life that I might take it again; I have power to lay it down and I have power to take it again" (John 10:17,18). No wonder our Lord's foes remembered such promises as these! The marvel is that His friends forgot them!

THE PROOFS

Luke tells us in the prologue to the Book of Acts that Christ "showed Himself alive after His passion by many infallible proofs" (1:3). The word "infallible" is not in the original and it is really redundant. If a thing is a proof it is infallible and that's an end of it. But, if any proofs were ever infallible, they are these. What are they?

They are ninefold: (1) *the vacated tomb*; (2) *the deflated shroud*; (3) *the translated Lord*; (4) *the disseminated Spirit*; (5) *the elated disciples*; (6) *the dictated Book*; (7) *the dedicated day*; (8) *the fabricated Church*; and, most impressive of all by far, (9) *the incarnated God*.

Take them each in turn.

(1) *The vacated tomb.* That is a vitally valid piece of evidence. Some time ago a liberal theologian was asked on television: "Would Christianity survive should a tomb

containing Christ's body be discovered?" He answered: "Yes." But would it? Perhaps it would as a system of moral philosophy or a programme of social reform, but not as the dynamic personal faith it essentially is. Initially, it was an awful shock to Mary Magdalene to find the grave empty. But, ultimately, would it not have been an infinitely severer shock had she found it occupied?

O, the anguish of Mary!
O, the depth of despair!
Had she gone to the tomb,
And the dead Lord was *there.*

It is true, of course, as Carroll E. Simcox contends, that "the Gospel of Easter is not the empty tomb, but the Risen Christ", nevertheless the vacancy of the sepulchre is a central fact of the case. No atom of Christ's body was left within the tomb. It was a nest forsaken. The Bird of Paradise had flown. The sweet scent of the spices clung around the rockhewn burial-place, but the cavern was just an echoing void. The corpse had vanished. Henry Parry Liddon, the great Anglican preacher, did not hesitate to declare: "No other spot on earth says so much to Christian faith as does the empty tomb of our Lord." "Come, see the place" (Matthew 28:6) – the funerary cave – is still a focal part of the Easter Gospel.

(2) *The deflated shroud.* Another most potent piece of evidence for the Resurrection was the grave-clothes. It wasn't just that they were there; it was the shape and the position they had assumed. At the entombment on the evening of the first Good Friday, the winding-sheet had been wrapped around the Lord's body after the fashion of the folds in the materials of an Egyptian mummy. Sprinkled upon this cloth cocoon were one hundred pounds' weight of spices, and when Jesus rose He passed through the shroud without its being unwound. It was

this that convinced the first observers of the scene. There was no way in which that could have happened but by resurrection. Had the winding-sheet been unfolded, torn apart, or burst open from within, the funereal spices would have been scattered all over the floor of the grave. As it was, nothing was disturbed. The only observable change was that the shroud, now unsupported by the body, had fallen flat under the weight of the embalming unguents, while the turban, not having had anything heavy placed upon it, retained its convex shape in a place apart. It was probably this, more than anything else at the time, which persuaded Peter and John that Jesus was alive.

(3) *The translated Lord.* The writer to the Hebrews employs the term "translation" (Greek *metathesis*) in relation to Enoch (11:5). But surely the word is supremely applicable to the Saviour Himself! At the Resurrection His humanity underwent *metathesis.* It was translated into a glorious new dimension of being. Of this the translated Lord furnished proof by twelve recorded appearances during the Great Forty Days. By the Resurrection He became "a life-giving Spirit" (1 Corinthians 15:45).

Note that the character of Christ Himself made such posthumous self-revelations presumptively probable. Had they been reported of Herod, they would have been rejected out of hand as palpably false. With Jesus, however, it was altogether different. He was perfect God and perfect Man. When reported of Him, such manifestations are not only credible but inevitable. Jesus was not the Resurrection because He rose from the dead: He rose from the dead because He was the Resurrection. As Carroll E. Simcox tersely and tellingly expresses it: "Man must die as man, but the God-Man, if He dies, must rise again." "It is no miracle that Jesus rose from the dead," says George Matheson, "it would have been a miracle if He had not risen." Since Jesus was absolute God, it was as inconceivable that He should be defeated by death as that a baby should blow out the sun. "It was not possible that He should be holden of death" (Acts 2:24).

Moreover, our blessed Lord was morally perfect. "Which of you convinceth Me of sin?" He challenged (John 8:46). During His earthly life the most supernatural thing about Him was what we too negatively call His sinlessness. It alone made the Resurrection not only believable but absolutely certain. For, as Henry Drummond suggestively inquired: "What if it should be the normal thing for a man without sin to rise from the dead?"

In his treatment of this theme Karl Adam argues compellingly: "What we are dealing with is not the raising up of a mere man, but the resurrection of the Christ, not the mere flaring up of an extinct natural life, but the creative breaking through of the Divine life, which Jesus from the very beginning knew to be His own." In other words, He who "hath delivered us from the power of darkness and hath translated us into the kingdom of His dear Son" (Colossians 1:13), first delivered and translated the "dear Son" Himself in that way.

(4) *The disseminated Spirit.* A frequently-forgotten but immensely expressive part of the evidence for the resurrection of Christ was the diffusion at Pentecost of the Holy Spirit. A dead Christ could never have "baptized with the Holy Ghost and with fire" (Luke 3:16). As Peter told his hearers in his Pentecostal sermon, it was: "This Jesus whom God raised up, who hath shed forth this which ye now see and hear" (Acts 2:32,33). The disciples themselves did not fully grasp the implications of Christ's rising from the dead until they had had the distinctively charismatic experience. Before that, they knew of the resurrection of Christ, but until then they really did not know the Christ of the Resurrection. It was when he was "in the Spirit" (Revelation 1:10) that the Seer of Patmos saw the Living One, for it is the Spirit who makes the Resurrection real.

(5) *The elated disciples.* That a dramatic and determinative

change came over the first followers of Jesus on Easter Day no observant and candid reader of the New Testament will be in the least likely to dispute. Hugh T. Kerr does not exaggerate when he speaks of it as a "transcendent transformation". "I wonder," wrote Karen Muller, "why those doubting disciples thought that Leader of theirs could be stopped by a single boulder blocking the door of His tomb, when He had revealed a faith big enough to remove mountains?" Nevertheless, they did! But there can be no doubt that when –

Triumphant o'er His foes and woes,
The Son of God by moonlight rose,
By all but heaven unseen –

something tremendous happened to the personalities of those men. If we did not know of the Resurrection, we should be obliged, on the ground of this evidence alone, to postulate some stupendous occurrence to account for the extraordinary change in the character and behaviour of the disciples. If, for instance, one day you see a man looking sad, dejected, melancholy and the next you find him exhilarated, excited, exuberant, you look for a reason and, should you discover that in the meantime he has "come into a fortune", you say: "That explains it!" Those disciples of Jesus were like that. You must posit nothing short of a Resurrection to account for the phenomenal transformation in these men.

(6) *The dictated Book.* Someone has graphically said that Jesus rose from the grave with the New Testament in His hand. Certain it is that if He had not risen the New Testament could never have been written. To quote Hugh T. Kerr again: "It was the fact of the Resurrection that gave us the New Testament and not the New Testament that gave us the story of the Resurrection." Or, as Lumsden Barkway clinchingly puts it: "Without the Resurrection the New Testament would never have been written, for there

would have been nothing to write about and no one to write it." Our Lord did not, of course, in every case dictate the Scriptures after the manner of a modern businessman dictating a letter to a secretary or dictating-machine. What He did was to indwell and inspire its human authors so that their writings were supernatural.

Part of such inspiration consists of accurate and honest reporting and on this question of the Resurrection itself the Christian Scriptures certainly ring true. How else account for Matthew's amazing admission in his picture of Christ's final appearing in this age to His disciples on a mountain in Galilee: "When they saw Him, they worshipped Him: but some doubted" (Matthew 28:17). It is as certain as anything can be that no false or fictitious narrative could ever have contained that candid footnote.

(7) *The dedicated day*. Up to the dawn of the day on which Christ rose from the dead the first day of the week had had no more reverential recognition paid to it than any other day of the week. The only thing notable about it was that it happened to *be* the first day of the week! It was to the seventh day that the Hebrews were divinely attracted and to which they gave such honour and attached such significance. In the Epistle of Barnabas, a second century document, the author states: "Therefore we keep the eighth day of joyfulness, the day on which Jesus rose from the dead." Between Easter Day and Sunday there is obviously a close correspondence. As R.H. Malden beautifully expresses it: "Every Sunday is a little Easter." To this John Keble alludes in his classic *The Christian Year*. Apostrophizing the Day of the Resurrection, he cries:

Thou shedd'st thy light on all the year:
Sundays by thee more glorious break,
An Easter Day in every week.

That the disciples, strict observers of the Mosaic law as they were, should have come to hallow the first day in preference to the seventh, can only be rationally attributed to some dramatic and dynamic occurrence which revolutionized the ingrained habits of a lifetime. That happening was the Resurrection. "Every Sunday, as it comes round," observes James Denney, "is a new argument for the Resurrection. The decisive event in the inauguration of the new religion took place on that day – an event so decisive and sure that it displaced even the Sabbath."

(8) *The fabricated Church.* When the Lord Jesus said: "I will build My Church" (Matthew 16:18), only a few months remained of His earthly life. He knew that perfectly well and He knew that it would take not months but millennia to build His Church. Yet He said: "I will build My Church." The work was not to be delegated to another. It was to be His exclusive personal responsibility and prerogative. Does not that very assertion postulate the Resurrection? Does not His very declaration of intent presuppose a rising from the dead? And has not the Living Lord in fact carried that omnipotent resolve into effect in subsequent centuries? The fabricated Church is proof positive that Jesus lives.

(9) *The incarnated God.* By far the most compulsive evidence of the reality of the Resurrection of Christ is the fact that the body which occupied that grave in the garden of the Arimathaean was no ordinary corpse. It was in truth the body of the incarnate God. That such a body could not dissolve into dust was a foregone conclusion. In his *The Ancient Creeds in Modern Life* H.B. Swete puts this point well: "The resurrection of Christ, as a physical fact, is entirely in harmony with His supernatural conception. Granting the truth of the Incarnation and conception by the Holy Spirit, it is unthinkable that the body so formed and united from the first with the Person of the Logos could have seen corruption and lain in the tomb until it was mingled with the dust of Israel." That single argument closes and clinches the case for the factuality of Christ's rising from the dead.

THE PRESENCE

The spiritual presence of Jesus is both a local and a cosmic phenomenon. It is guaranteed by Himself to the irreducible congregational minimum: "Where two or three are gathered together in My name, there am I in the midst of them" (Matthew 18:20) and its universal reality is proclaimed: "Go ye, therefore, and teach all nations, baptizing them in the name of the Father, and of the Son, and of the Holy Ghost: teaching them to observe all things whatsoever I have commanded you: and, lo, I am with you alway, even unto the end of the world" (Matthew 28:19,20).

The spiritual presence of Jesus is a familiar experience in the fellowship of the few. It is noteworthy that, although our Lord was a magnetic preacher, although for the greater part of His public ministry the crowds followed Him, when thinking of the gatherings of His people on earth, He did so in terms of the tiniest of groups. "Two or three." You cannot have a smaller company than that, for the single lesser number is a unit and not a company at all; and it is typical of the humility of Jesus to envisage and anticipate the lowest imaginable attendance as meeting in His name. "A blind man can always tell when there is a poor congregation," writes F.W. Boreham. "In such a case the minister invariably quotes a certain text: 'Where two or three are gathered together in My name, there am I in the midst of them.' But the text is as much out of place as the missing worshippers. We have no right to drag it in drearily, dolefully, dismally, whenever the empty pews are particularly conspicuous. It is not an apology for human absence. It is the triumphant proclamation of a divine presence." That presence is locally realizable.

It is also cosmically real. For Christ *kenosis* was followed by *pleroma*. He who came to the Place of a Skull – the very epitome of emptiness – became Head over all things, filling the universe with His presence. Of this the New

Testament categorically assures us. "He ascended up far above all heavens, that He might fill all things" (Ephesians 4:10). "Since He is exalted," states Homer A. Kent, Jnr, "He is able to fill all things with His presence. This includes the earth and the realm of the Christian dead as well as His exalted position in heaven." Bishop Jackson in his classic exposition of the Creed puts the point perfectly in an unforgettable epigram: "As perfect God, our Lord is present *everywhere*, as glorified Man, He can be present *anywhere*" (Bk 11:3). The universal presence of Christ, as experienced throughout the Christian centuries in the fellowship of the faithful, is a unique religious phenomenon and for believers it provides convincing proof in itself of the reality of the Resurrection.

THE POWER

"Jesus Christ," affirms Paul, "was declared to be the Son of God with power by His resurrection from the dead" (Romans 1:3,4). That word "declared" is strikingly picturesque. In the original it is *horisthentos*, a term from which by almost direct transcription we get our word "horizon". What the apostle is saying, therefore, is that at the Resurrection Jesus was *horizoned* with power. A modern illustration of it can be found in what takes place in a television-studio when the high-powered lights and lynxeyed cameras are switched on. Just before that, the body of the person sitting there occupies only a few cubic feet of space. At much less than a mile it would be invisible and inaudible. But when the lights are turned on and the cameras begin to function, that person is literally *horizoned*. Instantly, it may be, he is seen and heard by millions all over the world. Something analogous occurred at the Resurrection. In the act of rising from the tomb our blessed Lord was horizoned to fill all space and time. In the ringing words of J. Ithel Jones: "He was 'declared to be the Son of God *with power* by His resurrection from the dead'. God said on the day of Christ's baptism and again on the day of His transfiguration: 'This is My beloved Son'. But on the day of the Resurrection God shouted it at the world. He took the seal from the grave and put it on the Gospel. The rising from the dead is God's great confirmation of Jesus' claims." At the Resurrection Christ was horizoned with power.

Travelling by train in the United States, Bishop William Quayle fell into conversation with some of his fellow passengers. The bishop was in mufti and one of the passengers was curious to know what he did for a living. "What is your line of business?" he inquired. "What do you travel in?" Quaintly, the bishop replied: "Horizons!" He was right. Everyone who proclaims the Gospel of the Risen Christ is in "horizons".

For Paul, however, the thrill of the Resurrection lay not only in the fact that it was an explosive event in history but also in that it was a dynamic event in experience, both individual and corporate. Wistfully, he cried: "That I may know Him, and the power of His resurrection" (Philippians 3:10) – an echo of which may be heard in these resounding lines from the pen of a modern minstrel:

That I may know Him! Ah, I long to know
Not just a Christ of far-gone years ago;
Nor even reigning on a heavenly throne,
Too high and distant to be really known.

I long to know Him closely – this is how –
Alive and in the ever-pressing Now;
A Living One within my heart this hour,
Communicating His all-conquering power,
Who now no longer lives from me apart
But shares His resurrection in my heart.

Power from a tomb! That is a strangely unexpected place for power to come from. Power from a throne is a congruous and credible conjunction of concepts, but power from a grave seems fantastically improbable. Yet it was from a grave that Christ came horizoned with power.

Once in Jerusalem I seemed to have a vision. It was at the Garden Tomb. I saw, as it were, the Risen Christ marching from the sepulchre as on the morning of the Resurrection, His face shining like the sun. Behind Him, silhouetted against the dawn sky, was Golgotha, with its vacant Cross and Jesus, as He went His way, turned and looked back at that empty gibbet; and then, averting His gaze, sped on towards Galilee and Glory.

By the Resurrection Jesus was demonstrated to be Deity by the display of Divine power. All the forces of earth and hell conspired to keep Him in the tomb. The whole universe appeared organized to affect Him negatively where His claims to divinity were concerned. Human beings were part of that attempted nullification. Judas cried: "You shall not be!" as He sold Him for thirty pieces of silver. Caiaphas exclaimed: "You must not be!" as he pronounced Him worthy of death. Pilate gave sentence: "You no longer shall be," as he signed His death-warrant. But on the morning of the Resurrection the Almighty Lord rose from the dead, crying: "I am!"

The apostle not only proclaims the Resurrection as power for personal living but also as Divine energy for the revival of the Church. In the personal context the Resurrection means regeneration: in the collective context, it means revival. For his converts at Ephesus the apostle prayed: "That ye may know what is the exceeding greatness of His power to usward who believe, according to the working of His mighty power, which He wrought in Christ when He raised Him from the dead" (Ephesians 1:18–20). That is a stupendous prayer. It seeks to link human impotence to Divine omnipotence.

THE PROSPECT

Edwin Markham, the distinguished American poet, has some lines entitled "A Guard at the Sepulchre", which linger long in the mind. They purport to be a confession of one of the soldiers posted on those nervous nights at the tomb of Jesus. He says:

> *I saw your Risen Christ, for I am he*
> *Who reached the hyssop to Him on the Tree,*
> *And I am one of two who watched beside*
> *The sepulchre of Him we crucified.*
>
> *Years have I wandered, carrying my shame;*
> *Now let the tooth of time eat out my name,*
> *For we who all the wonder might have told,*
> *Kept silent, for our mouths were stuffed with gold.*

That is, of course, purely poetic licence. No one, either friend or foe, did in fact see Jesus rise. So far as the world knows, He is still in the sepulchre. The world has never seen Him in His risen power. It can behold no splendour streaming from the empty tomb. Its Easter Day has yet to dawn. "Clearly," wrote G.R. Beasley-Murray, "if Christ is alive, the world is mistaken."

A day is soon coming, however, when the world *will know* that Jesus lives. His feet shall stand in that day upon the Mount of Olives" (Zechariah 14:4). "Every eye shall see Him" (Revelation 1:7). This is the point of Paul Althaus's percipient comment: "The Second Coming removes the hiddenness of Easter for history."

Nor is the prospect of resurrection appearance limited to our Lord. It extends to all His true disciples: "When He shall appear, then shall ye also appear with Him in glory" (Colossians 3:4). "The hour is coming, in which all that are in the graves shall hear the voice of the Son of Man, and shall come forth" (John 5:28,29). "Behold I show you a mystery; we shall not all sleep, but we shall all be changed, in a moment, in the twinkling of an eye, at the last trump; for the trumpet shall sound, and the dead shall be raised incorruptible, and we shall be changed. Thanks be to God, which giveth us the victory through our Lord Jesus Christ" (1 Corinthians 15:51,52,57). "He must reign till He hath put all enemies under His feet. The last enemy that shall be destroyed is death" (1 Corinthians 15:26,27). "Jesus Christ hath abolished death, and brought life and immortality to light through the Gospel" (2 Timothy 1:10).

Thus did the Captain of our Salvation, by His conquering comeback, turn the tide of moral war in the cosmos, win for the forces of righteousness a glorious victory over the hosts of darkness and rout death and hell for ever. His death and resurrection are the prelude and promise of our own.

For the garden tomb is empty
And the east is silver grey,
As the angels of the morning
Trumpet in another day:
See, the wounded God go walking
Down the world's eternal way,
For His work is not yet done.

8
THE RETURN OF THE NATIVE

The Christian Doctrine of the Ascension

Hail the day that sees Him rise
To His throne above the skies;
Christ awhile to mortals given
Reascends His native heaven.

Charles Wesley

God is gone up with a shout, the Lord with the sound of a trumpet.

Psalm 47:5

When the righteous triumph, there is great glory.

Proverbs 28:12

He was received up.

Luke 2:2

What if ye should behold the Son of Man ascending where He was before?

John 6:62 RSV

I leave the world and go to the Father.

John 16:28

He led them out as far as to Bethany, and He lifted up His hands, and blessed them. And it came to pass, while He blessed them, He was parted from them and carried up into heaven.

Luke 24:50,51

The day in which He was taken up.

Acts 1:2

Jesus, whom the heaven must receive.

Acts 3:21

He ascended up far above all heavens.

Ephesians 4:10

He was received up into Glory.

1 Timothy 3:16

We have a great High Priest, that is passed into the heavens.

Hebrews 4:14

Christ, who is at the right hand of God, having gone into heaven.

1 Peter 3:22.

IN HIS AUTOBIOGRAPHY *A King's Story* the Duke of Windsor tells of a strange thing that happened at the funeral of his father, King George V. He describes how, when the body was being conveyed on a draped gun-carriage, through the silent, crowded streets of London, a mishap took place, which was to him unforgettable, although witnessed by only a few: "The imperial crown, heavily encrusted with precious stones, had been removed from its glass case in the Tower and secured to the lid of the coffin over the folds of the Royal Standard. In spite of the rubber-tyred wheels, the jolting of the heavy vehicle must have caused the Maltese Cross on top of the crown – set with a square of sapphires, eight mediumsized diamonds and one hundred and ninety-two smaller diamonds – to fall. For suddenly, out of the corner of my eye, I caught a flash of light dancing along the pavement."

Writing in his *The Life to Live* Frederick M. Meek takes up the narrative at that point. "One of the sailors, marching behind the gun-carriage, picked it up, took it to the commanding officer and, saluting, said: 'This cross fell off, sir. It must be replaced.' The officer was a little bewildered by the untoward happening, and he asked: 'Must it be replaced now?' 'Yes! sir', replied the sailor, 'the crown is never complete without the cross.'"

Theologically, the converse is also true. The Cross is never complete without the Crown. The Coronation inevitably follows the Crucifixion; the Ascension, the Atonement.

The Ascension! But was there only one Ascension? Or were there two? Some think there were two. The reason for their making that assumption is that there is such a marked difference between the attitude of the Risen Lord to Mary Magdalene when He met her for the second time on the day of the Resurrection and the attitude He had adopted toward her on the first occasion. In the earlier interview He had said: "Touch Me not, for I am not yet ascended to My Father" (John 20:17). In the later, described by Matthew, here is what transpired: "And as they (Mary Magdalene and the other Mary) went to tell His disciples, behold, Jesus met them, saying, All hail. And they came and held Him by the feet and worshipped Him" (28:9). Was there perhaps an ascension between these two appearances? C.I. Scofield inclines to that opinion. In a footnote to the relevant section of his edition of the Bible he writes: "Jesus speaks to Mary as the High Priest fulfilling the Day of the Atonement (Leviticus 16). Having accomplished the sacrifice, He was on His way to present the sacred blood in heaven and, between the meeting with Mary in the Garden and the meeting of Matthew 28:9, He had ascended and returned – a view in harmony with the types."

There is certainly a marked difference between the manner in which at the meeting with Mary Magdalene alone our Lord gently restrained her from physical contact with Him and that in which afterwards He allowed her and the other Mary to clasp Him by the feet. The unrecorded private ascension postulated by Dr Scofield could account for this apparent *volte face*. But notice precisely what Jesus said. He did not say: "Touch Me *now*. This will be your last earthly chance to do so." No. What He *did* say was: "Touch Me *not, for* I have not yet ascended to My Father." Alexander Maclaren used to maintain that there is great force in the *fors* of the New Testament. Certainly this *for* is of absolutely determinative significance. The paradox is that He withdrew from the world bodily in order to be more accessible to us spiritually. As the poet puts it:

Touch Me not, awhile believe Me;
Touch Me not, till heaven receive Me:
Then draw near and never leave Me.

"He is touched," declares the writer to the Hebrews, "with the feeling of our infirmities" (4:15). Whatever be the truth as to whether or not there was not one but two ascensions, there can be no question that the historic Church has always had an Ascension on its calendar. The day was officially commemorated as "Holy Thursday" and there were never any doubts in ancient times as to its factuality.

It is not always the same now. One senses a certain embarrassment in some ministers where the subject of the Ascension is concerned. They tend to shy clear of the topic or to dismiss it lightly as no more than a graphic myth or triumphalist parable. But the Ascension, far from being of merely marginal or secondary importance, is a cardinal fact of the Christian faith. Not only is it extensively reported by Luke, both in his Gospel and in the Book of Acts, it is incidentally referred to or assumed to have taken place in scores of passages in the New Testament. Its theme is woven like a golden thread into the very warp and woof of Holy Scripture. It is not so much a matter of text as of texture.

Nor is the Old Testament without analogical anticipations of it. Enoch and Elijah present proleptic parallels and the entry of the High Priest in the Hebrew sanctuary into the Holy of Holies on the great Day of Atonement provides the writer to the Hebrews with marvellous illustrative material.

Moreover, our Lord's own Transfiguration was a sort of dress-rehearsal for the Ascension. "Jesus taketh Peter, James and John his brother, and bringeth them up into an high mountain apart, and He was transfigured before them: and His face did shine as the sun, and His raiment was white as the light" (Matthew 17:1,2).

Here are the historical particulars regarding the Ascension. "He led them out as far as to Bethany, and He lifted up His hands, and blessed them. And it came to pass, while He blessed them, He was parted from them and carried up into heaven" (Luke 21:50,51). "While they beheld, He was taken up; and a cloud received Him out of their sight. And while they looked steadfastly toward heaven as He went up, behold, two men stood by them in white apparel, which also said, Ye Men of Galilee, why stand ye gazing up into heaven? This same Jesus, which is taken up from you into heaven, shall so come in like manner as ye have seen Him go into heaven" (Acts 1:9–11).

"A cloud received Him out of their sight." It hid *Him* from *them*, but as W.E. Sangster happily comments, it did not hide *them* from *Him*. The cloud is still there. We cannot see our blessed Lord with the eye of sense. Faith, however, like a heavenly radar, can penetrate the cloud and watch with reverent wonder the heavenly ministry of our ascended Lord.

The New Testament represents the Ascension as a sublime drama in three acts – *secession, procession* and *accession*.

Take them in that order.

SECESSION

The first thing to note about the Ascension is that it was a deliberate, predetermined, public withdrawal from the world. Our Lord had not only to leave the planet, He had to be *seen* to leave it. No one saw Him rise from the *clods*, but all the eleven disciples witnessed His ascent into the *clouds*. As J.T. Graves sings:

O Prince of Peace, who once did'st rise
In splendid triumph to the skies
Before the rapt disciples' eyes.

Yes, they saw Him go. They *had* to see Him go. The secession was not secret. They were eye-witnesses.

Nevertheless, despite the testimony of such credible observers, some actually do dispute the historicity of the Ascension. The story of Christ's departure from Planet Earth, they tell us, is the product of an age which naively accepted the idea of a sort of sandwich universe, with heaven and hell as the slices of bread, so to speak, and earth as the meat in the middle. The New Testament, they allege, credits and presupposes a cosmogony impossible to the informed modern mind. Patently, conceiving of the earth as flat, people then tended to think of heaven as "up" and of hell as "down". Now, of course, we know better. Science has taught us to believe in the world we inhabit as a huge ball, spinning in space, and in view of this, they suggest, we need to overhaul our concept of the Ascension.

In his *The Christian Faith* Claude Beaufort Moss does not hesitate to say: "We are not to think of Him disappearing into the blue sky, like a skylark... He did not go up as one ascends in an aeroplane: He went up as the heir to the throne becomes king, as the boy goes up from the fourth form to the fifth form, as a soldier rises when he becomes a general."

No doubt such a figurative use of the narrative in preaching is permissible, but it must not be allowed to detract from the literal factuality of the Ascension narrative as recorded in the New Testament. We may dare to controvert its historical authenticity, alleging that it was mistaken or even deliberately fraudulent in its account of what happened: the one thing we cannot do is to deny that it definitely describes the occurrence as an event in time, an event as solid and concrete as the wood of the Cross or the stone at the tomb. Jesus rose bodily into the skies from the skull of Olivet: and, as an old Welsh preacher picturesquely expressed it, His disciples actually saw the holes in the soles of His feet and in the palms of His hands as He went up. We are grateful here for the unequivocal witness of James Dodds. In his *Expositions of the Apostles' Creed* he remarks: "Unlike the Ascension, the Resurrection of Christ took place unseen by mortal eye. Eye-witnesses of His rising from the dead were not needed. The fact that they had seen Jesus after He rose qualified them to be witnesses of the Resurrection. But it was only because they had seen Him taken up that they could bear personal witness to His Ascension."

The place of the Ascension is specifically identified. It was the Mount of Olives. The date is also intimated. It was forty days after the Resurrection. The time of day at which it occurred is not recorded. We do not know, for we are not told. We do know exactly when He was crucified and approximately the hour when He rose from the tomb, but the timing of His ascent to the skies is not stated. If, however, in this, as in so much else, our Lord were to synchronize His activities in accordance with the representations of the Temple ritual, He would pass into the presence of God at the hour of the morning sacrifice. We may imagine that the first red light of a rushing dawn was streaming from the heavens as He entered the high portals of the hidden sanctuary.

From the fact, which Luke relates in Acts, that Christ's followers had a meal with Him before what would now be called His "vertical take-off", it seems likelier that the Ascension occurred late in the afternoon – just before darkness fell. As we have observed, they had to be actual spectators of His departure. That was the over-riding consideration. Whether it was a farewell breakfast or a supper He shared with His disciples it had to fall within the parameters of daylight.

Nonetheless, despite the obvious historical factuality of the narrative, some actually do cast doubt upon its objective reality. In his book *He Ascended into Heaven* J.G. Davies writes: "If we take the description in the first chapter of Acts literally and regard the cloud as a conveyance which carried Christ up to a localized heaven much as an elevator may carry a man up to the highest skyscraper in New York, we are bound to conclude that such an occurrence is not only improbable but impossible. Although we may perhaps consider that, as the Resurrection appearances can perhaps be understood as accommodations to the sense-perceptions of the disciples, so this event may be taken as an accommodation to their precopernican cosmology."

According to this theory, the Ascension is simply a myth, a symbol, a figure of speech. It never really happened, although the credulous disciples may have sincerely believed that it happened. The story of Christ's rising to the skies is simply a verbal picture, a visual aid, designed to illustrate His moral and spiritual triumph over the world.

We are reminded that, in ordinary, everyday speech, we employ language which, although scientifically inexact, is nonetheless useful for our purpose and perfectly plain to those to whom it is addressed. "When a schoolboy tells you he has been promoted to a higher class," remarks John Howat in his *Concerning the Faith in Christ*, "you do him an injustice if you take him to mean no more than that he has been transferred from a classroom on the ground floor to one upstairs." Even in the most sophisticated meteorological offices, one finds references to the sun rising and setting, although of course every schoolboy knows that it does nothing of the kind. Just so is it, we are asked to believe, with the story of the Ascension of Jesus. It is merely a parable of the ultimate victory of the virtues and values of Christ.

No student of Christian history, however, can be in any manner of doubt that from the beginning the Church has looked upon the Ascension of Christ as solid historical fact. All through the centuries that has been the classic, orthodox, official position. In a once-famous book entitled *On the Creed*, Bishop Pearson put the case with the utmost frankness and fulness: "I am fully persuaded that the only begotten, eternal Son of God, after He rose from the dead, did with the same body and soul with which He rose, by a true and local translation, convey Himself from the earth on which He lived, through all the regions of the air, through all the celestial orbs, until He came unto the heaven of heavens, the most glorious presence of the Majesty of God."

In line with this is the following dogmatic declaration by John Burr: "Like His resurrection, the Ascension of our Lord is part of the history of the world, an event beheld by actual human vision and vouched for by actual human evidence." Incontrovertibly, that is how the New Testament intends us to interpret the Ascension. That is how the early Church understood it; and that is how we are meant to comprehend it. The fact that in the fourth century it was decided by the Church annually to commemorate the Ascension on the sixth Thursday after Easter indicates that it was officially regarded as a real event.

Why is it so vital to believe that this was so? Why had the Ascension to be an observed historical fact?

Mainly for three reasons: (1) *that His departure might be*

dramatized; (2) *that His presence might be universalized;* and (3) *that the believer's life of faith might be realized.*

His Departure Dramatized

As we have already observed on several occasions, Jesus had not only to withdraw from the world: He had to be *seen* to do so. During the Great Forty Days He had been alternately appearing and disappearing, materializing and dematerializing – in a garden, on a road, in a room, on the shore of a lake, on the summit of a hill – and now He was going to appear in that manner no more until the Second Advent. This truth had to be driven into the minds of His disciples. There had to be something decisive and terminal about the Ascension to convince them of its factuality and finality. Otherwise they might easily have been mystified or misled by false hopes. If Jesus had just walked over the horizon like some celestial Captain Oates, His followers would have been expecting Him all the time suddenly to flash again into visibility. His ascent from the Mount of Olives made it transparently clear that He would not do so. "As they watched Him," writes C.G. Killick, "listening eagerly to His beloved voice, they saw His body rise from the earth, in a heavenward direction, until it was hidden from their sight by a cloud. No less pictorial method of withdrawal could have so surely convinced His followers that this was final so far as that age was concerned." There had been other occasions when our Lord had bidden farewell to His disciples, so to say, horizontally – at Nazareth, in Galilee when He departed into a mountain to pray, at Emmaus, and so on. But this was different. This time He was bidding them "Goodbye", as it were, vertically.

In his *Christian Belief* R.H. Malden says he does not see the need for this. "The words which appear in our Bible 'He parted from them' might be rendered 'He stepped aside', and from this what we call the Ascension may have happened horizontally, Christ vanishing into the low-lying morning mist almost before they were aware of it." Most emphatically, however, the Ascension was not just a repetition of what happened at Emmaus. For the Ascension to mean to the Master's disciples what it was meant to mean He had to ascend literally from earth's surface and had to be observed in the act of doing so. Nothing, I repeat, could be more actual and factual than the story of the Ascension. Oddly enough, although the New Testament narrative tells of Christ's being taken up to heaven, it is itself, so to say, absolutely "down to earth". And it is immensely significant that the two men in white, undogmatically identified by G. Campbell Morgan as Moses and Elijah, linked the Ascension with the Advent. "He shall so come as ye have seen Him go" (Acts 1:11) they said, the implication surely being that they would not see Him again in that way until His glorious Return.

His Presence Universalized

During the days of his flesh the Redeemer was physically limited to certain locations. Had He abode in that condition complications would almost certainly have arisen. "Sooner or later," says John Eddison, "His continued presence on earth would have created problems. As the news about Him spread throughout the world, people would have flocked in their thousands to Palestine to see Him, and thousands more would have been disappointed.

Here an illustration may help. Suppose someone in your town or village, your office or your school, were to become famous overnight; how he does it may be left to your imagination, but through some invention, discovery or achievement this person's name becomes a household word on everyone's lips and adorning with banner-headlines every newspaper. Very quickly an impossible situation arises and things get completely out of hand as people from all over the world begin to pour into the neighbourhood by road, rail and air. Life comes to a complete standstill as millions try to get a glimpse of this great celebrity. It is then, we will suppose, that the BBC steps in. A helicopter lands conveniently near, the person is bundled into it and whisked off to the television studios. You and I, who have struggled into the area, hoping for a photograph or even an autograph, feel cheated and disappointed. Just when we expected to enjoy fellowship with him, he was snatched from our presence. But I think we would see the sense of what had taken place if that night on a programme of national news this famous person were to speak to the whole country. We would realize that he had been taken away from the few that he might be given back to the many."

Paradoxically, Christ had to withdraw from the world in order to be accessible to His people living in the world. As we have noted, when He said to Mary, "Touch Me not" (John 20:17), he added the strangest of all reasons for the prohibition, "For I am not yet ascended to My Father." That is so completely contrary to what one might have expected Him to say in the circumstances. Would it not have been natural for Him to tell Mary not to miss her last chance of clasping Him? "Touch Me *now*" rather than "Touch Me *not*" is what we might have anticipated Him saying. But no. He does not. He says: "Touch Me not, for I am not yet ascended": in other words, "After I have ascended, I shall be far more available than I now am. My departure will only serve to escalate My accessibility. My withdrawal from your hands will but bring Me closer to your hearts." To quote Bishop Jackson again: "As God the Living Christ is everywhere: as resurrected Man, He can be anywhere." "He departed from our eyes," comments the great Augustine, "that we should return to our hearts and find Him there. He would not tarry long with us, yet did He never leave us." "Though Christ, as He is God is in all places at once," observes Thomas Watson, "yet as Man He is not. When He was on earth, His manhood was not in heaven; now His manhood is not on earth, though His Godhead be." "When He had finished that which He came to do," writes W. Russell Maltby, "and had shown Himself so that we knew Him, it was expedient for us that He should go back out of the Here into the Everywhere, out of some men's sight that He might be near to all men's hearts."

Just think what a spectacular ascent Christ could have effected and what a correspondingly electrifying impression He could have produced in the people of His time if He had leapt up to the skies from a pinnacle of the Temple in full view of the assembled populace of Jerusalem, or if He had gone back to Calvary, climbed up on to His empty Cross and, before the astonished gaze of thousands of spectators, mounted to heaven. He didn't. No. He went out, out from the bustling, busy capital to the comparative quiet of Olivet and, so far as we know, the only witnesses of His Ascension were the eleven disciples. "God raised Him up the third day," cried Peter, "and showed Him openly; not to all the people, but unto witnesses chosen before of God, even to us, who did eat and drink with Him after He rose from the dead" (Acts 10:40,41).

Our Life of Faith Realized

Two things our Lord is reported to have said come to mind in this connection. The first was uttered when, addressing His disciples, after interpreting for them the Parable of the Sower, He declared: "Blessed are your eyes, for they see" (Matthew 13:16). The second was spoken to Thomas following our Lord's exposure of His wounds to the doubter in the Upper Room: "Because thou hast seen Me, thou hast believed: blessed are they that have not seen, and yet have believed" (John 20:29). There is a blessedness of sighted faith: there is a still greater blessedness of blind believing; and it was in order to make possible such sightless beatitude that the Redeemer withdrew His physical form from human vision. "We walk by faith, and not by sight" (2 Corinthians 5:7). For more than three years Peter had had the priceless privilege of seeing his Master in bodily presence; yet, when writing to his converts, who had not enjoyed that privilege, the apostle does not speak as if that had involved for them any grave deprivation: "Whom, having not seen, ye love; in whom, though now ye see Him not, yet believing ye rejoice with joy unspeakable and full of glory" (1 Peter 1:8). Such is the blessedness of blind believing.

PROCESSION

But more. The Ascension was also a procession. So the inspired apostle Paul depicts it: "Wherefore He saith, when He ascended up on high, He led a multitude of captives" (Ephesians 4:8 margin).

Our Lord was often at the head of a procession. Not only on Palm Sunday when, for the only time in His brief earthly life, He was accorded what we may call the "Green Carpet Treatment", did He assume such primacy. It was often His position. He was not like W.S. Gilbert's Duke of Plaza Toro in *The Gondoliers,* who "led his regiment from behind because he found it less exciting". Always He was in the van. Aptly His men were called "followers" because that was what they were. They had responded with their lives to His oft-repeated challenge: "Follow Me!" He was their Leader as well as their Lord. "He led them out" (Luke 24:50). That might well be taken as the epitome of His entire earthly ministry. He was always pioneering the path, blazing the trail, opening up fresh avenues of experience and service. And when, at last, He set His face like a flint and conducted them towards Calvary, "They were amazed; and as they followed, they were afraid" (Mark 10:32).

Beyond the Cross and the tomb He was still at the head of the procesion. "Behold, He goeth before you" (Matthew 28:7). Then, finally, He "led them out as far as to Bethany" (Luke 24:50) and there began what may be termed the Celestial Palm Sunday, as He rode into the heavenly Jerusalem not on a *colt* but on a *cloud*.

The procession did not end on earth. He did not pass alone into the heavens, but as the Head of a great company. Paul visualizes the whole Christian life under the figure of that procession: "Wherever I go, thank God," he cries, "He makes my life a constant pageant of triumph in Christ" (2 Corinthians 2:14 Moffatt). And the same apostle envisioned the Ascension as just such a sublime processional. Quoting from Psalm 68:18, he wrote: "When He ascended on high, He led a host of captives". So Moffatt. The New English Bible is even more picturesque: "He ascended into the heights with captives in His train." Arthur S. Way's translation adds yet a further graphic touch: "He went up to heaven's height; He led captive a train of vanquished foes."

The picture is a striking and arresting one. It is that of the hero's welcome accorded to a Roman conqueror on his return in triumph to the imperial city after a successful military campaign, amid a shower of flower-petals, a flourish of trumpets, the ringing of bells and the shouts of the populace. Roped behind him were the prisoners of war, not a few sullenly defiant, others pale with fear. Some have identified the captives Paul here speaks of with the "spirits in prison" (1 Peter 3:19) to whom Peter tells us Christ went and preached following the ordeal of the Cross. Further mention of them others find in Matthew 27:52,53: "The graves were opened; and many bodies of the saints which slept arose, and came out of the graves after His Resurrection." Our Lord did not ascend alone. He led a great procession.

Just as when a British Coronation Service is being televised, the outside cameras cover the glittering procession as it passes in pomp through the peopled streets of London; and then, when it vanishes through the great doors of Westminster Abbey, the inside cameras begin to take over and the internal colourful coverage proceeds. So in the Scriptural account of the Ascension of Christ. Luke, the evangelist, pictures our Lord leading His disciples out of the eastern gate of the Holy City, down into the Valley of the Kedron and then up the slanting slope of the Mount of Olives on the other side. He portrays the ascent of the Saviour as He is slowly elevated to the skies and a cloud conceals Him from their view. Then the apostle Paul comes in. He shows what happens on the farther side of the cloud: "He ascended up above all heavens, that He might fill all things" (Eph 4:10).

See, the Conqueror mounts in triumph!
See the King in royal state,
Riding in the clouds His chariot,
To His heavenly palace gate.

Nor was the ascent without militant opposition. Infernal forces in heavenly places sought to bar the Conqueror's way. Paul mentions them in Ephesians 6:12: "We wrestle not against flesh and blood, but against principalities, against powers, against the rulers of the darkness of this world, against spiritual wickedness in heavenly places." But the mighty ascending Lord was more than a match for all His adversaries. "Having spoiled principalities and powers, He made a show of them openly, triumphing over them" (Colossians 2:15). And then there arose a great cry: "Lift up your heads, O ye gates; and be ye lift up, ye everlasting doors, and the King of Glory shall come in" (Psalms 24:7–9).

ACCESSION

The secession and procession were succeeded by an accession. One scholar has said that Psalm 110:1: "The Lord said unto My Lord, Sit Thou at My right hand" is the passage in the Old Testament most frequently quoted in the New. He professes to have traced in the Christian Scriptures between twenty and thirty references to it, direct or indirect. Certain it is that the New Testament reports three persons on earth as actually having seen Christ at the right hand of God – Stephen at his martyrdom, Saul on the Road to Damascus and John on the Isle of Patmos.

"On the right hand of God." What does the phrase really mean? We are sometimes prone to construe it crudely. "As a boy," confesses C.S. Lewis, "I used to think of God as a sort of Old Man seated upon a carved chair, and by His side there was a younger Man who was His Son." That is the sort of image the language of Scripture in relation to Christ's exaltation may evoke in immature minds. Not long ago I heard of a small boy who, when asked what God was doing in heaven, replied brightly that He was sitting on a throne, swaying a sceptre with His left hand. And when inquiry was made as to why the Almighty was supposed to be lefthanded, the lad answered that that was plain enough since the Bible says that Jesus is seated on His right hand! Definitely, we are not to think of Christ's accession in that sort of crude anthropomorphic way!

How, then, *are* we to think of it? A quotation from the Old Testament may serve to make things clear: "Bathsheba therefore went unto King Solomon to speak unto him for Adonijah. And the king rose up to meet her, and bowed himself unto her, and sat down on his throne, and caused a seat to be set for the king's mother; and she sat on his right hand" (1 Kings 2:19). Two further such references may also assist: "At Thy right hand there are pleasures for evermore" (Psalm 16:11). "Let Thy hand be upon the Man of Thy right hand, upon the Man whom Thou mad'st strong for Thyself" (Psalm 80:17). James Dodd in fact goes the length of declaring: "Christianity *is* Christ Himself sitting at the right hand of God." Jesus is, if one may say so without irreverence, God's Right Hand Man.

What precise rôles does He play as He occupies this highly-exalted position?

It is possible to discern in the Word of God six such august functions: He is (1) *Victor;* (2) *Ruler;* (3) *Intercessor;* (4) *Donor;* (5) *Preparer;* (6) *Precursor.*

Take them briefly in that order.

Victor

Several Biblical passages make it plain that our Lord sits at God's right hand as Victor, or in order to be Victor. Consider the following catena of cognate verses: "I saw in the night visions; and, behold, one like the Son of Man came with the clouds of heaven, and came to the Ancient of Days; and they brought Him near before Him. And there was given Him dominion and glory, and a kingdom, that all people, nations and languages should serve Him. His dominion is an everlasting dominion, which shall not pass away; and His kingdom that which shall not be destroyed" (Daniel 7:13,14). "He raised Him from the dead, and set Him at His own right hand in the heavenly places, far above all principality and power, and might, and dominion, and every name that is named, not only in this world but also in that which is to come" (Ephesians 1:20,21). "Wherefore God also hath highly exalted Him, and given Him a name which is above every name; that at the name of Jesus every knee should bow, of things in heaven, and things in earth, and things under the earth; and that every tongue confess that Jesus Christ is Lord to the glory of God the Father" (Philippians 2:9–11). "He is exalted to be a Prince" (Revelation 1:5). "I overcame and sat down with My Father in His throne" (Revelation 3:21).

Sometimes our Lord's session at the right hand of God is spoken of in Scripture not so much as the spoil of victory as the place from which victory is to be achieved: "The Lord said unto My Lord, Sit Thou at My right hand until I make Thine enemies thy footstool" (Psalm 110:1). "He must reign till He hath put all enemies under His feet" (1 Corinthians 15:25). In whatever way it is represented, however, it always denotes a position of favour, honour, victory, dominion. "I will make Him, My Firstborn, higher than the kings of the earth" (Psalm 89:27).

Jesus is Victor. This is the first great truth implied by the fact that He is at the right hand of the Majesty on High.

Ruler

"Ascension Day," as Maurice C. Burrell has remarked, "is primarily the Festival of Christ the King." He is Ruler as well as Victor, King as well as Conqueror; Monarch as well as Warrior.

Three times during His earthly life our Lord was offered a crown. The first was proferred by the Devil. Matthew records that, during the Temptation in the Wilderness, Satan took Jesus to the top of a high mountain and showed Him in panoramic vision all the kingdoms of the world and the glory of them. "All these things will I give Thee," cried the Tempter, "if Thou wilt fall down and worship me" (4:9). The second crown was offered to Christ by the people. "Jesus perceived that they would come, and take Him by force, to make Him a King" (John 6:15). The third crown was offered to Jesus by God. It is noteworthy that the First Gospel begins with a statement that Christ is King. It opens with the inquiry of the Wise Men: "Where is He that is born King?" (2:2). And it closes with the same assertion of His sovereignty inscribed on the placard affixed to the Cross above the head of the Crucified: "This is Jesus the King" (22:37).

Not everyone now acknowledges the sovereignty of Jesus. "We see not yet all things put under Him" (Hebrews 2:8). To His own, however, He is King of kings and Lord of lords. "We see Jesus crowned" (Hebrews 2:9). Soviets do not accept the sovereignty of Queen Elizabeth II, though her loyal subjects do; and just as the penitent thief on Golgotha recognized the Kingship of Christ ("Lord, remember me when Thou comest into Thy kingdom", Luke 23:42), while Pilate just as obviously did not ("Art Thou a King, then?" John 18:37), so Christians everywhere bow to the authority of the Lord Jesus while nonChristians completely disregard it. But a time is coming, as we shall see, when the whole world will submit to His royal sway.

Intercessor

This, according to the New Testament, would seem to be the main aspect and activity of His heavenly ministry. Not only is the sceptre His, the censer is His also. He is God's Attorney", our "Spokesman at the throne of God", our Advocate, Mediator, Daysman. To this the Christian Scriptures repeatedly testify. "It is Christ that died, yea, rather, that is risen again: who is even at the right hand of God, who also maketh intercession for us" (Romans 8:34). "Having then a great High Priest, who hath passed through the heavens, let us hold fast our confession" (Hebrews 4:14). "Christ entered not into a Holy Place made with hands, like in pattern to the true; but into heaven itself, now to appear before the face of God for us" (Hebrews 9:24). "Wherefore also He is able to save to the uttermost them that draw near to God through Him, seeing He ever liveth to make intercession for them" (Hebrews 7:25).

For us He wears the mitre,
For us His robes are whiter
Than heaven's unsullied light.

F.B. Meyer somewhere paints a vivid verbal miniature of the scene on the Mount of the Ascension. He portrays the little company of disciples standing on the crest of Olivet, our Lord in the midst of them, His hands uplifted in blessing; next the slow ascent and envelopment in the concealing cloud; and then, with an exquisite imaginative touch, He likens it to the passing of the Hebrew high priest into the Holy of Holies and the closure of the curtain behind him.

Our Saviour was always a Man of prayer. One of the wonders of His earthly life was that so often, although He was incarnate omnipotence, He betook Himself to the practice of intercession.

> *When the cold mountains and the midnight air*
> *Witnessed the holy fervour of His prayer.*

He prayed in the fields; He prayed on the hills; He prayed in a garden; He prayed in the streets; He prayed in houses; He prayed in the Temple, and now He prays at the right hand of God. S.D. Gordon has some weighty words on the subject: "The Lord Jesus is still praying. Thirty years of living; three years of serving; one tremendous act of dying – nineteen hundred years of praying! What an emphasis on prayer!" "He ever liveth to make intercession," says the writer to the Hebrews (7:25). Prayer is the very pulse of His heavenly life.

And now think what all this means in the lives of His followers. "Our hope does not rest on a dead Christ," writes H.B. Swete, "but on One who is alive for evermore. Nor, again, on a Christ who merely lives, but on One who lives and reigns with God; nor, once more, simply on the fact of His exaltation, but on the knowledge that this exalted Person uses to lay our case before God."

It is a great preventive of sin to realize that Christ is continually praying for us. As Arthur Skevington Wood finely says: "In the days of His flesh, He prayed for Peter that his faith might not fail. Now in His ascended state, He prays for every Peter, weak and apt to stray." Martin Luther found that to be true. "In deep spiritual temptations," he confessed, "nothing has helped me better than that Christ, the true, eternal Son of God is 'bone of our bones, and flesh of our flesh'; and that He sits on the right hand of God, and pleads for us."

Always the Christian lives between the Accuser and the Advocate. Revelation 12:10 calls the Devil the "Accuser of our brethren, which accused them before God day and night." And in 1 John 2:1 we read: "If any man sin, we have an Advocate with the Father, Jesus Christ the righteous." The former is perpetually indicting us: the latter is constantly acquitting us. If we listen to the one, we shall be plunged into the abyss of self-disgust and moral despair: if we hearken to the other, we shall rejoice at the freeness, the fulness and the foreverness of the forgiveness of God.

There is a memorable passage among the published writings of Robert Murray McCheyne which here rises into recollection. This is it: "If I could hear Jesus pleading for me in the next room, I should not fear a host of enemies: but distance makes no difference. He *is* pleading for me."

Further, it is a great restorative to any Christian lamenting a lapse into sin. You may remember in this context a comforting couplet from John Keble's *Christian Year:*

> *What! fallen again? Yet cheerful rise.*
> *Thine Intercessor never dies.*

Yet again it is heartening to recall this continuous high priestly ministry of Jesus against the background of the folly and faultiness of many of our prayers. John Burr uses in this connection a beautiful illustration. "The exalted Christ," he says, "plays the part of a mother of a child desirous of presenting his father with a bouquet. The child gathers an armful of flowers and weeds, all mixed together. The mother selects, arranges and binds the flowers, rejects the weeds, and so makes the gift fair and acceptable. So does Christ, the Intercessor, sort out our prayers and praises, and present them acceptably to His Father."

A striking type of the heavenly ministry of the ascended Christ is afforded by the Old Testament story of how Aaron and Hur held up the hands of Moses in Rephidim during a battle between Israel and Amalek, as recorded in

Exodus 17:8–16. William Cowper has poetically paraphrased it in these familiar lines:

> *While Moses stood with arms spread wide*
> *Success was found on Israel's side:*
> *But when through weariness they failed,*
> *That moment Amalek prevailed.*

In our celestial Moses there is no wilting weakness. He is never either faint or weary: His bow abides in strength.

Donor

Once again, He is Donor. This comes out clearly in several texts: "Thou hast ascended on high, Thou hast led captivity captive: Thou hast received gifts for men" (Psalm 68:18). "This Jesus hath God raised up, whereof we all are witnesses. Therefore being by the right hand of God exalted, and having received of the Father the promise of the Holy Ghost, He hath shed forth this which ye now see and hear" (Acts 2:32,33). "When He ascended up on high, He led captivity captive, and gave gifts unto men" (Ephesians 4:8).

This is an allusion to a custom which obtained in Roman times. When a conquering hero, having returned from the wars, swept in his chariot along the thronged thoroughfares of the Imperial City, he flung out largesse to the people lining the streets, freshly-minted coins which had been specially struck to celebrate the occasion.

So, says the apostle, the Lord Jesus from His seat of eternal power has dispensed to His Church the gift of the Holy Spirit and the gifts of holy offices for its inspiration and instruction in the persons of apostles, prophets, evangelists, pastors and teachers.

"Our God is a giving God," says David Taylor Rennie, "God the Father gave the Son, God the Son gave the Spirit, and God the Spirit gives gifts to men." He is the Divine Donor.

Preparer

In the consciousness of Christ Himself one of the principal reasons for His ascension to heaven was that He might prepare a place for His people. "I go," He said, "to prepare a place for you" (John 14:2). It is touching to reflect that He who had no place to lay His head (Matthew 8:20) has gone to prepare a place for all His own (John 14:2). There would have been no accommodation for us in Paradise unless our Lord had ascended to make it ready for us. "Heaven," as the wellknown aphorism has it, "is a prepared place for a prepared people," and Frances Ridley Havergal maintained that all the ministries of the Christian Church are designed to prepare us for what Christ has prepared for us in the world to come.

When we enter this life – weak, vulnerable, helpless, utterly unable to fend for ourselves – we find that preparations have been made for our arrival. We are the product of our parents' love; they make a home for us; they protect, provide, plan for and please us in every way they can. Like the birds, we have a nest awaiting us, where we are warmed and fed and reared to adulthood. Everything is done that can be done for our well-being, education, culture, development.

If that be the case in this fallen world, how much more marvellous must be the preparation being made for us in heaven! With a word, Christ spoke the worlds from nought in a split second: He has been nearly two thousand years getting Paradise ready for us. What a place that must be! "Eye hath not seen, nor ear heard, neither have entered into the heart of man, the things which God hath prepared for them that love Him" (1 Corinthians 2:9). He is the Preparer.

Precursor

Finally, He is Precursor. What is a precursor? According to the dictionary, he is a forerunner; and that is precisely the term which the New Testament applies to this climactic ministry of our ascended Lord. "The hope set before us we have as an anchor of the soul, both sure and stedfast, and which entereth into that within the veil, whither the Forerunner is for us entered, even Jesus, made an high priest for ever after the order of Melchisedec" (Hebrews 6:18–20). That word *prodromos*, meaning an advance runner, is employed nowhere else in the Christian Scriptures. It paints an appealing picture of our Lord, as a sort of celestial Outrider, "bringing many sons to Glory" (Hebrews 2:10), and reminds us of a petition in our Saviour's great high-priestly prayer: "Father, I will that they also, whom Thou hast given Me, be with Me where I am" (John 17:24). As Henry Wadsworth Longfellow has it in *The Golden Legend:*

When Christ ascended
Triumphantly, from star to star
He left the gates of heaven ajar.

No! Not just ajar – wide open! "When Thou hadst overcome the sharpness of death, Thou didst open the kingdom of heaven *to all believers.*"

It has been comfortingly pointed out that, whatever the future holds for us – whether death or Rapture, clods or clouds – we can be sure that the Lord Jesus has trodden the way before us. He has died and He has ascended.

Among the astronomers of France few are as famous as M. Leverrier, discoverer of the planet Neptune. Born in 1811 at St Lo in Normandy he became well-known throughout the world in 1846 after having issued an astronomical paper in which he inferred the existence of Neptune from aberrations in the orbital behaviour of the planet Uranus. Once he was present in a large assembly of brilliant people, and every-one was eager to pay him respects. The Bishop of Coutances offered him a graceful compliment. "Sir," he remarked, "it cannot be said of you what is said of many others, that you have raised yourself to the clouds. Of you it may be said that you have raised yourself to the stars." "That is not sufficient," replied Leverrier. "I mean to ascend still higher." All listened with rapt attention expecting to hear of some exciting new astronomical discovery. "Yes," went on Leverrier, "I mean to rise higher than the stars. I mean to ascend to heaven itself, and I hope you will help me with your prayers."

Not only was there an Ascension in the life of Christ: there is to be an ascension in the life of every true believer. "We shall be caught up together in the clouds, to meet the Lord in the air: and so shall we ever be with the Lord" (1 Thessalonians 4:17). Of that more anon.

But we need not wait till the final trumpet blows for our elevation to the heavenly places. Spiritually, we are there *now.*

Soar we now *where Christ hath led,*
Following our exalted Head:
Made like Him, like Him we rise;
Ours the Cross, the grave, the skies.

9
THE LIVELY ORACLES

The Christian Doctrine of the Word of God

Our fathers received the lively oracles to give unto us.

Acts 7:38

Unto (the Jews) were committed the oracles of God.

Romans 3:2

Ye have need that one teach you again which be the first principles of the oracles of God.

Hebrews 5:12

The Spirit of the Lord spake by me, and His Word was in my tongue.

2 Samuel 23:2

All this the Lord made me understand in writing.

1 Chronicles 28:19

I have esteemed the words of His mouth more than my necessary food.

Job 23:12

For ever, O Lord, Thy Word is settled in heaven.

Psalm 119:89

Thy Word is true from the beginning: and every one of Thy righteous judgments endureth for ever.

Psalm 119:160

Every Word of God is pure.

Proverbs 30:1

The Word of our God shall stand for ever.

Isaiah 40:8

I will show thee that which is noted in the Scripture of truth.

Daniel 10:21

The Word of God Most High is the fountain of wisdom, and His words are everlasting commandments.

Ecclesiasticus 1:5

Heaven and earth shall pass away, but My Word shall not pass away.

Matthew 24:35

Man shall not live by bread alone, but by every Word of God.

Luke 4:4

The Scripture cannot be broken.

John 10:35

All Scripture is given by inspiration of God, and is profitable for doctrine, for reproof, for correction, for instruction in righteousness.

2 Timothy 3:16

Prophecy came not in old time by the will of man: but holy men of God spake as they were moved by the Holy Ghost.

2 Peter 1:21

My ground is the Bible. Yes, I am a Bible bigot: I follow it in all things, great and small: I receive the written Word as the whole and the sole rule of my faith.

John Wesley

The Bible is always a new Book. There is not a stale page in the Word of God. It is just as fresh as though the ink were not yet dry.

Charles Haddon Spurgeon

The Word of God is in the Bible as the soul is in the body.

Peter Taylor Forsyth

Do not believe what I say simply because I say it, unless you find the proof of it in the Holy Scriptures.

Cyril of Jerusalem

The Bible contains many truths as yet undiscovered.

Joseph Butler

The Lord hath yet more light and truth to shed forth out of His holy Word.

John Robinson

Each part of the Scripture should be read with the help of the same Holy Spirit with which it was written.

Thomas a Kempis

"LIVELY ORACLES!" The word "oracle" is capable of various connotations. The ancient Hebrews referred to their Temple as "the oracle". In his poem entitled "The Island" Lord Byron described conscience as "the oracle" while in the field of television a giant computer is so named, and viewers are encouraged to "Page the Oracle".

The oracles spoken of by Stephen as he took his stand before the Sanhedrim reported in Acts 7 occupy a unique category. They are, as the apostle Paul declared, "the oracles of God" (Romans 3:2), and they may fitly serve as frontispiece to this study of the Christian Doctrine of the Word of God. In the interests of clarity and comprehension it will be advisable to divide the subject into seven main sections, each with its own heading thus: (1) *the Author*; (2) *the writers*; (3) *the Book*; (4) *the translators*; (5) *the interpreters*; (6) *the message*; (7) *the readers*.

Take them each in turn.

THE AUTHOR

The most important thing about any book is its author – not its title, its topic, its calf binding, its gilt lettering, its pica type, its India paper, its glossy jacket and attractive layout, but its author. The ultimate worth of any work depends on the one who wrote it.

That generalization includes the Bible. Who is its author? Some years ago there appeared in an American magazine a satirical cartoon purporting to portray a scene at the counter of a public lending library in the twenty-first century. An applicant has just asked for a Bible. "Bible?" muses the attendant. "Bible! Never heard of it. Do you know the author's name?" In studying Holy Writ that is ever the primary and pivotal question. Whose Book is it?

To that inquiry the Bible itself supplies the answer. Here it is: "All Scripture is given by inspiration of God, and is profitable for doctrine, for reproof, for correction, for instruction in righteousness" (2 Timothy 3:16). "No prophecy of the Scripture is of any private interpretation. For the prophecy came not in old time by the will of man: but holy men of God spake as they were moved by the Holy Ghost" (2 Peter 1:21,21). "These words the Lord wrote, and delivered them unto me" (Deuteronomy 5:22). "Ye received the Word which ye heard of us, not as the word of men, but as it is in truth the Word of God" (1 Thessalonians 2:13). Yes, beyond all dubiety the Bible itself claims to be the Word of the living God, and if God is not in fact its Author, what a field-day it affords to megalomaniacs. Listen: "I, even My hands, have stretched out the heavens, and all their host have I commanded" (Isaiah 45:12). Who wrote that? Was it Isaiah or Jehovah? Certainly, God employed men as His amanuenses, but He reserves for Himself the prerogative of authorship. He does not violate or nullify the personalities of these secretaries of the Spirit; but, despite their indispensable and invaluable contribution to the sacred volume, He remains the Author.

How can this be? Let me see if I can make the point plain by means of a simple illustration. Every great dramatist – Shakespeare, Ibsen, Shaw, and so on – when he writes a play, peoples it with characters of all sorts, and on each of the characters bestows traits, responses, qualities in line with his overall purpose. The likelihood is that he will have at least one villain and possibly several other shady individuals. They are necessary to the unfolding of his plot. Naturally, the playwright will make these seedy characters of his say things and do things of which he himself would not approve. But, in a well-constructed drama, things never get out of hand. In spite of all that takes place in the play of which the dramatist would disapprove, he remains throughout the author of the play.

So with God and the Bible. In its pages we hear the voices of Satan, the demons, Judas, Caiaphas, Pilate, and a multiplicity of persons of all moral sorts and conditions. But things never get out of hand. God is in charge throughout. As the Psalmist puts it: "Surely the wrath of man shall praise Thee: the remainder of wrath shalt Thou restrain" (Psalm 76:10). Someone has estimated that the phrase "Thus saith the Lord" occurs over two thousand times in the Bible. Surely a contribution of such magnitude entitles the Divine Being to be regarded as the Author of the volume. In the words of Daniel J. Boorstin: "God is the Celebrity-Author of the world's best-seller."

THE WRITERS

Nevertheless, although the author of the Bible is God, it was men who actually wrote it. Scripture does in fact record three occasions on which God wrote with His own hand – on Sinai, on the wall of Belshazzar's palace in Babylon and on the sand of the Temple court in Jerusalem – but it nowhere claims that God personally wrote the Bible Himself.

William C. Procter has packed this truth into a neat epigram. "In the Bible," he says, "we have God's authorship and man's penmanship." That puts the point well.

The Scriptures were written over a period of some one thousand five hundred years by about forty penmen and yet, although of such a composite character, the Book displays an amazing basic and essential unity. The most wonderful thing about the written Word is that, threaded through it from beginning to end, as in a golden tapestry, the living Word can be seen. During that historic walk to Emmaus Luke tells us of the Risen Christ: "Beginning at Moses (He could go no further back in the Bible than that!) and all the prophets, He expounded to the two disciples the things concerning Himself" (24:27). Christ in all the Scriptures! There you have the ultimate mystery of the Bible.

It is as if to a great book contributions were to be made by Francis Bacon, William Shakespeare, King James I and VI and John Donne in the sixteenth century; by John Bunyan, John Locke, John Milton, Isaac Newton, Jeremy Taylor, Robert Walpole, Isaac Watts, George Fox, Oliver Cromwell and Richard Baxter in the seventeenth century; by Jeremy Bentham, Edmund Burke, Edward Gibbon, Samuel Johnson, Immanuel Kant, William Pitt, George Washington, John Wesley, George Whitefield, Howell Harris, William Wilberforce, William Wordsworth and

William Pitt in the eighteenth century; by Benjamin Disraeli, John Bright, Robert Peel, Richard Cobden, William Ewart Gladstone, John Richard Green, Abraham Lincoln, David Livingstone, Thomas Babington Macaulay, Charles Haddon Spurgeon, William Booth, Alfred Tennyson, Henry Ward Beecher and Henry Parry Liddon in the nineteenth century – and the book turned out to be at last a complete biography of Winston Spencer Churchill!

One of the saddest passages in the New Testament occurs in John 5 where our Lord laments: "Ye search the Scriptures; for in them ye think ye have eternal life: and they are they which testify of Me. And ye will not come unto Me that ye might have life" (vv.39,40). Between them and Christ there was a Paper Curtain. They had found the Book, but they had not found the Man behind the Book. That is why they were bewildered, perplexed, mystified by it. The Man was in the Book. "You can no more take Christ out of the Bible," wrote Horace Bushnell, "then you can take the watermark out of a sheet of paper." But they could not find Him, and so could not make sense of life. For history is, as A.T. Pierson said, His story, or it is sheer mystery.

THE BOOK

Nearly every brand of religion is based on a book. Whether ancient or modern, mystical or historical, ceremonial or ethical, it is almost certain to be founded on some allegedly sacred volume. From the *Vedas* of Hinduism to the *Book of Mormon;* from the *Koran* of Islam to the *Science and Health* of Christian Science; from the *Zend Avesta* of Parseeism to *Das Kapital*, which has been called "the Red Bible of Communism", there are many illustrations of this fact. Nearly every brand of religion is based on a book.

That is supremely true of the Christian religion. It, too, is based on a Book, a Holy Book, and the name of that Book is the "Bible". "The word 'Bible' ", someone has written, "came from the town of Byblos on the coast of Lebanon, where papyrus was produced for the writers of the ancient world. The papyrus scrolls acquired the name of *biblia* or books from association with the town from which they came, much as china or porcelain took its name from the country in which it was first made. The extensive copying of the Hebrew and Christian Scriptures tended to connect the word *biblia* with that particular collection of documents and so gave the name 'Bible' to the whole."

It is worth noting that the Bible has a number of names for itself – "the Law and the prophets" (Isaiah 8:20); "the Scripture of truth" (Daniel 10:35); "the Word of God" (1 Thessalonians 2:13); "the Holy Scriptures" (2 Timothy 3:15), and so on.

There is, however, one title, thrice-repeated in the New Testament, which we have taken as heading of this chapter. It is "oracle". The term is derived from the Latin *oraculum*, signifying "a message from a god". In the original Greek the word is *logion*, an expression patently allied to *logos*, and therefore peculiarly and particularly suitable as a designation of the Divine documents.

We have seen that, while God is the Author of the Bible, He chose to collaborate in its production with some forty penmen. This raises the complex question of inspiration and as to how precisely it operated. "In the Christian view of the Bible," observes J.K. Mozley, "it is finally true that it is the Word of God just as it is finally true about Christ that He is the Word of God." And it is almost as difficult in the matter of the inspiration of the Bible as in that of the Incarnation of our Lord to draw a true differential between the Divine and the human.

There are various views. One is that of *natural inspiration*. This holds, as do the Unitarians, that the Bible is inspired in just the same way as any work of genius is inspired. It is on a par with Dante's *Divine Comedy*, Milton's *Paradise Lost* and Bunyan's *Pilgrim's Progress*.

Another is *partial inspiration*. This argues that the Bible is not a scientific textbook and so is not to be trusted in relation to such matters as the birth of the universe, the origin of the species and the possible destiny of this planet. It contains a number of errors and inaccuracies of the sort one would expect to find in such an ancient, composite volume, but it is divinely inspired and therefore inerrant in matters relating to the redemptive purpose of God for mankind – so-called "Salvation History". The third view is that of *dictational inspiration*. This is the theory that God actually dictated the entire Bible to its writers verbatim, as a modern businessman dictates a letter to his secretary, the secretary contributing nothing to the message but merely communicating it. According to this view, the Biblical writers were in the process of transmission and presentation, as one author strikingly put it, "as passive as a pen". The fourth view is that of *verbal inspiration*. Many pious people claim to adhere to this theory without really thinking what they are saying. To maintain that the Bible is not only the Word of God but the very words of God is to overlook the fact that the Scriptures are a veritable whispering gallery of voices. In its pages we hear the accents of the Devil, demons, Judas, Caiaphas, Pilate and many more whose sentiments are not such as one could possibly associate with God. Whatever the doctrine of the plenary inspiration of Holy Scripture may mean, it cannot conceivably mean that. The fifth and final view is that of *supervisal inspiration*. This teaches, in short, that nothing is included in the Bible but what God willed to be there and that nothing is omitted from the Bible which God meant to find a place within the Sacred Book.

Let this be the criterion. Test the other theories against it. *Natural inspiration* is ruled out, for one has only to compare the greatest works of human genius with the Bible to discover that there is a categorical difference between them. But *supervisal inspiration* does leave room for *dictational inspiration*. We are expressly told in the Word of God itself that large parts of the Bible were directly and personally dictated by God to His amanuenses. The Ten Commandments are, of course, the classic instance, but there is much more of such direct Divine dictation in the Holy Scriptures. "God," as a modern writer has said, "is a great believer in putting things down." He certainly is; and the Bible records not a few occasions when He has bidden His servants do the same. "The Lord said unto Moses, Write this for a memorial in a book" (Exodus 17:14). "Samuel wrote a book and laid it up before the Lord" (1 Samuel 10:25). "Thus speaketh the Lord God of Israel, saying, Write thee all the words that I have spoken unto thee in a book" (Jeremiah 30:2). "What thou seest write in a book" (Revelation 1:11). As Augustine says: "Christ's members gave out the knowledge which they had received through the dictation of the Head; whatever He willed us to read concerning His own words and acts, He bade them write, as though they were His own very words." Where such passages are concerned, it goes without saying that they are infallible, inerrant, and absolutely authoritative insofar as they correspond exactly with the original autographs.

With regard to *partial inspiration,* supervisal inspiration ensures that the original writers and subsequent translators were divinely safeguarded against error in the discharge of the tasks which were respectively laid upon them in relation to the Holy Scriptures – making certain that what the Lord dictated was accurately recorded and also the literary assignments given them inerrantly carried out. This involved three things: *reporting; researching;* and, as we have already remarked, *receiving.*

First, *reporting.* Some of the sacred penmen are reporters. "This is the disciple which testifieth these things: and we know that his testimony is true" (John 21:25). "That which we have heard, which we have seen with our eyes, which we have looked upon and our hands have handled, that which we have seen and heard, declare we unto you" (1

John 1:1,3). That is the first strand in the rope of Holy Scripture as it fell to the lot of its human writers – firsthand reporting.

What does supervisal inspiration mean here? It means that the biblical writers were, for the purpose of composition, as was Mary in the Incarnation, divinely indemnified against errors of observation, lapses of memory and unintentional misrepresentation of facts. What they wrote was honest, adequate, accurate reporting.

Next, *research*. Supervisal inspiration, although the paramount factor in the making of the Bible, did not exempt its human contributors from the labour of exact and exhaustive investigation. On the contrary, it inescapably involved them in such literary and historical research. As Luke records in the prologue to his Gospel: "Forasmuch as many have taken in hand to set forth in order a declaration of those things which are most surely believed among us, even as they delivered them unto us, which from the beginning were eye-witnesses and ministers of the Word; it seemed good to me also, having had perfect understanding of all things from the very first, to write unto thee in order, most excellent Theophilus, that thou mayest know the certainty of those things, wherein thou hast been instructed" (1:1–4). Further, there is an account given in Galatians 1 of how Paul *historied* Peter (as the original has it), spent a fortnight with him and during that time elicited from him as much information as possible about the beginnings and meanings of the faith. "I went into Arabia, and returned again unto Damascus. Then after three years I went up to Jerusalem to see Peter, and abode with him fifteen days" (1:17,18). See also 1 Kings 11:41; 14:29; 1 Chronicles 29:29. Mark is said to have sought information at the same source and Luke to have similarly interrogated Mary the mother of Jesus.

What does supervisal inspiration mean here? It means that God led the minds and hearts of the sacred penmen to the right sources, enabled them to extract from them the requisite data and protected them from exposure to error, fraud, deceit, imposture.

Beyond these elements of reporting and researching there was, as we have noted, an element of *receiving*. In this connection there was no need for supervisal inspiration to operate, as every word they took down was divinely dictated. The Bible tells us that the words were inspired so far as the divinely dictated portions are concerned and that the writers were inspired as they set them down. About this there is a division of opinion. "The claim to inspiration is not made for the writers," says William C. Procter, "but for the writings." "The Scriptures teach that persons are inspired, not parchments," declares Alexander Clark, "and that the writers are agents not automata." But surely both are true. "Holy men of God spake as they were moved by the Holy Ghost" (2 Peter 1:21). "The letter killeth, but the Spirit giveth life" (2 Corinthians 3:6). It is not a case of Either–Or. Both men and message were and are inspired.

Yet although, as in the mystery of the Incarnation, God linked Himself to humanity, so in the mystery of the inspiration of Holy Scripture God made use of human channels, yet He never surrendered His Divine authorship or permitted the Book to become the word of man rather than the Word of God.

H.O. Mackey has a memorable illustration which brings this truth out admirably. "Who built St Paul's Cathedral?" he asks dramatically, and then he replies to his own question: "So many masons, carpenters, iron-workers, carvers, painters – and then there was Wren. Yes, there was Sir Christopher Wren. He was not a mason, nor a carpenter, nor an iron-worker. He never laid a single stone, drove a nail, or forged a railing. What did he do? *He did it all*! He planned the splendid edifice, inspired with his thought and purpose all their toil, and wrought through every worker. They were his 'hands', and people today flock in their thousands from all over the world to see Sir Christopher Wren's masterpiece."

Who wrote the Bible? Moses, David, Isaiah, Jeremiah, Peter, John, Paul? Yes, but it is God's Book. He merely used them as instruments of His inspirational purpose. All Scripture is given by inspiration of God, and is profitable for doctrine, for reproof, for correction, for instruction in righteousness; that the man of God may be perfect, throughly furnished unto all good works" (2 Timothy 3:16,17). "Prophecy came not in old time by the will of man: but holy men of God spake as they were moved by the Holy Ghost" (2 Peter 1:21). "Ye received the Word of God, not as the word of men, but as it is in truth the Word of God, which effectually worketh also in you that believe" (1 Thessalonians 2:13). "If any man think himself to be a prophet, or spiritual, let him acknowledge that the things that I write unto you are the commandments of the Lord" (1 Corinthians 14:37). "I certify you, brethren, that the Gospel which was preached of me is not after man, for I neither received it of man, neither was I taught it, but by the revelation of Jesus Christ" (Galatians 1:11,12).

So much for the inspiration of the Book.

Turn now to its *formation*. From a consideration of the *breath* of Holy Scripture, we proceed, logically enough, to think of the *body* of Holy Scripture.

It has been percipiently said that, just as, in order to make a proper survey of this planet, one must first take a total view of it from outer space, recognizing that it is a sphere and then proceeding to observe that it is divided into two hemispheres: just so in any workmanlike examination of the Word of God, one must begin by seeing it as a whole, and then go on to notice that it is comprised of two main sections – the Old Testament and the New.

Here it should be mentioned that the Bible is made up of sixty-six books – thirty-seven in the Old Testament and twenty-nine in the New; the Authorized Version contains one thousand one hundred and eighty-nine chapters; thirty-one thousand one hundred and seventy-three verses; seven hundred and seventy-three thousand, seven hundred and forty-six words. What a Book! How does it happen to have the proportions we see it to possess today? Patently, alike in Judaism and in Christianity, there must have been across the centuries a vast amount of religious writing, good, bad and indifferent, some spurious, some genuine. What makes the items which comprise this particular collection so special? By what means were they singled out for inclusion in the sacred volume? In other words, how did they come to compose what we call the "canon" of Scripture?

The term "canon" is almost a direct transcription of the Greek *kanon*, meaning a "reed" or "rod" which served as an instrument of measurement.

In the case of the Old Testament no one knows precisely when the canon was closed. All that is known for certain is that the collection, as it now stands, had been finalized before 200 B.C., when the Septuagint, the first complete Greek version of the Hebrew Scriptures, is fabled to have been produced by seventy, or rather seventy-two, scholars at Alexandria in as many days. You are probably familiar with the shorthand of the title consisting of Roman capital numerals – LXX.

A number of doubtful documents labelled the "Apocrypha" – by no means equal in excellence – were excluded by the compilers of the Hebrew Scriptures. They consist of 1 and 2 Esdras, Tobit, Judith, parts of Esther, Wisdom of Solomon, Ecclesiasticus, Baruch, Song of the Three Holy Children, History of Susanna, Bel and the Dragon, the Prayer of Manasses, King of Judah, and 1 and 2 Maccabees. Significantly, there is not a single recorded reference by Christ or any of His apostles to one of these books.

The New Testament canon, authoritatively formulated at the Third Council of Carthage (397), was anticipated in a pastoral letter issued at Easter 365 by the famous Athanasius. Part of the encyclical read like this: "It seemed good to me to publish the books which are admitted in the canon and have been delivered unto us, and are believed to be divine: Genesis, Exodus, Leviticus, Numbers, Deuteronomy, Joshua, Judges, Ruth, 1 Samuel, 2 Samuel, 1 Kings, 2 Kings, 1 Chronicles, 2 Chronicles, Ezra, Nehemiah, Esther, Job, Psalms, Proverbs, Ecclesiastes, Song of Solomon, Isaiah, Jeremiah, Lamentations, Ezekiel, Daniel, Hosea, Joel, Amos, Obadiah, Jonah, Micah, Nahum, Habakkuk, Zephaniah, Haggai, Zechariah, Malachi. Matthew, Mark, Luke, John, Acts, Romans, 1 Corinthians, 2 Corinthians, Galatians, Ephesians, Philippians, Colossians, 1 Thessalonians, 2 Thessalonians, 1 Timothy, 2 Timothy, Titus, Philemon, Hebrews, James, 1 Peter, 2 Peter, 1 John, 2 John, 3 John, Jude, Revelation." Thirtytwo years later, the list received official conciliar ratification.

Perhaps a brief note may be placed here about three matters relevant to the making of the Bible. First, *the criteria employed in the selection of the books*; next, *the completeness achieved in that selection*; and then *the comprehensiveness exhibited in the collection*.

First, *the criteria*. Although the Church Council put its official stamp of approval on the final compilation, it must not be supposed that the hierarchy was in any way directly responsible for the collection. The books were sifted and sorted out by the people of God and so, as one has expressed it, they may almost be said to have canonized themselves! The conspectus is a product of the concensus. The works won their way into the canon by their own sheer worth.

Next, *the completeness*. The Bible itself proclaims the finality of its form and content in no uncertain terms. "Ye shall not add unto the Word which I commanded you, neither shall ye diminish ought from it" (Deuteronomy 4:2). "Add not to His words, lest He reprove thee" (Proverbs 30:6). "If any man shall add unto these things,

God shall add unto him the plagues that are written in this book: and if any man shall take away from the book of this prophecy, God shall take away his part out of the book of life" (Revelation 22:18,19). Addition and subtraction are alike prohibited under pain of dreadful penalties.

Once more, *comprehensiveness.* Is it not absolutely astounding that every doctrine of the historic, orthodox Christian faith found its fount and foundation in the Bible? The Scriptures are all-embracing in their survey and supply of spiritual truth. Nothing necessary to salvation, whether in time or eternity, is not either directly derivable or logically deducible from the Divine documents. "To the law and to the testimony! If they do not speak according to this Word, it is because they have no dawn" (Isaiah 8:20 NASB).

As to the structure of the Scriptures, the Lord Himself has set His seal to the threefold analysis of the Old Testament – legal, prophetical, poetical. "These are the words which I spake unto you, while I was yet with you, that all things must be fulfilled, which were written in the law of Moses, and in the prophets, and in the Psalms concerning Me" (Luke 24:44).

The New Testament is made up of four main divisions in accordance with the Saviour's promise of a quadrilateral ministry of the Holy Spirit – evangelical, historical, polemical and prophetical. Here are the terms of Jesus' assurances: "He shall testify of Me" (John 15:26). That is the Gospels. "He shall bring all things to your remembrance" (John 14:26). That is the Acts. "He will guide you into all truth" (John 16:13). That is the epistles. "He will show you things to come" (John 16:15). That is the Revelation. As notated in the original autographs the Hebrew Scriptures were written in unpointed script; that is, in an alphabet containing no vowels. The text was just one long line of consonants, the reader orally providing the vowels. Later at Tiberias the Massoretes, Jewish biblical scholars added the vowel points, and later still punctuation, verse divisions, paragraphing and chapter divisions were successively introduced.

The language in which the New Testament was penned was not the classical Greek of the Athenian academy, but the *koine*, or colloquial Greek, spoken in the market-place. The verbal cradle in which the Word was laid was as crude as the manger of Bethlehem. Its analogue in our own tongue is not the English of Oxford but that of Billingsgate. As General Jan Smuts reminded us: "I cannot help remembering that, if it had depended upon the intelligentsia of the day, our knowledge of Christ would have been a casual and contemptuous remark of Tacitus. A few fishermen of Galilee prevented it."

THE TRANSLATORS

According to an Italian aphorism: "Translation is treason." If that be indeed so, the Bible must have been subjected to more treachery than any other book, for it has been oftener translated than any other. Some time ago the French Academy published the findings of a group of linguistic experts, who had taken a census of the living languages of the world. The census revealed that more than 2,000 languages and dialects are in active use today. One recalls with what jubilation the British and Foreign Bible Society celebrated the completion of the thousandth translation of the Scriptures, thus investing with fresh meaning the first line of Charles Wesley's great hymn: "O, for a thousand tongues!" Recently it was announced that the Bible has been rendered into over two thousand languages and the work of translation still goes on and is indeed likely to be given a great boost in the not too distant future. Experts in the field of electronics are now working on a highly-sophisticated device, a computer, which will be able to translate instantly from one language to another.

That day is not yet, though it may not be long in coming. Meantime, modern readers of the Bible are placed under a heavy debt of gratitude to those who, rendering the text in plain and pleasant language and setting up the type in an easily readable and readily referable manner, have performed for us all an invaluable service. We have already noted how the Massoretes contributed to the readability of the ancient Hebrew documents by the introduction of vowel points. In 1250 A.D. Cardinal Hugo divided the text into chapters, for the purpose of a Latin concordance he was then compiling. Just three hundred years later – in 1551 to be precise – Sir Robert Stephen chopped the text up into verses – not always with the happiest results – during a journey by carriage from Paris to Lyons. The practice of paragraphing was first adopted in the Revised Version of 1881, since when it has been the mode of printing favoured in most of the new translations. It is the layout in practically all the modern versions.

What a plethora of such versions there is today! Here are some of them: *The Twentieth Century, Weymouth, Moffatt, Goodspeed, Phillips, Ferrar Fenton, Cutler Torrey, Amplified, New English Bible, the Jerusalem Bible, Berkeley, the Living Bible, Barclay, Way, Rieu, New American Standard Version, The New International Version, the New King James Version.* In all of these the content of the Bible is presented paragraphically, making reading a pleasure.

Nevertheless the Authorized Version continues to retain its immense popularity. With some it has become almost a fetish. For them it has grown into something of the same sort of thing as that burlesqued by Washington Gladden: "The Bible is a Book written in heaven in the English language, divided there into chapters and verses, with headlines and reference marks, printed in small pica, bound in calf, and sent down by angels in its present form." As such its format is naturally sacrosanct! To misquote it is not just an error, it is a sin. A.E. Garvie tells of "an old lady purchasing a Bible, who was asked if she wanted an Authorized Version or a Revised Version, and indignantly replied that she did not want any version, but the Bible as God gave it!" Nor is the wide popularity of the Authorized Version among the rank and file of the membership of the churches to be wondered at. You may remember Thomas Babington Macaulay's proud claim for that Bible: "It is a Book which, if everything else in our language should perish, could alone suffice to show the whole extent of its beauty and power."

Yet the new translations keep pouring through the presses! From this it may be inferred that there is a public demand for them – not so much, one suspects, for devotional reading, but for suggestive variant renderings of passages familiar in the older version and closer to the working vocabulary of today.

This extraordinary proliferation of present-day versions has been partly responsible for the phenomenal circulation of the Scriptures in our time. No fewer than fourteen million copies are distributed annually. One society alone – the American Bible Society – presented Gerald Ford, during his term of office as President of the USA, with the two thousand millionth copy to come from its Press. In March 1976 the world welcomed its four thousand millionth inhabitant. One Bible Society has, therefore, by itself produced sufficient copies of the Scriptures to supply half the world's population! It has been responsibly estimated that the average life of a book is three or four years, only one in three reaching a second edition, and only one in a thousand lasting a century. But this Book, this Divine Library, has lasted for thousands of years and has run through countless editions and is still far and away the world's best-seller. In a college with which I was once connected, which catered for continental students, there was one student, I recall, struggling with the study of English, who in morning prayers never forgot to thank God for the translators of the Bible. A fellow-feeling made her wondrous kind.

THE INTERPRETERS

Jorge Luis Borges, the distinguished Anglo-Argentinian litterateur, once made this discerning remark: "Every book which is read for the first time is a new book, for the new reader finds in it fresh meanings never before discovered." That is uniquely true of the study of the Scriptures. "The Bible is always a new Book," says R.C. Chapman whimsically, "to those well acquainted with it!"

The fact that the Bible was originally written in three languages and had to be copied by hand made scholarship absolutely essential to its production and perpetuation. The majority of simple people, innocent of any language but their own mother-tongue, when confronted by a biblical passage in Hebrew, Aramaic or Greek, are fain, when challenged by the question addressed by Philip to the Ethiopian eunuch, "Understandest thou what thou readest?" to reply: "How can I, except some man should guide me?" (Acts 8:30,31). This service the scholars of the centuries have rendered us. Not always do we remember or recognize this. We are like the old Scots Highland lady, who remarked to her minister: "I do like the writings of St Paul. He has such grand Gaelic!"

Then there are the commentators – Matther Henry, Adam Clarke, Brook Fosse Westcott, and so on – and the concordance-compilers – Cruden, Young, Strong, etc. – and the innumerable company of Christian writers and preachers. What light they shed upon the sacred page! Not long after World War II I remember being present at a great historical pageant at the Palace of Versailles near Paris. It was evening and the facade of the magnificent building was at first in darkness. Then in one room after another lights were switched on, as over loud-speakers André Maurois gave a résumé of the story of the palace and its historical associations, until at last every window was illuminated and the whole building a blaze of lights. That is the sort of thing which happens to one's knowledge and appreciation of the Bible as one studies it across the years. Commentators and expositors turn on the lights in chapter after chapter of the sacred volume and, infinitely better still, the Holy Spirit illuminates its pages. How dark the Word of God would be to us but for such enlightening ministry! Thank God for the lamps enkindled in Interpreter's House!

Unhappily, all biblical scholarship has not been of this brilliantly illuminative character. No more tragic commentary on the truth expressed in 2 Corinthians 3:6, "The letter killeth", can be found than exists in what is called Higher Criticism. We speak sometimes of the "dead letter" in this connection, but that is too negative a phrase. It is not what the Bible says. The Bible speaks of the letter that *kills*. To assume, as many seem to do, that the best way to understand the Bible, if not indeed the only way, is to investigate its historical sources and subject its text to a species of literary vivisection, is rather like trying to locate the genius of Albert Einstein by performing an autopsy upon his dead body! Some *tomes* are *tombs* – the sepulchres of their dead authors. Not so the Bible. It is living and powerful.

"The letter killeth." In his little book *A Christian in East Germany* Pastor Johannes Hamel relates how Wellhausen, the famous destructive higher critic, commenced his last public lecture before professional retirement. Entering the lecture-hall, he mounted the rostrum and held up the empty covers of his Bible. With a piercing voice, he cried: "This, gentlemen, is what I bequeath to my successor!"

Or take the second story. "A garbled remark alleged to have been made about Billy Graham in his early days plunged him into conflict," records John Pollock in his definitive biography of the great evangelist. "It had to do with his attitude to the Bible. Billy was deeply disturbed and hurt. After supper, instead of attending evening service, he retired to his log cabin and read again the Bible passages concerning its authority. He recalled hearing that the prophets used phrases such as 'The Word of the Lord came' more than two thousand times. He meditated on the attitude of Christ, who fulfilled the law and the prophets! He loved the Scriptures, quoting them constantly, and never once intimated that they might be wrong. Billy went out into the forest, and wandered up the mountain, praying as he walked 'Lord, what shall I do? What shall be the direction of my life?' He then saw what be believed to be a crisis: 'So I went back and got my Bible, and I went out in the moonlight. And I got to a stump, and put the Bible on the stump, and I knelt down, and I said, O, God, I cannot prove certain things. I cannot answer some of the questions people are raising, but I accept this Book by faith as the Word of God.' He stayed at the stump, praying wordlessly, his eyes moist. 'I had a tremendous sense of God's presence. I had a great peace that the decision I had made was right' " (London: Hodder & Stoughton, 1966, pp.80,81).

It is not hard to see which of these two modes of regarding Holy Scripture is the better. One spells abject failure: the other phenomenal success. One thing is piercingly clear – you can't use as the sword of the Spirit a volume on which you have savagely used the scissors of literary criticism. Some see the Word of God as little more than a Book of puzzles to be solved. They are paralytically preoccupied with such inquiries as: Did Adam have a navel? Where did Cain get his wife? Is the Pentateuch Mosaic or merely *a* mosaic? The credibility of Genesis and the edibility of Jonah are to them such teasing problems that they miss the beauty and comfort of Psalm 23, John 14 and 1 Corinthians 13. Truly, the letter killeth. There is about as much spiritual profit in such Bible study as in the solving of a crossword puzzle!

THE MESSAGE

Imagine a vast meadow in summer teeming with wild flowers of seemingly endless varieties. To the untrained eye it appears to contain a bewildering floral miscellany of which no proper classification could possibly be made. But the expert botanist knows better. After due investigation, he is able to divide the mass of flora into the categories to which they respectively belong.

Not otherwise is it with the Word of God. The Bible does not resemble a trim little garden-plot in which the plants are neatly classified and tabulated. It is like God's other Book – the Book of Nature – packed with a plethora of wonderful things. The expert expositor can, however, distinguish in the medley certain basic principles underlying it and revealing its fundamental integrity, consistency and harmony.

Three great words sum up the basic message of the Bible – love, law, life. Significantly, they are all discoverable in our Lord's sublime cameo of Christian truth: "For God so loved the world" – that's the love! – "that He gave His only-begotten Son, that whosoever believeth in Him should not perish" – that's the law! – "but have everlasting life" – that's the life! (John 3:16).

THE READERS

There are three ways in which the truth of the Bible is impressed upon the mind of the general reader – the witness of archaeology, the witness of prophecy and the witness of personal experience. As to the witness of archaeology, it has been officially stated by one eminent in this field that, despite the intense investigation which has been conducted in this sphere for more than a hundred years, no excavation in Bible lands has proved the Scriptures false in any particular! On the contrary, it has most remarkably confirmed its testimony and vouched for its veracity. As to the witness of biblical prophecy, we shall have occasion to deal at some length with this subject in the last chapter of the present book. Suffice it here to say that such biblical predictions as those relative to the return of the Jews to Israel, the rise of Russia as a world-power, the formation of the European Economic Community, the emergence of Ecumenism, and so on, are cogent and compelling arguments for its supernatural origin and Divine authority.

It is, however, in the realm of personal experience that conviction concerning the truth of the Bible is most powerfully brought home to us. However intellectually interested we are in Scripture as a piece of literature, we shall be like a man with lockjaw at a banquet unless we open our hearts to receive its saving message. In this connection seven crisp counsels may be given: (a) *Read it through;* (b) *Get it off;* (c) *Pray it in;* (d) *Note it down;* (e) *Hold it fast;* (f) *Work it out* and (g) *Pass it on.*

Just a word about each of these.

(a) *Read it through.* Bulky books are out of fashion. People today have neither the time nor the patience to read them. Thin paperbacks are the order of the day and there is a lot of literary slimming going on. Well, the Bible is a big Book. For this reason many readers find the thought of ploughing through it from Genesis to Revelation somewhat daunting. John Ruskin's mother had a rather ruthless and relentless method of inculcating in her son the habit of Bible-reading. "She began with the first verse of Genesis," he records, "and went through to the last verse of the Apocalypse – hard names, numbers, Levitical law, and all – and began at Genesis the next day." No doubt young Ruskin found the course off-putting. Yet there is a great deal to be said for discipline in Bible study. Just to dip into it here and there is to have at last but a truncated version composed of one's own favourite passages and missing out many parts of the Bible which are of first importance. The only way to make sure that such passages are *not* missed is to wade systematically through the Word and take in its message as a whole. Read it through. No-one can live on nibbles. I once saw an arresting poster. It bore this inscription: "Read the Bible. Free Gift Inside."

"I have heard of a young man who was left heir to his father's property," writes H.J. Wilmot-Buxton, "but, when the father died, another disputed the son's claim.

The matter came into the law-court and the young man was told that if only he could produce his father's will, his inheritance would be secure. One day he opened a Bible seeking comfort and guidance in his troubles, and from between its pages a paper fell out. It was his father's will in which the property was distinctly left to him." That sort of thing, spiritually speaking, is a regular occurrence among devout readers of the Bible. Like the Psalmist, they are able to say: "I rejoice at Thy Word, as one that findeth great spoil" (119:162).

It is the Spirit who thus illuminates the Word. "What does it matter," cried George Fox to Cromwell, "that we have the Scriptures, if we have lost the Spirit who wrote them?" "The Bible without the Spirit," said Samuel Taylor Coleridge, "is like a sun-dial by moonlight!" "In Thy light shall we see light" (Psalm 36:9).

The simplest mind can receive this divine illumination. To such a person a text can suddenly be lit up like a neon sign. But this does not exempt us from the task of search and research in the Book of God. It is significant that the term "search" is used as it is in the Bible itself with reference to the reading of the Word. "Search the Scriptures" (John 5:39). "They searched the Scriptures daily" (Acts 17:11). "The prophets have inquired and searched diligently" (1 Peter 1:10). In this context John Bengel offers some capital counsel: "Apply yourself to the whole text, and apply the whole text to yourself." One of the best guarantees of anybody's theological soundness is the material unsoundness of his Bible. "If a man's Bible is coming apart," someone has quipped, "it is a fairly good indication that he himself is well put together."

(b) *Get it off*. There is no finer way of taking firm possession of the Scriptures than by committing them to memory. Not very long ago a youth behind the Iron Curtain was discovered by the Communist authorities to be secreting a number of copies of the Bible. At once they confiscated them, stripping him of every volume he had. As they did so, he said: "Well, anyhow, you can't take away the three chapters I've learned by heart." It is one thing to have the Bible in your *hand*, it is another to have it in your *heart*, and the best method of getting it into your heart is to get it *off by heart*.

(c) *Pray it in*. The most effective type of devotional Bible study I know is adopted and advocated by D.L. Moody. Here is how he describes it: "I took the word 'love', and I do not know how many weeks I spent studying the passages in the Bible in which it occurs, till at last I could not help loving people. It just flowed out of my fingers. I got to thinking of the compassion of Christ. So I took the Bible and began to study it over to find out what it said on the subject. At last the thought of His infinite compassion overwhelmed me. I could only lie on the floor of my study with my face in the open Bible and cry like a child." Some only *pry* into the Bible: others *pray* over it. If there is any meal that merits grace before meat it is that in which we partake of the manna of the Word.

(d) *Note it down*. When Robert Chapman was told to mark his Bible, he replied: "I prefer my Bible to mark me." "Writing maketh an exact man" according to Francis Bacon, and it is not until one commences the practice of transcription that one realizes how true that is. Precision flows from the pen. "Some men," wrote Byron, "have only enough learning to misquote." There is an appalling amount of loose and inaccurate quotation of Scripture – even in public. If the Bible is indeed the Word of God, we ought to take wise care how we cite it. Note-taking helps to make one word-perfect when quoting the perfect Word.

(e) *Hold it fast*. Our grasp of anything is an unconscious indication of the sort of store we set by it. Our clutch reveals much. We tighten our grip on the things we prize most. Manifestly, in this apparently ambiguous world we have got to get a hold of something, and there is not much in it that we can hold for long. The Bible names certain realities which we can hold tenaciously. "Hold fast that which is good" (1 Thessalonians 5:21). "Hold fast the profession of your faith" (Hebrews 10:23). "Hold fast the form of sound words" (2 Timothy 1:13). And, summing it all up, "Hold fast the faithful Word" (Titus1:9).

(f) *Work it out*. Experiment is an excellent expositor. The Bible is a work that works and when you put its teaching to the pragmatic test you discover with delight that life backs it. "Life will only work in one way," wrote William Russell Maltby, "and that is God's way." To get to know God's way you must consult God's Word. The Bible is like the manual of instructions issued by the manufacturer with every complex and highly technological piece of machinery. We may try to persuade the apparatus to operate as we think it should: but, sooner or later, if success is to be assured, we shall have to come back to the maker's directions. Just so with the Bible. We have to put it into practice if we want personally to prove it true.

(g) *Pass it on*. There is a stirring romance in the story of the ingenious expedients to which Christians have had recourse through the years in their efforts to disseminate the Word of God in places where it is not published and where its circulation is proscribed. One thinks of how the Bible was baked in a loaf, its pages pulled out and packed in tiny rolls into bamboo-poles, smuggled into countries where it was officially contraband benearh the floorboards and within the panelling of motor-vehicles. "Holding forth the Word of Life" (Philippians 2:16) has meant handing it over the Berlin Wall, the Iron Curtain, the Bamboo Barrier. Hands are stretching out for it all over the globe: other hands must pass it on. It is Paper Manna, Bread from Heaven, and for lack of it the world would die.

As a footnote to this chapter, take this striking tale. It is about Bernard Dodd, Travelling Secretary of a Bible Society serving the navy, army and air-force, who related some time ago how a young soldier stationed in Belfast read through the New Testament in fourteen hours, and then observed: "This is super. Is there a sequel?" Yes, there is a sequel. Let Paul tell us what it is: "Ye are manifestly declared to be the epistle of Christ, ministered by us, written not with ink, but with the Spirit of the living God; not in tables of stone, but in fleshy tablets of the heart" (2 Corinthians 3:3). So, once more, the Word is made flesh.

10
THE MASTER'S MASTERPIECE

The Christian Doctrine of the Church

The Church of Jesus Christ is the Divine Masterpiece.
Thomas Rees

I will build My Church, and the gates of hell shall not prevail against it.
Matthew 16:18

All that believed were together.
Acts 2:44

The Lord added to the Church daily such as should be saved.
Acts 2:47

The multitude of them that believed.
Acts 4:32

God did visit the Gentiles to take out of them a people for His name.
Acts 15:14

All that in every place call upon the name of our Lord Jesus Christ, both theirs and ours.

1 Corinthians 1:2

The churches of Christ.

Romans 16:16

The Church that is in their house.

1 Corinthians 16:19

God hath set in the Church, first apostles, secondarily, prophets, thirdly, teachers.

1 Corinthians 12:28

God gave Him to be Head over all things to the Church, which is His body, the fulness of Him that filleth all in all.

Ephesians 1:22,23

To the intent that now unto the principalities and powers in heavenly places might be known by the Church the manifold wisdom of God, according to the eternal purpose which He purposed in Christ Jesus our Lord.

Ephesians 3:10

Unto Him be glory in the Church throughout all ages, world without end.

Ephesians 3:21

He gave some, apostles; and some, prophets; and some, evangelists; and some, pastors and teachers; for the perfecting of the saints, for the work of the ministry, for the edifying of the body of Christ.

Ephesians 4:11,12

That He might present it to Himself a glorious Church.

Ephesians 5:27

He is the Head of the body, the Church, that in all things He might have the pre-eminence.

Colossians 1:18

Ye are come unto Mount Zion and unto the City of the Living God, the heavenly Jerusalem; and to an innumerable company of angels, and to the general assembly and Church of the first born.

Hebrews 12:22,23

I, John, saw the Holy City, New Jerusalem, coming down from God out of heaven, prepared as a bride adorned for her husband.

Revelation 21:2.

AMONG THE CLOSING SCENES IN the Life of the great British architect, Sir Christopher Wren, is one which appeals strongly to the imagination and which may fitly serve as frontispiece to our study of the Christian doctrine of the Church. In it Wren appears as a very old man – he lived to be ninety – sitting, spy-glass in hand, on sunny summer evenings in the doorway of his house at Camberwell, London, looking out across the Thames at St Paul's Cathedral, which it had been the crowning glory of his career to construct. Erected between 1675 and 1710, at a cost of a million pounds – a colossal sum in those days – the cathedral is the most spectacularly splendid building in Britain. No wonder its architect surveyed it with pleasure and with pride.

The master complacently contemplating his masterpiece! There you have a picture of Christ, the Divine Architect, gazing at last on the faultless perfection of His Church, a picture recalling a glowing sentence in Ephesians: "Christ loved the Church, and gave Himself for it, that He might present it to Himself a glorious Church, not having spot, or wrinkle or any such thing" (5:27)! The Church is the Master's masterpiece. Throughout all ages it will be the object of His rapturous gaze – to use a term which is peculiarly exact – "con–templ–ation."

But *what* is the Church? The term is what Sangster would have called a "blurred word". To get it into sharp focus, we must first banish whatever verbal fog there is about it by stating quite definitely and categorically what it is *not*.

(a) *the Church is not a building.* Naturally enough, many think of it as such. To them a church is a special sort of structure – ancient or modern, simple or ornate, a "barn" or a basilica – intended for public worship. You may remember George Crabbe's jaunty jingle:

> *What is a church? Our honest sexton tells,*
> *'Tis a tall building with a tower and bells.*

But it isn't. It isn't property: it's people.

Here it may be pertinent to point out that, whereas the Jew had his Tabernacle, his Temple and his synagogue, the Muslim his mosque, and the Brahmin his pagoda, for the first one hundred and fifty years of its existence, the Christian Church had no consecrated building in which to conduct its services.

Since then, to be sure, the pendulum has swung the other way. Christianity has now become, perhaps, the world's richest property-owner, numbering among its edifices the noblest ever built. This is rather ironical in view of the fact that the Lord Jesus does not seem to have been very interested in or impressed by architecture. When the disciples came to Him excitedly, calling attention to the materials and construction of Herod the Great's gorgeous Temple, His only comment was a prediction of its impending destruction. "Master," they cried, "see what manner of stones, and what buildings, are here!" Jesus foretold that soon it would all be thrown down. But He did not weep at the prospect, as Titus, the Roman general, is reported to have done later. He reserved His tears for the fearful fate which He foresaw awaiting a nation which had rejected Him. For many people, however, the word "church" *has* come to be mentally identified with a material structure.

No one will be disposed to dispute that ecclesiastical architecture *can* act as an aid to worship. The pillared aisle, the soaring column, the vaulted roof – all tend to lift the mind to loftier levels. Experience shows, nevertheless, that they do not always or inevitably have that effect. As H. Martyn Cundy frankly admits: "God is with five humble Christians praying round their fireside in a far more intimate way than He is in the greatest cathedral thronged with sightseers."

At the commencement of Church history Christians were probably too poor to afford premises of their own, and later the Church became an officially banned society, and was thus prohibited from possessing property. Initially, its Jewish members worshipped in the Temple at Jerusalem, and in synagogues up and down the Roman Empire. Gentile members would sometimes foregather in a large room in a house belonging to one of them. In times of persecution, when the Church became an Underground Movement, its people met in catacombs and caves, or amid the ruins of pagan shrines. In Ephesus, as we know from the account in Acts, Paul conducted services on hot afternoons from eleven to four – when the students were having a siesta – in the schoolroom of Tyrannus. Evidently, there was nowhere else available. The Church is not a building.

(b) *the Church is not Israel.* A great deal of confusion has resulted from the identification of the Church with God's ancient people. The two are not to be equated. It is true that, as someone has said, "the Church was in the bosom of Judaism like the unborn child in its mother's womb", but it is a mistake to identify the two, just as it would be an error to mix up William Shakespeare with the wife of a certain wool-merchant in Stratford-upon-Avon. It must be admitted, of course, that some scriptural passages *do* seem to provide warrant for it. For example, there is a reference in Acts 7:38 to "the Church in the wilderness"; and in Hebrews 2:12 a sentence from Psalm 22:22 is quoted: "In the midst of the Church will I sing praise unto Thee." Four times in the Gospels our Lord is described as "the King of Israel" (Matthew 27:42; Mark 15:32; John 1:49; 12:13). In Romans 9:6 Paul declares: "They are not all Israel which are of Israel", and in Galatians 6:16 he alludes to the Church as "the Israel of God." The Lord Jesus promised the Twelve that "in the Regeneration when the Son of Man should come in His glory, they would sit upon thrones, judging the twelve tribes of Israel" (19:28). And in the Book of Revelation we read that "the wall of the city had twelve foundations, and in them the names of the twelve apostles of the Lamb" (21:21). From such quotations it is easy to see that those who teach that in the Church there is the total fulfilment of the Divine territorial promises made to the Hebrew patriarchs, do appear to have a solid biblical basis for their thesis. Nevertheless, it is a grave error to identify the Church with Israel. God has a programme for each, but His plan for the one is quite distinct from His design for the other. It is true, of course, that within the Church Jew and Gentile are one, for there national differentiation disappears. But Paul's threefold division of humanity – "the Jew, the Gentile and the Church of God" (1 Corinthians 10:32) – makes it patent that the Hebrew nation and the Christian Church are distinct and separate entities. The Church is not Israel.

(c) *the Church is not Christendom.* Claude Beaufort Moss speaks of those who "belong to Christendom but not to the Church". The distinction is valid and well-drawn. Ever since 334 A.D., when Constantine officially proclaimed Christianity the official religion of the Roman Empire, there has existed what is known as "Christendom" – that is, the realm or domain of the christened. Theoretically, that suggests that they have been *Christ*-ened, made to belong to Christ; but practically it does not always work out that way. There is a piquant story about a Cambridge professor with a lisp, who was wont on occasion to remark: "Ath a child I wath chrithened and vacthinated. Neither of them took!" That, unhappily, is the state of multitudes today. They have been christened, but not *Christ*-ened; baptized as babies but not born again as responsible adults. Christendom is not the Church. In Christendom the tares are mingled with the wheat (Matthew 13:30); the chaff with the grain (Matthew 13:12); the bad fish with the good (Matthew 13:47); the goats with the sheep (Matthew 25:32). The true Church contains no such heterogeneous ingredients. It is not Christendom.

(d) *the Church is not a denomination.* In everyday speech we refer to the Anglican Church, the Baptist Church, the Methodist Church, the Presbyterian Church, and so on. But this use of the word is what Disraeli would have called a "terminological inexactitude". True, each of these great divisions of organized Christianity form part of the Church of God, but the Church is far bigger than any of its branches.

Just as it is proverbially possible not to see the wood for the trees, so it is ecclesiastically possible not to see the tree for the branches. "To which branch of the Christian Church do you belong?" a believer was asked. "I don't belong to any branch," he replied. "I belong to the trunk!" Many church-goers, however, are so lost amid the luxuriant foliage of their local branch that they cannot see the total tree. They make a great fuss of the church with a small "c", but have very little conception of or concern for the Church with a big "C". We must not seek to imprison the cosmic Christ in a solitary congregation or even in a denomination. Certainly, our Lord is with us at the local level, but we must not limit Him to the local level. Michael Faraday, the famous scientist, was an elder in a small evangelical group. On one occasion Cardinal Wiseman, a once-well-known Roman prelate, asked him whether, in his deepest conviction, he really believed that the Church of Christ – holy, catholic, apostolic – was shut up in that little company. "O, no," answered Faraday, "but I do believe from the bottom of my soul that Christ is with us." That puts things in their proper persepective and proportion. The Church is not only "the multitude which no man can number" (Revelation 7:9); it is also the "two or three gathered together" of Matthew 18:20. It once met in the home of the mother of John Mark at Jerusalem; there were house-churches, too, in the dwelling at Corinth of Aquila and Priscilla and in that of Aristobulus in Rome. A housechurch is permissible only if no other accommodation is available. But no denomination, under whatever name it goes, is the Church. "You cannot see the Church," wrote Luther, "even if you have put on spectacles." The Church is not a denomination.

How, then, *are* we to think of the Church? In what precise terms are we to conceive of it? If it is not a building, not Israel, not Christendom, not a denomination, what is it?

So vast and so varied is the theme that if we are to do it anything like justice we shall have to survey it from a multiplicity of vantage-points. There are in fact no fewer than ten angles from which we may profitably contemplate it. We may label them as follows: (1) *definitions and descriptions*; (2) *mystery and history*; (3) *universality and locality*; (4) *unity and sanctity*; (5) *energy and authority*; (6) *gifts and government*; (7) *faith and fellowship*; (8) *services and sacraments*; (9) *work and witness* and (10) *departure and destiny*.

Consider them as they come.

DEFINITIONS AND DESCRIPTIONS

Let us start with New Testament definitions. Here is a representative handful of them: "Those whom Thou hast given Me" (John 17:11). "All that believed" (Acts 2:44). "The multitude of them that believed" (Acts 4:32). "A people for His name" (Acts 15:14). "All that in every place call upon the name of the Lord Jesus Christ" (1 Corinthians 1:2). "The general assembly and Church of the firstborn" (Hebrews 12:23). "A people for God's own possession" (1 Peter 2:9).

Or turn to the formal statements contained in the primitive creeds. The creed of Irenaeus (AD 180) presupposes the existence of the Church but does not name it. Neither does the creed of Cyprian (AD 250), nor that of Novatian (AD 260). In the creed of Marcellus of Ancyra (AD 341) there is the briefest possible mention of it: "I believe in the holy Church." The so-called Apostles' Creed expands that a little: "I believe in the holy, catholic (universal) Church." The Nicean Creed further amplifies the reference: "I believe in one holy, catholic (universal) and apostolic church". Item 19 in the Thirty-nine Articles of the Church of England reads thus: "The visible Church of Christ is a congregation of faithful persons, in which the pure Word of God is preached and the sacraments be duly administered, according to Christ's ordinance in all those things that of necessity are requisite to the same." The Westminster Confession of Faith is even more explicit: "The catholic or universal Church consists of the whole number of the elect that have been, are, or shall be gathered into one under Christ, the Head thereof, and is the spouse, the body, the fulness of Him that filleth all in all. The visible Church, which is also catholic or universal, under the Gospel (not confined to one nation, as before under the Law) consists of all those throughout the world that profess the true religion, together with their children, and is the Kingdom of the Lord Jesus Christ, the House and Family of God, out of which there is no ordinary possibility of salvation."

Or consider some personal formulations of faith about the Church. Take this of Martin Luther: "The Church is the spiritual home of all who believe in Christ." Or this from John Calvin: "The Church is the multitude of men and women, diffused throughout the world, who profess to worship one God in Christ and are initiated into their faith by baptism, testifying their unity in true doctrine and charity by partaking of the sacraments, have consent in the Word of God, and for the preaching of that Word maintain the ministry ordained of God." Or take this from Henry Barrow: "A true planted and rightly established Church of Christ is a company of faithful people, separated from unbelievers, gathered in the name of Christ, whom they truly worship and really obey. They are a brotherhood and sisterhood, a communion of saints, each of them standing in and for their Christian liberty to practise whatsoever God has commanded and revealed unto them in the Holy Ghost."

In our quest for an adequate definition of the Christian society we may enlist the aid of two English words. One is the word "Church" itself. What does it mean? It comes from the Greek adjective *kuriakos,* which signifies "the Lord's" or "that which belongs to the Lord" and *oikos,* "house" – thus *kuriake oikia,* equals "the Lord's House". The second English word is "ecclesiastic". It is derived from the Greek *ekklesia,* connoting "called out". Of it the French *église* and the Welsh *eglwys* are recognizable first cousins.

The expression *ekklesia,* as it appears in the New Testament, has a double background. The first is Hebrew. In the Septuagint, or Greek version of the Old Testament, it stood for the congregation of Israel. The second is classical Greek. In this context it was used to connote an assembly of the magistrates of a city state, democratically elected to administer its affairs, and summoned to each session by the town-crier. Karl Barth has a graphic picture of the *ekklesia* as "citizens called out by the trumpet and rushing from everywhere".

Etymologically, therefore, the Church is a company of people, called out of the world because they belong to the Lord. So much for definitions.

Pass now to *descriptions*. No student of the New Testament can fail to notice that it does not so much define the Church as describe it, and it does so with a profusion of richly evocative imagery. The Christian Scriptures know nothing of images *in* the Church, but they abound with images *of* the Church. From the kaleidoscopically varied plethora of analogies, let us choose twelve for snapshot treatment. The word "Church" occurs over one hundred times in the New Testament, and it is portrayed by a whole gallery of figures. It is pictured as (a) a *body*; (b) *a temple*; (c) *a bride*; (d) *a mother*; (c) *a family*; (f) *a fold*; (g) *salt*; (h) a *loaf*; (i) *a garden*; (j) *a pillar*; (k) *an army*; (l) *a colony* and (m) *a city*.

Let us look at each of these in turn for a little.

(a) *The Church as a body*. "As we have many members in one body, and all members have not the same office, so we, being many, are one body in Christ, and everyone members one of another" (Romans 12:4,5). "Ye are the body of Christ, and members in particular" (1 Corinthians 12:27). "The Church which is His body" (Ephesians 1:22,23). "There is one body" (Ephesians 4:4). "We are members of His body, of His flesh, and of His bones" (Ephesians 5:30). "He is the Head of the body" (Colossians 1:18). "Ye are called in one body" (Colossians 3:15).

This is Paul's favourite figure, and in the New Testament no one but he uses it. Neither Peter nor John, nor James, nor Jude employs such imagery. It is peculiar to Paul, and it is strikingly suggestive. Students of the Scriptures will no doubt find the following ideas suggested by this figure: *animation – assimilation – articulation – identification – specialization – organization – subordination – operation – co-operation – propagation.*

G.R. Balleine's definition of the Divine society could hardly be bettered: "The Christian Church is a great body, made up of a lot of little people, who must all function properly if the body is to keep healthy and if the body's work is to be done."

(b) *the Church as a Temple*. "Ye are the temple of God" (1 Corinthians 3:16). "Ye are the temple of the living God" (2 Corinthians 6:16). "All the building, fitly framed together, groweth unto an holy temple in the Lord: in whom ye also are builded together for an habitation of God through the Spirit" (Ephesians 2:21,22). "Christ, whose house are we" (Hebrews 3:6). "The Church," as one old preacher remarks, "is a nonesuch building. Other structures are made of wood and stone and other suchlike materials, but this building is made of men and women, souls united to Christ by faith" (1 Peter 2:5).

It has been ably and memorably said that "just as, under the Old Economy, God had a Temple for His people, so, under the New Economy, He has a people for His Temple." The term "temple" presupposes the setting apart of a sacred site for certain holy purposes. We read in Revelation that in the New Jerusalem John saw no temple (21:22), the reason being that in that perfect era the whole world will be a temple. "The word 'temple' ", writes F.B. Meyer, "means 'to cut'. Before the Romans erected a temple to any of their gods, the services of the augur were called in, to cut off a piece of soil by sacred rites from the common ground around." The physical demarcation was meant to symbolize moral and spiritual separation. The basic concept of a temple is, therefore, one of isolation with a view to consecration.

When we contemplate the Church in this light, we are doing what the word itself implies. At the heart of it you can see the word "temple" – con–*temple*–ate! To an imaginative and reflective mind such contemplation suggests four things: (i) *a temple is a costly building*; (ii) *a temple is a consecrated building*; (iii) *a temple is a communal building*; and (iv) *a temple is a continuing building.* It partakes of permanence.

One of the romances of modern architectural literature is the story of the building of the Anglican Cathedral at Liverpool. "This towering cathedral," it has been said, "is the overpowering achievement of one man." In 1901 a young architect, Giles Gilbert Scott, aged 22, submitted a design for the proposed cathedral. He entered it in a competition. His entry was adjudged the best, and he was given the assignment. The remainder of his life was spent in turning that dream into solid stone. Scott died in 1960. Now, suppose that, just before he passed away, someone had suggested to him that the cathedral was unlikely to last for long, he would have questioned his sanity. I like the story about the old couple who, not long after the completion of the building of the cathedral, paid a visit to it and submitted it to critical inspection. The husband was a bit afraid that the red sandstone was not durable enough material for such a structure. Prodding it with the point of his umbrella, he remarked to his wife: "I wonder if such soft stone will stand the strain of centuries of wear and tear?" With a smile, his wife replied: "I expect the architect thought of that, my dear!" And, if the human architect did, how much more the Architect Divine!

In Him it is ordained to raise
A temple to Jehovah's praise,
Composed of all the saints who own
No Saviour but the Living Stone.

Vast is the building! See it rise!
The work, how great! The plan, how wise!
O, wondrous fabric, power unknown
That rears it on the Living Stone!

There is an eloquent passage among the published

works of John Henry Newman which is in place here. "A temple there has been," he says, "on earth, a spiritual temple, made up of living stones; a temple, as I may say, composed of souls, a temple with God for its light, and Christ for its high priest, with the wings of angels for its arches, with saints and teachers for its pillars, and with worshippers for its pavement. Wherever there is faith and love this temple is."

"Not only are we building a temple," wrote Joseph Parker, "but each person is himself a temple. We should build a great temple for a great God. That is to say, we ourselves should be great temples because a great God has come to dwell within us."

(c) *the Church as bride.* Few New Testament figures depictive of the Church are more felicitous in both senses of the word than this one. It is as apt as it is attractive, and the Christian Scriptures are replete with references to it. Here are some of them: "He that hath the bride is the Bridegroom" (John 3:29). "I have espoused you to one husband that I may present you as a chaste virgin to Christ" (2 Corinthians 11:2). "Christ loved the Church and gave Himself for it" (Ephesians 5:25). "He that loveth his wife loveth himself. This is a great mystery, but I speak concerning Christ and the Church" (Ephesians 5:28,32). "The marriage of the Lamb is come, and His wife hath made herself ready" (Revelation 19:7). "I, John, saw the Holy City, New Jerusalem, coming down from God out of heaven, prepared as a bride adorned for her husband" (Revelation 21:2). "Come hither; I will show thee the Bride, the Lamb's Wife" (Revelation 21:9). "The Bride says, Come" (Revelation 22:17).

What facets of the Church's faith, form and fellowship are adumbrated by this analogy? It is perhaps not too fanciful to find the following: *beauty – purity – gaiety – affinity – monopoly – dependence – productivity – expectancy.* Unlike Jacob, the Lord Jesus will not be content to take

Leah in the room of Rachel. He will have a bride "not having spot, or wrinkle, or any such thing" (Ephesians 5:27). And, as William Macdonald reasonably enough maintains, "If Christ loves the Church, then obviously the Church should be filled with bridal affection for Him."

(d) *the Church as mother.* One of the tenderest New Testament metaphors illustrative of the character and ministry of the Church is that of mother. In Galatians 4:26 Paul refers to it as "Jerusalem, which is the mother of us all." We must not carry this figure too far as do the Roman Catholics, who describe their own denomination as "the holy, catholic and apostolic Roman Church, Mother and *magistra* (mistress) of all churches." Nevertheless, the true Church *is* the mother of believers. There is point and pertinence in a great saying attributed with minor variations to Irenaeus, Cyprian, Tertullian and Calvin: "No one can have God for his Father unless he has the Church for his mother." There may be isolated occasions when God reveals Himself directly in the life of one who knows nothing about the Bible or the Church, but that must be a very rare exception. Generally, it is through the motherhood of the Church with its Bible, ministry, fellowship and sacraments, that we get to know the saving Fatherhood of God.

Just *how* is the Church like a mother?

In four ways.

(i) *Because through her we are born again;* (ii) *Because from her we receive the sincere milk of the Word;* (iii) *Because it is she who teaches us to talk to God;* (iv) *Because she it is who trains our faltering feet to walk in the way of faith.* The Greater Catechism states that "the Church is the mother which, through the Word of God, gives birth to every Christian and supports him." The Church as such cannot save us, but it can and does succour us once we *are* saved. She is the mother of us all.

(e) *the Church as a family.* A further fecund New Testament figure illustrative of the Church is that of a family. Curiously enough, the word *family* (Greek *patria*) occurs once only in the Christian Scriptures. But it may be said without the slightest exaggeration that the concept of the Church as a family pervades the Book.

Take some typical texts: "The whole family in heaven and earth" (Ephesians 3:15). "That He should gather together in one the children of God" (John 11:52). "Now therefore ye are no more strangers and foreigners, but fellow citizens with the saints and of the household of God" (Ephesians 2:19). "Let us do good unto all men, especially unto them who are of the household of faith" (Galatians 6:10).

How does the Church resemble a family? There are five angles of analogy: (i) *the Church is like a family in its common ancestry*; (ii) *the Church is like a family in its recognizable identity*; (iii) *the Church is like a family in its personal intimacy*; (iv) *the Church is like a family in its social solidarity*; (v) *the Church is like a family in its communal activity*.

Sociologists have often been at pains to point out that there are basically two sorts of human society – the organic and the contractual. A contractual society is one which a person enters either by his own volition or by being co-opted into it. An organic society is one to which a person belongs by birth. The Church is both. We have to choose to enter it, but we can only truly do so by being born again.

(f) *the Church as a fold.* Yet another suggestive simile to illustrate the significance of the Church is that which likens it to a fold. Because the Bible is so largely pastoral in its background, it is hardly surprising that it contains so many references to rural scenes. Much mention is made in it of shepherds and shepherding. "The Lord is my Shepherd" (Psalm 23:1). "Thou leddest Thy people like a flock" (Psalm 77:20). "We are His people and the sheep of His pasture" (Psalm 100:3). "He shall feed His flock like a shepherd" (Isaiah 40:11). All these verses describe the Lord's relation to the Hebrew people and their relation to Him.

In the New Testament the figure is applied to the Church. "Fear not, little flock" (Luke 12:32). "Take heed to all the flock" (Acts 20:28). "Feed the flock of God" (1 Peter 5:2). "Be ensamples to the flock" (1 Peter 5:3).

Of the Church as a fold the Scriptures do not so frequently speak. The Revised Version, however, makes a significant emendation in the text of John 10:16, where the Authorized Version reads: "There shall be one *fold* and one Shepherd." For the word "fold" (Greek *aule*, meaning a yard or enclosure, the Revisers substitute "flock" (Greek *poimne*), thus righting a wrong rendering. Nevertheless, the Church *is* a fold as well as a flock. Twice in John 10 our Lord Himself refers to the Church as a fold. "Other sheep I have, which are not of this fold" (v.16); "He that entereth not by the door into the sheepfold, the same is a thief and a robber" (v.1). So the Church is a fold as well as a flock. "The Jewish nation was a fold," wrote William Macdonald, "the Church is a flock." "There are many folds," comments F.B. Meyer, "but there is only one flock." This is, of course, true; and yet it was to His Church, and to His Church as a whole, that our Lord was alluding when in these three verses He spoke of His Church as a fold.

What correspondences are there between the Church and a fold? Three at once spring to mind: (i) *the Church is like a fold in that it is collective*; (ii) *the Church is like a fold in that it is selective.* A fold does not enclose all. It excludes as well as includes. When in modern Israel the sheep and goats which have been grazing together all day find darkness approaching, the shepherd leads the sheep within the stone enclosure, but leaves the goats outside for the night. (iii) *the Church is like a fold in that it is protective.* That is its principal purpose. Sir George Adam Smith, while on a visit to Palestine, watched a shepherd penning his sheep within a rectangular dry-stone enclosure. The enclosure had no door. The visitor pointed this out to the shepherd, and asked for an explanation. "Where is the door?" he inquired. The shepherd's answer was startlingly biblical. Laying himself down on the threshold, he said "I am the door."

(g) *The Church as salt.* Salt furnishes a further figure by which the New Testament brings out the nature and function of the Church. "Ye are the salt of the earth" (Matthew 5:13). Note the plural. "Ye are" – not "Thou art". A single grain of salt is practically worthless, but even the proverbial pinch of salt can make all the difference to a meal. As the little girl said: "Salt is something you only notice when it isn't there!" "All salt seems to have come from the ocean," observes A.C. Dixon. "The rock salt deposits were gradually made by the evaporation of bodies of water, caused by the earth's overflow during times of convulsion. So the character of the Christian Church comes from the ocean fulness of God."

What points of parallel are presented here? Four! (i) *the Church is like salt in its uniqueness.* "Salt is a thing on its own," writes Lionel Fletcher, "a thing without a substitute." We have a substitute for sugar: we call it saccharine; we have a substitute for butter: we call it margarine; but we have no substitute for salt. (ii) *the Church is like salt in its whiteness.* "To her was granted that she should be arrayed in fine linen, clean and white; for the fine linen is the righteousness of the saints" (Revelation 19:8). (iii) *the Church is like salt in its usefulness.* Salt has many functions. It preserves. It flavours. It heals. In Old Testament worship it was employed liturgically. "Every oblation of thy meat-offering shalt thou season with salt; neither shalt thou suffer the salt of the covenant of thy God to be lacking. With all thine offerings thou shalt offer salt" (Leviticus 2:13). Not long ago medical spokesmen were saying disturbing things about salt, even deprecating its use. Now, it appears, they have revised their opinion. "Salt is good," said Jesus (Mark 9:50), and He is never wrong. (iv) *the Church is like salt in that it produces thirst.* A Sunday School teacher once asked her class what purpose salt served. Several answers were given. Then a small girl put up her hand. "Please, miss," she said, "salt makes people thirsty." That is just what the Church is meant to do – make people thirsty for God.

(h) *the Church as a loaf.* Another thought-provoking New Testament analogy represents the Church as a loaf. "We, being many, are one bread" writes Paul (1 Corinthians 10:17). It is a fitting and felicitous figure, extrapolating four ideas or points of correspondence:

(i) like a loaf, the Church is a unity made up of many units; (ii) like a loaf, the Church is a product of earth and heaven. J.F.C. Pellow has a charming little lyric which brings this out well:

Earth bore me,
Water fed me,
Air bathed me,
Fire stirred me.

Earth my substance,
Water my fulness,
Air my strength,
Fire my joy.

I was lifted up,
I was cast down,
I was broken,
I was buried.

Earth I was,
Water bound me,
Air leavened me,

Fire formed me.

All the four elements
Of the round world
Meet in me
For man's feeding.

(iii) like a loaf, the Church is not a dispensable luxury but an indispensable necessity; and (iv) like a loaf, the Church can only fulfil its function through fraction. It must be broken in God's hands if it is to be of service to the world.

(i) *the Church as a garden.* "You are God's garden" (1 Corinthians 3:9 Barclay). "A garden inclosed is my spouse" (Song of Solomon 4:12). "A garden is a lovesome thing, God wot," sang T.E. Brown, and no garden means so much to the Master as the garden of His Church. One of Charles Haddon Spurgeon's finest sermons has for subject the text, "Supposing Him to be the Gardener" (John 20:15). The supposition is supported by the facts. God *is* a gardener. With a word He brought worlds into being: but He *planted* a garden (Genesis 2:8). "My Father *is* the Gardener," said Jesus (John 15:1 TLB). Since Jesus is God, He too is a Gardener and the Church is His Garden.

Let us think of four ways in which the comparison may be sustained: (i) *the Church, like a garden, is walled off from the world;* (ii) *the Church, like a garden, is subject to successive seasons;* (iii) *the Church, like a garden, is both beautiful and useful;* (iv) *the Church, like a garden, has to be tilled, planted and tended.*

(j) *the Church as a pillar.* In his immortal allegory, *Pilgrim's Progress,* John Bunyan introduces a character named "Reformation", whose task it is to clear the inscription on a pillar called "History". "The Church of the living God, which is the pillar and ground of the truth" (1 Timothy 3:15). On this topic Clovis G. Chappell archly comments: "God means the Church to be a pill*ar*, not a pill*ow*." "I was wrapped up as in a rapture," relates George Fox, in his famous *Journal*, "and I stepped up in a place and asked the priest: 'Dost thou call this place a church?' Instead of answering me, he asked me what a church was. I told him the Church was the pillar and ground of the truth."

It is on record that, when someone inquired of Winston Churchill if he supported the Church, he replied: "Yes, but not as a pillar on the inside, but rather as a buttress that holds it up on the outside." But the Church does not need a buttress. It is itself an imperishable pillar.

Absalom, King David's disobedient son, "in his lifetime had taken and reared up for himself a pillar, which was in the king's dale; for he said, I have no son to keep my name in remembrance; and he called the pillar after his own name" (2 Samuel 18:18). Great David's greater Son, who was "obedient unto death, even the death of the Cross" (Philippians 2:8), has for His memorial the pillar of the Church which will perpetuate His name throughout the ages of eternity.

What likenesses can we discover here? There are five: (i) *the Church is like a pillar in its sturdy permanence;* (ii) *the Church is like a pillar in its supportive power;* (iii) *the Church is like a pillar in its upward thrust;* (iv) *the Church will ultimately by like a pillar in its polished perfection.* A pillar is not just a columnal rock. It is not simply an accidental geological formation, like the columns of the Giant's Causeway in Ulster. It is graven by tool and man's device and polished to perfection. Chrysostom, the golden-mouthed orator of the Early Church, has a fine figure depicting the fusion of fellowship in the Christian Church. He says: "It is just as if someone made two pillars, the one of silver and the other of lead, then melted them together and, by a miracle, they came out one golden pillar." (v) *the Church is like a pillar in its public prominence.* There *are* indoor columns, but the pillars we most often see are those ornamenting and supporting buildings from the outside. "In addition to being a support for the building," writes William Macdonald, "a pillar was often used in early days for posting public notices." Just so the Church of Jesus is a pillar on which is inscribed eternal truth.

(k) *the Church as an army.* It is customary to speak of the Church on earth as "the Church Militant". Yet, curiously enough, the only time in the New Testament when the Church is actually described as an army refers to the Church in heaven, the "Church Triumphant", as we should say. Nevertheless, much mention is made of military matters in relation to the members of the Church. By implication Paul portrays himself as a soldier, when he alludes to Epaphroditus (Philippians 2:25) and Archippus (Philemon 2) as "fellow-soldiers", and admonishes Timothy to "endure hardness as a good soldier of Jesus Christ" (2 Timothy 2:3). The same apostle also specifies the pieces of armour which the Christian is to wear and bids him buckle them on. "Put on the armour of light" (Romans 13:12). "Put on the whole armour of God" (Ephesians 6:11). "Take unto you the whole armour of God, that ye may be able to stand against the wiles of the Devil, your loins girt about with truth, and having on the breastplate of righteousness; and your feet shod with the preparation of the Gospel of peace; above all, taking the shield of faith, wherewith ye shall be able to quench all the fiery darts of the wicked. And take the helmet of salvation and the sword of the Spirit, which is the Word of God" (Ephesians 6:13–17). "The Church that is not militant," said Joseph Parker, "is dead."

This thought of the Church as an army suggests five things: (i) *enlistment.* "There may be civilians braver and more resourceful and more patriotic than anybody in the army," declares Donald M. Mathers, in *The Word and the Way,* "but that does not change the fact that to be a real soldier you must be enlisted." (ii) *commitment.* The young

Israeli recruit has to go to Masada, that famous hill on the South Western shore of the Dead Sea, where one of the great epics of Jewish history was enacted and swear unreserved and undying allegiance to the flag. So the Christian soldier must vow unqualified loyalty to his Lord. (iii) *equipment*. As we have seen, the soldier of Christ is well-accoutred. He is covered with protective panoply and furnished with weapons of attack. (iv) *armament*. "They overcame him (the Devil) by the blood of the Lamb and by the word of their testimony" (Revelation 12:11). (v) *engagement*. Dean Church in his *Human Life and its Conditions* claims that "the Christian society has a commission as definite as a soldier's" and Napoleon maintained that "a soldier is only a machine to obey orders". There is nothing vague or unclear about a warrior's briefing. He knows exactly what he has to do and goes right ahead and does it. So ought the Church of God to mobilize and move under the orders of its great Commander.

Armies of prayer, your promise claim,
Prove the full power of Jesus's name
And take the victory.

(1) *the Church as a colony*. In Moffatt's translation of the New Testament there is a fine and felicitous rendering of Philippians 3:20. The Authorized Version reads: "Our conversation is in heaven." Aside from the fact that, in this usage, the term "conversation" is archaic, the word in the original *politeuma* has social overtones not necessarily involved in the old rendering. Thus the Revised Version has "citizenship" with "commonwealth" in the marginal reading. Moffatt's is better here than any: "We are a colony of heaven."

In what senses is this so? Three: (i) *the Church, like a colony, is remote from its homeland*. In *The Shepherd of Hermas* we have the following picture of the members of the primitive Church: "They dwell in their own country, but only as sojourners; they bear their share in all things as citizens; and they endure all hardships, as strangers. Every foreign country is a fatherland to them, and every fatherland is foreign. They obey the established laws and they surpass the laws in their own lives. Their existence is on earth, but their citizenship is in heaven."

Earth is a desert drear,
Heaven is my home.

(ii) *the Church, like a colony, is a reproduction of the homeland.* One historian states that in every Roman colony Rome itself could be seen in miniature. The Church is meant to be heaven on a small scale. "As Paul entered the gates of Philippi," observes R.M.L. Waugh, "he saw everything with a Roman stamp on it – shops and police, laws and roads, togas and baths, villas and soldiers, but, great as was his pride in being a Roman citizen, his thrill was greater in knowing that he was a colonist from a heavenly city. He was enrolled as a burgess of heaven."
(iii) *the Church, like a colony, is a venue for the King.* The sovereign paid regular visits to the colony to strengthen links of loyalty and to proclaim the rights of the crown. To his coming the colonists eagerly looked forward. Not otherwise is it with Christ and His Church.

(m) *the Church as a city.* It has often been pointed out that the Bible begins with a garden and ends with a city. That is deeply significant. Starting with a one-man Paradise it closes with a Paradise packed with happy people. "I, John, saw the Holy City, New Jerusalem, coming down from God out of heaven, prepared as a bride adorned for her husband" (Revelation 21:2). That is the Church in its final perfection.

Like many cities the Church is built on both banks of a river. It has both an earthly and a heavenly identity. "A city that is set on a hill cannot be hid" (Matthew 5:14). "Ye are come unto Mount Zion, the city of the living God, the heavenly Jerusalem" (Hebrews 12:22). "The Church resembles a city built on both sides of a river," comments R. Hill. "It is militant on the one side and triumphant on the other. It is the river of death which runs between."

What is there about a city to make it an apt emblem of the Church of God? Five things: (i) *Like a city, the Church has a history.* Cities do not spring up overnight like mushrooms. It may take a millennium or more to make a city. "Rome," says the adage, "was not built in a day." So it is with the Church. (ii) *like a city, the Church has identity.* On a political map there are large empty spaces, but the towns are plainly marked. (iii) *like a city, the Church has community.* It is not merely an urban mob. Its social life is highly organized. (iv) *like a city, the Church partakes of permanency.* It is not just a camp of tents: it is a collection of solid and durable buildings. (v) *like a city, the Church has security.* In ancient times, people exposed to attack by a foreign foe fled to the cities. There, behind stout bastions, they could together withstand the enemy. "I will build My Church," our Lord declared, "and the gates of hell shall not prevail against it" (Matthew 16:18). It is the real City of Refuge.

So much, then for definitions and descriptions. We turn now to the second main section of our study.

MYSTERY AND HISTORY

In 1550 AD a Spaniard Vincente Yanez Pinzon, pushing the prow of his ship towards the sunset, sailed into the mouth of the River Amazon. No white man had ever done so before. Pinzon and his men did not know where they were. Mistaking South America for the West Indies, one of the ship's company suggested that they had discovered an island. Pinzon dissented. "No," he said, "a river so great as this must drain a continent." Contemplating the Church of Christ, and thinking of its long procession through the centuries, one is constrained to the conclusion that its source must lie somewhere away back among the mists of eternity. That this is so the New Testament leaves us in no sort of doubt. Paul traces this Amazon back to the Andes. He speaks of the Church as "the mystery which was kept secret since the world began, but now is made manifest" (Romans 16:25,26). "The mystery which in other ages was not revealed unto the sons of men, as it is now revealed unto His holy apostles and prophets by the Spirit" (Ephesians 3:4,5). "The mystery which from the beginning of the world hath been hid in God" (Ephesians 3:9). "The mystery, which hath been hid from all ages and from generations, but now is made manifest to His saints" (Colossians 1:26). The Church is no Divine afterthought, no mere incidental by-product of the redemptive process, no addendum to the plan of salvation. The Church was in God's mind "before the hills in order stood or earth received its frame". He willed it from the beginning. It was His "bright design" from the dawn of Creation. Christ made the worlds that He might build the Church. He framed the stars that He might form the fellowship. Like the mighty, rolling Amazon, the Church begins among the mysteries where, as on lofty mountains, the high mists hang.

In the Church of God mystery and history meet, like lightning flashing betwixt heaven and earth. What starts in mystery moves into history. In the epistles we read of the former: in the Acts, of the latter.

This is not the place in which to embark upon a detailed account of the history of the Church, nor even to essay a brief sketch of it. All one need do is to indicate four major milestones on the road along which it has travelled: (a) *formation*; (b) *malformation*; (c) *Reformation*; and (d) *transformation*.

Take them in that order.

(a) *formation*. Differing views are expressed by expositors as to precisely when the Church began on earth. Some trace its origin to the nation of Israel, stemming from the call of Abram. Others profess to discover it in the baptismal ministry of John the Baptist. In other forms of baptism associated with Jewish religion the candidate plunged himself into the ritual water. John was the first to baptize others; and, as baptism in water is a rite of entry into the Christian Church, some maintain that this is where the Church took its rise. Others, again, find the founding of the Church in the revelation vouchsafed to the Apostle Paul. In support of their contention they quote Ephesians 3:4–6: "The mystery of Christ, which in other ages was not made known unto the sons of men, as it is now revealed unto His holy apostles and prophets by the Spirit, that the Gentiles should be fellow-heirs and of the same body." The preponderance of informed opinion, however, identifies the birth of the Church with the Day of Pentecost.

That Israel cannot be the Church is patent from the fact that in Matthew 16:18 our Lord speaks of the building of the Church as an event still future; that the baptism of John does not mark the birth of the Church is manifest from Acts 19:1–7, which makes it plain that the two baptisms are quite distinct and that John's baptism was pre-Christian; that Paul's revelation of the Church as the body of Christ, epoch-making though it was, did not signal the Church's nativity is clear from the circumstance that nobody would have known what he was talking about when he spoke of the Church if the Church had not been in existence at the time.

Beyond all reasonable cavil, the Church commenced on the day of Pentecost. The statistics of its beginnings, as Luke presents them, are as follows: "The number of names together were about an hundred and twenty" (Acts 1:15). "There were added unto them about three thousand souls" (Acts 2:41). "Many of them which heard the Word believed; and the number of the men was about five thousand" (Acts 6:7). In the arithmetic of the Church's membership addition gave way to multiplication. Even the high priest had to acknowledge: "Ye have filled Jerusalem with your doctrine" (Acts 5:28). And it was not long until the whole habitable world had heard the Gospel and crowds of converts swelled the ranks of the Church.

Such, in briefest outline, was the formation of the Church. With the passing of the first apostles, however, this happy state of affairs came to a temporary end.

(b) *malformation*. The Church lost its charismatic character. The fount of Pentecostal prophecy dried up or was officially checked or choked; and this changed the Church completely. We shall have occasion later to note that in the Early Church there were two distinct types of ministry – that of those who were humanly nominated, elected and ordained, provided they possessed certain moral and social credentials, and that of those who were appointed by prophetic directive, concerning whom no such testimonials were required, since "the Lord knoweth them that are His" (2 Timothy 2:19).

When the Spirit was spurned and the spring of prophecy ceased to flow, inevitably this supernatural type of ministry dwindled and diminished and eventually disappeared. The apostles were replaced by monarchical bishops and the prophets by itinerant spongers who went about spouting and exploiting the generosity of the Lord's people. Instead of being filled with the wind of the Spirit they were but bellowing windbags.

In process of time the Church's teaching became impregnated with Hellenistic philosophy and its worship by pagan practices; until at last it was completely absorbed into secular society by the edict of Constantine. Then followed the Dark Ages succeeded by the Middle Ages, when the lamp burned dim beside the sacred ark and when there was no open vision. Ecclesiastical leaders, vying with one another for precedence, made "the Word of God of none effect through their tradition" (Mark 7:13), and by their crass materialism and even, in some instances, gross immorality dragged the flag of the faith in the dust. "Every harlot was a virgin once", as William Blake has reminded us, and no one could have recognized in the painted prostitute which Christendom had become, the "chaste virgin" whose purity Paul had once guarded with such fatherly care.

(c) *Reformation*. Then broke the bright dawn of the Reformation. John Wycliffe was its "morning star", and with Luther, Calvin and Knox broad daylight came. The Bible was restored to its rightful place as rule of faith and practice in the Church and final moral monitor in the individual life of the believer. Errors and abuses such as mariolatry, purgatory, indulgences, prayer for the dead, and so on, were swept away and the Christian Church was brought back in large measure to its pristine purity. The great evangelical doctrines of the New Testament – justification by faith alone, the priesthood of all believers, the authority of the Word of God – were rediscovered and proclaimed with passionate fervour. The Church was born again.

(d) *transformation*. But reformation was not enough. There was a return to the Word, but not to the Spirit. As Rome had reinstituted something analogous to the worship of the Hebrew Temple, so the Reformed churches came to bear an unmistakable resemblance to the synagogue. The letter proved lethal. Scholarship became preoccupied with the minutiae of literary construction. Grammar came to be more esteemed than grace. Human authorship, and dates of composition, appeared more important than divine authority; and finally Higher Criticism reduced biblical studies to the level of the solving of a theological crossword puzzle. The Dove seemed to have flown back to heaven.

Round about the turn of the twentieth century, however, a remarkable transformation began to take place. The Reformation had rehabilitated the Word; the transformation was to recall the Church to the Spirit. Pentecost had come again. The time of the singing of birds had returned. The Dove was once more resting on the Church.

UNIVERSALITY AND LOCALITY

The term "church" (*ekklesia*) can stand in the New Testament for anything from a cosmic concourse to a congregational couple. It can apply to the whole body of believers, "some on earth, in glory some", and also to the local group of Christians, which may consist of no more than two persons (Matthew 18:20).

When Thomas Hobbes' *Leviathan* – a book whose theme is political economy – was first published in the days of the Cromwellian protectorate, it bore on its first page a picture of a titanic man and, when one looked closely, one saw that the body of the giant was made up of hundreds of tiny men. This was intended to illustrate the author's thesis that a nation is just a huge person comprised of millions of little people.

By the same token, the Church universal is a body composed of a multitude of bodies. As Augustine epigramatically expressed it: "The universal Church consists of many churches."

Take, first, *the Church universal*. References to this abound in the Christian Scriptures. "I will build My Church; and the gates of hell shall not prevail against it" (Matthew 16:18). "God hath put all things under His feet, and gave Him to be Head over all things to the Church, which is His body, the fulness of Him that filleth all in all" (Ephesians 1:22,23). "Christ is the Head of the Church; Christ also loved the Church, and gave Himself for it; that He might sanctify and cleanse it with the washing of water by the Word, that He might present it to Himself, a glorious Church, not having spot, or wrinkle, or any such thing" (Ephesians 5:23–27). "Ye are come unto Mount Zion, unto the city of the living God, the heavenly Jerusalem, and to an innumerable company of angels, to the general assembly and Church of the firstborn, which are written in heaven, and to God the Judge of all, and to the spirits of just men made perfect, and to Jesus, the Mediator of the new covenant, and to the blood of sprinkling, which speaketh better things than that of Abel" (Hebrews 12:22–24).

The first to apply the label *katholicos* (catholic) to the universal Church was Ignatius. The term is a Greek adjective, formed from *kata*, "throughout" and *holos*, "the whole". As Donald M. Mathers contends, however, it is one of the curiosities of Church history that "the word 'catholic' should have come to be a party name". There are in fact three main branches of Christendom each of which claims to be catholic – the Greek Catholic, the Roman Catholic and the Anglo-Catholic. Greek, Roman and English like to label themselves, oddly enough, with a word – "catholic" – which does not occur in the New Testament, but obviously if they are Greek, Roman or English they are not truly catholic and if they are catholic they are not merely Greek, Roman or English. The true catholic or universal Church is comprised of that body of believers, known only to God, who have been born again by His Spirit and baptized into His body.

Let us consider, next, the *local church*. Much mention is made of it in the New Testament. "Where two or three are gathered together in My name, there am I in the midst of them" (Matthew 18:20). During the "Killing Times" in Scotland the prophet Alexander (better known as "Sandy") Peden wrote: "Where is the Church of Christ in Scotland today? It is not among the great clergy. But I will tell you where the Church is today. Wherever there is a praying young man or a praying young woman by a dykeside in Scotland today, that's where the Church is." Locality no less than universality is a mark of the Christian Church, as witness the following texts: "Paul, called to be an apostle of Jesus Christ, unto the church of God, which is at Corinth, to them that are sanctified in Christ Jesus, called to be saints" (1 Corinthains 1:1,2). "Paul, unto the church of the Thessalonians, which is in God the Father, and in the Lord Jesus Christ" (1 Thessalonians 1:1). "Paul, unto Philemon, our dearly beloved fellow-labourer, and to the church in thy house" (Philemon 1,2).

The apostle Paul uses the word "church" (*ekklesia*) sixty-six times in his epistles. Sometimes he applies it to the whole company of Christians scattered throughout the habitable earth, and in the world unseen, as in Colossians 1:18: "He is the Head of the body, the Church." Sometimes he relates it to a community of Christians resident in a particular city, as in 2 Corinthians 1:1: "Paul, an apostle of Jesus Christ by the will of God, unto the church of God which is at Corinth." Sometimes he addresses it to a small group of Christians, gathering in a house. Four times in the New Testament occurs the phrase "the church which is in thy (their, his) house" (Romans 16:5; 1 Corinthians 16:19; Colossians 4:5 and Philemon 2). This is hardly surprising in view of the fact that the Church was born in a house. One would not wish to dogmatize on such a point, and yet it is probably in order to say that, for Christians, assembling in a house is permissible, or commendable, only when no public place of worship is available. The house-group, it is claimed by its advocates, can help to *build* a church up: sad experience shows that it can also *break* a church up.

Such companies, large or small, met in a wide variety of locations all over the habitable world. Yet, however remote from one another geographically these churches might be, mystically they were one. As Richard Hooker picturesquely puts it in his classic *Ecclesiastical Polity*: "The main body of the sea, being one, yet within divers precincts hath divers names, so the Church catholic is in like manner divided into a number of distinct societies, every one of them is termed a church within itself" (III:1,14).

UNITY AND SANCTITY

This boast of the unity of the body of believers, although

not falsified by distance or death, does seem to be belied by the existence of what are called "denominations". The Church is rent asunder by manifold divisions. There are groups which name themselves, or are so named by others, after their founders. Lutheranism, Calvinism, Wesleyanism, and so on, are examples of these. There are groups which distinguish themselves by the names of the nations to which they belong – Church of England, Church of Scotland, Church of Canada, Church of South India, etc. There are groups which mark themselves off from others in accordance with their respective systems of government – Episcopalians, Presbyterians, Congregationalists. There are other groups whose labels are in line with the distinctive practices they adopt or experiences to which they lay claim or fellowship they enjoy – Baptists, Brethren, Holiness groups, Pentecostals, and so on.

What are we to say about such denominational divisions?

There is a variety of views.

Some say they are good, serving a useful, if interim, purpose and subserving God's over-all plan and programme for the Church. Of this mind on the matter is George B. Duncan. He states: "The divisions between the Christian churches are not necessarily an argument against the validity and the truth of Christianity. I don't discard the grocery trade because I have several different firms with their own different brands of shops in my town! There can be a scandal in division, if this is accompanied by bitter enmity. There need be no scandal in division if this secures a diversity and variety that enriches the sum total of what is offered to the world by the Church." That is one view.

Others say that denominational divisions are bad. They denounce them roundly as directly contrary to the desire and design of Christ, and as constituting an insuperable handicap to the Church's work and witness. I once heard Toyohiko Kagawa, the well-known Japanese Christian leader, speaking publicly in London. He had a very harsh, rasping, grating voice, whose munched syllables were hard to make out. This he himself playfully admitted. "I speak English very badly," he confessed, "and when I say 'denomination', some people think I am saying 'damnation'. I am not surprised. To me they are very much the same thing!"

Marcus Rainsford adopted the same stance. "I believe sects and denominations to be the result of the Devil's attempt to mar and hinder, as far as possible, the visible union of the Church of God," he declared, "and that they have their root in our spiritual pride and selfishness, our self-sufficiency and our sin."

Others maintain that it does not much matter whether or not there are denominational barriers so long as they are not Berlin Walls. Provided they do not cut us off from fellowship with one another, their presence is, more or less, an irrelevance. If we are on good terms with one another, if we unite for great rallies and crusades, if we work together in the interests of the Kingdom of God, we need not bother our heads about sectarianism. "I do not object to denominational walls," declared Alexander Maclaren, "but to the broken bottles on top of them."

And yet, somehow, the Christian conscience is not easy about these divisions. Universal unity is not the be-all and end-all. It is better to be divided and right than united and wrong. But surely there is something better still – to be united and *right*! Still, the Church's fractions seem *vulgar* fractions. We are ashamed of them *vis-a-vis* the critics of Christianity. The adjective with which we most often qualify our divisions is "unhappy". In former days Thomas Guthrie castigated them in trenchant terms: "Christ has but one Church," he cried. "The Second Adam, like the First, is the Husband of one wife. Just as the Church cannot have two Heads, so the one Head cannot have two bodies; for as that body were a monster that had two heads, so the head which had two separate bodies."

The New Testament certainly emphasizes the essential unity of the Church. "There is one body" (Ephesians 4:4). "We, being many, are one body" (1 Corinthians 10:17). "The body is one" (1 Corinthians 12:12). "That He should gather together in one the children of God that were scattered abroad" (John 11:52). "That they all may be one" (John 17:21). "We were all baptized into one body" (1 Corinthians 12:13). "Ye are all one in Christ Jesus" (Galatians 3:26). Yes, there is certainly strong stress laid in the New Testament upon the unity of the body of Christ.

Nevertheless, unity can be bought too dear. For it we can pay too high a price. In the human body there are billions of minute cells, each less than one three-thousandth of an inch in diameter. There are more cells in a single brain than there are people on the planet. But each of these cells is placed in the body by the spirit. It is the spirit alone that can integrate and build a body. Any other kind of addition is not growth but *a* growth.

There is such a thing as an unnatural union. Of this Siamese twins constitute the classic example. The only hope of survival for such twins lies not in union but in severage. What is far too often forgotten in these ecumenical days is that it can be as much a Christian duty to disjoin as to unite. Union for the sake of union may be disastrous.

Never must it be overlooked that the New Testament begins with one Church and ends with two. It starts with our Lord's great declaration of intent: "I will build My Church" (Matthew 16:18), and it closes in the Book of Revelation chapters 18 and 19 with the Harlot and the Bride – the Church of Man and the Church of God respectively. Unless this is clearly kept in mind, if it were possible the very elect would be deceived by the plausible arguments of ecumenism.

One thing is certain. There can be no true unity apart from the recognition of the pre-eminence in his Church of the Lord Jesus Christ. As Elizabeth Wordsworth has sagely said: "How is the hand united with the foot? By the brain, which is always sending and receiving messages through the nerves. Cut off the head and intercourse between the members will soon come to an end. Just so in the Christian Church. There can be no true unity apart from the acknowledged Headship of Christ."

It is not without significance that in the great Ephesian chapter where Paul speaks of "the unity of the faith" (4:13) and of "the unity of the Spirit" (4:3), he also admonishes his readers to "grow up into Christ in all things, which is the Head, even Christ" (4:15). Christ is alive. He needs no "vicar". He requires no deputy. He is here Himself in Person as Head of His Church. If a hand tries to direct the body, it fails; if a foot tries to control the body, it is frustrated. There is no substitute for the head, and, as we have seen, no mere man can ever be head of the Church, for the simple reason that every eligible man is a member of the body and no more.

And now think of the *sanctity of the Church.* "Unity and sanctity." These are two of what are traditionally known as "the notes" of the Church. "I believe in one holy Church." The concepts are organically linked. The Christian Church will never be one unless and until it is holy. In the museum at Blackburn, Lancashire, hangs an impressive water-colour by Thomas Unwin R.A. (1782–1857). It is called "The Saint-Maker's Shop", and it depicts a scene in a carpentry in the middle of which sits a carver, mallet and chisel in hand, at work on a life-sized wooden figure, while all around lie other products of his masterly craftsmanship.

"The saint-maker's shop." Would not that be an apt name for the Church? Primarily, it exists for the glory of God and for the doing of His will in the world. But it can never achieve these goals unless its members are holy. For, as John S. Banks has cogently contended, "The holiness of the Church is the aggregate of the holiness of its members. All other holiness is merely nominal."

ENERGY AND AUTHORITY

The ideas are cognate. In the original New Testament they are *exousia* and *energeia* – authority and power. One is pointless and may be destructive without the other.

Take an illustration. Here, let us say, is a royal castle. It has need of a sentry to guard its gate. There are two aspirants for the post; yet both are, in their different ways, incompetent and therefore ineligible. One is a civilian, a prize-fighter, possessing plenty of physical power: the other is a soldier, who at the time of the adjudication has contracted pneumonia, and is forbidden by his doctor to get out of bed. Neither of them can fill the bill. The former possesses power without authority: the latter, authority without power. Both are essential, and the Church can have both if only she will lay claim to them.

Consider, first, *authority*. This operates in four ways: (i) *doctrinally*; (ii) *procedurally*; (iii) *morally*; (iv) *judicially*.

(i) *The Church is to exercise authority doctrinally*. This it has done through the centuries of its existence. It has drawn up creeds and confessions, systematizing and formulating its beliefs as set forth in the Word of God. The Church has, of course, no authority to tamper with the truth of Scripture, or arbitrarily to impose upon it meanings which it was manifestly never intended to convey. But it does have authority, nay, more, a duty to expound and to apply the teaching of the Bible.

(ii) *the Church is to exert its authority procedurally*. It has a Divine right, under the Headship of Christ, to administer its own affairs, to extend the Right Hand of Fellowship to approved new members, to determine policy, practice and procedure, to impose discipline and to regulate its communal life in accordance with the principles laid down in the Word of God. "We have no such custom," writes Paul, "neither the churches of God" (1 Corinthians 11:16).

(iii) *The Church should exert authority morally*. It ought

to be the conscience of the community. It should speak out boldly and impartially and disinterestedly on ethical issues. It should mould, confirm, correct the moral judgment of its members. Beyond its borders, and within them, it should make real the living law of God. In any dispute, where morals are concerned, it should, with the Word of God open in its hand, be the final court of appeal. "Tell it unto the Church" (Matthew 18:17).

(iv) *The Church should exert its authority judicially.* It is invested with the power of the keys. It has the authority to execute discipline. The awful anathema of excommunication is not the monopoly of any religious leader, although it can be so exerted, but is within the competence of the Church itself. Referring to 1 Corinthians 5:3ff., Sidney Cave comments: "Paul did not himself expel the incestuous member of the Corinthian church. That excommunication was to be the act of the whole community of its members." The total fellowship is to tell the persistent and impenitent offender: "Get right or get out!" Such people have to be "sent to Coventry" before they are fit to return to Zion. The Church must maintain its own moral standards. If it condones or connives at sin, it is false to itself and disloyal to its Divine Lord.

And now a word about *energy.* As we have noted, authority means nothing unless accompanied by power. Right must be reinforced by might. The Church is like a spacecraft. It was launched by a burst of supernatural energy and it cannot continue on its course unless constantly propelled by that Divine dynamic. The initial explosive power which projected it on its way must be its perpetual driving force. And that power which brought the Lord Jesus out of the tomb and propelled Him to the highest place that heaven affords, is available to the Church. For his Ephesian converts the apostle prays: "That ye may know what is the hope of His calling, and what the riches of the glory of His inheritance in the saints, and what is the exceeding greatness of His power to usward who believe, according to the working of His mighty power, which he wrought in Christ, when He raised Him from the dead, and set Him at His own right hand in the heavenly places, far above all principality and power and might and dominion, and every name that is named, not only in this world but also in that which is to come" (1:18–21).

GIFTS AND GOVERNMENT

"He gave gifts unto men" (Ephesians 4:8). "God hath set in the Church governments" (1 Corinthians 12:28). Government in the Church of God is not a prize to be grasped at but a gift to be received.

It cannot have escaped the notice of the most casual student of the New Testament that in its pages there are presented two categorically distinct orders of ministry. It would be too much to state that the one is natural and the other supernatural, but the difference between them is nevertheless firmly and fixedly drawn. The first type is subject to selection, investigation, nomination: the other is not. In the former class are (a) the *episkopos*, bishop or overseer; (b) the *presbuteros*, presbyter or elder; and (c) the *diakonos*, deacon or minister. Candidates for such offices, or nominees for such positions, had to have their credentials carefully examined and their characters scrutinized and their qualifications reviewed. "A bishop must be grave, the husband of one wife, vigilant, sober, of good behaviour, given to hospitality, apt to teach; not given to wine, no striker, not greedy of filthy lucre," and so on (1 Timothy 3:2,2ff). "A bishop must be blameless, as the steward of God; not self-willed, not soon angry, not given to wine, no striker, not given to filthy lucre" (Titus 1:7). "Against an elder receive not an accusation, but before two or three witnesses" (1 Timothy 5:19). "Ordain elders in every city, if they be blameless, the husband of one wife, having faithful children, not accused of riot or unruly" (Titus 1:6,7). "The elders which are among you I exhort, Feed the flock of God, taking the oversight thereof, not by constraint but willingly, not for filthy lucre, but of a ready mind: neither as being lords over God's heritage, but being ensamples to the flock" (1 Peter 5:1–3). "Likewise must the deacons be grave, not double-tongued, not given to much wine, not greedy of filthy lucre; holding the mystery of the faith in a pure conscience" (1 Timothy 3:8,9).

The second group of offices is listed in 1 Corinthians 12:28: "God hath set some in the Church, first apostles, secondarily prophets, thirdly teachers." And again in Ephesians 4:11: "He gave some, apostles; and some, evangelists; and some, prophets; and some, pastors and teachers." Notice that no qualities or qualifications are stipulated as being prerequisite to the appointment of these officials. That is not because such things are not as essential in an apostle as in a bishop, in a prophet as in an elder, in a pastor as in a deacon! Of course, they are. It is because, being Divinely called to office, by prophetic revelation, they did not require such human testimonials. "Jesus needed not that any man should testify of man: for He knew what was in man" (John 2:2,25). "The Lord knoweth them that are His" (2 Timothy 2:19).

Why did this distinction between the two types of offices disappear? There is no evidence in the New Testament to support the contention that God willed it to be so. These supernatural ministries and functions were gifts to the Church, and a gift differs vastly from an offer. If not accepted, an offer may be withdrawn: a gift never. These offices or gifts of the Risen Christ were not bestowed on the Church until after the Ascension. They cannot therefore refer to the apostles who companied with our Lord during His earthly ministry. And is it reasonable to believe that they were conferred simply for the first few decades of the Church's history? We have scriptural warrant for asserting the contrary. "He gave apostles – post-Ascension apostles – till we all come in the unity of the faith and of the knowledge of the Son of God, unto a perfect man, unto the measure of the stature of the fulness of Christ" (Ephesians 4:11,13). And if anybody thinks we have reached that level of spiritual maturity in the modern Church he must be strangely lacking in spiritual judgment. Patently, those gifts were bestowed on the Church in perpetuity, and indeed may it not well be that the unity for which so many in the Church today are longing and looking may be contingent upon the reintroduction to the Church of these divinely-appointed ministries? How ironical that the nominal Church has dignitaries called Patriarchs, Popes, Cardinals, and the like, of which not one word is spoken in the New Testament, and yet fails to have the offices which it so definitely specifies as being an essential part of its constitution!

According to Anglican theology, the Church is "an extension of the Incarnation". That is a deeply significant description. It implies, among other things, that the full-orbed ministry of our blessed Lord cannot be wholly expressed without these five offices. Christ personally embodies them all. He is "the apostle and high priest of our profession" (Hebrews 3:1). Hence He needs the apostle in the Church to perpetuate that feature of His ministry. He is "that Prophet that should come into the world" (John 6:14). So He requires the prophet in the Church to prolong this aspect of His work. He is not only the Evangelist, but the Evangel, wherefore He must have in His Church the evangelist to fulfil this function. He is the Chief Pastor (Gk *archepoimen*, leading shepherd). Therefore a pastor is necessary to carry on this branch of His activity. He is "the Teacher come from God" (John 3:2). Consequently, without a teacher in the Church one vital aspect of Christ's task would be unrepresented. In other words, all these ministries and offices are indispensable to the total expression of the many-sided ministry of our blessed Lord.

Physiologists tell us that the human body is very highly centralized, that there are in fact no fewer than nine major systems within the overall system itself. Among these five may be marked out as of special importance: (1) *the nervous system*; (2) *the respiratory system*; (3) *the reproductive system*; (4) *the circulatory system*; and (5) *the digestive system*. It may not be too fanciful to see in each a resemblance to one or other of the five offices in the body of Christ. Let us for a little develop this thought.

(1) *The Apostle*. He represents the nervous system. He is, under the Divine Head, the controlling office, the executive function. At this point, however, three questions arise: (a) What does the term "apostle" mean? (b) Were there not just twelve apostles? and (c) How do they operate?

(a) What does the term "apostle" mean? It comes from the Greek *apostolos*, and signifies an emissary, one who is sent on a mission. Indeed in his translation of the New Testament John Foster turns the substantive into a verb thus: "There was a man *apostled* from God, whose name was John" (John 1:6). Etymologically, the word "apostle" is simply the Greek equivalent of the Latin word "missionary". "In classical Greek," writes William Barclay, "the term had a nautical flavour. It was used of the dispatch of a naval squadron, and later of the leader of such an expedition – what we should call an admiral." The apostle is, then, an envoy, an emissary, someone sent out on official business or enterprise of some sort.

(b) Were there not just twelve apostles? That is the popular notion despite the fact that Matthias replaced Judas and that Paul's apostleship is universally recognized. It is important here to bear in mind the distinction between the two categories of apostles – "the apostles of the Lamb", that is, those appointed by Christ during His earthly ministry, and "the apostles of the Church", that is, those offices donated by our Lord after His Ascension, the largesse, so to speak, of freshly-minted coins disbursed by the Conqueror as He mounted in triumph to the skies.

This accounts for the fact that scholars have actually traced as many as twenty-two apostles in the New Testament.

From the fact that the Saviour bestowed apostles on his Church at the close of His earthly career it may warrantably be inferred that He intended them to continue in His Church until His Second Coming. Certainly, they were not divinely donated for but a few brief decades. Paul puts the matter beyond all possible dispute when he says: "He gave apostles... till we all come in the unity of the faith, and of the knowledge of the Son of God, unto a perfect man, unto the measure of the stature of the fulness of Christ" (Ephesians 4:11).

Are there, then, meant to be apostles in the Church today? Christendom has its patriarchs, popes, cardinals, and all the rest of the hierarchy, not one of which is named in the New Testament. But is it meant to have apostles? And, if so, where are they?

About that there are various views.

The first is that of those who hold that *there are no apostles in the Church today*. They are all dead and gone and the Church, which Paul affirms is built on them, is based on a boneyard. Apostleship, these people explain, was an office peculiar to the primitive Church. It was not divinely destined for continuance, but came to an end with the passing of the apostle John.

The second view is that nowadays the term "apostle" is nothing more than a courtesy title conferred on the great Christian leaders of the centuries. On his tombstone John Wesley is described as "the venerable and apostolic Wesley". William Carey is commonly hailed as "the Apostle of India"; David Brainerd has been labelled "the Apostle to the American Indians"; of John Fletcher of Madeley, Robert Southey wrote: "No age or country has ever produced a man of more fervent piety or more perfect charity; no church has ever possessed a more apostolic minister." Who could reasonably object to the courtesy title being bestowed on such Christlike characters as these?

The third view is that there *are* apostles in the modern Church but that they are men of mystery. Nobody can know who they are. They are apostles anonymous. Whether or not that be the case, it cannot be contested that the apostles of the primitive Church took no pains whatever to conceal their pastoral identity. Here is Peter: "Peter, an apostle of Jesus Christ" (1 Peter 1:1). And here is Paul: "Paul, an apostle of Jesus Christ by the will of God" (Ephesians 1:1). There is not the slightest shred of evidence to support the contention that the apostles of the Early Church made the smallest effort to conceal their ministerial status and identity. After all, why should they?

The fourth view is that there are apostles in the Church today, but that they have been renamed and are to be discovered in the episcopate or sacerdotal orders. Historically, they were in fact replaced by the monarchical bishops and in recent times Pope Paul VI spoke of himself as "an apostle on the move". P.T. Forsyth, for his part, held that "the apostolate died with the primitive apostles, and that its permanent continuation in the Church is not in the episcopate or in the sacramental system, but in the Scriptures which constitute the apostolic deposit." No candid commentator on the issue, however, is likely to express himself as satisfied with this ambivalent attitude to apostleship.

The fifth view is that there are, and certainly should be, in the Church today, as in that of old, living apostles as an extension of Christ's supreme apostleship. Why are we so shy of the word "apostle"? Doubtless our reserve and reticence are due to the traditional concept of the Twelve as the Saviour's Supermen, a band of beatified human beings. That is a romanticized and glamorized notion of the apostolic party. They were not at all like that. The records show that they were, on the contrary, very ordinary mortals. Our tendency to rhapsodize has led us to invest them with shining haloes. It is no misrepresentation of them to say that more than half of them were complete nonentities. They uttered, so far as we know, no saying worthy of permanent record and did no deed deserving of admiring recollection. Despite the apparent flippancy of the following lines, there is point and pertinence in them. They are titled simply: "Apostles" and are from the scholarly pen of A.T. Cadoux:

You sometimes feel you'd like to chuck it?
Thomas desponded, but he stuck it.

You've fallen short of your ideal?
St Peter felt how that could feel.

You find you're full of wrong ambition?
Once James and John mistook their mission.

There's very little you can do?
Andrew kept jogging others through.

Christian and businessman don't fit?
Ask Levi what he made of it.

You're dry for fellowship's elixir?
St Philip made himself a mixer.

You feel you're not appreciated?
Of all the rest there's naught related,

Save Judas: have him in your mind
When suicidally inclined.

Are circumstances very blue?
Remember what St Paul pulled through.

No! The apostles were not exceptionally saintly men. They were men of like passions with ourselves.

But to return to our question: *Are* they in the Church today? If not there, they should be, for God has set the apostles in the Church as He has set the stars in the sky, and as the darkness draws in at the close of this age, they will burn all the brighter in the firmament of the future. Yet, when one looks at the professing Church today, where are they?

Many years ago a brilliant American journalist-businessman, Bruce Barton by name, published two startlingly unconventional religious books, entitled respectively *The Man Nobody Knows* and *The Book Nobody Knows*. One was a life of Christ; the other, a study of the Bible. Barton's central thesis, in both volumes, was that the conventional portraits of Jesus, literary and artistic, and those of His Church, were largely misrepresentations, and that the traditional concepts of the Scriptures were also wide of the mark. Years ago I read both books; and, after reading them, I remember thinking: "This author ought to write a third book, completing the trilogy, and called *The Church Nobody Knows*". For years I waited in vain for the appearance of that volume. I didn't find it. And then, quite recently, while rooting around among the musty tomes on the shelves of a secondhand bookstore, I discovered what I had for so long been seeking. Barton had, after all, written that third book. Only, for some reason, he had not issued it under that title. He had incorporated it in a larger volume labelled *What* Can *a Man Believe?* That was why I missed the work *The Church Nobody Knows*. The Church has been missing it for ages – a Church with a living apostleship.

Nor does the New Testament disguise or conceal the fact that there are such things as false apostles. The Greek has a word for them, *pseudapostoloi*. To say nothing of the classic example of Judas Iscariot, Paul writes in 2 Corinthians 11:13: "For such are false apostles, deceitful workers, transforming themselves into the apostles of Christ." In addressing the church at Ephesus as recorded in Revelation 2:2, the Risen Christ commends it thus: "Thou hast tried them which say that they are apostles, and are not, and hast found them liars." Yes, there *are* false apostles. So, too, are there false coins. But people do not reject good currency because of the existence of counterfeit. So with apostles.

(c) How do they operate? That is our third query. From a study of the relevant Scriptural passages, it may fairly be inferred that there were four major functions served by the apostles in the primitive Church: (i) *the foundation of churches*; (ii) *revelation of the truth to the churches;* (iii) *ordination of ministers in the churches*; and (iv) the *administration of church affairs.*

In contradistinction to bishops, elders and deacons, which were purely local callings, that of the apostles was what might in modern parlance be termed diocesan. The apostle was, under God, in complete spiritual control of the groups of Christians he had himself been instrumental in establishing into local churches. "Grace is given to me of God that I should be the minister of Jesus Christ to the Gentiles, ministering the Gospel of God. So I have strived to preach the Gospel, not where Christ is named, lest I should build upon another man's foundation" (Romans 15:15,20). "According to the grace of God which is given unto me, as a wise master-builder, I have laid the foundation" (1 Corinthians 3:10). "We are come as far as to you also in preaching the Gospel of Christ; not boasting of things without our measure, that is, of other men's labours; but having hope, when your faith is increased, that we shall be enlarged by you, according to our rule, abundantly, to preach the Gospel in the regions beyond you, and not to boast in another man's line of things, made ready to our hand" (2 Corinthians 10:14–16).

A further function of the apostleship was to impart *revelation to the churches.* To this Paul alludes in Ephesians 3:3: "How that by revelation He made known unto me the mystery, which in other ages was not made known unto the sons of men, as it is now revealed unto His holy apostles and prophets by the Spirit." Not only were the apostles well-versed in the historical data of the Christian faith, there was also disclosed to them a divine revelation, which it was their duty, as far as in them lay, to communicate to their converts and congregations. The apostle was not only an historian: he was a theologian. He was to inform and instruct the churches he had founded.

Yet another function of the apostleship was *ordination.* In the account in Acts 6:1–6 of the election of the seven deacons, we have a noteworthy combination of the democratic and the apostolic. The people chose the deacons and then "set them before the apostles: and when they had prayed, they laid their hands upon them". Of Paul and Barnabas we read: "When they had ordained them elders in every church, and had prayed with fasting, they commended them to the Lord, on whom they believed" (Acts 14:23). Paul gave this directive to Titus: "Set in order the things that are wanting, and ordain elders in every city" (Titus 1:5). Herbert Lockyer quotes a nameless ancient author as saying: "When you provide apostles, to choose elders for us, we shall be exceedingly obliged for both. How can we have elders appointed according to Scripture unless we have apostles or their delegates?"

The fourth function of apostleship was *administration.* "Order," wrote the poet, "is heaven's first law." "I have given order unto the churches," announced the apostle Paul (1 Corinthians 16:1). "Let all things be done decently and in order," he commanded his converts (1 Corinthians 14:40); and to the Colossians he wrote: "Though I be absent in the flesh, yet am I with you in the Spirit, joying and beholding your order" (2:5). We see Peter exercising this authority in Acts 5:1–6, which reports the tragic story of Ananias and Sapphira and their financial falsity and double-dealing; we see it, too, in 1 Corinthians 5:3–5, where Paul adjudicates in the matter of the incestuous member. We see it, once more, in 1 Timothy 1:20 where the apostle handles a case of blasphemy.

Under this heading also may be comprehended the conferment of gifts. Those gifts were, of course, *charismata,* spiritual gifts. Paul did, it is true, on occasion carry material gifts from one church to another, but the donations of which we are now thinking were infinitely more important. In Acts 8 we read of Peter and John bestowing the gift of the Holy Spirit upon the Samaritans (vv14–17), and again in Acts 19:6 of Paul communicating to the dubious dozen at Ephesus the Pentecostal endowment. In Romans 1:11 the apostle observes: "I long to see you, that I may impart unto you some spiritual gift", and in 2 Timothy 1:6 he encourages his junior colleague to "stir up the gift that is in thee, by the putting on of my hands."

Another branch of apostolic responsibility in the ancient Church was *the management of its affairs.* Paul did not act as "lord over God's heritage" (1 Peter 1:3), but he did supervise the Lord's inheritance. Not only did he impart revelation and instruction, he also issued orders; he not only advised: he commanded; in matters marital, domestic, social, industrial, as well as in matters ecclesiastical, he spoke with authority in the name of God and as one who expected to be obeyed. He was no mere figurehead: he was the figure through whom the Head expressed His supreme authority.

From all this it should be patent to the honest reader of the New Testament that there should be apostles in the Church today. The God who set the stars in the firmament has set apostles in the Christian community, and they will still be there when the stars have fallen from the sky. It is instructive to note that in Revelation 18:20, at the time of the destruction of the great city of Babylon, there are still said to be apostles and prophets in the glorified Church. "Rejoice over her, thou heaven, and *ye holy apostles and prophets*".

(2) *The Prophet.* He represents the respiratory system in

the body of Christ. Inhaling and exhaling the breath of God, he oxygenates the fellowship with the living Word.

In the primitive Church prophecy manifested itself in four ways: There was (a) the *sign* of prophecy, when it was evidence of reception of the baptism in the Holy Spirit; (b) the *spirit* of prophecy, a divine afflatus which descended upon certain persons at particular times, but was not a permanent donation – an enduement but not necessarily an endowment; (c) the *gift* of prophecy, a charisma given irrevocably, a heavenly bestowal never to be withdrawn; (d) distinct from each and all of these was the *office* of prophet. "Now there were in the church that was at Antioch certain prophets. As they ministered to the Lord and fasted, the Holy Ghost said, Separate Me Barnabas and Saul for the work whereunto I have called them" (Acts 13:1,2). That this practice was common in the Early Church a study of the relevant literature makes plain. To take only one example, Clement of Alexandria reports that the apostle John in old age "went about Asia Minor appointing bishops, instituting entire new churches and appointing to the ministry those who were *pointed out by the Holy Ghost*", in other words, by prophecy.

Admittedly, this is dangerous doctrine. All too easily we can exchange prophecy for popery. Because the primitive Church rejected prophecy, it landed itself with the Papacy. Yet every sensitive person cannot but feel that, while politically the best available, democratic methods of government are out of keeping with the supernatural character of the Church of God. They are pre-Pentecostal. Before the Day of Pentecost lots were cast and votes taken when appointments were made to office in the Church, but after that date things were different. The democratic principle did not apply except in cases where persons were appointed to such posts as handling the money, where it was important for the congregation to have a say in the election.

The historic tragedy was that in the primitive Church

the spring of pure prophecy dried up because of the depentecostalization of the fellowship.

The harp of prophecy, so long
By sacred impulse fired,
Hath breathed its last enchanting song
And with the seer expired.

As Vance Havner wittily comments: "Prophets are almost extinct in the religious world today. The present-day Church is a non-*prophet* organization."

If that be indeed so, we shall require to have recourse to nominations, references, ballots, elections – all the paraphernalia of a competitive society. But if, when He ascended, Christ gave prophets in perpetuity to His Church – not prophets to the nations like Jeremiah, but prophets to the Church like Agabus, why should not the people of God have the direct divine guidance they so sorely need in these dark and difficult days? That the sheep should choose the shepherd seems ludicrous. It is the prerogative of the Chief Shepherd to appoint the under-shepherds. "He calleth His own sheep by name" (John 10:3) is the Scriptural principle; and if He thus calls them personally in salvation, will He not also call them personally in administration?

(3) *The Evangelist.* He represents the reproductive system in the body of Christ. It is his special privilege to preach the Gospel throughout the world with a view to winning souls for Christ, thus adding to the Church. The stench of death is on any Christian group which loses its outlook and outreach. To place newborn converts in such a spiritually moribund environment is, as Samuel Chadwick strikingly expressed it, "rather like putting a living baby into the arms of a dead mother". No list of Christian ministers would be complete which did not have room for the evange*list*.

(4) *The Pastor.* He represents the circulatory system in the body of Christ. Like the blood in a human body, he is always getting around. He is, as we say, in circulation. He is not like the hapless minister of whom we have so often heard who is "invisible through the week and incomprehensible on Sunday". He is always in the midst of his people and they read his mind perfectly. They feel his love for them, not a professional pose but a sincere affection. With a fatherly concern for his folk, he moves in and out among them, alike loving and beloved. There is in him a selflessness – say, rather, a self-giving – which yields rich returns. The ministers who, under God, build churches in contrast to those who merely draw congregations are the men of pastoral heart, the men of prayer and care. It has been well said that a minister needs lungs and legs, and the legs are almost as necessary as the lungs. A critic once alleged that a certain clergyman had "foot and mouth disease", and when asked to explain himself, replied: "He doesn't visit and he can't preach!" There was probably an organic connection between the symptoms. The minister who does not move about among his people, seeing through their eyes and feeling with their hearts, bearing their burdens, sharing their problems, is liable to offer them from the pulpit a more or less irrelevant message. The pastor, on the other hand, knows better. He speaks, as George Fox used to say, "to their condition".

(5) *The Teacher.* He is the digestive system in the Body of Christ. He feeds the minds and souls of the faithful with food convenient. We hear a lot nowadays about what are called "convenience foods". Agur anticipated that. "Feed me with food convenient," he pleaded (Proverbs 30:8). Such is the teacher's task. He has milk for the babes and meat for the men. "Rightly dividing the Word of truth" (2 Timothy 2:55), he does not set before his hearers processed pabulum prepared by others. He goes direct to the Word itself, availing himself of whatever scholarly aids are

accessible, praying over the passage with which he is dealing until its meaning stands out stark and plain, and he is able to deliver it clearly to his congregation. (What is not really clear to him can never be made clear to them!) As far as secular education is concerned, we all owe our understanding of things to a teacher of one kind or another. It is teachers who, by lip and literature, keep the coinage of truth in currency. Thinkers may be misers: by the very nature of things teachers, if true to their office and function, are bound to be benefactors. A minister may have a mind like a mint, but no ready cash, rather like a penniless millionaire, who has loads of money in the bank but none in his pocket. The true teacher can never be like that. He is a good communicator, an articulate expositor, who always has largesse to give away.

FAITH AND FELLOWSHIP

Faith and fellowship are bound up together inextricably in the Christian life. There can be no true fellowship without faith and no true faith without fellowship. "They continued steadfastly in the apostles' doctrine and fellowship" (Acts 2:42). David Martyn Lloyd-Jones used percipiently to point out that the doctrine must precede the fellowship, and not the reverse. Nor is real fellowship founded on economic considerations. "All that believed were together, and had all things common" (Acts 2:44). R.V.G. Tasker notes significantly: "The early Christians at Jerusalem were not brought into fellowship because they had all things common. They behaved generously to one another because they were redeemed." The bond between them was basically spiritual.

By nature *homo sapiens* is what anthropologists call "a gregarious animal". He longs to belong. He forms clubs, classes, groups, societies, federations. The paradox is, however, that, as Byron said about women: "People cannot live without others and yet they cannot live with others." Man's social predicament has been picturesquely compared to porcupines huddled together on a cold day for warmth: they need proximity for heat, but proximity brings its own pointed problems. Here are two pertinent quotations: "Forsooth, brothers, " cried William Morris, "fellowship is heaven and lack of fellowship is hell." And here is Jean Paul Sartre: "Hell is other people."

Only in the Church of Christ can that radical anomaly be fully resolved. Faith in Christ produces a fellowship to which, at its best, earth has no rival. It finds its focus in the Lord Himself: "I believe in Church loyalty," writes Paul S. Rees, "but not in church idolatry. Some years ago I was teamed up with a dear and noble preacher in a series of meetings. One day, as my friend was ministering the Word, he turned and dramatically addressed a brother who was sitting off to the speaker's left at the front of the building. He knew him well. 'Jones', he said, 'you belong to the Methodist Church, don't you?' I will never forget his answer. 'No, sir, I am a member of the Methodist Church: I belong to Jesus Christ.' "

Because you belong to Christ,
You also belong to me.

The fact is this – in finding Christ you find fellowship and in finding fellowship you find Christ, the Christ in the centre of every company assembled in His name, the Christ incorporated in every member of the holy fellowship.

In his famous *Journal* John Wesley has an entry in which he records advice given to him by an anonymous counsellor: "Sir, you wish to serve God and go to heaven? Remember that you cannot serve Him alone. You must therefore find companions or make them. The Bible knows nothing of solitary religion."

The fellowship is not far to find. It has branches in almost every street and in places all over the world. "Anyone who is to find Christ must first find the Church," says Martin Luther. "For how can one know where Christ is unless one knows where His followers are? Whoever wishes to know something about Christ must not trust to himself, nor by the help of his own reason build a bridge of his own to heaven, but must go to the Church, must visit it and make inquiry. Now, the Church is not wood and stone, but the company of people who believe in Christ. He must keep company with them, and see how they believe and teach and live." "I would rather belong to the most imperfect church I ever knew," remarks Reuben A. Torrey, "than not to belong to any church at all." But one must organically belong to it, not just casually visit it, or support it, as Winston Churchill said he did, "like a flying buttress, *from the outside*". There are no artificial limbs in the body of Christ, no glass eyes. You've got to be real to belong to it.

SERVICES AND SACRAMENTS

Years ago one used to hear in certain quarters the parrot-cry: "Let us have fewer services and more service." Experience shows, however, that when service is divorced from services, it tends to become secular and to lose its spiritual potency. Of course, everything hinges on the sort of services one has in mind. The fewer of certain stereotyped, formal, listless, heartless, lifeless services we have the better – the sort of services tilted at in the following satirical lines:

They do it every Sunday,
They'll be all right on Monday –
It's just a little habit they've acquired.

But real services in which God's Word is powerfully proclaimed, prayer fervently presented, worship devoutly offered and warm fellowship experienced and extended is the sort of background out of which are born the finest forms of public service. There is nothing like it. Secular society provides many amenities for the sick, the poor, the aged, but the trouble is that it stops short, as it is bound to stop short, just at the point of the beneficiaries' greatest need. Only committed Christians, accustomed to regular attendance at church services, are capable of rendering the class of service most required.

There are, or should be, three broad types of service in the Church. The first should have an upward reference, devotional, aspirational, with its gaze turned heavenward. The second should have an inward reference – doctrinal, ethical, with its vision directed toward self-examination. The third should have an outward reference – evangelistic, missionary, social, with its sights on the outside world. Heaven, heart and heathen will thus each in turn come into view. Whatever their primary point of reference, all true services will end in service.

The size of the congregation, the visible company, is, to be sure, largely irrelevant, although, of course, it is desirable, not to say obligatory, that as many attend as possible. "Let us consider one another," urges the writer to the Hebrews, "to provoke unto love and to good works: not forsaking the assembling of ourselves together, as the manner of some is" (10:24,25). One has heard of a congregation so small that when the vicar said in the pulpit, "Dearly Beloved," a spinster on the front pew thought he was proposing marriage! Yet, however numerically insignificant the visible congregation may be, the invisible congregation, which never fails to be present, is an innumerable company.

A famous archbishop – Robert Leighton – was once asked if many had attended a church service at which he had just officiated. He replied that the church was full. Actually, there had been a very small attendance. But the archbishop was not lying. It was of the Church invisible, the great cloud of witnesses, that he was thinking.

There is a similar story about an old minister who used to live in a little village and went every day into his church to conduct public worship. On most days nobody turned up. Undaunted, he proceeded with the service as if the place was packed. One day a visitor entered the church and found the old man ministering, as usual, to empty pews. When the proceedings had closed, he went up to him. "What a pity the church was empty!" he said. "Empty!" cried the old minister. "Empty! Why, the church was full!" "I beg your pardon," protested the stranger, "there wasn't a soul in the building except ourselves!" "Ah," returned the minister, "that is what you think because you do not understand. Your eyes are blind. Every seat was occupied. The very aisles were crowded with members of the Church invisible."

Not unnaturally, most ministers prefer to *see* their congregations; and, if they are wise, they will adapt their message to the known needs of their parishioners.

As to the sacraments, the Roman Church acknowledges seven, historic Protestantism only two – the Dominical Sacraments, those instituted by our Lord Himself – baptism and the Lord's Supper.

(1) baptism. This is the rite of entry into the Christian Church. By example and by precept our Lord commended and commanded it. "Then cometh Jesus to be baptized" (Matthew 3:13). "Go ye, therefore, and teach all nations, baptizing them" (Matthew 28:38). "After these things came Jesus and His disciples into the land of Judaea; and there He tarried with them and baptized" (John 3:22) "Repent, and be baptized every one of you in the name of Jesus Christ for the remission of sins, and ye shall receive the gift of the Holy Ghost" (Acts 2:38). "Peter commanded them to be baptized in the name of the Lord" (Acts 10:48). And in the words of the dubious Marcan epilogue: "He that believeth, and is baptized, shall be saved" (Mark 16:16).

To whom and in what way is the rite to be administered? Some say it is to be performed on infants, others insist on adults only. Quite clearly, if repentance is a prerequisite to baptism, as several texts testify, one might as well confer on a baby a Ph.D. as baptize it in water. As to the mode, there are three prevalent practices – sprinkling, effusion and immersion. There are those who will have it that the amount of water used in the ordinance is a matter of indifference. Not long ago a man accepted Christ as Saviour and was duly baptized by immersion. Some time later he happened to be in a mixed company of believers and unbelievers where in the course of general conversation the subject of baptism cropped up. There was an animated discussion as to which was the proper mode. Then one person said: "Some people eat with knife and fork, some with spoons, some with chop-sticks, some with fingers – all eat." The obvious inference was that it did not matter how you were baptized so long as you *were* baptized. The new convert appealed to a seasoned Christian who happened to be present: "What do *you* think is the proper mode or does it very much matter which is adopted?" The other replied: "Please go and ask them how many ways there are of burying a person. Baptism is burial." Paul writes: "We are buried with Christ by baptism into death" (Romans 6:4) and again: "Buried with Him in baptism, wherein also ye are risen with Him through the faith of the operation of God, who hath raised Him from the dead" (Colossians 2:12).

Had either effusion or sprinkling been the Scriptural mode of administering the rite, what need would there have been for John's converts to travel from all over Judaea to Aenon where, as John tells us, there was "much water" (John 3:23)? There would have been enough water in the Pool of Siloam to sprinkle the whole population of Jerusalem without any observable diminution in the supply. Patently, dipping not dripping is the biblical method. "Know ye not that so many of us as were baptized, were baptized into His death? Therefore we are buried with Him by baptism into death: that like as Christ was raised up from the dead by the glory of the Father, even we also should walk in newness of life" (Romans 6:3,4). No-one has ever thought it sufficient, in disposing of the dead, to sprinkle a few drops of H_2O on the face of a corpse! Charles Haddon Spurgeon had the right idea: "I am about to preach the Gospel," he once said. "Warm the water!"

Along with this baptism in water is meant to go a baptism of fire. The Christ who confronts us on the pages of the New Testament is a Pentecostal Christ, the Divine Incendiary bringing fire to earth. Each of the four evangelists quotes John the Baptist's reference to Jesus as "He that shall baptize with the Holy Ghost" (Matthew 3:11; Mark 1:8; Luke 3:16; John 1:33). Evidently they regarded that as one of our Lord's primary functions. From the records we see that Jesus delegated the task of water baptism to His disciples – "Jesus Himself baptized not, but His disciples" (John 4:2) – yet He reserved for Himself the prerogative of baptizing with fire.

It is that baptism rather than baptism in water which is declared in the New Testament to be the door into the fellowship of the Church. "For in one Spirit are we all baptized into one body" (1 Corinthians 12:13). On the basis of that baptism the right hand of fellowship into the Church is conferred. "When James, Cephas and John, who seemed to be pillars, perceived the grace that was given unto me, they gave to me and Barnabas the right hands of fellowship" (Galatians 2:9).

(2) *the Lord's Supper*. It is ironical that this sacrament, which was divinely designed to be the seal and symbol of the Church's unity, has proved to be almost the most divisive issue of all. From the magical to the merely memorial, from the austerely simple to the exotically ornate, it has been observed in a wide variety of ways.

There are three major views.

The first is that of those who think that this ordinance is dispensable. Denominations to which, despite their attitude to this rite, no responsible Christian would deny the name of Christ, nevertheless have, in their respective systems of worship, no place for this ordinance. One thinks of the Quakers and the Salvation Army. Neither of these admirable bodies practises the Breaking of Bread.

The second view is that of those who, like Leslie Weatherhead, doubt whether our Lord ever meant the sacrament to be celebrated in perpetuity. To such the Last Supper was indeed intended to be the Last Supper – only a valedictory meal shared by the Master with His men.

The third view is that which holds that the ordinance *was* divinely designed to be perpetuated by frequently repeated acts within the fellowship of the Church. But here, again, we run up against a broad diversity of opinion as to what precise mode the sacrament is to take. A number of names given to the ordinance indicate the wide divergence of views as to its essential nature – the Breaking of Bread, the Eucharist, the Mass, the Lord's Supper, the Lord's Table, and so on.

As might be expected, the theology of the sacrament reflects this disparity of concept. The Roman view – known as Transubstantiation – dating from the ninth century, maintains that, after the priestly benediction, the physical elements are magically transmuted into the actual body and blood of the Lord. The Lutheran view – Consubstantiation – teaches that, after the blessing has been invoked, the elements remain exactly what they were before materially, but acquire a new supernatural quality, much as magnetized metal remains metal but has added to it the property of magnetism. The Calvinistic view is summarily expressed in the following paragraph: "Worthy believers, outwardly partaking of the visible sacraments, do then also inwardly by faith really and indeed, yet not carnally and corporeally, but spiritually, receive and feed upon Christ crucified and all the benefits of His death: the body of Christ being then not corporeally in, with or under the bread and wine: yet as really but spiritually present to the faith of believers in that ordinance as the elements themselves are to their outward senses." The name of Ulrich Zwingli is often improperly linked with a fourth view, but it might be more correctly labelled Socinian. According to it, the Lord's Supper is nothing more than a memorial rite. The elements throughout the ceremony are and remain "bare signs and nude emblems". It is only a commemorative ordinance.

An illustration which I have found extremely helpful in this connection occurs in *Christian Belief* by R.H. Malden (London: S.P.C.K., 1958, p.52). "It has to do with paper money," he writes. "A treasury note (say) for the sum of £10 is a piece of paper. By every chemical test which can be applied it can be shown to be a piece of paper. As such its value is relatively small. But it is paper which has been treated in a particular way by a competent authority. Therefore, whoever receives it becomes richer than he was before. To be able to explain exactly how and why this piece of paper enriches the recipient would need considerable knowledge of the rules which govern currency and of the whole system of banking and credit. Some people must possess this knowledge, but the ordinary person need not concern himself with it unless he chooses. Lack of it does not deter him from accepting the note, nor prevent him from proving its real value. If he likes he can say: 'The Queen has ordained that it shall be so'. Anyone can understand this, and the illustration can be pressed to a considerable distance before it breaks down."

Detailed discussion of this vital subject is beyond the bounds of this survey. But perhaps we may sum up its significance in terms of three terse and simple sentences: (1) *It is commemoration of an absent Lord*; (2) *It is communication with a present Lord*. And (3) *It is contemplation of a coming Lord*. It looks back; it looks out; it looks on. It is a veritable focus of the Faith. As Horatius Bonar finely sings:

For that Coming here foreshown,
For that Day to man unknown,
For the glory and the throne,
We give Thee thanks, O Lord.

WORK AND WITNESS

The Church, as we have noted, is the Body of Christ, and a body is quite different from a statue. A statue is carved to be gazed at as a work of art – a body is designed for toil. Michelangelo's great figure "David" never did a stroke of work in its life. That is no reflection on the marble masterpiece. But if Michangelo's body had not done a great many strokes of work we should never have had the statue. The Church of Christ is meant for work and to a large extent that work consists of witness.

"Social service," comments Dr John Dow, "follows preaching as the right foot follows the left." But service to the community, it must always be remembered, the best service that can be rendered, is the preaching of sin and judgment as a means of inducing in the hearer true repentance. It is much less costly to serve one's neighbour in a practical way, and thus gain his gratitude and appreciation, than to tell him bluntly that he is a sinner who needs to repent. Service has, of course, its legitimate place. But the best service one can render is to induce in the hearer sincere sorrow for his sin and a willingness to turn in faith to Christ for salvation.

The New Testament reports the Master's staccato directives: "Behold, I send you" (Luke 10:3). "Go ye therefore, and teach all nations" (Matthew 28:28). "So send I you" (John 20:21). Paradoxically, the Church's standing orders are marching orders. The command is to preach the Gospel to every creature. And, as Charles Reynolds Brown reminds us in *The Main Points*, "The only place where this command is being taken seriously is in the Church of Christ."

Nor can the Church of Christ be true to itself if it fails to fulfil this mission. "It is the sincere and deep conviction of my soul," wrote Phillips Brooks, "that if the Christian faith does not culminate and complete itself in the effort to make itself known to all the world, that faith appears to me to be a thoroughly unreal and insignificant thing, and incapable of being convincingly proved to be true."

In the New Testament we are given no grounds to hope that this evangelistic outreach on the part of the Church will result in the conversion of humanity. "This Gospel of the kingdom shall be preached in all the world for a witness unto all nations" (Matthew 24:14). "Though our task is not to bring all the world to Christ," observes Dr A.J. Gordon in a memorable epigram, "our task is unquestionably to bring Christ to all the world."

Nor is this solely the task of the divinely-appointed ministers listed in Ephesians 4:11. The same passage informs us that it is to prepare the people of God for *their* ministry that these officers are appointed. "For the mending of the saints *unto* (no comma, no 'for') the ministry" is the correct translation. It is to be their ministry. We hear a lot nowadays about "audience participation". That was the practice and procedure in New Testament times. "When ye come together, every one of you hath a psalm, hath a doctrine, hath a tongue, hath a revelation, hath an interpretation. Let all things be done unto edifying" (1 Corinthians 14:26).

Considering that the following paragraph was penned close on a century ago, there is something almost prophetic about these weighty words of Alexander Maclaren: "I cannot but believe that the present practice of confining the public teaching of the Church to an official class has done harm. Why should one man be for ever speaking, and hundreds of people who are able to teach, sitting dumb to listen or pretend to listen to him? I hate forcible revolution, and do not believe that any institutions, whether political or ecclesiastical which need violence to sweep them away, are ready to be removed. But I believe that if the level of spiritual life were raised among us, new forms would naturally be evolved, in which there should be a more adequate recognition of the great principle on which the democracy of Christianity is founded, namely, 'I will pour out My Spirit upon all flesh' (Joel 2:28; Acts 2:17). 'On My servants and on My handmaidens I will pour out in those days of My Spirit, and they shall prophesy'" *Expositor's Bible* (Colossians – Philemon) (London: Hodder & Stoughton, 1903), pp.328–30.

DEPARTURE AND DESTINY

Of this we shall have more to say in our final chapter. Here, however, some brief and cursory mention must be made of these great matters.

Departure! It is the custom of earthly governments to evacuate their nations from threatened territory. If a revolution is about to break out or an invasion to break in, they commonly send aircraft or ships to get their people out of the danger zone before the trouble starts. That is what the Americans did in the Philippines, the British in Uganda and the Portugese in Angola.

This is also the policy of God. Before the awful "time of Jacob's trouble" (Jeremiah 30:7) erupts Christ will appear and gather His people to Himself. Translation for the saints will precede tribulation for the world.

At this point, however, we must be mindful of the fact to which we have earlier alluded that the New Testament begins with one Church and ends with two. For the false church – the Church of Man – there will be a departure from the faith: for the true Church a departure from the earth. As Professor John F. Walvoord has said: "The true Church will not go through the Great Tribulation, but the false Church will." Christendom, as such, will not be raptured, but the Church which is His body will be "caught up to meet the Lord in the air" (1 Thessalonians 4:17).

But the Church has a great future beyond that dramatic departure. During the Millennium it is to reign with Christ on earth and on into eternity its glorious destiny extends. Evangelical writers are likely to be accused of rhapsodizing when they dilate with lyrical abandon on the splendours of the Church's future. Listen to these glowing words of Paul E. Billheimer: "The nations of the world are but puppets manipulated by God for the purposes of His Church. Creation has no other aim. History has no other goal. From before the foundation of the world until the dawn of eternal ages God has been working toward one grand event, one supreme end – the glorious wedding of His Son, the Marriage Supper of the Lamb. The one purpose of the universe from all eternity is the production and preparation of an eternal companion for His Son, called the Bride, the Lamb's Wife. She is to share the thronc of the universe with her Divine Lover and Lord" (*Destined for the Throne*, pp. 26,15). Here is how the apostle Paul puts it: "That in the ages to come He might shew the exceeding riches of His grace in His kindness toward us through Christ Jesus" (Ephesians 2:7)). "That He might present it to Himself, a glorious Church" (Ephesians 5:27).

The Divine Architect will thus contemplate His masterpiece with complacency for ever.

11
THE LIFE OF GRACE

The Christian Doctrine of Salvation

Grace is love at its loveliest falling on the unlovable and making it lovely.

Anon

The Christian life is grace from beginning to end.

Bruce Milne

That grand word "grace".

Charles Duthie

To make a saint, it must indeed be by grace, and whoever doubts this, does not know what a saint is, or a man.

Blaise Pascal

The true grace of God is the soil out of which all great service for God grows and develops.

D.L. Moody

With this our pride repress
And give us grace, a growing store,
That, day by day, we may do more
And may esteem it less.

Of His fulness have all we received, and grace for grace.

John 1:16

The law was given by Moses, but grace and truth came by Jesus Christ.

John 1:17

Justified freely by His grace.

Romans 3:24

Grace hath abounded unto many.

Romans 5:15

There is a remnant according to the election of grace.

Romans 11:15

By the grace of God I am what I am.

1 Corinthians 15:10

God is able to make all grace abound towards you.

2 Corinthians 15:10

My grace is sufficient for thee.

2 Corinthians 12:9

We have redemption through His blood, the forgiveness of sins, according to the riches of His grace.

Ephesians 1:7

By grace are ye saved, through faith, and that not of yourselves; it is the gift of God, lest any man should boast.

Ephesians 2:8,9

That in the ages to come He might show the exceeding riches of His grace in His kindness toward us through Christ Jesus.

Ephesians 2:7

God hath given us good hope through grace.

2 Thessalonians 2:16

The grace of God that bringeth salvation hath appeared to all men.

Titus 2:11

Therefore, being justified by His grace, we should be made heirs according to the hope of eternal life.

Titus 3:7

Let us come boldly to the throne of grace.

Hebrews 4:16

The God of all grace called us unto His eternal glory by Christ Jesus.

1 Peter 5:10

THERE IS A CHARMING, if probably apocryphal story, which has come down to us from the childhood of Her Majesty Queen Elizabeth II. It tells how, as a small girl, she was much puzzled as to what words her father, King George VI, used during the singing of the national anthem. As all the world knows, the anthem contains the Biblical quotation, "God save the King"; and, as he was himself the king, she wondered whether he did not find the anthem somewhat confusing, perplexing, embarrassing. How did he get over the difficulty? Did he remain silent perhaps? Or did he sing: "God save my gracious *me*"?

One thing is certain: if God does not make our "me" gracious, the whole Divine plan of salvation goes by the board so far as we are concerned, for that is what it is all about. But He can, and He does. That is to be our theme in this study. We are to be occupied with what the old theologians were wont to call *ordo salutis*.

At the outset we may well make our own the beautiful prayer of an old Scots saint, which stresses the pre-eminence of grace in the Christian life: "Lord Jesus, from whom all grace comes, give me grace to feel my need of grace, and give me grace to ask for grace, then give me grace to receive grace, and when grace is given me give me grace to be grateful and to use grace. Amen."

In our attempt to deal with this major Christian doctrine, there are four lines we may follow, four headings which may help to direct and systematize our thought: (1) *the Majesty of the Grace that made us;* (2) *the Mystery of the Grace that Chose us;* (3) *the Mercy of the Grace that Saved us;* and (4) *the Ministry of the Grace that Shapes us.*

Think of them in that order.

THE MAJESTY OF THE GRACE THAT MADE US

Not always is it fully realized or recognized that Creation was an act of pure grace on the part of God. So far as our mortal minds can see, there was absolutely no constraint or pressure put upon Him – how could there be? – to produce this magnificent material order. Modern astronomers claim to be able, with their highly-sophisticated, scientific apparatus, to hear in the universe echoes of the Big Bang in which it is supposed to have originated. The Bible tells us, as we have noted, that it was not with a Bang but with a Being that it began. It did not explode into existence: it emerged from nothingness as an expression of the creative grace of God. Robert Louis Stevenson did not exaggerate when he exclaimed: "There is nothing but God's grace. We walk upon it; we breathe it; we live and die by it. It makes the nails and axles of the universe." The language of James 1:18 is as applicable to creation as it patently is to regeneration: "Of His own will begat He us with the Word, that we should be a kind of firstfruits of His creatures." We are born of grace no less than we are born again of grace; and Ilion T. Jones did not lack warrant for his claim: "The word 'grace' is unquestionably the most significant single word in the Bible."

The New Testament refers to the "throne of grace" (Hebrews 4:16). It sees grace as sovereign. Grace is bound to be sovereign since it cannot, by its very nature, be subject to any compulsion. "There is no reason to be given for grace," remarks Ralph Venning, "but grace. This is why we often apply to those who rule in church or state the appellation 'Your Grace'". In this connection the great Puritan divine Thomas Goodwin has a pertinent word for us: "Grace is more than mercy and love. It superadds to them. It denotes not simply love, but love of a sovereign, transcendently superior, One that may do what He will, that may freely choose whether He will love or no. There may be love between equals and an inferior may love a superior, but love in a Superior, and so superior that He may do what He will, in such a One love is called 'grace'; and therefore grace is attributed to princes; they are said to be 'gracious' to their subjects, whereas subjects cannot be gracious to princes."

Now God, who is an infinite Sovereign, had power to choose whether or not He would make us. For Him to love us into existence was an exercise of free grace. As a definition of grace it would be hard to beat or better that of R.W. Dale: "Grace is kindness bestowed upon the undeserving; kindness where there is no claim or merit; kindness without hope of return." The Bible bids us believe that on the throne of the universe there is a Being like that.

THE MYSTERY OF THE GRACE THAT CHOSE US

As a mighty river takes its rise among the mists that mantle the mountains, so salvation finds its source in the foreknowledge, predestination and election of God.

It starts with God's foreknowledge. There is no time in God. He is eternal. To Him the future is immeasurably more clear than is the past to us. He knows every thought, word and deed of every creature He has made, not only *after* they have happened but dateless ages *before* they have happened. "Such knowledge is too wonderful for me," says the Psalmist (Psalm 139:6), but it is a fact all the same. Well, then, this being so, God knows exactly how each individual, when confronted with the offer of free grace in Christ Jesus, will respond; and, on the basis of that Divine prescience, He predestinates to salvation those who believe and elects them to be "to the praise of His glory" (Ephesians 1:12). Herein lies the paradox of Divine predestination and human freewill. Man's will is free, but in exercising his freedom man does not determine his own destiny: God has *pre*destined that on the basis of His foreknowledge.

Next, election. This is a great enigma, and yet we see the principle of election plainly illustrated in nature, in history and in the Bible. We see it in nature. In autumn the forest-floor is strewn with nuts, seeds and spores of all sorts. Not all reach maturity. Some *root*, others *rot*. In the slimy ooze of the pond there are myriads of micro-organisms. What percentage of them become finished creatures? Proportionally, not many, only a responsive few. And in the human reproductive process millions of potential members of the species never survive the seminal stage of their existence.

History, likewise, has its impressive illustrations of the working of this principle. "If we desire to trace election on a wider than the individual scale," observes James Wright, "we might see how it applies to nations. The Greek nation is selected for culture and art; the Roman, for law; the Anglo-Saxon, for enterprise, political and religious freedom. Above all, the Jews, for revelation."

The Bible also has its illustrative instances. Here are Cain and Abel: Abel is accepted, Cain rejected; here are Jacob and Esau: Jacob is accepted, Esau rejected; here are Saul and David: David is accepted, Saul is rejected.

Thankfully, however, a belief in the doctrine of predestination does not commit one to belief in the dreadful doctrine of *double* predestination, the notion that some human beings have been brought into existence for the express purpose of being damned. That is outrageous. To anyone pressing that point of view we should feel prompted to reply in the recorded words of John Wesley: "Ah, I see. Your god is my Devil!"

Nevertheless, there seem to be those who appear to find a perverse pleasure in contemplating the final fate of the non-elect. An old Calvinistic preacher gave it as his considered opinion that only one in twenty of the human race were elected to salvation, the remaining nineteen being reprobate. "Holy Willie" in Burns' satirical stanza is a little more liberal:

O Thou, wha in the heavens dost dwell,
Wha, as it pleases best Thysel'

Sends ane to heaven and ten tae hell
A' for Thy glory,
An' no for ony guid or ill
They've din afore Ye.

One in ten as against one in twenty!

But we are not bound to believe in the terrible teaching of double predestination because of our belief in predestination itself. This is brought out very remarkably in Matthew 25:31–46, where Christ portrays Himself as a King on the throne of His glory, dividing humanity into two basic categories – sheep and goats: "Then shall the King say unto them on His right hand, Come, ye blessed of My Father, inherit the kingdom prepared for you from the foundation of the world" (v.34). But now notice what follows: "Then shall He also say unto them on His left hand, Depart from Me, ye cursed, into everlasting fire, prepared for" – whom? You? No. "Prepared for the Devil and his angels" (v.41). Hell was never meant for human beings: it was meant for Satan and his minions. Yet God so respects man's freewill that He will not over-ride it, even to save him from eternal perdition. Man's will is free. Everything turns upon that empirically verifiable fact, so far as his salvation is concerned. He is free to accept God's offer of mercy or to reject it.

Predestination and freewill are the obverse and reverse faces of a single coin. Much acrimonious debate might have been avoided if only the presence in spiritual truth of the element of paradox had been duly recognized. There is a story about two knights who almost engaged in mortal combat because one said that a shield suspended above them was made of gold and the other that it was made of silver. Both forgot that they were looking at opposite sides of the same shield.

One of the finest illustrations of the paradox of freewill and predestination in Christian thinking is the work of a Puritan preacher. He pictures a man approaching a gate surmounted by a stone arch. On the masonry above the arch he sees carved in stone the words: "Whosever will may come" (Revelation 22:17). On passing through the gate, and looking back, however, he sees engraved: "Elect from before the foundation of the world" (Ephesians 1:4).

"Elected," comments Emil Brunner, "does not mean predetermined, so that we would be simply pawns pushed hither and thither by God without our being able to do anything about it, but elected means eternally beloved of God in Jesus Christ, His Son." As someone has paradoxically put it: "God predestines freewill." Nevertheless, election is not to be thought of as founded on Divine favouritism or caprice: it is based on human free-will and decision. No one is chosen because he is choice: each is choice because he is chosen, and because he has responded positively to the call of God.

From the Scriptures we learn that the elect, having been "chosen according to the foreknowledge of God" (1 Peter 1:2), are rendered unimpugnable through the merits of Christ their Redeemer: "Who shall lay anything to the charge of God's elect" (Romans 8:33)?; that they are characterized by the possession and exercise of faith (Titus 1:1); and that it is incumbent upon them to put on "mercy, kindness, humility, meekness, longsuffering, forgiveness and love" (Colossians 3:12–14), because they are "Divinely predestinated to be conformed to the image of His Son" (Romans 8:29).

And if anybody protests that this is discriminatory and that he doubts his own election, let me remind him of the man who went once to consult a minister of Christ about a spiritual problem. The minister asked him if he was a Christian. "I do not know whether or not I am elected," he replied. "Then," the minister demanded, "are you a candidate? I have never heard of anyone being elected who was not first a candidate!" Even if we do, by the grace of God, believe ourselves to be numbered with the elect, it is still our bounden duty to "make our calling and election sure" (2 Peter 1:10).

Someone has suggested the following succinct summary of the matter: "God elects whom He foreknows; He predestinates whom He elects; He conforms to the image of His Son those whom He elects." But that does not absolve the elect from co-operation with the Divine will in their lives.

What the old theologians described as "the Effectual Call" is still, thank God, heard by God's elect. As Martin Buber maintains: "We are being addressed." Have you noticed how in the Bible, when God is summoning a person to Himself or to His service, He frequently repeats the name, so that there can be no faintest doubt as to whom the message is directed? "Moses, Moses!" "Samuel, Samuel!" "Martha, Martha!" "Simon, Simon!" "Saul, Saul!" and so on. There is nothing more thrilling in the whole range of Christian experience than this sense of being personally addressed by Almighty God.

THE MERCY OF THE GRACE THAT SAVED US

"By grace are ye saved, through faith, and that not of yourselves: it is the gift of God, not of works, lest any man should boast, for we are His workmanship (Gk *poiema*), created in Christ Jesus unto good works, which God hath before ordained that we should walk in them" (Ephesians 2:8–10).

We start, where we are bound to start, with man's fallen nature. No realistic attempt at the philosophy of a good life can begin without a frank recognition of the radical evil of the human heart. This is one of the most disturbing, but at the same time, one of the most heartening and comforting, articles in the creed. As diagnosis is, medically, prerequisite to cure, so conviction of sin, an overwhelming sense of its gravity as an offence against God, our neighbour and ourself is a necessary preliminary to salvation.

Repeatedly, the Bible reminds us that man is radically

depraved. Here are some pertinent texts: "The imagination of man's heart is evil from his youth" (Genesis 8:21). "There is no man that sinneth not" (2 Chronicles 6:36). "There is no man that doeth good, no, not one" (Psalm 14:13). "They go astray as soon as they are born" (Psalm 58:3). "Who can say, I have made my heart clean; I am pure from my sin" (Proverbs 20:9)? "Surely, there is not a righteous man upon earth, that doeth good and sinneth not" (Ecclesiastes 7:20). "The heart of the sons of men is fully set in them to do evil" (Ecclesiastes 8:11). "All have sinned and come short of the glory of God" (Romans 3:23). To minimize the malady is to detract from the marvel of the remedy. That is why Scripture so surgically probes the nature of sin. The more serious its diagnosis of the character of evil, the more marvellous the salvation it offers as the sole cure.

At the same time, it is important to recognize that, by affirming the fact of human depravity, the Word of God must not be construed as teaching that man is totally bad in the sense that he is utterly incapable of performing any good act. To suggest that would be to fly in the face of coercive evidence to the contrary. Nor does the Bible intend to convey the impression that the Almighty is indifferent to ethical issues or blind to moral distinctions. What the Scriptures do imply is the tragic truth about man is that the best thing about him is the worst thing because it gets in the way of God's grace, and so prevents him from accepting Christ as Saviour. "Of sin, because they believe not on Me" (John 16:9). Note that it is our *righteousnesses,* not our *unrighteousnesses,* which are described as in God's sight "filthy rags" (Isaiah 64:6). It was not criminals but clergy who put Christ on the Cross, not rogues but Rabbis. As William Blake poetically expressed it:

Caiaphas was in his own mind
A benefactor of mankind.

Yes, the paradox is that man's best is his worst. In this sense, he is totally depraved, utterly unable to effect his own salvation, or experience that provided for him by God. It is tempting at this point to introduce what seems a pat reference from the Psalms: "O, my soul, thou hast said unto the Lord, Thou art my Lord: my goodness extendeth not to Thee" (16:2), but I am afraid the Hebrew will not admit of such an interpretation. In this sense man *is* totally depraved, completely unable to save himself. In the light of the Cross how contemptibly mean our highest moral attainments appear! "It has been the Cross which has revealed to good men that their goodness has not been good enough," says Johann Hieronymus Schroeder; "in the presence of the Cross man dares not speculate about the degree of his goodness: rather he is at once cast down by his own sin and overwhelmed by the joyous insight that God is the Kinsman of the way."

This moral impotence on the part of man is exacerbated by the fact that, not only does he inherit a fallen nature, but he lives in a fallen world. One of the characters in Dylan Thomas's *Under Milk Wood* complains: "I want to be good, but nobody will let me." And, of course, chief among those who make it hard for us to be good is our adversary the Devil, who "as a roaring lion, walketh about, seeking whom he may devour" (1 Peter 5:8).

Inevitably, this combination of factors – a fallen nature, an evil environment and a malevolent Devil – involve man in temptation. "Temptation is common to man," writes Paul (1 Corinthians 10:13). Indeed it is! "There is no order so holy, no place so sacred," declares Thomas a Kempis, "as that there be no temptations in it." With this Samuel Rutherford heartily concurs. "Temptations that I supposed to be stricken dead and laid upon their backs," he confesses, "rise again and revive upon me; yea, I see that while I live temptations will not die." Not even the great and the good escape. "Calvin and I have temptations that would kill most men," affirms Luther. "Paul had temptations that would have killed us; and Christ had temptations that would have killed Paul."

Michael Green does well to remind us, however, that the Biblical word for temptation can equally mean testing. It is morally neutral. Were this not so, the sinlessness of Christ would be impugned and His redemptive ministry impossible (Luke 4:1–14). The writer to the Hebrews informs us that the Lord was "in all points tempted like as we are, yet without sin" (4:15); and in truth our Saviour referred to His whole earthly career as "My temptations" (Luke 22:28). As it has been trenchantly said: "It belongs to devils to be overcome by evil temptations and to sin from very wickedness; it belongs to angels not to feel temptation; it belongs to mankind both to feel temptations and to conquer." Thus, in becoming a Man, Christ laid Himself wide open to the solicitations of evil, without however succumbing to them.

An old Scots preacher, John Macrae, has a graphic word-picture of man's moral predicament: "I compare the Christian in his perilous journey through this world to a man walking through a narrow passage between two rows of close fires with a sack of gunpowder on his back. He must be careful at every step that he does not go nearer to one side than the other, lest the smallest spark of the fire should touch the powder and blow him to pieces."

At this juncture conscience comes into play. But what *is* conscience? Etymologically, it means "knowledge with oneself", or "complete knowledge". Theologically, it means more. As Archbishop Trench points out: "Conscience is not merely that which I know, but that which I know with *Some Other*, that Other being God, who makes His law and His presence felt and acknowledged in the heart." Alexander MacColl defines conscience grandly thus: "Conscience is the supreme court of the universe, set up in the human spirit."

There are those who would dearly like to escape from its monitorial attentions. Was it not Byron who wrote:

Why should not conscience have vacation
As well as other courts o' the nation,
Have equal power to adjourn,
Appoint appearance and return?

But no. Conscience never takes time off. Speaking of the pagan world of his time, Paul says that God had "planted the law in their hearts, their conscience also bearing them witness, and their thoughts the meanwhile accusing or else excusing one another" (Romans 2:15).

Yet, strangely enough, conscience is not always a reliable moral guide. It can always tell us to do what is right, but it cannot always tell us what it is right to do. Some of the blackest crimes on the calendar have been committed in the name of conscience. The New Testament uses some curious and apparently incongruous adjectives to qualify conscience. It speaks of a "weak conscience" (1 Corinthians 8:7); a "seared conscience" (1 Timothy 4:2); a "defiled conscience" (Titus 1:15); even an "evil conscience" (Hebrew 10:22). Conscience needs sensitizing, enlightening, reinforcing, "Your conscience is a watchdog," writes Hugh Redwood. "Don't feed it on sleeping tablets." Nourish it rather on the Word of God; let it be sensitized by the Holy Spirit; and it will grow strong, tender, authoritative, dominant. "Conscience," says Stanislaus, "warns us as a friend before it punishes us as a judge."

Unhappily, men do not always heed, as they should, the cautionary counsel of conscience. When conscience and temptation are in the ring together, it is usually conscience that goes to the ropes. Margaret Percival has done well to remind us that "the time for reasoning is *before* we have approached near enough to the forbidden fruit to look at it and admire". Proximity to attractive sin tends to paralyze moral judgment. Thomas Adams laments: "I see the Devil's hook and yet cannot help nibbling at his bait." You may recall Thomas a Kempis' concise summary of the natural history of temptation: "First, there cometh to the mind a bare thought of evil, then a strong imagination thereof, afterwards delight and evil emotion, and then consent." Once the anticipated pleasure has been awakened, the dictates of conscience are hardly likely to be regarded until it is too late.

Thus man falls into *sin*. Sin is a word which has almost vanished from the popular vocabulary of today. Yet the reality for which it stands was never more blatantly in evidence. What *is* sin essentially? Various definitions have been attempted. Some allude to it as "the growing pains of humanity", a sort of measles or mumps of the soul, destined sooner or later, to be outgrown; others identify it as an evolutionary hangover, a survival of the law of the jungle; others, again, as "a blundering quest for God"; others, still, as a mere negation, the absence of something rather than the presence of anything:

> *Evil is null, is nought,*
> *Is silence implying sound,*

and so on.

But what does the Bible say about sin? Investigation of the original constrains one to the conclusion that its attitude towards sin, and its assessment of it, may be compressed into five pictorial phrases: (a) *missing a mark*; (b) *crossing a line*; (c) *forging a chain*; (d) *contracting a disease*; and (e) *taking a drug*.

Take them each in turn.

(a) *missing a mark*. It is no mere coincidence that the two main words for sin in the Bible are the Hebrew *chata* and the Greek *hamartia*. Both mean missing the mark. In ancient times there was a popular game with the strange name of "Saints and Sinners". The players took sides, and the sport consisted in shooting arrows through a hoop hung up at some distance from the archers. If the competitor got all his arrows through the hoop, he took his place among the "Saints"; if, however, he failed to get even a single arrow through, he was classed with the "Sinners". In the great game of life there is no such thing as natural "Saints". As we have noted, all have come short of the glory of God. That applies to those who have the temerity or insensitivity to claim that they are morally "right on target".

There is a funny story in a book called *The Parables* by Gerald Kennedy. He tells of an old man in Arkansas who was a compulsive sharp-shooter, always trigger-happy. Everywhere he went he had his rifle at the ready, taking pot shots at anything in sight. A skilled marksman, following his trail, was amazed to find that the old fellow always hit a bull's-eye. Wherever he found signs of the sharp-shooter's exploits – on barn-door, ranch-fencing, or wherever – there was always a circle traced in white chalk and, right in the centre of it, a bullet-hole. This impressed the observer immensely. Meeting the sharp-shooter some time later, he complimented him on his superb marksmanship. The sharp-shooter, with a toss of his head, made light of it. "Shucks!" he cried. " 'Taint nothin'. I jess shoots first and draws a circle afterwards!"

Something of the same procedure is followed by many modern men and women in the matter of morals. They set up their own private standards and, conforming to them, are quite complacent about their mode of living. But, as the apostle Paul puts it, "they, measuring themselves by themselves, and comparing themselves among themselves, are not wise" (2 Corinthians 10:12). God's standard is the ultimate criterion; and, where that standard is concerned, we all miss the mark. It is told of the Roman emperor Galerian that he once watched an archer shooting twenty arrows in swift succession at a target, and missing with the lot. "May I compliment you," he remarked afterwards to the luckless archer, "on your splendid talent for missing?" That is a talent, morally speaking, shared by the whole mass of mankind.

(b) Other Hebrew words for sin, such as *chata* and the Greek *hamartano*, convey the idea of going astray, trespassing on forbidden territory, *crossing a line*. The English word "sin" is itself derived, so scholars tell us, from a Norse root *sund*, signifying "to separate". We see a survival of the old term in such expressions as "sundering", and in Plymouth *Sound*, that is, "the water that separates".

Now around certain areas of human experience God has set up protective fences, and behind them there is this inscription: "Trespassers will be Prosecuted". Sin, in one aspect of it, consists in leaping over those fences and disregarding the Divine warning.

Years ago, when I lived in Yorkshire, an outbreak of foot and mouth disease occurred among the cattle in the country district where I resided. After the discovery was made, a certain neighbourhood was officially designated an infected zone, and around the fields in that locality electrified fences were put up to prevent animals from straying on to the contaminated ground.

So God has graciously fenced off from man the enchanted territory of sin. He has proscribed his entry into it and forbidden indulgence in it. For humanity He has made it "out of bounds"; and sin, in this view of it, is a crossing of the line of demarcation, a trespassing on prohibited property, a breach of the Divine hedge; and "whoso breaketh an hedge, a serpent shall bite him" (Ecclesiastes 10:8). That is precisely what happened in Paradise.

(c) *forging a chain*. Not only is sin a failure to attain a moral ideal or Divine standard, or a wandering off into forbidden territory, it is also the forging of a chain. Inevitably, sin brings bondage. "Whosoever committeth sin is a slave of sin" (John 8:34).

The beginning of all life may be described in terms of a bursting of bonds, a breaking out of prison. By the bud slowly unfolding its sticky petals on the bough; the grub struggling to extricate itself from the cocoon; the baby forcing its way from the womb, and by many more such instances, this principle is vividly illustrated.

Now, sin is just a reverse of that. It presents the tragic picture of a person forging a chain and fettering himself with it, like a man in a madhouse deliberately donning a strait-jacket. While the process is in progress, the sinner may not, and probably does not, know what he is doing. To his infatuated and bedizened fancy, the bond with which he is binding himself may seem no thicker than the flimsy strand of a spider's web – and so, at the start, it may very well be – but ultimately he discovers to his dismay that sin has him as securely fastened as the Lilliputians with their ropes of gossamer had Gulliver. Drink, drugs, gambling, sex can get just such a strangling grip on the human soul. Sin is the forging of a chain.

(d) *contracting a disease.* There is something about contracting a disease which is closely analogous to man's entanglement with sin. Several points of illuminating correspondence at once suggest themselves in this connection: (i) sin, like some diseases, is congenital. The predisposition is there from earliest infancy. (ii) sin, like some diseases, is infectious. No quarantine can effectively prescribe or limit its incidence. "Sin," as someone has said, "is a great epidemic which has infected the whole human race." (iii) sin, like some diseases, is disfiguring. One recalls with revulsion seeing the ravages of sin registered on the face of Bonnie Prince Charlie in a portrait in oils of him, executed in old age, exhibited in a public art gallery. (iv) sin, like some diseases, is humanly incurable. There is no man-made remedy for spiritual heart-trouble. (v) sin, like some diseases, is fatal in its consequences. "Sin, when it is finished, bringeth forth death" (James 1:15). John

Newton has a neat lyrical compendium of the range of resemblances between sin and disease:

The worst of all diseases
Is light compared with sin;
On every part it seizes,
But rages most within.

'Tis leprosy and fever
And palsy all combined,
And none but the believer
The least relief can find.

According to recently-published statistics, no fewer than fifteen million people throughout the world are infected with physical leprosy, but by nature the whole of the human race suffers from its spiritual counterpart. Sin is like contracting a disease.

(e) *taking a drug.* One of the saddest anomalies of the moral life is that the more one commits sin the less one knows about its real nature. Evil casts a spell upon the soul. It injects into it a numbing tranquillizer, inducing in it a state of spiritual stupefaction. Sin, not religion, is what Karl Marx should have dubbed "the opiate of the people". The first time an evil deed is perpetrated the feeling of guilt and shame is almost insupportable. So conscience-stricken is the culprit that he can hardly look anyone in the face. But, as he persists in the practice, and the thing becomes a habit, his moral sense becomes atrophied and in time he can perform the immoral act without a qualm. That is why the present age, when sin is so rampant, has little awareness of its reality. Asked what was the great want of Victorian England, William Ewart Gladstone is reported to have replied: "Ah, a sense of sin!" What would he say were he to come back today? Robert Burns, Scotland's national bard, deserves a hearing on this subject:

I waive the quantum o' the sin,
The hazard o' concealin';
But, och, it hardens a' within
An' petrifies the feelin'.

It sure does. "Every man's sin works like a drug," writes John Henry Jowett, "and continued sin tends to stupefaction."

It is pertinent at this point to turn our attention for a little to the three broad types of sin: (a) *sins of transmission;* (b) *sins of omission;* and (c) *sins of commission.*

(a) *sins of transmission.* The Bible goes to great lengths to impress us with the fact that at birth we inherit a nature with a bias towards evil, in other words, with a fallen nature. "Thy first father hath sinned" (Isaiah 43:27). "By one man sin entered into the world" (Romans 5:12). "Behold, I was shapen in iniquity, and in sin did my mother conceive me" (Psalm 51:5). "Thou wast altogether born in sin" (John 9:34). "Sin dwelleth in me" (Romans 7:17). "It's all that stuff about original sin that I can't swallow," a man once remarked to Seth Joshua. "You don't have to swallow it," he answered. "It's inside you already!"

We must, of course, not even seem to subscribe to the dreadful Augustinian doctrine of the transmission of guilt. A dogma which can seriously describe babies as "little devils clinging to their mothers' breasts" is surely self-condemned. We cannot too strongly stress that what is transmitted in human generation is not guilt but bias, not culpability but corruption. "The son shall not bear the iniquity of his father, neither shall the father bear the iniquity of the son" (Ezekiel 18:20). It is true that the entail of sin is often communicated to the offspring of those who offend against God's law: "The Lord God, visiting the iniquity of the fathers upon the children, and upon the children's children, unto the third and to the fourth generation" (Exodus 34:6,7), but the guilt is not transferred. Such punishments and penalties as are inherited from a sinful ancestry, the grim legacy of lust and greed and violence, do not pass on to the descendants moral liability for the wrongs committed and the evils perpetrated. "The soul that sinneth *it* shall die" (Ezekiel 18:4). There is an awful incommunicability about guilt. As Rudyard Kipling writes:

The sins that they do two by two
They pay for one by one.

Culpability is strictly non-transferable.

That we *do* have a fallen nature is a matter of universal experience. Always and everywhere it is easier to do wrong than to do right, just as it is easier to walk downhill than uphill. If there were no Fall mentioned in the Bible, it would be necessary to invent one to account for man's moral condition. Nevertheless, possession of a corrupt nature, with a bias towards evil, does not involve guilt, even although it may, and probably should, entail shame. A teen-aged girl, born with a club-foot, albeit not in any way responsible for her pedal deformity, and perhaps not even able to account for it, is yet at great pains to hide it, as far as possible, from public view. Although feeling ashamed of it, she is not at all responsible for it. Just so with what theologians call "Original Sin". We are, or certainly ought to be, ashamed of it, but we need not feel in the least guilty about it.

So far from concealing their sinful nature, the saints seem to have a holy fear of being thought better than they really are. Always they are ready to expose their inward rottenness, baring their souls with "all the gusto of a showman". Corresponding to that is the indisputable fact that other people seem to have a sort of Divine right to know the worst about us. Paradoxically, the most public thing about anyone is his private life. "It is as if a man had an inalienable right to behold all that is dark, imperfect, stupid and guilty in his fellow-beings," declares the distinguished Swiss psychoanalyst Carl J. Jung. Another eminent psychologist, the American William James, has laid down as an indispensable prerequisite to spiritual health a willingness, as he puts it, to "exteriorize one's rottenness". The ripest and rarest of Christians have always been the readiest to do that.

Here are a few characteristic confessions. Take Paul: "In me, that is in my flesh, dwelleth no good thing" (Romans 7:18). Or take John Knox: "In youth, middle age, and now after many battles, I find nothing in me but corruption". Or, again, take John Wesley: "I am fallen short of the glory of God. My whole heart is altogether corrupt and abominable, and consequently my whole life." Or, once more, take Augustus Toplady: "I am myself nothing but sin and weakness. In my whole flesh naturally dwelleth no good thing." Or, yet again, take Charles Haddon Spurgeon: "My experience is a daily struggle with evil within. I wish I could find in myself something friendly to grace; but hitherto I have searched my nature through, and have found everything in rebellion against God." Or, take finally Alexander Whyte: "I am the worst man in Scotland. If the people passing me in Princes Street, Edinburgh, could read the thoughts of my heart, they would spit in my face." Summing up in vigorous verse the nature of "that vile three-letter word", Charles Wesley says:

Thou art darkness in my mind,
Perverseness in my will,
Love inordinate and blind,
That always cleaves to ill;
Every passion's wild excess,
Anger, lust and pride thou art;
Thou art sin and sinfulness
And unbelief of heart.

How radically different from these frank self-exposures on

the part of the saints is the popular view of sin today! As we have observed, the very word has almost disappeared from our vocabulary. We speak often of "vice", "crime", "delinquency", and so on, but seldom of sin. When Walter Cronkite, the well-known US political analyst, was asked whether human beings were basically good or basically bad, he gave his opinion in these words: "Most people are good. There aren't many really evil people." Not so speak the saints.

Transmitted sin, better described as "sinfulness", as we shall later see, constitutes the most persistent, intractable and embarrassing problem of the spiritual life. Meanwhile, we may remind ourselves of Thomas Adams' neat aphorism: "Iniquity can plead antiquity." It certainly can. Human sin began almost as soon as humanity itself.

(b) *sins of omission.* Despite its negative appearance, this aspect of sin is, to sensitive and imaginative people, certainly one of the most appalling of all. The evil that we have done is bad enough, but the good we have left undone is of far greater magnitude – "duties unattempted, opportunities unimproved, grace disregarded". Archbishop Ussher, we are told, "prayed often and with great humility that God would forgive him his sins of omission, his failings in his duty." Another notable Anglican uttered a similar request: "O, Lord, forgive my sins, especially my sins of omission." You may remember in this context the self-accusatory lines of Margaret Wilkinson, entitled "Guilty!":

I never cut my neighbour's throat,
My neighbour's purse I never stole;
I never spoiled his house and lands,
But God have mercy on my soul!

For I am haunted night and day
By all the deeds I have not done,
That unattempted loveliness,
O, costly valour never won!

There are some who refer to what they call "unconscious sins". I do not think the adjective appropriate or even admissible. The phrase is surely a misnomer. They are no unconscious sins, for the simple reason that there are no sins, as such, where the will is not engaged, and the will can never be engaged unconsciously. But there are vast numbers of sins of omission, which do not register, as they should, in the conscience of insensitive people, either because they rationalize their inaction or because the consequences of such negative sins are not always noticeable to others. In any case, we should do well to make our own this lyrical litany:

Since what I dream and what I do
In my weak life are always two;
Help me, oppressed by things undone,
O Thou, whose dreams and deeds are one.

(c) *sins of commission.* This brings us to what is commonly meant by the word "sin"; that is, deliberate acts of wrongdoing, voluntary violations of the law of God. And there are three things to note about it: (i) its universality. "No man living is acquitted before Thee" (Psalm 143:2). "Who can say, I have made my heart clean, I am pure from my sin" (Proverbs 20:9)? (ii) its degree. All sin is wrong, but all sin is not wrong to the same extent. (iii) its social consequences. We recognize and are enabled by the grace of God to lament the sins which we ourselves have committed, but have no means of computing the moral damage we have done by our evildoing in the lives of others. In his private diary Thomas Shepherd of Cambridge, Connecticut, USA, has written: "I began to consider whether all the country did not fare the worse for my sins; and I saw it was, and this was an humbling thought to me."

Then, when the sin has been committed, conscience suddenly and dramatically reverses its rôle, as we have reminded ourselves, and instead of being a friendly counsellor, it becomes a stern and implacable judge. No longer is it adviser, but accuser. Conscience is the Sinai of the soul. As soon as the law of God has been broken, conscience becomes an erupting volcano, belching forth fire and brimstone.

This judgmental function of conscience is dynamized by the Spirit. Of Him our Lord declares: "When He is come, He will reprove the world of sin, and of righteousness, and of judgment: of sin, because they believe not on Me; of righteousness, because I go to My Father, and ye see Me no more; of judgment, because the prince of this world is judged" (John 15:8–11). Many other passages of Scripture make the same point. "God is angry with the wicked every day" (Psalm 7:11). "The wrath of God is revealed from heaven against all ungodliness and unrighteousness of men, who hold the truth in unrighteousness" (Romans 1:18). This engenders what theologians call "conviction of sin". The soul is wrung with a strangling realization of the wrongs it has done. A phoney sense of integrity is replaced by a real sense of iniquity. Almost all the leading Evangelicals have passed through that shattering experience – Augustine, Luther, Bunyan, and so on. Obstetricians tell us that in natural birth the baby suffers as well as the mother. To that there is, or ought to be, a spiritual parallel. But, alas, there are far too many cases of painless spiritual childbirth. Many seem to be born again in what used to be described as "Twilight Sleep". People lightly profess to be converted to Christ without experiencing the pangs of conviction of sin. No wonder the rate of spiritual infantile mortality among them is so high.

Now, just as physical pain tends to produce a cry, so conviction of sin produces, or should produce, *confession of sin*. Most creatures cry out under torture. (That is, incidentally, one of the strongest proofs that there is a good and loving God. Otherwise, why cry?) And one of the climactic moments in our spiritual experience is that in which we turn, as it were, King's Evidence against ourselves. To do so is utterly unlike human nature. We love to stand erect in conscious rectitude rather than bow in acknowledgement of the fact that we are sinners. Yet, such frank self-exposure is an indispensable precondition of salvation. "We own our sins," says an old Puritan, "that we may disown them." We must disclose the symptoms if the Divine Physician is to effect a cure. "When anyone is ready to uncover his sins," it has been sagely said, "God is ready to cover them." To this the Scriptures set their seal. "He that covereth his sins shall not prosper: but whoso confesseth and forsaketh them shall find mercy" (Proverbs 28:13). To spell sin properly we must always put "I" in the middle of it. General confessions are not worth much. They are vague, amorphous and unspecific. It is when confessions become intensely, even embarrassingly, personal that God absolves us. "Honest confession is good for the soul," says an old Scots proverb. The Psalmist found that to be true. "I acknowledged my sin unto Thee, and mine iniquity have I not hid. I said, I will confess my transgressions unto the Lord; and Thou forgavest the iniquity of my sin" (Psalm 32:5).

From confession we pass to repentance. The Greek word *metanoia*, means "after-knowledge" in contradistinction from *pronoia* which signifies "foreknowledge".

Several other states of mind which are superficially similar to repentance are frequently mistaken for it. Before proceeding further with our study, it may be well, as far as possible, to clear away any such misunderstandings.

For one thing, repentance is not *regret*. Regret is being sorry for oneself, deploring the consequences of one's sinful actions. When Frederick Temple, Archbishop of Canterbury, famous sire of a more famous son, asked a candidate for ordination to define repentance, the candidate answered: "A heart broken because of sin." "Stuff and nonsense!" exploded the archbishop. "It is a heart that has broken *away* from sin". Repentance is not merely regret.

For another thing, repentance is not *remorse*. Remorse is repentance with no hope at its heart. In this regard William Nevins institutes an illuminating contrast between Judas and Peter. "There are two kinds of repentance," he says, "one is that of Judas; the other, that of Peter. The one is ice broken, the other is ice melted". Repentance unto life will mean repentance in the life. Tertullian dubbed remorse "an emotion of disgust". It eats its old heart out instead of seeking a new heart.

For a further thing, repentance is not *reformation*. Some folk seem to think that a change of life-style for the better is all that is required, that amendment can be a sufficient substitute for Atonement. Analogous to this is the Papist practice of penance, in which a sinner tries to compound for his transgression by afflicting his soul or flagellating his body. But true repentance is not something that can be earned or won or merited in any way: it is a *gift* (2 Timothy 2:25). It is all of grace. Reformation will certainly follow genuine repentance, but it is no real part of repentance itself.

For a final thing, repentance is not *reparation*. To be sure, anyone who, like Zacchaeus, truly repents will, like him, where possible, make amends to the person he has wronged. Restitution is practical proof of the reality of repentance, but it must not be mistaken for repentance. One recalls reading how, once at the Keswick Convention, after a powerful and searching message on this subject, the local Post Office was reported to be sold out of Postal Orders, purchased by people eager to make reparation for monetary irregularities of which they had been guilty. But, buying the Postal Orders was the consequence and not the cause of the moral revolution wrought in them.

What, then, *is* repentance? The New Testament word is *metanoia*, which means literally "change of mind". But theologically, the word means much more. Perhaps one might properly define it as a revulsion against sin resulting from a revelation of the righteousness and love of God. To repent is something we are commanded to do, not an optional exercise. "Repent ye, and believe the Gospel" (Mark 1:15). It is, as we have seen, a gift. "God hath also granted repentance unto life" (Acts 11:18). "Him hath God exalted with His right hand to be a prince and a Saviour, for to give repentance to Israel" (Acts 5:31). "God hath also to the Gentiles granted repentance unto life" (Acts 11:18).

Years ago, when we lived near the town of Dumfries in the south of Scotland, a local man pointed out to me a "peel", as the Borderers call them, known as "The Tower of Repentance". Someone, it is said, once asked a Christian living in those parts, "What is the way to heaven?" Pointing to the peel, the Christian replied: "It is round by that tower." It certainly is. For, on the highest authority, "Except ye repent, ye shall all perish" (Luke 13:3).

Repentance, we have stated, is a revulsion due to a revelation. "Godly sorrow worketh repentance" (2 Corinthians 7:10). "The goodness of God leadeth thee to repentance" (Romans 2:4). "Then shall ye remember your own evil ways, and your doings that were not good, and shall loathe yourselves in your own sight, for your iniquities and for your abominations" (Ezekiel 36:31). In all real repentance there is, of course, a decisive break with sin. "There can be no true repentance," remarks R.W. Green, "while a secret love of sin continues in the heart." We are all human enough to know that, as Josh Billings slyly says: "It is much easier to repent of sins that we have committed than to repent of those we intend to commit." "He hath ill repented," observes Augustine, "whose sins are repeated." Sincere repentance always entails a resolute turning away from sin. "There is no pardon," affirms an old Puritan, "for the persistent sinner."

Moreover, genuine repentance is usually marked by a

note of urgency. There is no time to be lost. Doom looms. Things must be put right at once. A learned Rabbi was once asked: "When should I repent?" "The day before you die," was the answer. "But how can I know on what day I shall die?" demanded the questioner. "That's just the point," responded the Rabbi. "You do not know the date of your death, so you had better repent today." "You cannot repent too soon," comments Thomas Fuller, "because you do not know how soon it will be too late." Those who, like Fichte, protest, "I have no time for penitence," will one day find that they have eternity for despair. Better weep now than then! "The true holy water," as Thomas Watson quaintly observes, "is not that which the Pope sprinkles, but is distilled from the penitent eye."

Furthermore, the Bible speaks of "the fruits of repentance" (Matthew 3:8). It is a bitter root, but it bears fragrant flowers and luscious fruit. The poet Sterling puts the point lyrically:

Repentance clothes with grass and flowers
The grave in which the past is laid.

And Francis Quarles quaintly adds: "When Peter's cock begins to crow, 'tis day!"

Earlier in our study, we noted that one of the main factors in producing repentance is the Word of God. That Word has doubtless been responsible for begetting conviction of sin in the heart, but at this point it becomes involved in a new way in the life of the person concerned. Repentance and faith are the two wings on which the soul flies to God. We have looked a little at the former: now turn to the latter.

Faith! The term reverberates like the toll of a great bell all through the New Testament. It is presented and represented in four principal ways: (a) *as discernment.* "Now faith is the substance of things hoped for, the evidence of things not seen" (Hebrews 11:1). (b) *as adjustment*. Four times in the Word of God does this critically significant sentence appear: "The just shall live by faith" (Habakkuk 2:4; Romans 1:17; Galatians 3:11; and Hebrews 10:38. Note the differing emphases in the quotations). (c) *as endowment*. "To another faith by the same Spirit" (1 Corinthians 12:9); and (d) *as commitment*. "I live by faith in the Son of God, who loved me and gave Himself for me" (Galatians 2:20 Moffatt).

It is with the second and fourth of these sorts of faith that we are to be here principally preoccupied – faith as *adjustment* and faith as *commitment*. But how is faith to be obtained? This brings us right back to the Bible. A striking story from the Life of D.L. Moody will help our present purpose. He tells that, as a youth, he was in the habit of praying fervently for faith, and that he expected it to strike him like a bolt from the blue. It did not. Then, one day, while reading Romans, his eye lit on the text: "Faith cometh by hearing and hearing by the Word of God" (Romans 10:17). "I closed my Bible," says Moody, "and prayed for faith; I opened my Bible, and began to study, and faith has been growing ever since." By hearing or reading the Holy Scriptures faith is born within the soul. As we proceed, we shall see how that faith works. In Acts 14:24 Paul and Barnabas speak of "the door of faith". It is an apt figure. Faith *is* the entrance to the life of grace.

As such, the first thing it produces is a sense of forgiveness. About forgiveness there are four views. Some say that forgiveness is *unnecessary*. When Walt Whitman's aunt, solicitous for his spiritual well-being, asked him if he had made his peace with God, he answered: "I did not know that we had quarrelled!" Some say that forgiveness is *easy*. Heinrich Heine, the German-Jewish poet, was once interrogated by a friend as to whether he expected God to forgive him for the sort of life he was then leading. He casually responded: "Of course, God will forgive me. It is His trade!" Some say that forgiveness is *impossible*.

Luther when young felt like that. Troubled about his sins, he consulted an old monk on the problem in the monastery at Erfurt in Germany. The monk inquired: "Do you believe in the Creed?" "Yes," said Luther, "I do ." "Do you, then, accept as true that article in the Creed which says: 'I believe in the forgiveness of sins?'" queried the monk. "Yes", returned Luther. "Then," went on the monk, "when you sing it in church, sing it like this: 'I believe in the forgiveness of *my* sins!'" But no. It made little difference. Luther still smartingly felt that his sins were unpardonable. That is the perspective on sin engendered by the convicting Spirit of God. It is thus that sin looks in the light of the Cross, and it is how it must seem in the sight of Him who is "of purer eyes than to behold evil, and cannot look upon iniquity" (Habakkuk 1:13) – no mere petty, pardonable peccadillo, but a heinous crime, nothing less than man murdering his Maker. As Thomas Payne truly said: "Sin in its essence is Deicide." Sin is so dreadful an offence that but for the sacrifice of Christ, it could never to all eternity have been forgiven. "Neither in this world, neither in the world to come" (Matthew 12:32). There is such a thing as "the unpardonable sin". "There is a sin unto death: I do not say that he shall pray for it" (1 John 5:16). "Whosoever speaketh against the Holy Ghost, it shall not be forgiven him." (Matthew 12:32). "It is impossible for those who were once enlightened, and have tasted of the heavenly gift, and were made partakers of the Holy Ghost, and have tasted the good Word of God, and the powers of the world to come, if they shall fall away, to renew them again unto repentance" (Hebrews 6:4–6). Whatever these awful words may mean, they certainly do not imply any limit to the love of God, but only the limit in human beings of response to it. With confidence, therefore, we may state the positive truth. "All manner of sin shall be forgiven." As R.H. Malden remarks: "It is a great thing to know that sin, however grievous, can be forgiven, to know that God is a pardoning God, whose mercy is even as His Majesty."

John Wesley observes: "The forgiveness of sins is one of the first unseen things whereof faith is the evidence." Repentance and faith, as we have noticed, are according to the New Testament the divinely-appointed preconditions of forgiveness. Perhaps we should add, as a third condition, forgivingness. In parable and precept Jesus plainly teaches that to be forgiven we must be forgiving. "If ye forgive men their trespasses, your Father will also forgive you. But if ye forgive not their trespasses, neither will your Father forgive your trespasses" (Matthew 18:35). "When ye stand praying, forgive, if ye have ought against any: that your Father also which is in heaven may forgive you your trespasses" (Mark 11:25). "Forgive, and ye shall be forgiven" (Luke 6:37). "Forgive us our sins; for we also forgive every one that is indebted to us" (Luke 11:4). With these terms met, pardon is Divinely bestowed. As George Bernard says: "God tells us Himself that we are forgiven."

But this is not all. There is more, much more – justification, reconciliation, regeneration, adoption, assurance. Salvation is infinitely more than mere acquittal at the high court of heaven.

Pass on to *justification*. There is often an antiphonal relationship between the Old Testament and the New. So here. To the Old Testament's query: "How then can man be justified with God" (Job 25:4)? the New Testament returns six replies: it says he is *justified by grace*. "Being justified freely by His grace" (Romans 2:24); *justified by blood*. "Being now justified by His blood" (Romans 5:9); *justified by His resurrection*. "Christ was raised again for our justification" (Romans 4:25); *justified by faith*. "Therefore being justified by faith we have peace with God through our Lord Jesus Christ" (Romans 5:11); *justified by works* (before men). "By works a man is justified" (James 2:24); *justified by words*. "By thy words thou shalt be justified" (Matthew 12:37).

What does it mean to justify? We get a clue if we

examine other verbs with the same ending. To beautify is to make beautiful. To pacify is to make peaceful. To solidify is to make solid, and so on. Does to justify, then, mean to make just? Yes, it does. It means to make consciously right not on the basis of one's own moral achievements but on the ground of what Christ accomplished on the Cross; that is, not on attainment but on Atonement. Stripped of all the technical jargon of theology, what justification amounts to is this – not only that, as Whyte used to put it, "God has no ill will at us", but that He has credited us with the moral merits of our Redeemer. The clever Evangelical *cliche* that "to be justified means to be just-as-if-I'd never sinned" is far too negative. Justification implies, not only that we have been exonerated, acquitted, absolved, but that it is as if we had actually lived the life that Jesus lived as recorded in the Gospels. Justification is thus much more than mere forgiveness.

Nevertheless, as David Thomas quite properly argues, "no man can be happy if he is merely treated as righteous when he is not righteous". Patently, there can be no question of any legal fiction, any mere pretence on the part of God that things are otherwise than they are. And so we proceed from justification to regeneration. This is the pivotal point in the whole plan of salvation; this, and not any issue of dogma or polity, is what splits Christendom in two. So-called Christian institutions, however popular, powerful and venerable, which do not recognize the absolute cruciality of regeneration, are no part of the true Church of God. To one of the early Methodist preachers, Conyers by name, the then Archbishop of York, Dr Drummond, said sharply: "You would be better employed preaching the morality of Socrates than canting about the New Birth." That exalted church dignitary was plainly not himself a Christian in the New Testament sense. For on the threshold of all genuine Christian experience stands the Divine imperative: "Ye must be born again" (John 3:7). Just as human birth is the necessary precondition of all man's experience and achievement, so rebirth, being made "a new creature in Christ Jesus" (2 Corinthians 5:17), is the indispensable prerequisite of everything in the Christian life. Regeneration is not just a figure: it is a fact. By believing in Jesus Christ as Saviour and Lord we are indeed made new.

Our experience is like that of a newborn child. It is a passive experience: we cannot bring ourselves to birth either naturally or spiritually. Marcus Loane refers to the New Birth as "the great obstetric metaphor", but it is surely much more than that: it is a transforming experience, literally a New Birth.

Physically, the most marvellous journey anyone can take is not some space probe to a far-flung star, nor some odyssey to the moon or voyage to Mars: the most marvellous journey anyone can undertake is only a few inches long – the journey from the womb to the world – a journey from darkness to light, from bondage to freedom, from nonentity to identity, from silence to sound, from solitude to society, from dependence to independence, and so on. Christ is God's "only begotten Son" (John 3:16), but through Him we are "begotten again unto a lively hope by the resurrection of Jesus Christ from the dead" (1 Peter 1:3). "And of His own will begat He us with the Word of truth, that we should be a kind of first fruits of His creatures" (James 1:18).

The next stage in the life of grace is *adoption*. "God, having predestinated us unto the adoption of children by Jesus Christ" (Ephesians 1:5), "we have not received the spirit of bondage again to fear; but ye have received the Spirit of adoption, whereby we cry Abba, Father" (Romans 8:15). "That we might receive the adoption of sons" (Galatians 4:5). "And because ye are sons, God hath sent forth the Spirit of His Son into your hearts, crying, Abba, Father" (Galatians 4:6).

Some critics aver that in this connection there is a

conflict between the teaching of John and that of Paul. John, they say, tells us that we become children of God by *birth*: Paul, by *adoption*. A *prima facie* case can be made out for this, but there is really no disparity or disagreement. The misunderstanding arises from importing into Paul's figure of adoption ideas totally alien to it. It comes of reading the text through English instead of through Greek spectacles. To the Greek of Paul's time adoption meant "the placing in the estate of a son of one who was already a child of the family". In the old Greek household it was a formal ceremony. The minor never wore the toga until the day of his attaining his majority. On that day, in the presence of his elders, the toga was placed upon his shoulders in token of his having come into all the rights and privileges of a fullgrown son. Adoption did not *make* him a child. He was born that. Adoption was the formal recognition of his legal standing as a son and heir.

This sense of belonging to the family of God and inheriting its favours induces in the believer a sense of *assurance*. "We believe," cries Peter, "and *are sure*." (John 6:59). There is indeed a faith of *assent* and a faith of *adherence*, but the New Testament points to something finer far – the faith of *assurance*. The Greeks had a compound word for it. Among recent verbal importations from that great language into English is the term *euphoria*, meaning "high spirits, a sense of well-being". The Christian Scriptures have a still better term *plerophoria* – "full assurance", "much assurance" (Hebrews 10:22; Colossians 2:2; Hebrews 6:11; 1 Thessalonians 1:5). This assurance is communicated to the soul by three agencies – (i) *the witness of the historic Word*; (ii) *the witness of the Spirit within*; and (iii) *the witness of the works without*.

(i) *The Witness of the Word*. "As many as received Him, to them gave He power to become the sons of God" (John 1:12). "Because ye are sons, God hath sent forth the Spirit of His Son into your hearts, crying, Abba, Father" (Galatians 4:6). "Beloved, now are we the sons of God" (1 John

3:2).

(ii) *The Witness of the Spirit within.* You remember Samuel Wesley's dying words to his son John: "The inward witness, son, the inward witness – that is the proof, the strongest proof, of Christianity." The witness confirms and corroborates the Word. Years ago when we lived in the centre of London, we used, on summer evenings, to have in our home a vivid illustration of this. Standing at the open door, we could hear the great bell of Big Ben booming out the time across the Thames and, at precisely the same moment, hear its chimes sounding out on the radio within. So the Word says: "You are sons of God" and the inward witness endorses that. "Yes, you are," it says.

(iii) *The Witness of the works.* Any confidence of personal acceptance with God not attested to by corresponding behaviour is worse than worthless. "I would not give a straw," declares John Newton, "for that assurance which sin will not damp. If David had come from his adultery and still had talked of his assurance, I should have despised his speech."

Confirmatory of this assurance is the convert's compliance with our Lord's command to be *baptized in water*. By both practice and precept Christ commanded this ordinance. "Jesus was baptized of John in Jordan" (Mark 1:9). "Go ye therefore and teach all nations, baptizing them in the name of the Father, and of the Son, and of the Holy Ghost" (Matthew 28:19). His apostles followed His example. They also taught water baptism. "Repent, and be baptized every one of you in the name of Jesus Christ" (Acts 2:38), cries Peter. Paul was himself baptized (Acts 9:18) and uses baptism with great effect as an illustration of the principle of death-union with Christ (Romans 6:3,4). No fewer than ten individual baptisms are recorded in the Book of Acts.

In our study of the Church we noted that three modes of baptism are practised in Christendom today – *sprinkling,* effusion and immersion. Also there are *infant baptism and adult baptism.* Infant baptism is performed by sprinkling in the Roman and in some Protestant churches: in the Greek churches the infant is totally immersed three times in the name of the Father, and of the Son, and of the Holy Ghost.

No unbiased student of the New Testament is likely to dispute the truth of the statement that the mode of baptism it employs and enjoins is the total immersion of adults – what is known as "Believer's Baptism". Infant baptism, however pretty and appealing as a piece of ceremonial, would seem to be without warrant or backing in the Word of God. As Alan Wright perceptively points out: "The Bible does not say: 'Be baptized and repent': it says 'Repent and be baptized.' " Now, no baby can fulfil that scriptural precondition!

Besides, baptism is a lustration which is also an illustration. Sprinkling or effusion present no picture of death and burial and rising again with Christ. Roman Catholics are not content with sprinkling holy water on the face of the corpse: they insist upon interment! No. It is adult baptism that the New Testament prescribes.

Is, then, baptism necessary to salvation? Some say it is. Calvin knew better. He reminded us that the thief on the Cross went straight to Paradise without having had the opportunity to subscribe to the ordinance. Nevertheless, although not requisite to salvation, baptism is certainly essential to complete conformity to the command of Christ. "Go ye, and baptize" is the Divine directive.

Experientially conjoined with baptism in water are two other baptisms – a *baptism of power* and a *baptism of love.* Of the latter we shall have something to say later on. To the baptism of power we now turn for a moment or two.

This baptism is specifically referred to in the New Testament by four different persons – John the Baptist, the Lord Jesus, Peter and Paul. Here are the references: "He shall baptize you with the Holy Ghost and with fire" (Luke 3:16). "Ye shall be baptized with the Holy Ghost not many days hence" (Acts 1:5). "Ye shall be baptized with the Holy Ghost" (Acts 11:16). "For in one Spirit are we all baptized into one body" (1 Corinthians 12:13).

Unhappily, this baptism which was Divinely intended to be the sign, seal and sacrament of Christian unity, has become in some circles a stone of stumbling. About it there is a wide diversity of opinions. Some say (a) *it was for yesterday, but not for today*; some say (b) *it was for certain races, but not for others*; some say (c) *it was for men, but not for women*; some say (d) *it was for the illiterate, but not for the educated*; some say (e) *it was for the spiritually immature, but not for ripe saints*; and some say (f) *it will be for tomorrow, but is not for today*.

As if to sweep away all such gratuitous argumentation, Peter makes a categorical affirmation to the contrary: "The promise is unto you, and to your children, and to all that are afar off, even as many as the Lord our God shall call" (Acts 2:39).

What, then, *is* this baptism? It is a repetition in the experience of the individual believer of what happened collectively to the disciples on the Day of Pentecost – an effusion on them and an infusion into them of the Spirit of the living God. Both our blessed Lord and the apostle Peter referred to this baptism as a *gift*. Paradoxically, however, it is a gift which has to be asked for! "If ye, then, being evil, know how to give good gifts unto your children, how much more shall your heavenly Father give the Holy Spirit to them that ask Him" (Luke 11:13)? These reported words of the Redeemer Himself demolish several of the theories put about today respecting the baptism in the Holy Spirit. They scupper the historical proxy theory, the automatic communication theory and the theory of millennial fulfilment – to name but three. "To them that ask." That brief but comprehensive clause makes this clear.

Distinction is sometimes drawn between the extraordinary and the ordinary signs displayed on the Day of

Pentecost. The former were exclusive to the time and place and were not in fact repeated. The sound as of a mighty rushing wind and the cloven tongues of fire fall into this category. They did not recur. But the other tongues which the simple followers of Jesus spoke, although supernatural, did not pass with the historic occasion. They were later reproduced in Samaria, Caesarea, Corinth, and elsewhere throughout the primitive Church. Only by the most tortuous and ingenious exegetical sophistry can the implications of this be explained away. Tongues, *glossolalia*, may be identified in Scripture as (i) *sign*; (ii) *sporadic "spirit"* and (iii) *permanent gift*. Tongues are like the whistle of a kettle which tells you that the water is boiling. You cannot drink the whistle, but neither can you brew tea properly in the absence of that sign. This vitalizing spiritual experience is the inalienable birthright of every believer till the final trumpet blows.

On what terms?

(a) *Prayer*. It was while our Lord was praying in the Jordan that the Dove descended upon Him, and it is still in answer to prayer that the Spirit is bestowed. Ten days of corporate prayer preceded the coming of the Comforter long ago and His infusion into the being of the believer is still indissociably linked to intercession. "Now when the apostles which were at Jerusalem heard that Samaria had received the Word of God, they sent unto them Peter and John: who, when they were come down, prayed for them that they might receive the Holy Ghost, for as yet He was fallen upon none of them" (Acts 8:14,15).

(b) *The preaching of the Word*. "While Peter yet spake these words (Gk *rhemata*), the Holy Ghost fell on all them which heard the Word (*logon*)" (Acts 10:44). In every Christian congregation there are those who hear only the *words*, and there are those who hear the *Word*, the *logos*: it is on the latter that the Spirit falls.

(c) *The laying on of hands*. "When Paul had laid his hands upon them, the Holy Ghost came on them; and they spake with tongues and prophesied" (Acts 19:6).

(d) *Obedience.* "The Holy Ghost, whom God has given to them that obey Him" (Acts 5:32). God's power is conveyed with a view to the execution of God's purpose.

The primary purpose of this baptism in the Spirit is not, as is sometimes supposed, the purification of the soul of the recipient – that is the special preserve of the baptism of love, of which mention will be made in the next main section of this study – but the impartation of power for public ministry. This we have on the authority of our Lord Himself: "Ye shall receive power, after that the Holy Ghost is come upon you: and ye shall be witnesses unto Me both in Jerusalem, and in all Judaea, and in Samaria, and unto the uttermost part of the earth" (Acts 1:8).

THE MINISTRY OF THE GRACE THAT SHAPES US

What is the greatest thing that anybody can ever be? About that there is bound to be a broad spectrum of opinion. An astronaut? A discoverer? An inventor? A statesman? An author? A military leader? A business tycoon? No. the greatest thing anybody can ever be is a saint.

But what *is* a saint?

Some say there are no saints. Psychoanalysis has caused them to disintegrate. It can break them up into little bits, as did the fall of Humpty Dumpty, but it cannot put them together. G.A. Studdert-Kennedy has some archly satirical lines, entitled "The Psychologist", which bring this out well:

He takes the saint to pieces
And labels all the parts;
He tabulates the secrets
Of loving, loyal hearts:
His reasoning is perfect,
His proofs as plain as paint;
He has but one small weakness –
He cannot make a saint.

An eminent psychologist, asked recently for a definition of a saint, is reported to have replied: "A saint is a moral myth. He has no existence outside the romantic fancy of the pious." And, according to a cynical Chinese proverb: "There are only two good men – one is dead the other is not yet born."

Some say that saints *are* to be had – at a price! "The task of preparing the evidence for Cardinal Newman's sanctity is enormous," comments Sue Macgregor, the wellknown radio personality. "There is no one alive who knew him, to testify of him; and, although half a dozen priests have been examining every shred of written evidence for the past twenty years, they still have twenty more years to scrutinize. It could also be a costly business. When Elizabeth Stanton was canonized in September, 1974, the promoters of her cause – unbelievably the *Wall Street Journal!* – estimated that the process took ninety-three years and cost nearly half a million pounds. Researchers, typists, translators, multi-lingual proof-readers, lawyers and doctors – all had to be paid; and a good deal of the money goes on the ancient canonization ceremonies in and outside St Peter's." Even so, as Sir Thomas Browne observes, "There are many (questionless) canonized on earth that shall never be saints in heaven." Charles Caleb Colton has history on his side when he roguishly remarks: "Some reputed saints that have been canonized should have been cannonaded!"

Some say, with the backing of the New Testament, that every born again believer is a saint. Paul addresses his pastoral correspondence to the "saints" or "those called to be saints" in Rome, Corinth, Ephesus, Philippi, Colosse. When so doing, he is not directing his epistles to a few haloed paragons of virtue: no; he is writing to the whole Christian community in every case.

The first followers of Jesus were known among their contemporaries by various names – disciples, believers,

Christians, brethren, and so on. But, whatever appellations might be attached to them, their supreme differentiating quality was that they were saints.

The New Testament saint is a unique human phenomenon. He is not just what is commonly known as a morally "good" person: he is in a class by himself because he is a product of Divine grace. "To make a saint, must indeed by be grace," comments Blaise Pascal, "and whoever doubts this, does not know what a saint is, or a man."

One Sunday, when he was too infirm and feeble to attend church, "Rabbi" Duncan's daughter returned from a service and he asked her what the sermon had been about. "Sanctification," she replied. "And did it begin with regeneration?" inquired her father.

He might equally well have mentioned justification. "I have now made a new question, whether Christ is more to be loved for giving sanctification or for free justification," writes Samuel Rutherford, "and I hold that He is more and most to be loved for sanctification. It is in some respects greater love in Him to sanctify than to justify, for He maketh us most like Himself in His own essential portraiture and image in sanctifying us. Justification doth but make us happy, which is to be like angels only. To be sanctified is to be like God Himself."

But the "Rabbi" was right. There can be no sanctification without regeneration. True Christian sanctity starts there. Not always, however, is it recognized or realized that regeneration is not just a change in the old nature, but the reception of a new nature. We who were by nature "the children of wrath" (Ephesians 2:3) have become "partakers of the Divine nature" (2 Peter 1:4). Every man, irrespective of regeneration, is, in H.G. Wells' phrase, "a civil war". Constantly, by his very moral makeup, he is engaged in the *duel* of the *dual*. Plato likened man to a charioteer to whose car two horses were harnessed – one white, one black; the white, winged and leaping heavenward; the black, ever seeking to drag its driver down into the depths of depravity.

The best illustration of this dichotomy I know is from the pen of W.L. Watkinson. Here it is: "Some misguided scientists have recently succeeded in producing what has been called a 'diabolical fad'. By grafting a portion of the body of one insect upon another, they were able to make new organisms. The result, however, is hideous in the extreme. The grafting is done when the insect is in the pupa state. The insect-grafter may commence work on either the chrysalis or the perfect insect itself; but the chrysalis or grub of the insect offers the best facilities. The vivisector takes the pupa of a spider and, by a delicate surgical operation, grafts it upon the pupa of a fly and when the freak has passed the chrysalis state and merged into a perfect insect, we have a monster indeed. We may fancy the strange and distressing conflict which ensues within the violated organism – the clash of irreconcilable impulse and instinct in a creature compounded of, say, butterfly and spider – a passion for the sunshine and a love of darkness, a longing for roses and a thirst for blood demanding inconsistent satisfaction – the creature perplexed within itself, afraid of itself, devouring itself."

Such is man by nature. Consider, then, how much more strenuous and unremitting the conflict when there is implanted into him the Divine nature. Paul uses a most vigorous vocabulary when picturing this inner war. "I see a law in my members warring against the law of my mind" (Romans 7:23). "I keep under my body, and bring it into subjection" (1 Corinthians 9:27). "The flesh lusteth against the spirit, and the spirit against the flesh" (Galatians 5:17). Sanctification consists by the grace of God in winning this internal conflict.

How is it to be done? There are three classic answers to that question: (a) *eradication*; (b) *suppression*; and (c) *counteraction*.

Take them one by one.

(a) *eradication*. As the word itself implies, this means

plucking the evil in human nature up by the roots, cutting it off at one fell swoop, passing through a critical moral experience which for ever ends the inner battle. There are Christians who claim that this has happened to them; and, in the case of some of them at least, no reasonable person would be likely to contest the claim.

What are we to say to this? Well, candour compels us to confess that it is certainly the swiftest and most expeditious way of solving the problem.

I well remember, across a widening gap of years, an illustration which an old Welsh preacher employed in this connection. He told of a man who had a monkey of which he was extremely fond. His affection could not have been greater for a human friend. Unluckily, the monkey contracted a disease of the tail that the veterinary surgeon said necessitated amputation if the animal's life was to be saved. This deeply distressed the owner. He was a kind-hearted man, and he could not bear to think of his monkey being subjected to so much suffering. To hack off the whole tail at one stroke would be too painful. So he decided that he would have the tail cut off in a series of operations – bit by bit!

Every reader of the New Testament knows that our Lord *does* speak about moral amputation. "If thy right hand offend thee, cut if off and cast it from thee; for it is profitable for thee that one of thy members should perish, and not that thy whole body should be cast into hell" (Matthew 5:30).

Manifestly, however, such moral amputation relates to *sins* and not to *sin*. Its reference is to bad habits rather than to the bad heart from which they spring.

One of the most strenuous advocates of this mode of sanctification in a former generation was Daniel Steele. He claimed that, at one stroke, all evil was eradicated from his nature. If anybody can honestly make that colossal claim, he is to be heartily congratulated. But not many would be bold enough to do it.

(b) *suppression*. Here we have the second theory regarding the process of sanctification. If the first conjured up the idea of a surgeon removing a cancerous tumour from a body, rooting it out with merciful ruthlessness, the second evokes the picture of the captain of a ship, whose crew has mutinied, battening down the rebels beneath the hatches.

This practice is not without its proponents. Inquired of as to what he made of sin, Ernest Renan is said to have answered: "I suppress it." Good for him! But, unless the records grossly malign him, he does not seem to have been too successful. Suppression is always a precarious business. One never knows when the mutineers are going to break out and take over; and, in any case, the strain of keeping them in check is positively exhausting. Moreover, the process is self-defeating – paralyzingly negative. Captain Bligh of the *Bounty* was for a time so taken up with managing the mutineers that he could not get on with the voyage. Something was always hatching under the hatches. Psychologists often warn us of the dangers of repression, but suppression also has its perils. Its effect on personality can be devastating. Suppressed instincts and impulses can explode in one's face like a letter-bomb! To change the figure, one may screw the 'old man', down in his coffin, but he has a nasty habit of bursting the lid open. "I have several times been invited to attend the funeral of somebody or other's 'old man'," says Spurgeon, "but, on attending it, I have been startled to find the corpse suddenly getting up and making a fighting speech!"

It is true, of course, that with the passing of the years, the suppression of certain instincts and passions becomes easier. Because of this some old saints tend to mistake senility for sanctity. In the expressive language of C.S. Lewis, they are "like eunuchs boasting of their chastity".

(c) *counteraction*. Here, again, the figure changes. Instead of seeing a surgeon extracting a cancer from the body of a patient or a captain battening down mutineers beneath the hatches, we think of a room full of darkness, whose gloom is instantly dispelled by the turning on of a light. The best way of banishing the blackness is not to pick up a broom and try to brush it out: it is to press a switch and let the brightness in.

Or, take another figure. You go to an airport to board a plane. On the tarmac outside the building you see a giant aircraft, weighing hundreds of tons, awaiting departure. You know that there is such a thing as the law of gravity. You know that that law is operating on the huge plane and that it will take a terrific force to lift it by an inch much less raise it to the clouds. Yet you get into the aircraft quite confidently, assured that it is able to convey you to your destination. Why? Because you believe in the operation of another law – the law of the spirit of petroleum. Your confidence is justified. The mighty engines are turned on. The turbo-jets begin to roar. You're off!

That illustrates the principle of counteraction. In spiritual terms Paul speaks of it in Romans 8:12: "The law of the Spirit of life in Christ Jesus hath made me free from the law of sin and death"; and again Galatians 5:16: "Walk in the Spirit, and ye shall not fulfil the lusts of the flesh."

It is pertinent at this point to revert to the third of the baptisms to which reference was earlier made – the baptism of love.

Such is the mystery of the Divine indwelling – the sovereign remedy for indwelling sin. "Sin dwelleth in me," Paul was compelled to confess (Romans 7:17), but he was able to tell his Ephesian converts that he was praying that "Christ might dwell in their hearts" (Ephesians 3:17). The latter is the only adequate antidote to the former. There is a beautiful old English aphorism: "To love is the perfect tense of the verb to live."

For each of these methods of sanctification there is something to be said, although the superiority, realism and scripturalness of the last-named must surely be obvious. Equally sincere people have practised different modes, and have claimed to find them effective. God deals with His creatures in diverse ways.

Many years ago I went one winter's day to visit two patients in Lochmaben Hospital, Dumfriesshire, Scotland. It was bitterly cold. I could hear players curling on the frozen loch as I went by. The doctors, I discovered on arrival, had placed one of the patients in bed on an open verandah. There was a tarpaulin sheet on the bed and there was snow on the tarpaulin. The other patient was located in a super-heated cubicle whose temperature was tropical. What were these doctors up to? Had they taken leave of their senses? Or did they want to kill the one patient and cure the other? The fact is that their aim was to restore health to both patients; and, although the treatment prescribed in each case was totally different from that given to the other, the objective was the same.

Just so with this matter of sanctification. We find saints like D.M. Panton maintaining that for the Christian moral tensions intensify as life goes on: we find others, like Evan Hopkins, declaring that such tensions are due to unconfessed sin or an unsurrendered life. We find some, like E.H. Bickersteth, opting for peace almost at any price, and others, like John Henry Newman, adopting as moral motto: "Purity rather than peace." So John Keble writes:

Then grudge not thou the anguish keen
Which makes thee like thy Lord.

One of the richest and rarest religious biographies published this century is the Life of Alexander Whyte by G.H. Barbour. It contains an account of an interview Whyte once had with a young minister, fresh from an exhilarating experience at the Keswick Convention. "I've had a wonderful time," he related. "The sin-question in my life has been dealt with once for all. I am perfectly sanctified." Whyte listened with patient and sympathetic interest to the rapturous recital. Then, shaking his old grey head, he said with a sigh: "It's a sair fecht tae the end."

Both were right. As George Macdonald has it: "God descends into every life by His own secret stair." We must permit the Divine physician to prescribe what He deems best for each individual life. For some sanctification is a crisis. Sinfulness is eradicated as a tumour is removed from a body: for others it is a process, painful and protracted. It is crucifixion of the old man by slow degrees. "I am crucified with Christ," cries Paul (Galatians 2:20), but also: "I die daily" (1 Corinthians 15:31).

What is the explanation of the paradox? It is this. In relation to sanctification there is a difference between a Christian's *standing* and his *state*. Positionally, in Christ he is already perfectly sanctified, as holy as his Lord: "Christ is made unto us wisdom, and righteousness, and sanctification and redemption" (1 Corinthians 1:30). "We are sanctified through the offering of the body of Jesus Christ once for all" (Hebrews 10:10). By one offering He hath perfected for ever them that are sanctified" (Hebrews 10:14). Pragmatically, however, the Christian is still imperfect. "I never saw a perfect man," says Spurgeon. "You can't find a perfect Christian anywhere in the world today," states Billy Graham. Personally, I have only known one man who was perfect, and he was perfect because Perfect was his name! Even Paul confessed to personal imperfection: "Not as though I had already attained, either were already perfect" (Philippians 3:12). That is the paradox. Perhaps a simple illustration may help to explain it.

Suppose that I present you with a bulky, leatherbound, handsome volume of the complete works of William Shakespeare. You take the book from me, and you say: "Thank you. The volume is now mine." You are quite right. It is yours – yours as so much tooled leather, indiapaper, printer's ink, and so on – yours immediately you accept it. Ah, but there is another sense in which it is not yours and never will be yours, until you have spent a lifetime studying it.

So with sanctification. The moment we take Christ as our sanctification, we are "perfect and complete in Him" (Colossians 4:12), but it will require the whole of life's long day to work it out. To that end six gracious ministries contribute: (1) *the Ministry of the Spirit*; (2) *the Ministry of the Word*; (3) *The Ministry of the Disciplines of life*; (4) *the Ministry of Private Devotion*; (5) *the Ministry of Public Worship*; (6) *the Ministry of the Advent hope*.

(1) *The Ministry of the Holy Spirit.* To this we have already referred, but we may now quote relevant New Testament texts: "Grace is given to me of God, that I should be the minister of Jesus Christ to the Gentiles, ministering the Gospel of God, that the offering up of the Gentiles might be acceptable, being sanctified by the Holy Ghost" (Romans 15:15,16). "Elect according to the foreknowledge of God the Father, through sanctification of the Spirit" (1 Peter 1:2).

(2) *The Ministry of the Word.* "This is the will of God, even your sanctification" (1 Thessalonians 4:3). The will of God is expressed through the Word of God, and the Word of God has an immense moral impact on the lives of those who come under its authority. "Now ye are clean through the Word, which I have spoken unto you" (John 15:3). "Sanctify them through Thy truth. Thy Word is truth" (John 17:17). "Sanctified by the Word of God" (1 Timothy 4:5) is a phrase used of things, but it applies *a fortiori* to people.

(3) *The Ministry of the Disciplines of Life.* The trials and tragedies, disappointments and disenchantments, the headaches and the heart-aches are not, in the case of the Christian, mere arbitrary and fortuitous occurrences, without any relation to his moral and spiritual character. They are the hands of the Potter, shaping into perfection the plastic and pliable clay. "My grace is sufficient for thee" (2 Corinthians 12:9). "Tribulation worketh patience, and patience experience, and experience hope" (Romans 5::3,4). "The trying of your faith worketh patience. But let

patience have her perfect work, that ye may be perfect and entire, wanting nothing" (James 1:3,4).

Imitation does, to be sure, find a place in the promotion of personal holiness. The Christian life is, in one aspect of it, as Thomas a Kempis envisaged it, the *Imitation of Christ.* "Be ye followers of me, even as I also am of Christ" (1 Corinthians 11:1). "Christ left us an example," says Peter, "that ye should follow His steps" (1 Peter 1:21). But imitation has limitation. With the best will in the world I cannot by mere volition become like my blessed Lord. Just as no-one can perfectly copy Michelangelo in art, Beethoven in music, Shakespeare in poetry, so, unaided, no human being can ever, even by the most sedulous imitation, become like the Perfect Man. Imitation has its modest place, but it is no substitute for incarnation: "Christ in you, the hope of glory" (Colossians 1:27).

(4) *The Ministry of Private Devotion.* It is safe to say that among Christians nothing is praised more and practised less than private prayer. "Prayer-time," as Frederick William Faber was wont to say, "is God's punishment-time." We can be sure of this – prayer will make a person stop sinning or sinning will make him stop praying. The two are incompatible, mutually exclusive. Of our blessed Lord it is told that as He prayed on the summit of Hermon amid the starlit snow "the fashion of His countenance was altered" (Luke 9:29). That illustrates what may happen to us, in our meaner measure, if, like our Master, we go aside to pray.

(5) *The Ministry of Public Worship.* One of the most potent of sanctifying agencies is public worship. Its membership, its fellowship, its partnership – all conspire to make the participant more like his Lord. While, as for the ministry, among its main functions is the "mending of the saints" (Ephesians 4:12). How wise we were, therefore, to heed the admonition of the writer to the Hebrews: "Not forsaking the assembling of ourselves together, as the manner of some is; and so much the more as ye see the

Day approaching" (10:25).

And that brings us to the last of the ministering agencies (6) *The Ministry of the Advent Hope.* The imminent prospect of the Lord's Return is bound to exert an enormous moral influence upon the life of anyone who truly believes it. "Every man that hath this hope in Him, purifieth himself, even as He is pure" (1 John 3:3). And the Parousia will itself put the finishing touches to the portrait: "For when He shall appear, we shall be like Him; for we shall see Him as He is" (1 John 3:2). And so the life of grace will end in the likeness of glory.

Grace all the work will crown
Through everlasting days;
It lays in heaven the topmost stone
And well-deserves the praise.

12
THE WONDERFUL END

The Christian Doctrine of the Last Things

Right on to God's faithful Word,
Right on to the coming Lord;
Right on where the windings bend;
Right on to the Wonderful End.

Anon

We recognize the need for an End as well as a beginning for humanity – of a sea into which the river of man's life is to run, as well as a mountain up from which it is to spring.

Elizabeth Wordsworth

How long shall it be to the End?

Daniel 12:6

What shall be the End of these things?

Daniel 12:8

What shall be the sign of the End?

Matthew 24:3

Then cometh the End.

1 Corinthians 15:24

Even now, dear children, we are getting near the End of things
1 John 2:18 Phillips

I am the End.
Revelation 1:8

IN THAT BITTER but very moving book *Father and Son* by Edmund Gosse there is a passage of piercing poignancy in which the author describes how, having been brought up by his Christian Brethren parents to believe in the imminent personal Return of Christ, he found himself at sixteen with his mind in a perfect whirl about this aspect of his inherited faith. Things came to a head one beautiful summer afternoon as he lay on a sofa in a room at the borading-school he attended. "Over my soul," he records, "there swept an immense wave of emotion. Now, surely, the great final change must be approaching. I gazed up at the tenderly-coloured sky, and I broke irrepressibly into speech: 'Come now, Lord Jesus', I cried, 'come now, and take me to be with Thee for ever in Thy Paradise. I'm ready to come. My heart is purged from sin. There is nothing that keeps me rooted to this wicked world. Come now, *now*!' I waited for a while, and watched for the glorious apparition. Then I felt a faint shame at the attitude I had adopted, though I was alone. Presently, the colour deepened in the sky. 'The Lord has not come,' I muttered, 'the Lord will never come!' "

That incident in the recorded life of Edmund Gosse can be taken as typical of the experience of many in our time. They are in a quandary. The question which, above all others, they want to ask is this: Does Jesus Christ intend to revisit Planet Earth? Is He really coming back to this world? Or is all this talk about His Advent mere wishful thinking, a pathetic fallacy, the fantastic dream of a handful of apocalyptic fanatics?

About that there are four main views.

The first is that of those who, like Gosse, say that *the Lord Jesus is not coming back.* Albert Schweitzer was of this mind. In his *The Quest of the Historical Jesus* he states that our Lord was in error in relation to His Second Coming. He thought He was going to return to earth, but He was mistaken. Of the same opinion on the point was Dame Margaret Knight. She excused herself from subscribing to the doctrine of the Deity of Christ on the ground that, as she alleged, He was proved wrong about His Second Advent. Snapping his fingers vigorously in class, an American professor of divinity told his students: "I don't care *that* for the Second Coming of Christ. The doctrine of the Second Coming of Christ is a purely speculative doctrine. I do not believe that Christ will return to this earth." This is the first view – the view that Christ is not coming back.

The next is that *He has already come back.* Those adopting this stance on the subject fall into two broad categories.

One is composed of those who declare that Christ returned on the Day of Pentecost. They confuse the descent of the Spirit with that of the Son. According to their thinking, the Parousia occurred when the Paraclete entered the world in fulness on the morning of the first Whitsunday. Folland could actually argue with reference to the apostle's later writings: "John wrote after the occurrence of the Second Advent and under the power of the abiding Presence." Well, it is certainly true that the apostle penned his epistles in the context of the abiding Presence. The Saviour's sacred pledge was fulfilled: "Where two or three are gathered together in My name, there am I in the midst of them" (Matthew 18:20), and "Lo, I am with you alway, even unto the end of the age" (Matthew 28:20). Yet it is hard, not to say impossible, to see how any intelligent student of the New Testament could conceivably lend credence for a moment to such an interpretation. So many predictions of the Second Advent in the Christian Scriptures were made *after* Pentecost, and thus cannot have pointed *to* Pentecost. Moreover, our blessed Lord Himself promised: "I will pray the Father, and He shall give you another Comforter" (John 14:16). In Greek there are two words for "another" – *allos*, and *heteros*. The former means another of the same kind; the latter another of a different kind. Significantly, it is the former which we find here. To be sure, it was a Comforter of the same kind who was coming, but He was *another* Comforter all the same. And as Robert Glenn Gromacki reasonably enough contends, it requires a stretch of the imagination to say that Jesus sent Himself!

The other category is comprised of those who claim that Christ came at the time of the Fall of Jerusalem in A.D.70. No less a person than the great Puritan John Owen, commenting on "the Son of Man coming in the clouds of heaven," (Matthew 26:54), applies the words to the destruction of the Holy City. There is even a theory that a small company were caught up secretly to meet Christ in A.D.70, of which, of course, there is no record because there was no one left to make a record! No doubt part of our Lord's apocalyptic discourse recorded in Matthew 24, Mark 13 and Luke 21 *does* refer to this dreadful event in Jewish history. But to equate what the New Testament calls "that blessed hope" (Titus 2:13) with four years of besiegement and butchery is absurd. Besides, as Clarence E. Macartney relevantly remarks: "Christ's purpose in coming is not to destroy Jerusalem but to restore it." So much for the second view – that Christ has already come.

Some say that Christ is *always coming back*. "All history is His Coming," we are told. "The Coming of Christ is not an event," declares Frank Ballard, "it is a process which includes innumerable events, a perpetual advance of Christ in the activity of His kingdom. It has continued until now, and is still moving on, but He is truly the Coming One, for He is still coming and is yet to come." It is true, of course, in one sense, that Christ is always coming into human hearts and into history. We have His own word for it. There is such a thing as an "inner advent". "Behold, I stand at the door, and knock. If any man hear My voice, and open the door, I will come in to Him, and will sup with him, and he with Me" (Revelation 3:20). It is also true that He comes in the great crises of history, but that is a whole diameter from what we mean by the Second Coming.

Nor, again, is the Return of the Redeemer to be identified with *the death of the believer.* Marcus Dods held that it was. "The promise of Christ's Return," he wrote, "is fulfilled in the death of the Christian, and it has changed the aspect of death." A. Winkelhofer was of the same persuasion. "Whenever death occurs," he said, "there is the *parousia* of the Lord." But is that really so? A glance at John 21:22,23 proves that it is not. "Peter, seeing John, said to Jesus, And what shall this man do? Jesus said unto him, If I will that he tarry till I come, what is that to thee?" At this point in the narrative the evangelist interpolates an explanatory comment: "Then went this saying abroad among the brethren that this disciple should *not* die" (v.23). To equate Christ's Coming with the death of the individual believer is to make nonsense of that remark: "If I will that he live till he die"! Manifestly, the brethren interpreted Christ's words as meaning that John would live until the Second Advent, in which event he would not have died at all. Death, then, cannot be the Coming of the Lord. The approach of the "King of Terrors" (Job 18:4) cannot logically be identified with the Appearing of the "King of kings" (Revelation 19:16). W.E. Blackstone pertinently points out that "Christ's First Coming did not mean death", and S.G. Tragelles tersely and trenchantly observes: "It is a mistake to suppose the Coming of the Lord to mean death, for death is not our Lord."

If, then, the Second Advent is not something which will

never happen, nor something which has already happened, nor something which is always happening – what is it? *It is some thing which is about to happen*, as multiplying signs reveal and as the New Testament repeatedly and emphatically asserts.

Take, by way of confirmation, the following proof texts: "This same Jesus, which is taken up from you into heaven, shall so come in like manner as ye have seen Him go into heaven" (Acts 1;11). "Behold, I show you a mystery: we shall not all sleep, but we shall all be changed, in a moment, in the twinkling of an eye, at the last trump: for the trumpet shall sound, and the dead shall be raised incorruptible, and we shall be changed" (1 Corinthians 15:51,52). "Looking for that blessed hope, and the glorious Appearing of the great God and our Saviour Jesus Christ" (Titus 2:13). "Unto them that look for Him shall He appear the second time" (Hebrews 9:28). "I saw heaven opened, and behold a white horse and He that sat upon him was called Faithful and True; and in righteousness He doth judge and make war. His eyes were as a flame of fire and on His head were many crowns; and He had a name written that no man knew but He Himself; and He was clothed with a vesture dipped in blood, and His name is called the Word of God" (Revelation 19:11–13).

Without doing violence to the language of Scripture, it is impossible to interpret such texts in any but a literal way, as intimating a personal, corporeal, local, visible and audible descent of Christ from the skies. To construe them otherwise is flatly to contradict the infallible Word of God.

Now, this Coming of Christ will be the first of a train of tremendous events which is to make up the spectacular panorama of prophetic Scripture. In the interests of clarity and memorability we may perhaps enlist what Charles Churchill patly called "apt alliteration's artful aid" and consider the following twelve headings, the name of each of which in English conveniently commences with the letter *R*: (1) *Rapture*; (2) *Retribution*; (3) *Return*; (4) *Revelation*;

(5) *Recompense;* (6) *Recognition;* (7) *Realm;* (8) *Revolt;* (9) *Resurrection;* (10) *Reckoning;* (11) *Removal* and (12) *Renewal.*

Take them each in turn.

RAPTURE

Three words occur in the Greek New Testament in connection with the Second Coming of Christ. They are (a) *apocalupsis,* which means "unveiling"; (b) *epiphaneia,* which means "appearing"; and (c) *parousia,* which means "personal presence alongside". The terms are to some extent used interchangeably, but in the preponderance of instances it is the term *parousia* which is employed to designate the Rapture. The word "Rapture" does not itself appear in the English New Testament. It is derived from the Latin or Vulgate version of the Bible where the verb *rapere* is the infinitive of the word translated "caught up" in 1 Thessalonians 4:7.

Here is the classic passage on the *parousia* in the New Testament: "This we say unto you by the Word of the Lord, that we which are alive and remain unto the Coming of the Lord shall not precede them which are asleep. For the Lord Himself shall descend from heaven with a shout, with the voice of the archangel, and with the trump of God: and the dead in Christ shall rise first; then we which are alive and remain shall be caught up together with them in the clouds, to meet the Lord in the air: and so shall we ever be with the Lord" (1 Thessalonians 4:15–17). If we analyze the paragraph, break it up into clauses, we shall perhaps best elucidate its content.

Note particularly at the outset in passing that Paul prefaces the passage with the statement: "This we say unto you by the Word of the Lord" (v.15). Here we have not rabbinical tradition or Pauline speculation, but direct Divine revelation. This is Christ's own preview of the *parousia.* For this reason it is history prewritten, a prophetic picture of the Rapture.

Let us look at it more narrowly.

(a) *No deputy*. "The Lord Himself shall descend from heaven." "We do not want another Jesus," wrote F.B. Meyer, "we want the same one as went away." The New Testament is at great pains to make it unmistakably plain that the Christ of the Ascension and the Christ of the Advent are identical. "This same Jesus, which is taken up from you into heaven, shall so come in like manner as ye have seen Him go into heaven" (Acts 1:11).

He sent no angel to our race
Of higher or of lower place,
But wore the robe of human frame
And He Himself to this world came.

And, just so, He will come again.
(b) *No secrecy*. "With a shout, with the voice of the archangel, and with the trump of God." Sometimes the *parousia* is spoken of as a "Secret Rapture", but it is hard to see how the adjective can properly be applied to an event with such accompaniments.

At this point it may be well to interpolate a brief comment on "the shout, the voice and the trump". Among students of biblical prophecy it is a matter for debate as to whether distinction is to be drawn between those addressed respectively by these three audible concomitants of Christ's Coming. Some hold that the shout is directed to the Church, the voice of the archangel to the Jews, and the trump to the world in general, as a prelude to the outbreak of the Great Tribulation. Others maintain that all three are addressed to the Church alone and heard only by its members, each suddenly clothed with a resurrection body, invested with supersonic sensitivity. The former view would seem the more plausible. In any case, let us proceed to examine the sounds individually.

First, *the shout*. He who went with a shout will return with a shout. "Jesus cried with a loud voice" (Luke 23:46). "The Lord Himself shall descend from heaven with a shout" (1 Thessalonians 4:16). He whose mighty voice rent the black skies above Golgotha with the ringing cry: "It is finished" (John 19:30), will cleave the clouds with a shout at His Second Coming: "It is beginning – a new age is being born!" The text leads us to conclude that Christ is excited at the prospect of the *parousia*. When we are strangely moved we shout. Should not the Christian also be excited as he waits for the shout of His descending Redeemer? When our Lord appears, as someone has said, "the world will all at once hear a sound which it will not understand", as was the case on the occasion referred to in John 12:28,29: "Then came there a voice from heaven. The people that stood by and heard it said that it thundered." And again in Acts 9:4,7: "Suddenly there shined round about him (Saul) a light from heaven, and he heard a voice. The men which journeyed with him stood speechless, hearing a voice but seeing no man." First, then, there is the shout.

Second, *the voice of the archangel*. Who *is* the archangel? He is not difficult to identify, since only one archangel is named in Scripture. He is called "Michael" (Daniel 12:1; Jude 9; Revelation 12:7). Presumably, his will be the voice that we shall hear at the *parousia*. He is the mighty military archangel who, in Milton's magnificent line, "led the embattled seraphim to war". "At that time shall Michael stand up, the great prince which standeth for the children of thy (Daniel's) people" (Daniel 12:1). "There was war in heaven. Michael and his angels fought against the dragon, and the dragon fought and his angels" (Revelation 12:7). The saints, it seems, since they are passing through enemy territory at the Rapture, are to have a military escort. An angel announced Christ's First Coming: an angel will announce His Second Coming. There is the voice of the archangel.

Third, *the trump of God*. "It shall come to pass in that day that a great trumpet shall be blown" (Isaiah 27:13). God does not sound a thousand trumpets when the dawn comes up the sky, but when the Sun of Righteousness comes down the trumpet shall sound. Why is the *last* trump singled out for special mention? A quotation from J.T. Mawson will serve to explain: "Three trumpet-blasts were given when the Roman army had to move. The first blast meant 'Pack your baggage'; the second, 'Fall in' and the third, 'Quick March!' " At the Rapture, the whole Church, the risen dead and the remaining living, will for the first time in history be on the move together.

(c) *No mortality.* "The dead in Christ shall rise." "For the trumpet shall sound and the dead shall be raised" (1 Corinthians 15:52). No inquiry haunts the human heart so poignantly as the query as to where are the dead. You watch someone pass away in the room of a house. No door is unlatched; no window is opened, but there is no doubt that he is gone. Where?

Well, it all depends on whether or not he was a Christian. About the fate of those who are not, with the Bible open in our hand, we shall have something solemn to say later on. Meantime let us confine our inquiry to the case of the Christian. Where does he go when he exits from this world? We call him the "departed", but where has he gone?

There are some lines of melting pathos which, in this connection, come unbidden to the mind. Although regrettably bordering on the practice of praying for the dead, they are too beautiful to be omitted from this survey of the subject.

Somewhere thou livest and hast need of Him;
Somewhere thy soul sees higher heights to climb,
And somewhere still there may be valleys dim
That thou must pass to reach the hills sublime.

Then all the more because thou canst not hear,
Poor human words of blessing will I pray;
O true, brave heart, God bless thee wheresoe'er
Thou art in His wide universe today.

The English poet, Henry Vaughan, in his *Silex Scintillans* has expressed the same wistful sentiments:

He that hath found some fledged bird's nest may know
At first sight if the bird be flown;
But what fair dell or grove he sings in now
That is to him unknown.

There is a great deal about the future life which we should dearly like to know and of which we are kept in kindly ignorance. One thing, however, the New Testament makes clear beyond all cavil – the Christian dead are with Christ, which is far better" (Philippians 1:23). What does that little phrase "with Christ" imply? At least four things: (i) *a life that is conscious, not comatose*; (ii) *active, not passive*; (iii) *social, not solitary*; and (iv) *blissful, not purgatorial.*

It is appropriate here to point out that Christian doctrine teaches not only the immortality of the soul, but the resurrection of the body. The ancient Jews believed in the immortality of the soul. "God created man to be immortal, and made him to be an image of His own eternity" (Book of Wisdom 22:23). So also did the greatest of the Greeks. But the distinctive thing about the Christian religion is its insistence upon the resurrection of the body. It is true, as William C. Procter argues, that the identity between the body laid in the tomb and that which rises will be "one of personality, not of particles". And yet the fact remains that our Lord Himself spoke of the dead as "they that are in the graves" (John 5:28), and He further said: "They shall come forth, they that have done good unto the resurrection of life, and they that have done evil unto the resurrection of damnation" (v.29). As we know from elsewhere in Scripture, a period of more than a thousand years is to elapse between these two resurrections, but that the Bible predicts a rising of the body no reader is left in any doubt.

There is an unforgettable passage among the works of

Kohli Brugge, which seems almost to dispense with the need for a resurrection of the body. "I have no eyes, nevertheless, I behold Him ; I have no brain, nor mind, nonetheless, I comprehend Him; I have no lips, nevertheless I praise Him with all of you who call on His name; I lie outside in God's acre, nevertheless, I am in Paradise." Were it not that there is to be a millennial reign of Christ on earth in which the Christian is to share, such sentiments would almost seem to make a posthumous body superfluous. But when our Lord triumphed over death, it was not just His Spirit that survived: it was His total personality, and at the Rapture there will be not only a reunion of spirits, but a resurrection of the bodies of the faithful. Paul makes it plain that the posthumous body differs in some ways from the body that was buried. He writes: "That which thou sowest, thou sowest not the body that shall be, but bare grain. It may chance of wheat or of some other grain, but God giveth it a body, as it hath pleased Him, and to every seed his own body" (1 Corinthians 15:37,38).

Nevertheless, there must be some continuity of identity between the body which is buried and that which rises from the dead. As W.J. Sparrow Simpson points out: "The human body is like a river. The river remains the same while the water constantly changes." "God giveth it a body" (v.38). Every body is a gift of God. A man of seventy has in the course of his life had ten bodies. They have varied greatly in size, appearance and capacity, from the chubby baby in the cradle to the adult piloting a plane, addressing a senate, occupying a throne. Yet all through the years his consciousness is continuous. The apostle affirms that, on the farther side of the sepulchre, God will give another body. "For the trumpet shall sound, and the dead shall be raised incorruptible" (1 Corinthians 15:52). "The dead in Christ shall rise" (1 Thessalonians 4:16). That will be a great day! Henry Vaughan, the old poet, celebrates it in a bracing stanza:

A day so fresh, so bright, so brave,
'Twill show us each forgotten grave,
And make the dead like flowers arise,
Youthful and fair to see new skies.

As he speaks of it, Isaiah's princely prose trembles on the verge of song: "Thy dead shall live again. Their bodies shall arise. O, dwellers in the dust, awake and sing for joy" (26:19). The dear dead dust is not to be blown away for ever on the winds of time. "He will reconstruct the body of your abasement" (Philippians 3:21). "If I am somebody now," remarks Professor Moule, "I shall be the same body then."

Some time ago, when preaching on the resurrection of the dead, in a crowded church in Carmarthen, I suddenly had a strange experience. I seemed to see the people before me pulverized, as it were, into the particles of which their bodies were composed. Some of the particles I imaginatively traced to grain from Canada, some to coffee from Brazil, some to butter from Denmark, some to lamb from New Zealand, and so on. And then the thought struck me: Whether is it harder to bring these particles from all over the world to form the physical organisms before me or to build resurrection bodies from other particles on that "summer morn"? "Wherefore should it seem a thing incredible with you that *God* should raise the dead?" (Acts 26:8).

It is important to recognize that the resurrection of which we are now speaking is not the General Resurrection of the dead. That, as we have noted, will come later. This is what the New Testament repeatedly terms a rising *ek nekron*, that is "out from among the dead". No fewer than forty-nine times does the phrase occur in the Christian Scriptures.

Years ago, in the United States, a man was preaching on the Second Coming of Christ. Among those listening to him was a soldier, a veteran of Vietnam, a pathetic torso, whose arms and legs had been blown off in battle. He lay attending to the ministry in a spinal carriage. At the close of the service, the nurse who was in constant attendance upon him, wheeled him into the presence of the preacher. Pitifully, he looked up and asked: "Do you think the Lord will give me my limbs back when He comes?" With brimming eyes, the preacher opened his New Testament and, turning to Philippians 3:20,21, held it up for the war victim to see: "We look for the Saviour, who shall change our lowly body, that it may be fashioned like unto His glorious body." "There," he said, "is your answer."

Next on the prophetic programme is *the transformation of the living Christians*. "We shall all be changed" (1 Corinthians 15:51). "He shall change the body of our humiliation" (Philippians 3:20). "When we see Him we shall be like Him, for we shall see Him as He is" (1 John 3:2). At sight of the Saviour the saints will be instantly beatified and beautified.

There is in scientific circles today a species of genetic engineering called "cloning". Under the caption "Carbon Copy Humans to Order", a disturbing article appeared in the *Daily Mail* of February 18, 1976. It took the form of a recorded interview between Dr Derek Broomhall and June Southworth. In it the doctor described his researches in the realm of genetics, as a result of which he claimed to be able to produce human beings to order, all of the same basic design, if so desired. "People will say," he remarked, "that in time that could lead to scientists turning out ten thousand Einsteins. Well, there is little harm in that. We could use a few Einsteins. Cloning grabs the imagination. I have spent sleepless nights over this, but not from worry. I've been kept awake by excitement." How much more exciting is the prospect of the Christian! Every believer will have a body resembling that on which Christ rose from the dead on the first Easter dawn, or rather like that in which John saw Him on the Isle of Patmos.

There are two ways in which the Christian is being

changed and will be – gradual and sudden. Here is the former: "We all, with open face beholding as in a glass the glory of the Lord, are changed into the same image from glory to glory, even as by the Spirit of the Lord" (2 Corinthians 3:18). And here is the latter: "We shall all be changed, in a moment, in the twinkling of an eye" (1 Corinthians 15:51,52). "When He shall appear, we shall be like Him; for we shall see Him as He is" (1 John 3:2).

Many years ago there lived in London a woman named Eliza Kirk, who had attained the extraordinary age of 101. She celebrated her birthday by having all the mirrors removed from her home. Asked why, she explained: "I like to think of myself as I was, not as I am." Had she been a Christian, she could have found something better to contemplate – what she was going to be like when Jesus comes.

The happy consequence of the resurrection of the Christian dead and the transformation of the Christian living will be instant recognition and reunion. "Loved ones," sings E. Nathan, "shall meet in a joyful surprise." "As long as love kisses the lips of death" there will be in the human heart a passionate longing for "the touch of a vanished hand and the sound of a voice that is still". That longing will be, for those who love the Lord, gratified and satisfied at the Rapture.

On that happy Advent morning
All the graves their dead restore –
Father, sister, child and mother
Meet once more.

(d) *No priority.* "We shall be caught up together."

On December 17, 1977 Her Majesty the Queen performed the opening ceremony when an extension of the Piccadilly Line of the London Underground from the city centre to Heathrow was put into service. Immediately afterwards, it was my privilege to conduct a party of

Christians to Israel. Some of the party travelled by Tube and some were waiting in the departure lounge, but when the time of departure arrived, all got into a jumbo-jet and in one giant leap landed a few hours later at Ben Gurion airport, Tel Aviv.

To me the incident became a parable. Some of the saints will reach the Rapture by Underground, as it were, through the gateway of the grave: others will be alive when it happens. But, so far as the transportation is concerned, there will be no priority. "We shall be caught up together."

(e) *No gravity*. "To meet the Lord in the air." Happily, the ordinary human body is heavier than air. It is subject to the law of gravitation, which holds it down on the surface of the planet. Otherwise life on earth would be impossible. But that glorified body which the saints are to receive at the Rapture will be subservient to no such depressive force. It will be capable at will of levitation, able to rise unaided to the skies. "We shall be caught up in the clouds, to meet the Lord in the air" (1 Thessalonians 4:17). The *parousia* will be the Ascension of the saints.

The rapidity or otherwise of the Rapture is a matter for debate. Some think the reference to "in a moment, in the twinkling of an eye" is solely to the speed of the change: others hold that it applies also to the Rapture itself, so that, as A.J. Pollock observes, it will be so swift that "not even a stop-watch could record it".

A short while ago on television a nature film was shown. It featured the habits of insects, especially of those furnished with elongated hind legs, and thus equipped with heightened powers of vertical take-off. One such insect was said to leap with such astounding speed into the air that its ascent was invisible to the naked eye. The picture of its departure had to be slowed down by photography to two thousand times less a rate than it actually was in order to be observable by human vision.

So will it be at the *parousia*. When Christ comes Christians from all over the world will rise to meet Him in the twinkling of an eye, leaving nothing behind but their earthly garments, as they go, clothed with immortality to be for ever with the Lord. "I believe," says S. Andrews, "that just as when Peter and John, hastening to the sepulchre on Easter morning, saw the empty graveclothes lying, collapsed, on the stone ledge, so when Christ comes, there are going to be a lot of empty clothes around from which the transformed and translated bodies of the saints will have vanished." Paul speaks about being "clothed upon" (2 Corinthians 5:2). "At present," wrote John Calvin, "the created being wears only a working garb. Hereafter he will wear the clothing of Easter and Whitsunday," clad with immortality as with a garment he will cleave the heavens to meet his coming Lord.

At this point, however, an important question arises: Are *all* Christians to be transported at the *parousia* or only a proportion of them? There are eminent students of biblical prophecy who propound what is variously known as the "Partial Rapture Theory", the "Selective Rapture Theory" and the "Graded Rapture Theory". What are we to make of that? Well, it must be admitted that there are in the New Testament texts which *do* seem to support it. "Watch ye, therefore, and pray always that ye may be accounted worthy to escape all these things that shall come to pass, and to stand before the Son of Man" (Luke 21:36). "If by any means I might attain unto the resurrection of the dead" (Philippians 3:11). "Unto them that look for Him shall He appear the second time without sin unto salvation" (Hebrews 9:8). "Abide in Him that, when He shall appear, we may have confidence and not be ashamed before Him at His Coming" (1 John 2:28). There is, too, the sober warning inherent in the Parable of the Ten Bridesmaids, five wise and five otherwise, the latter being excluded firmly and finally from the marriage-feast.

Over against these, however, must be set several weighty considerations. There are likewise texts which make it abundantly clear that all true Christians will be caught up when Jesus comes. "Whom He justified, them He also glorified" (Romans 8:30). "We shall *all* be changed" (1 Corinthians 15:51). "The Coming of the Lord Jesus Christ with *all* His saints" (1 Thessalonians 3:13). Further, the Partial Rapture Theory postulates an intolerable division in the Church. No man weds his bride in instalments: nor will the Lord Jesus. Moreover, this theory tends to militate against the great Protestant Bible truth of salvation by grace alone. One can no more reach heaven on the principle of good works than a modern bird-man could fly to the moon on his flimsy wings. Translation, no less than salvation itself, will be on the basis of grace alone.

It is true that Paul does speak of grading of some sort. "Every man in his own order (Greek *tagma*, a term which is found nowhere else in the New Testament, 1 Corinthians 15:23). The reference is to the divisions in the Roman army. There were various ranks, and someone has envisaged the Rapture in terms of flights of Christians, rising from Europe, America, Africa, India, Australia, New Zealand, and so on, and all converging on the Coming Christ. What a picture that presents to the pious imagination! "Every man in his own order." But note that these divisions are *within* the ranks of the Raptured. There is no discrimination among the redeemed themselves. As J. Stuart Holden puts it with pointed persuasiveness: "Just as salvation was all of grace, so translation will be all of grace."

This is the age of the air. Men in earlier times had mastered the land and the sea, but not till modern times has man conquered his aerial environment. Never before have so many been caught up in the clouds – not only the living, but the dead! According to a recent Press release, a firm of undertakers (or morticians, as the Americans prefer to call them) in San Francisco, California, has devised a novel method of disposing of the dead. Instead of burying them in the earth, these morticians atomically project them into the heavens. The obsequies over, the corpse is catapulted into outer space, where it goes into endless gyrations around the planet. The cost of such an aerial funeral is said to be in the region of three thousand dollars.

That would seem to be a sort of parody of the *parousia*. Only, when the Lord comes for His people, it will not be cold cadavers that will be rising to the skies, but living saints.

(e) *No partibility*. "And so shall we ever be with the Lord." There is a powerful passage in Thomas Carlyle's *French Revolution* in which he portrays the scene at the parting of King Louis XVI and Marie Antoinette on January 21, 1793. The King was going to the guillotine and they were to see one another no more. It was a parting "for ever", and Carlyle breaks out: "O, Reader, canst thou measure that awful word!" That was a parting for ever, but here we are thinking of no parting for ever. In St Luke's account of the Ascension we read: "He led them out as far as to Bethany, and He lifted up His hands, and blessed them. And it came to pass, while He blessed them, He was parted from them" (Luke 24:50,51). In one sense He has been parted from His followers ever since. But, when they rise to meet Him in the air, there will be no partibility. There will be no farewell in that fellowship.

At this point in our study it may be well to stop for a minute or two to note that, while the New Testament gives us no warrant whatever for believing in a Third Advent, it does stress as strongly as possible that Christ's Second Advent is to take place in two distinct phases or stages. Usually – but not always – they are referred to respectively in Scripture as the *parousia* and the *epiphaneia*. At the first Christ will come *for* His saints: at the second, He will come *with* His saints. The former may be styled an Approach: the latter, an Appearance. It will be an event which is single and double at the same time; unitary, and yet dual.

And if anybody objects that this is impossible, an epochmaking incident from recent history may help to show that it is not without precedent. On July 13, 1969, Neil Armstrong and his companions were atomically propelled towards the moon in their spaceship Apollo 11. Ten days later, having completed their epic mission, they splashed down in the Pacific. Now, to those who watched the departure of the astronauts from the launching-pad and observed their return more than a week afterwards, there were two occurrences – the take-off and the splash-down, two totally different events with some two hundred and forty hours between them. Millions of things happened during that interval on this planet – births, deaths, marriages, and so on. But, to the intrepid astronauts themselves, it was only *one* event, a single happening involving no break in the continuity of consciousness.

Not otherwise will it be at the Return of Christ. At the Rapture, the line of biblical prophecy bifurcates, forming a sort of loop, on the upper side of which are listed the events to take place during that seven year period in the heavenlies, while on the underside are tabulated the events to take place collaterally on earth. Those in the heavenlies are (a) the *bema*; (b) *the presentation to the Father*; and (c) *the marriage supper of the Lamb*. As we shall see later, there are other events on the earthly plane. At the end of the seven-year period – the final "week" or heptad of Daniel's fifty – the loop returns to a single line at the *epiphaneia*.

Look, to begin with, at the first of these events in the heavenlies – the *bema* or Judgment Seat of Christ. Since "judgment must begin at the house of God" (1 Peter 4:17), it is fitting that this tribunal, at which the saints are to appear, should be the first of the five great final judgments: (2) *the judgment of the living nations*; (Matthew 25:31–46) (3) *the judgment of the Jews* (Ezekiel 20:37,38); (4) *the judgment of the Great White Throne* (Revelation 20:11-15);

and (5) *the judgment of the fallen angels* (Jude 6).

But how is it that the Christian is to be arraigned before this tribunal when we are expressly told that "he shall not come into judgment" (John 5:24)? The fact is that this is not a judgment in the legal or penal sense at all. It differs by a whole diameter from official judicial proceedings. To borrow A.J. Pollock's excellent illustration, it differs from these as widely as does a flower-show from a murder trial. I have been to both and I can vouch for the validity of the figure. A flower-show is a public display with a view to appraisal: a murder trial is a matter of life and death.

The principal New Testament references to the Judgment Seat of Christ are as follows: "Thou shalt be recompensed at the resurrection of the just" (Luke 16:14). "Every one of us shall give account of himself to God" (Romans 14:17). "Every man's work shall be made manifest, for the day shall declare it, because it shall be revealed by fire, and the fire shall try every man's work, of what sort it is" (1 Corinthians 3:13). "For we must all appear before the Judgment Seat of Christ, that every one may receive the things done in his body, according to that he hath done, whether it be good or bad" (2 Corinthians 5:10) The Greek word translated "Judgment Seat" is *bema*. It occurs twelve times in the original of the New Testament. In ancient days it figured in Greece both in the realm of law and in that of sport. On a *bema* it was that Pilate sat at the trial of Jesus. In Pauline usage, however, the reference is rather to the realm of athletics. Every two years the Isthmian Games were held in Corinth and it was doubtless these that the apostle had in mind in his illustration of the Judgment Seat of Christ. The *bema* was a dais or podium, on which the umpire sat when adjudicating at the gymnastic contests and from which he conferred upon the successful competitor a wreath of wild olive or a circlet of parsley. "They do it," wrote Paul, "to obtain a corruptible crown, but we an incorruptible" (1 Corinthians 9:25).

The *bema* will be to the Christian what the Ascension

was to Christ – the occasion of a crowning. Not legislation but coronation will be its *motif*. As John Blanchard finely says: "The heir to the throne may go almost unnoticed in the family photograph of the royal family, but when the moment comes for him to be crowned the whole world will recognize him." "Then shall every man have praise of God" (1 Corinthians 4:5). There will, of course, be those whose works will be designated "wood, hay and stubble" (1 Corinthians 3:12) and we are warned not to belong to them, but no one will go to perdition from the *bema* and the general overtone of the occasion is one of joy and jubilation.

Succeeding the *bema* will be the *presentation of the Church to the Father*. Here are a few apposite quotations: "I have espoused you to one Husband, that I may present you as a chaste virgin to Christ" (2 Corinthians 11:2). "That He might present (the Church) to Himself a glorious Church, not having spot or wrinkle, or any such thing, but that it should be holy and without blemish" (Ephesians 5:27). "You hath He quickened to present you holy and unblameable and unreproveable in His sight" (Colossians 1:21,22). "(He) is able to keep you from falling, and to present you faultless before the presence of His glory with exceeding joy" (Jude 24). "Without fault before the throne of God" (Revelation 14:5). He who is now *representing* us will then *present* us. Well, then, may we sing with Edward Mote:

When He shall come with trumpet sound,
O, may I then in Him be found,
Dressed in His righteousness alone,
Faultless to stand before the throne.

Of the *bema*, when God shall call for "every man's peculiar book", George Herbert wrote his poem entitled "Judgment":

What others mean to do I know not well,
Yet I hear tell
That some will turn Thee to some leaves therein
So void of sin
That they in merit shall excel.

But I resolve when Thou shalt call for mine,
That to decline
And thrust a Testament into Thine hand:
Let that be scanned,
Then Thou shalt find my faults are Thine.

The finest illustration I know of this second event, the presentation of the Church at the court of heaven, is this: Bertel Thorwaldsen was born in Denmark, the son of a poor Icelander. He became one of the world's greatest sculptors. Most of his life was spent in Italy, although he did live also for a while in Greece and Switzerland. And always, wherever he went, he spent his time modelling and chisselling masterpieces of his art. As his days drew in his heart turned home and he resolved to return to his native land. But he did not go empty-handed. With him he brought many of the magnificent statues he had carved or the plaster casts from which he had modelled them. Chartering a fleet of vessels, he took home to Copenhagen the treasures of his genius. It was a great day for him and a great day for the Danish capital. Flags fluttered bravely from the mastheads of the palace and other public buildings, bells pealed forth merrily and trumpets sounded stirringly to celebrate the occasion. Out from the wharf floated a flotilla of gaily decorated barges in one of which sailed the king and other members of the royal family while another carried burgesses and officers of state, prominent citizens, and so on. Amid scenes of rapturous jubilation, Thorwaldsen presented his masterpieces to the king. Then, taken ashore, the statues were placed on open wagons and drawn through the crowded streets of the capital to the admiration and adulation of the populace. Finally, they were placed on permanent display in a museum where they may be seen to this day.

What a splendid picture of Christ, the supreme Sculptor of human character, fashioning His saints in all parts of the world and bringing them together at last to present them perfect before the presence of His glory with exceeding joy!

The third event to take place in the heavenlies during the Danelian heptad is *the Marriage Supper of the Lamb.* "Let us be glad and rejoice, and give honour to Him, for the marriage of the Lamb is come, and His wife hath made herself ready; and to her was granted that she should be arrayed in fine linen, clean and white, for the fine linen is the righteousness of saints. And he said unto me, Blessed are they which are called unto the marriage supper of the Lamb" (Revelation 19:7–9). It is worth noting that the Bible starts with a story of the marriage of the First Adam and ends with the story of the marriage of the Last Adam, and all through the long interval between it is concerned in one way or another with the courtship by Christ of His Church. As Reginald Heber sings:

From heaven He came and sought her,
To be His holy bride;
With His own blood He bought her
And for her life He died.

A famous Continental thinker once likened nature to a bride, adorned in her nuptial attire, whose bridegroom had died on the wedding day, leaving her in tears ever since. The Church of Christ will never be like that. Her Bridegroom will never die again, and He will wipe away all tears from her eyes for ever. To celebrate the wedding there will be a great supper, beginning in heaven, as some prophetic students believe, and continued on earth during the Millennium, at which the crowded guests of God will feast. Discerningly, Merrill F. Unger points out that the Marriage Supper is Divinely designed for the honour of the Bridegroom, rather than for that of the bride. "The event is not said to be the marriage of the bride," he comments, "but that of the Lamb." For He is "all the glory in Emmanuel's land".

RETRIBUTION

From these events happening in the heavenlies during that momentous heptad, we turn to those occurring collaterally on earth. Under this heading we are to think of what is known as the "Great Tribulation". To this appalling judgmental period of human history there are numerous allusions in the Word of God. Here are some of them: "I will punish the world for their evil" (Isaiah 13:11). "I will call for a sword upon all the inhabitants of the earth, saith the Lord of hosts" (Jeremiah 25:27-29). "Alas, for that day is great, so that none is like it. It is even the time of Jacob's trouble, but he shall be saved out of it" (Jeremiah 30:7). "There shall be a time of trouble such as never was since there was a nation, even to that same time" (Daniel 12:1). "My determination is to gather the nations, that I may assemble the kingdoms, to pour upon them Mine indignation, even all My fierce anger; for all the earth shall be devoured by the fire of My jealousy" (Zephaniah 3:8). "Then shall be great tribulation, such as was not since the beginning of the world to this time, no, nor ever shall be; and except those days should be shortened, there should no flesh be saved; but for the elect's sake those days shall be shortened" (Matthew 24:21,22). "I also will keep thee from the hour of temptation, which shall come upon all the world, to try them that dwell upon the earth" (Revelation 3:10). "These are they which came out of the Great Tribulation" (literally, the Tribulation, the Great One), and have washed their robes and made them white in the blood of the Lamb" (Revelation 7:14). Such texts make it lucidly plain that, as William C. Procter put it epigramatically: "Pandemonium is to precede Millennium."

What is to be the duration of this dreadful period? Among students of biblical prophecy there is a consensus of opinion that it is to be roughly seven years. I say "roughly" because of our Lord's reference to "shortening". That consensus is founded on the clear teaching of Scripture. "I have given thee each day for a year – or, as the margin has it, "a day for a year, a day for a year" (Ezekiel 4:6). "From the going forth of the commandment to restore and to build Jerusalem unto the Messiah the Prince, shall be seven weeks, and three score and two weeks. The street shall be built again and the wall, even in troublous times. And after three score and two weeks shall Messiah be cut off, but not for Himself" (Daniel 9:25,26). In his masterly book on the subject *The Coming Prince* Sir Robert Anderson, a former Lord Chancellor of England, showed that this prophecy was literally fulfilled to the very day. "The edict for the rebuilding of Jerusalem," he wrote, "is to be assigned to 1st Nisan B.C.445. From that epoch until 'Messiah, the Prince', was to be sixty-nine sevens of prophetic years. (A prophetic year has 360 days). But 483 years of the 360 days contain 173,880 days; and 173,880 days, computed from the first day of Nisan in the twentieth year of Artaxerxes, ended on the 10th day of Nisan in the 18th year of Tiberius Caesar – the day when, in fulfilment of this and of Zechariah's prophecy, our Lord made His first and only public entry into Jerusalem."

But Daniel was directly told by the angel Gabriel that "70 weeks were determined upon his people and upon the Holy City", that is, 70 heptads, or weeks of years. Sixty-nine of those years expired when Messiah was cut off. Another heptad, or week of years, has yet to come. Our Lord, you will remember, broke abruptly off at a comma when expounding and explaining Isaiah 61:11,12 in the synagogue at Nazareth: "The Spirit of the Lord is upon Me, because He hath anointed Me to preach the Gospel to the poor, He hath sent Me to heal the broken-hearted, to preach deliverance to the captives, and the recovering of sight to the blind, to set at liberty them that are bruised, to preach the acceptable year of the Lord" (Luke 4:18,19). Then He halted. It was not a full-stop. It was only a comma. But He terminated the public reading summarily and decisively at that point, handing the scroll back to the minister. Isaiah, on the contrary, did not break off at that point. He went on: "And the day of vengeance of our God" (61:2). Our Lord, we may be sure, did not handle Holy Scripture in an arbitrary and irresponsible manner. This sudden termination of the reading was deliberate. The day of vengeance had not then dawned, nor has it even yet, but it may not be long before its flame-red sky lightens the world and the Great Tribulation begins.

It will be specifically the time of *Jacob's* trouble (Jeremiah 30:7) the climax of historic antisemitism, but it is nevertheless to come upon "all the earth" (Revelation 3:10), a period of universal woe.

Let us itemize some of the things that are to happen during that terrible time.

First, there is to be *the withdrawal of the Holy Spirit in His Pentecostal fulness from the world*. Mention of this is made in 2 Thessalonians 2:7 NEB: "Already the secret power of wickedness is at work, secret only for the present, until the Restrainer disappears from the scene." There is a wide range of speculation as to who or what this mysterious Withholder is. According to Alexander Reese he is the Roman Empire; Benjamin Warfield identifies him with the Jewish State; Mrs C. Needham holds that he is Satan, and so on. For the majority of commentators on biblical prophecy, however, his identity is unmistakable. He is the Holy Spirit.

"In the present age," as C.H. Mackintosh acutely observes, "the First Coming and the Second Coming of Christ are bound up together with the living link of the Holy Spirit's personal presence in the Church." After the

Rapture, the Paraclete will be withdrawn from the world in His Pentecostal fulness. Patently, it is impossible for an ominipresent Spirit to evacuate the world in the absolute sense. But just as, before the Day of Pentecost, the Holy Spirit was in the world, although not in total, tidal fulness, so, after the *parousia,* the *Paraclete* will withdraw in that fulness from human society. In the archaic language of the Authorized Version: "He who now letteth will let, until He be taken out of the way."

Naturally enough, after the recall to heaven of the Comforter, there will be a great apostasy (Greek *apostasia,* falling away) on earth. In the following Scriptural passages there are references to this: "As the days of Noe were so shall also the Coming of the Son of Man be" (Matthew 24:37). "When the Son of Man cometh, shall He find faith on the earth?" (Luke 18:8). "That day (the Day of Christ) shall not come except there come a falling away first" (2 Thessalonians 2:3). "Now the Spirit speaketh expressly that, in the latter times, some shall depart from the faith, giving heed to seducing spirits and doctrines of devils" (1 Timothy 4:1). It will be a period of unparalleled moral and spiritual declension.

Despite this – or perhaps because of it – there is to be *a great deal of evangelism during the Tribulation period*. The Jews are to be the evangelists. The remnant of them, 144,000, 12,000 representing each tribe, are to be, as Hal Lindsey says: "A company of Billy Grahams". "I will send those of them that escape into the nations, to the isles afar off, that have not heard My fame, neither have seen My glory, and they shall declare My glory among the Gentiles" (Isaiah 66:19). Their converts will be countless. "After this, I beheld, and, lo, a great multitude which no man could number, of all nations and kindreds and people and tongues, stood before the throne and before the Lamb, clothed with white robes and with palms in their hands. And he said to me, These are they which came out of the Great Tribulation" (Revelation 7:14).

And if anybody should protest that it is incredible that such a revival should occur after the withdrawal from the world of the Holy Spirit, one can only reply: "Do not overlook the evidential value of the event." Suppose that someone were to tell you: "I believe that Jesus Christ will come tomorrow", you might set him down out of hand as crank, fanatic, charlatan. But, if he were to say to you: "Jesus Christ came yesterday!" and were able to substantiate his testimony – ah, that would be another matter altogether! "Events," observed Jonathan Brierley, "are evangelists of the first order." Indeed they are! And none so powerfully persuasive as that stupendous event – the *parousia*. Hence this global response to the Gospel of the Kingdom during the Great Tribulation.

Half way through that seven-year period the Jewish missionaries of the Diaspora will be recalled to Israel. "He shall send forth His angels with a great sound of a trumpet, and they shall gather together His elect from the four winds, from one end of heaven to the other" (Matthew 24:31); and 144,000 Christian Jews will be there on Olivet to greet Christ when He appears.

Next on the prophetic agenda is *the emergencee of Antichrist*. Out of the pages of the Old Testament (Daniel 9, 11, etc.) and of the New Testament (Matthew 24: 2 Thessalonians, etc.,) glowers the grim yet glamorous face of Antichrist. He is the Devil incarnate, the reincarnation of Judas Iscariot, variously denominated in the Bible by a miscellany of horrific titles – "the Man of Sin", "the Son of Perdition", "the Anarchist", and so on. He is the Evil One's dazzling dictator, the second person in the diabolic trinity, the wicked World Ruler.

As to his nationality views vary. Some, like Sir Robert Anderson, regard him as a Greek; some, like Gavin Hamilton, consider him a Roman; some, like Dr Hollenbeck, dub him an Arab; and some, like Walter Scott, say he will be a Jew. The probability is that he will be an Italian Jew, an ethnic hybrid, combining in himself Gentile and

Jew. Biblical support for this view is that he is said (a) to belong to "the people of the prince that shall come" (Daniel 9:26), the prince referred to being Titus, a Roman, son of the Emperor Vespasian. Antichrist is also (b) stated "not to regard the God of his fathers" (Daniel 11:37a), a distinctive Hebraic phrase descriptive of an apostate Jew. And, further, not to be subject to "the desire of women" (Daniel 11:37a) – that is, according to certain commentators, the Messiah. For all of these reasons he would appear to be an Italian Jew.

On October 20, 1972, a BBC reporter, commenting on an EEC Summit Meeting, then being held in Paris, strikingly remarked that the aim of the conference was, in his own words, "to put a human face on the Common Market".

During the Great Tribulation the human face of the Common Market will be that of Antichrist. Head of a vast confederacy, the largest aggregation of human population on the face of the earth, he will despotically dominate an area of the surface of the planet probably comprising a prospective United States of Europe, the United States of America, Canada, South America, Australia, New Zealand, and so on – in short, all those parts of the world which have been populated and cultivated by emigrants from the continent of Europe.

To begin with, Antichrist will appear an amiable and attractive personality – suave, urbane, diplomatic, a mesmeric orator, a born leader. Perhaps because of his Jewish antecedents, Jews will be particularly drawn to him. They will actually accept him as their Messiah. Our Lord Himself foretold that: "Another shall come in his own name, him ye will receive" (John 5:43). With the Jews he will sign a seven-year pact. This also is Biblically predicted: "He will confirm the covenant with many for one week" (that is, one *heptad*)" (Daniel 9:27).

Initially, he will show great favour to the Jews. He will encourage them to rebuild their Temple in Jerusalem and to reinstitute the sacrifical rites of their ancestral religion.

They will consider him the best friend they have ever had. Yet, beneath the placid surface, trouble will be brewing.

Some idea of the appalling godlessness of the time is afforded by the account of the treatment meted out to the two witnesses referred to in Revelation 11:3-13. These are mystery men. Some take them for Enoch and Elijah, some for Moses and Elijah, some for Joshua the high priest and Zerubbabel. Whoever they are, they bear brave testimony for half a *heptad* – that is, for three and a half years – then they are brutally martyred, their bodies lying exposed on the streets of the Holy City, evidently with television cameras trained upon them, since "they of the people and kindreds and nations shall see their dead bodies three days and a half, and shall not suffer their dead bodies to be put in graves" (Revelation 11:9). Then observe the reaction to this atrocity of the profane populace of the day: "They that dwell upon the earth shall rejoice over them, and make merry, and shall send gifts to one another" (Revelation 11:10). In other words, they will make a sort of Christmas out of the assassinations. Three days later, however, the witnesses will be resurrected and be borne aloft to heaven.

Aiding and abetting the Antichrist will be the Second Beast or False Prophet, who is introduced to us in Revelation 13:11ff. He will reside in Jerusalem and will be the World Leader of the Coming Great World Church. When, three and a half years after the signing of the pact with the Jews, Antichrist doffs his disguise and displays himself in his true colours, the False Prophet will become his Public Relations Officer. He will make an image of Antichrist, to which he will impart life. The nearest thing I ever saw to this was in Disneyland, California, where a figure of Abraham Lincoln was so lifelike – rising from a chair, reciting well-known passages from Lincoln's famous speeches with oratorical gestures, and resuming his seat – that I felt sure a living actor was impersonating the great President. I was wrong. It was only a mechanical image.

"Imagine," says Charles C. Ryrie, "what would happen if that fake Lincoln actually came to life – and not just by getting up from a chair, but by actually walking right off the stage at Disneyland, mingling in the crowds, and making some prediction about the stock-market. Suppose Mr Disney (if he were living) should appear and say: 'I did it. I made him alive!'" What a sensation! Now that is what the Second Beast does. "In the midst of the week he (Antichrist) shall cause the sacrifice and the oblation to cease, and for the overspreading of abominations, he shall make it desolate, even until the consummation; and that determined shall be poured upon the desolate" (Daniel 9:27). "When ye therefore shall see the abomination of desolation, spoken of by Daniel the prophet, stand in the Holy Place" (Matthew 24:15). "That Man of Sin, the Son of Perdition, who opposeth and exalteth himself above all that is called God, or that is worshipped, so that he as God sitteth in the Temple of God, showing himself that he is God" (2 Thessalonians 2:3,4).

A system of commercial boycott will be introduced. All will be compelled on pain of death to have branded on their brow or right hand the Mark of the Beast, and the Mark of the Beast will control the Market of the Beast. For "no man might buy or sell save he that had the mark, or the name of the Beast, or the number of his name – 666" (Revelation 13:17).

To bow to the image of the Beast in the Temple will be mandatory. Those who refuse to accord it divine honour will have to pay for it with their lives. Some will *deify* Antichrist: others will *defy* him; and those who take the latter course will be subjected to a fearful fate.

Antichrist himself will reside in Rome, but he will have a holiday villa in the Holy Land between Jerusalem and the Mediterranean. At this home he will "make war on the saints" (Revelation 13:7). He will show himself to be a great military commander, so dexterous in the art of war that no one will be able to stand before him. The Second

Beast is his *aide de camp*. Incidentally, the mention of his bringing fire from heaven may have an atomic connotation.

However that may be, an aerial attack on the north of Israel by squadrons of Soviet aircraft is definitively foretold in Ezekiel 38, an assault repulsed with heavy casualties and whose success would seem to result from the use of atomic weaponry by the Israelis. The Soviets then resume their attack and run like a steam-roller through Israel down to Egypt. At this a future President of a United State of Africa, mustering all his resourses, counter-attacks and drives the Soviets north towards Megiddo. Here the tide of war halts, and it seems as if Israel, caught like a nut in a cracker, is about to be crushed out of existence. At this point it calls in the assistance of Antichrist, the President of the Western Confederacy, and the Battle of Armageddon, beginning in Jezreel sweeps south to Jerusalem. Just then the skies split open above Olivet and Christ, riding on a white horse, and at the head of a calvalcade of saints and angels, breaks in on the scene; He is greeted on the Mount of Olives by 144,000 Christian Jews, who doubtless join forces with Him. Crossing the Kedron Valley, they sweep up the Temple Mount and there, in personal encounter, Christ confronts Antichrist.

This is the climax of the Battle of Armageddon. Armageddon! The very word has become in English a synonym for total war. One thinks of James S. Stewart's striking depictment of modern man's moral dilemma: "Mankind in our time is staggering between Vanity Fair and Armageddon." One thinks of the *Financial Times* – of all papers! – editorializing: "A vital key to accurate forecasting of impending world events is an ability to spell the word Armageddon." One thinks of General Douglas Macarthur, commenting on the state of things at the close of World War II: "We have had our last chance. The Battle of Armageddon is next."

What *is* Armageddon? It is a locality mentioned in

Revelation 16:16: "He gathered them together into a place called in the Hebrew tongue Armageddon." Earlier references to the site may be found in Judges 5:19 and in Zechariah 12:11. The name is derived from two Hebrew words – *har,* meaning hill or mount – and *magedon,* meaning either God, or gathering, or slaughter. It is situated at the north western end of what the Israelis call *Emek Yizreel,* the Valley of Jezreel or Plain of Esdraelon. A broad "strath", 35 miles from east to west and 15 miles from north to south, it might well be described as the cockpit of humanity's military history. Napoleon labelled it "The world's greatest natural battlefield," and declared that all the armies of mankind could muster and manoeuvre there. When Lord Kitchener visited the area, pointing to the Plain of Esdraelon, he said: "This is the place where the final battle of the nations will be fought." He was almost right. Armageddon *will be* the last battle of this age, but not, as we shall see, of the ages.

Its story rings with the march of armed men – Joshua, Barak, Sisera, Gideon, Saul, Jonathan, Xerxes, Senacherib, Alexander the Great, Saladin, Napoleon, Allenby are notable names associated with this strategic military zone. Here, too, as we have noted, the last conflict of this age is to commence. The main antagonists will be the Antichrist at the head of the Great Western Confederacy, an outstanding Russian war-leader with his hordes, and a powerful military figure representing a future United States of Africa.

It would seem that the initiative of this final battle of the age will come from the Russians. The Soviets, having been repulsed with dreadful losses in men and materials in their first invasion, will run like a road-roller through Syria and Israel and drive south into the territory of the African leader, which the Russians will ravish and plunder. Tidings out of the east and the north will trouble the Soviet war-leader. Perhaps the tidings from the north will be news that Antichrist is mustering his forces at

Megiddo; and the tidings from the east may be the announcement of the approach of the 200,000,000 militia from the Lands of the Rising Sun. This is, of course, far too simplistic a sketch of how things may transpire at the final battle of the age, but it is a rough outline of the conduct of the war as foreshadowed in the Bible.

Behind the human actors in the titanic drama, however, will be the supernatural protagonists. There is a waxen seal of Megiddo, whose emblem is two lions rampant, at grips in grim hostility. What fitter figure could there be for Armageddon – the place where the two great lions – the Lion of the Tribe of Judah, spoken of in Revelation 5:5, and the one who "as a roaring lion walketh about seeking whom he may devour" (1 Peter 5:8) will meet in mortal combat? "The whole history of mankind," as Peter Beyerhaus points out, "is headed for the forthcoming clash between Christ and Antichrist."

Megiddo will be the point at which the armies first clash; but, after the battle has been in progress for a while, the tide of war will surge south towards the Holy City. According to the prophet Zechariah, this is where the last struggle is to be located: "I will gather all nations against Jerusalem to battle" (14:2). When this epic contest is at its height, there will be a terrible earthquake which will split Jerusalem into three parts. The metropolis will become a necropolis. Men will be butchered, women ravished, little children trampled to death. But, just as Israel seems on the brink of national extinction, a dramatic, Divine intervention will take place, which will radically alter the situation. For, when the Almighty bares His arm in battle, it does not much matter who bears arms against Him.

RETURN

This dramatic Divine intervention is predicted with detailed precision by the prophet Zechariah: "His feet shall stand in that day upon the Mount of Olives" (14:4). Regarding Christ's First Coming, Micah had prophetically pin-pointed the place with the utmost particularity: "Bethlehem!" (5:2). With no less exactitude and emphasis, Zechariah says: "Olivet!" (14:4).

REVELATION

During a visit to Israel in September 1983 I was electrified to hear of an Israeli Professor of Hebrew in the University of Jerusalem who publicly professed his faith in the imminence of the Coming of Messiah, and who said that when it happened, he would like to go up to the top of the Mount of Olives to meet Him and to extend to Him a welcome to the Holy Land, adding: "I would like to take Him by the hand, and to say: 'Excuse me, Sir, is this your first or your second visit to Planet Earth?'" We know what His answer will be!

This Return of the Redeemer to our world will be no hole-in-the-corner, clandestine affair. It will have world-wide publicity. "*Every* eye shall see Him" (Revelation 1:7). Six hundred million are reported to have watched Neil Armstrong alight on the moon, but not *every* eye. How will it be possible for the whole population of the planet to witness that stupendous spectacle? There are three theories. One is that the event will be globally televised and so seen by all. Another theory is that, at the time of His descent, our Lord will continue long enough suspended in the air, for the earth to rotate on its axis, thus giving each of its inhabitants a chance to observe His Advent. The third theory is that a vision of the Coming King will be *spiritually* transmitted to mankind, in some supernatural manner not necessitating recourse to technological aids.

When the Battle of Jerusalem is raging most fiercely, Christ will suddenly and spectacularly intervene. Commenting on our Lord's Triumphal Entry into the Holy City, John Bengel laconically observed: "He *shall* use the horse one day." The seer in the Book of Revelation watched Him do it. "I saw heaven opened, and behold a white horse, and He that sat upon him was called Faithful and True; and in righteousness He doth judge and make war. His eyes were as a flame of fire and on His head were many crowns, and He hath a name written that no man knew but He Himself; and He was clothed with a vesture dipped in blood, and His name is called the Word of God. And the armies which were in heaven followed Him upon white horses, clothed in fine linen, white and clean, and out of His mouth goeth a sharp sword, that with it He should smite the nations; and He hath on His vesture and on His thigh a name written, King of kings and Lord of lords" (Revelation 19:11–16).

Doubtless there will come a time during the battle when the two leaders, Christ and Antichrist, will find themselves in direct confrontation, eye-ball to eye-ball, as the rather gruesome modern phrase has it. "The Lord," wrote Paul, "shall consume him (Antichrist) with the Spirit of His Mouth, and shall destroy him with the brightness of His Coming" (2 Thessalonians 2:8). Five sixths of the Russian hordes will be exterminated and two thirds of the Jews will be slaughtered or driven into exile. Just as when, on the night of His arrest in Gethsemane, in response to His demand: "Whom seek ye?" the band of men with their weapons and torches, cried: "Jesus of Nazareth!" and He replied: "I am!", as His Deity flashed forth, "They went backward and fell to the ground" (John 18:6), so when they meet in final confrontation will Antichrist, the Great World Ruler, be paralyzed by the outshining of Christ's *parousia*, afterwards being consigned along with his nefarious ally the False Prophet to everlasting destruction. It will be noted that these arch-villains are not accorded the privilege of a trial. They are consigned unjudged to eternal perdition.

RECOMPENSE

Immediately after descending to Olivet with his shining cohorts, and after having routed Antichrist, our blessed Lord will conduct the survivors of the battle, representing the nations of the world, down into the Valley of Jehoshaphat, so called because it contains the traditional grave of that king, which lies at the southern extremity of the Kedron ravine. There He will set up His tribunal. This is known to students of biblical prophecy as "The Judgment of the Living Nations". It would patently be impossible for the whole population of the globe to assemble in that narrow gorge, but that is not necessary. It is nations, not individuals, who will be judged at this assize. We commonly say that the United Nations meets in New York, and so they do – but only in the persons of their representatives. Not otherwise will it be here. According to Joel 3:2, that great judgment will take place at the southern end of that ravine: "I will also gather all nations, and bring them down into the Valley of Jehoshaphat, and will plead with them there for My people, and for My heritage, Israel, whom they have scattered among the nations, and parted My land." Our Redeemer Himself gives this account of it: "When the Son of Man shall come in His glory, and all the holy angels with Him, then shall He sit upon the throne of His glory: and before Him shall be gathered all nations: and He shall separate them one from another, as a shepherd divideth his sheep from the goats." (Matthew 25:31ff.)

"Then shall the *King* say" (v.34). Dean Alford acutely remarks: "This is the only occasion recorded in the New Testament on which our Lord explicitly refers to Himself as 'King'." How careful and explicit and specific our Lord is in the wording of His references to the fate respectively of the sheep and the goats! To the sheep He says: "Come, ye blessed of My Father, inherit the Kingdom prepared for you from the foundation of the world" (v.34). To the goats, He says: "Depart from Me, ye cursed, into everlasting fire, prepared for – ?" Whom? "You!" No. "Prepared for the Devil and his angels" (v.41). Hell was not divinely designed for humans. Every member of our ransomed race who goes there will be a suicide.

RECOGNITION

One of the most mystifying tragedies of human history is the failure of the Jews to recognize in Jesus their true Messiah. "He came unto His own, and His own received Him not" (John 1:11). What infinite pathos there is in that single, simple sentence! It is an indictment, not just of Jesus' Jewish contemporaries, but of the whole Hebrew race. "We will not have this Man to reign over us" (Luke 19:14), words that first fell in parable from our Lord's own lips, have been their cry throughout the centuries. Subsequent to the Redeemer's Return, however, after He has touched down on Olivet, routing His enemies and judging the living nations, the Jews will see Him in a new light. One hundred and forty-four thousand of them will, as we have seen, be there to welcome Him when He returns. But not only they – the whole Hebrew race – will "own His title, praise His name". That is why the Seer in the apocalypse, after proclaiming Christ's universal visibility at the *epiphaneia*, "every eye shall see Him" (Revelation 1:1) – makes special mention of "them also which pierced Him" (1:1a).

Among the most tender and touching episodes in the Old Testament is that in which Joseph, now Prime Minister of Egypt, discloses himself to the brothers who have so grievously wronged him, but have now come begging bread. "Then Joseph could not restrain himself before all them that stood by him, and he cried, Cause every man to go out from me. And he wept aloud, and said unto his brethren, I am Joseph. Come near to me, I pray you" (Genesis 45:1-4).

That scene will be re-enacted on a grand scale at the Second Coming of Christ. It is predictively depicted for us several times in the Bible. Consider these confirmatory texts: "I will go and return to My place till they acknowledge their offence and seek My face" (Hosea 5:19). "It shall be said in that day, Lo, this is our God. We have waited for Him and He will save us" (Isaiah 29:9). "They shall look upon Me whom they have pierced, and they shall mourn for Him as one mourneth for his only son, and shall be in bitterness for Him, as one that is in bitterness for his firstborn" (Zechariah 12:10). "I will pour upon the house of David and upon the inhabitants of Jerusalem the Spirit of grace and supplications" (Zechariah 12:10). "In that day there shall be a fountain opened to the house of David, and to the inhabitants of Jerusalem, for sin and for uncleanness" (Zechariah 13:1). "The house of Israel shall know that I am the Lord their God, from that day and forward" (Ezekiel 39:22). "Shall a nation be born at once?" (Isaiah 66:8). "All Israel shall be saved" (Romans 11:26). "The Jews," remarks W. Haslam, "will be converted suddenly, as Saul of Tarsus was, by seeing the Lord in His glory."

An Israeli friend of mine, not yet a Christian, observed to me one day in the Holy Land: "You Christians are looking for Messiah; we Jews are also looking for Messiah; and if your Jesus should turn out to be our Messiah, we will welcome Him with open arms." They will when that day dawns!

REALM

It was a principle of the great Greek tragedians never to introduce a god into a drama unless the situation was so desperate that only a god could deal with it. That will be the world situation at the time Christ returns to reign. Already we begin to see signs of its approach. We need a world ruler. "Life has grown so complicated," wrote Clement Rogers, "government cannot be carried on by any ruler unless he is omnipresent." "What is needed today," declared H.G. Wells, "is a President of the Earth." Throughout its entire history the planet will have had three world rulers. The one who now controls its affairs and operates its evil system is known in the New Testament as "the god of this world" (2 Corinthians 2:4); the next world ruler will claim to be God. "He (Antichrist) sitteth in the Temple of God, showing himself that he is god" (2 Thessalonians 2:4). The third world ruler really will be God. "I saw heaven opened, and behold a white horse, and He that sat upon him was called the Word of God" (Revelation 19:11). "Yet have I set My King upon My holy hill of Zion" (Psalm 2:6). "The Lord shall be King over all the earth; in that day there shall be one Lord, and His name one" (Zechariah 14:9).

During the American Civil War a delegation from the deep south called on President Lincoln and spread out before him on a table a map of the United States, across which a line had been drawn. "South of that line," the spokesman told him, "it will be all right for people to have slaves, north of that line it will be illegal." Abraham Lincoln had a huge hand. Disregarding the arbitrary line, he laid his hand broadly on the map, covering it completely. "I claim it all in the name of freedom," he said.

In the Millennium the nail-pierced palm of the true Messiah will be placed on this planet. He will claim the whole world in the name of a freedom hitherto unknown.

For a thousand years our blessed Lord will reign on this earth which once rejected Him. Only a few hundred yards from where He wore a crown of thorns, He will wear the crown of glory. This is expressly and explicitly stated in Revelation 20:4–6, and it is what students of biblical prophecy describe as the Millennium.

Not everybody cares for the term. C.I. Scofield for one! "It is to be regretted," he remarked, "that this word ever supplanted the old biblical word 'Kingdom'. The Bible never uses the bastard term Millennium." Well, a bastard term it may be, minted from the Latin *mille*, thousand and *annus*, year. But it is now the official technical theological term for the thousand years' earthly reign of Christ, and it would be difficult, even if it were desirable, to displace it or replace it so late in the day. Its Greek equivalent is Chiliasm, from the word *chilias*, thousand.

There are three theories connected with the Millennium

to which we must at this point turn our attention. They are (1) *Amillennialism;* (2) *Postmillennialism;* and (3) *Premillennialism.* Take them in that order.

(1) *Amillennialism allegorizes the Millennium.* This view is held among others, by Philip Mauro, Oswald T. Allis and Archibald Hughes, and it is rapidly gaining ground in our time. It teaches that God has finished with the Jews as a chosen race, and that all the territorial promises made by God to the patriarchs are fulfilled in the Church. They are to be spiritualized and not taken literally. The binding of Satan, according to it, began with the earthly ministry of Christ; the Devil is now on a chain, presumably now some 25,000 miles long, since he is patently still prowling about the planet; the resurrection is regeneration and we are now going through the Millennium, whereas many of us feel we are just going through the mill! Surely an incredible creed!

(2) *Postmillennialism socializes the Millennium.* This optimistic utopianism is on its last legs – or was until recently. Two world wars and the constant threat of another one have just about put paid to it. It was initiated by Daniel Whitby, a Unitarian. "He came up with the idea," says John Walvoord, "that there would be a Millennium on the earth, but that it would not be a literal Millennium, following the Second Coming of Christ. Rather it would be an ideal social and political State, brought in through the preaching of the Gospel and through the influence of the power of the Church. The world would become Christianized and there would come a time when missionary effort would reach its ultimate and everyone would know the truth about Christ." Incredibly, Postmillennialism is being revived currently in America. One of its chief exponents maintains that it is a slight on the Gospel to suppose that it does not possess sufficient inherent momentum to win the world. But surely Paul Althaus has dealt a death-blow to this theory by pointing out, in his book *Die letzen Dinge (The Last Things)* that: "The concept of

Antichrist is a loud 'No' to all secular chiliasm, and to the optimistic faith in a progressive coming of the Kingdom of God on earth." That single insight, one would have thought, should be sufficient to close the coffin-lid on Postmillennialism.

Any who still subscribe to it are like the man who was inquiring into the subject of Biblical prophecy, but heard so much learned patter about Amillennialism, Postmillennialism and Premillennialism that he was utterly confused. "Which are you?" someone asked him. "I am a Panmillennialist," he replied. "A *Pan*millennialist!" exclaimed the questioner, "what is that?" "I don't altogether know," was the candid answer. "Only, I have come to expect that everything is going to *pan out* all right!" Such superficial, sentimental optimism is worlds away from the firm certitude which is founded on the Word of God.

(3) *Premillennialism actualizes it.* This is the only tenable eschatological position. The Millennium cannot come until Messiah comes. As John Knox sensibly argued: "To reform the face of the whole earth is a thing that will never be done until the King and Head appear for the restitution of all things." "The Word of God," observes William Hoste, "knows nothing of a Kingdom set up without the King." There is poetic justice in this Millennial teaching. "If there is no final victory of good over evil," someone has reasonably remarked, "then the Kingdom of God becomes just an empty dream; if there is no inheritance of the saints, then the Fatherhood of God just becomes a vain illusion."

There *is* to be a literal Millennium. Several weighty considerations make it mandatory – the rationality of history, the practicality of Christianity, the profitability of prayer, the credibility of the Bible, "I am a Chiliast," cried Franz Delitzsch, "Jesus Christ was a Chiliast!" Indeed our Lord was! "Thy will be done *on earth,*" He taught His disciples to pray. The request "Thy Kingdom come" is interpreted, as to its nature and location, by the phrase which follows it (Luke 11:2).

The Bible certainly predicts a Millennium. "In the days of those kings" – that is, translated into modern terminology, "in the days of the European Economic Community" – "shall the God of heaven set up a Kingdom which shall never be destroyed" (Daniel 2:44). The other world empires referred to in this prophetically pivotal chapter were literal kingdoms – Babylonian, Medo-Persian, Grecian, Roman – and this Kingdom, which God is to set up, will be literal too.

In the course of its long history the world has been ordered and controlled by almost every conceivable system of government – *autocratic*, that is government by a dictator, a despot; *aristocratic*, that is, as the Greek implies, government by the "best" people; *bureaucratic*, that is, government by civil servants; *plutocratic*, that is, government by wealth; and, finally, *democratic*, that is, government by the people. There is one form of government which has not yet been tried – *Christocratic*, government by Jesus Christ. When the Millennium comes, that is the government which will be in power.

What will life be like during those thousand years? The Bible does not provide us with a systematic blueprint of it. That is never God's way. He does not grow flowers in little trim botanical gardens: He grows them wild on the mountains; He does not scatter lumps of gold like pebbles on a beach: He buries it in the bowels of the earth; He does not strew pearls like bubbles on the surface of the sea: He secretes them in oysters in the oozy depths. Just so with scriptural truth. If we are rightly to answer the question as to conditions in the Millennium, we shall have to search and research in the pages of the Book of God. When we do so, we discover that there are at least fourteen descriptive statements which together form a composite picture of the Millennial Age.

Let us rapidly review them.

The Bible will be verified. "In the latter days ye shall consider it perfectly" (Jeremiah 23:20). The finest illustration I have come across in this connection occurs in a book called *Victory Pageant* by Robert Wallace Orr. He writes: "Let us suppose that we want to project a picture. We fix a large screen at the far end of the room. Then we insert a transparency in the slot in front of the lamp and switch on the electric current. When the apparatus is properly adjusted the picture will show up large and clear at the far end of the darkened room. Now we wish to find out what the picture looks like half way between the projector and the screen. So we take a large piece of white card and hold it up in the beam of light. We find that if we intercept the beam anywhere between the projector and the screen a blurred image is obtained. The true colours are indeed present, but the forms and the writing cannot be clearly seen until the light reaches the screen at the end."

So it is with biblical prophecy. The Bible predicted that the Jews were going back to the Promised Land, that there was going to be a great godless empire immediately to the north of Israel, that a revived Roman Empire was to appear. Now if, at the end of the last century, you had tried to interpret these Scriptures in the light ot the then current world situation, they would have seemed to be falsified by the facts. The Turks had an iron grip of Palestine; the tsars were in power in Russia under the sinister spell of a wily monk Rasputin; and nothing looked less likely than a federation of European states. Now, however, with the passing of time and the approach of the End of the Age, the ancient prophecies have leapt into lucid life. "In the latter days ye shall consider it perfectly" (Jeremiah 23:20).

Messiah will be identified. Earlier, as have seen, He will be recognized and accepted by the Jews, but in the Millennium He will be enthroned as Sovereign of the Earth. His Messianic office will no longer be restricted to the Hebrew nation, but will extend worldwide. As the great Messianic psalm (72) lyrically expresses it: "He shall have dominion from sea to sea, and from the river unto the ends of the earth. Yea, all kings shall fall down before Him; all nations shall serve Him" (vv.8,11). He will be identified as President of the Planet.

The Devil will be nullified. "An angel laid hold on the Devil, bound him for a thousand years, and cast him into the bottomless pit" (Revelation 20:1,2). "For a Millennium," says Geoffrey King, "two things are essential – the presence of the Lord and the absence of the Devil." The banishment of the Evil One is necessary to the establishment of the Divine Kingdom. That is why Satan is to be incarcerated for a thousand years. Imagine what the world would be like today if there had been no Devil since A.D.1000.

Natural light will be magnified. "The light of the moon shall be as the light of the sun, and the light of the sun shall be sevenfold" (Isaiah 30:26). On April 10, 1984, the Russians intimated their intention to suspend in outer space ten-mile squares of silver-coated tin-foil, the squares to be placed in such a position as to catch and reflect the sun's rays on the regions within Soviet territory, such as Siberia, thus substantially augmenting their light and heat and in this way speeding and increasing vegetable and arboreal growth and lengthening the outdoor working-day. The idea was mooted by the Germans during World War II, but was abandoned as quixotic, expensive, impracticable. It was revived at the time of the lunar landings by a Jewish professor in Sydney, Australia, but was not then implemented either. Some such augmentation of natural light and heat, without prejudice to human health, is forecast for this planet during the Millennium.

Earth will be fructified. Modern chemical fertilizers and intensive farming methods have done much to increase the gross agricultural product of the planet. But during the Millennium earth's productivity will be phenomenally increased. "The ploughman shall overtake the reaper, and the treader of grapes him that soweth seed" (Amos 3:19).

Such a year-round yield is practically the case in Israel today. There is no season without its crop; no month without its distinctive product. The sower is quite literally overtaking the reaper. How much more widespread and wonderful will be the productivity of Planet Earth during the thousand years' reign of Christ!

Creation will be pacified. "The wolf also shall dwell with the lamb, and the leopard shall lie down with the kid; and the calf and the young lion and the fatling together; and a little child shall lead them" (Isaiah 11:6). Even man has succeeded in persuading the lion and the lamb to lie down peacefully together. It happened in the famous Victorian circus, owned by "Lord" George Sanger. "One of the most noted acts," it is recorded, "was a lion that had been brought up to let a lamb nestle between its paws. The lamb could even butt the lion in the stomach without the King of the Jungle taking any notice." Moreover, in modern Jerusalem there is the Biblical Zoo, which is a sort of miniature Millennium in itself. Located in one of the suburbs of the Israeli capital, the Romema quarter, a richly-wooded part, it is unique among the zoological gardens of the world. Founded in 1929 by Professor Aharon Shulov, it aims to bring together within a roomy enclosure all the animals, birds and reptiles referred to in the Scriptures. "Approximately one hundred and thirty animals are named in the Bible," says the professor. "Besides repatriating to Israel all the animals mentioned in the Bible, the purpose of the zoo is to give the public, especially school-children, knowledge of the Bible by actually bringing it to life for them." In one corner of the zoo the prophecy of Isaiah 11:6, "The wolf shall lie down with the lamb, and the leopard shall lie down with the kid", is now almost fulfilled. The professor explains that he put a real live tiger in with the goats, while it was still young, and it has never occurred to it to do the goats any harm. Although somewhat apprehensive when the tiger was introduced into their domain, the goats have quite accepted the intrusive carnivore, and "actually eat their meals together and spend hours of play within the rocky enclosure." What is now transpiring on this narrowly limited scale, will one day take place universally. Here is the prophetic promise of the Word of God: "I will make with them (that is, with the animals) a covenant of peace, and will cause the evil beasts to cease out of the land, and they will dwell safely in the wilderness and sleep in the woods" (Ezekiel 34:25). During the Golden Age of the future all the carnivorous animals will have become herbivorous. The world will go vegetarian.

Human life will be amplified. "There shall be no more thence an infant of days, nor an old man that hath not filled his days; for the child shall die an hundred years old" (Isaiah 65:20). The oldest man alive today is said to be 139 years old. He is an extremely rare exception, although it is certainly true that human longevity is being markedly extended by medical science, dietary discoveries, and the like. There are far more retirees than ever before and the trend seems likely not only to continue but to increase. Centenarians are far more common than they used to be, but Millenarians will make their deaths appear like cases of infantile mortality. "A man shall die an hundred years old" (Isaiah 65:20). That will then be reckoned as premature passing.

Tribulation martyrs will be vivified. During that terrible time there will be a shocking slaughter of those who refuse to bear the Mark of the Beast. "And I saw thrones, and they sat upon them; and judgment was given unto them: and I saw the souls of them that were beheaded for the witness of Jesus, and for the Word of God, and which had not worshipped the Beast, neither his image, neither had received his mark upon their foreheads or in their hands; and they lived and reigned with Christ a thousand years" (Revelation 20:4).

The Jews will be occupied. For one thing, they will be busy rebuilding their Temple in Jerusalem. This will be the great Messianic Temple, the fifth in the long succession of sanctuaries which have stood on that magnificent site in the Holy City – first, Solomon's Temple, then Zerubbabel's Temple, then Herod's Temple, then Antichrist's Temple and finally Messiah's Temple. For another thing, the Jews will also be the leading evangelists of that era. "I will send those that escape of them unto the nations, to the isles afar off, that have not heard My fame, neither have seen My glory; and they shall declare My glory among the Gentiles" (Isaiah 66:19).

The Nations will be multiplied. One of the demographic facts to which experts in that field are today calling attention is that the population of the world is expanding at an alarming rate. Some even state that, if present trends continue, there will be standing room only on this planet in the not too distant future. Every time the clock ticks four babies are born and, despite the death rate, the race is reproducing itself in a positive crescendo of creative activity. By the year 2000 it is predicted to have reached 6,000,000,000. There will, of course, be a dreadful decimation of the world's population during the Great Tribulation, but during the Millennial Age conditions will be so conducive to healthy living that, among the inhabitants who do not have spiritual bodies, and are therefore reproducing themselves, there will be an enormous increase. "Imagine," wrote Clyne W. Buxton, "the vastness of the population of this planet if almost everyone born after 1000 AD were still alive."

Language will be unified. "Then will I turn to the people a pure language, that they may all call upon the name of the Lord, to serve Him with one consent" (Zephaniah 3:9). Note that it is a *pure* language – neither Aramaic nor Yiddish, but pure Hebrew. That language was virtually dead for two thousand years. It was the speech of the specialist, used only by the learned few. Then came Eliezer Ben Yehuda, born in 1858 in Lithuania of Jewish parents, who made it his lifework to seek to ensure that

Hebrew would be the language of modern Israel. He did his work so well that today Hebrew is the basic language in which the most highly sophisticated subjects are taught. There have been many Jews by the name of Moses, who have distinguished themselves in the history of their nation. Two stand out – Moses the Doyen of ancient Israel and Moses (Moshe) Dayan, the brilliant modern Israeli military commander. Although thousands of years separated them historically, they could have conversed in the same tongue.

Hebrew is by no means an easy language for Europeans to learn. Several of its features contribute to this. It has to be read from right to left, and not, as is usual with us, from left to right. Further, its vowel points have to be memorized and observed. Once more, its calligraphy is so completely different from anything with which we in the West are familiar. Yet it seems clear from Scripture that Hebrew will be the lingua franca in the millennial world. Charles de Gaulle would have liked it to be French and Winston Churchill English and Ludwig Zamenhof went the length of inventing a hybrid language Esperanto (from the Spanish word for "hope"). But the Bible says it will be Hebrew.

Some people are daunted by this. They cannot conceive of themselves ever mastering that mysterious tongue. But let them take heart. An ingenious electronic device has just been publicized. It is a small hearing-aid-like instrument, which can be affixed at night to the back of the ear, and during the hours of slumber can impart to the sleeper a perfect knowledge of any language he wants to learn. He can go to bed at night without knowing a single word of Hebrew and wake up with a working facility in it. This should prove of great help during the Millennium. If *man* can do that, how much more *God*.

It is said that the poet Alfred, Lord Tennyson, learned Hebrew in order to have the pleasure of reading the twenty-third Psalm in the original. It will be an infinitely greater pleasure to be able in that Golden Age to converse with the Lord Jesus in His native tongue!

The race will be sanctified. "The earth shall be filled with the knowledge of the glory of the Lord, as the waters cover the sea" (Habakkuk 2:14). Truly, those will be idyllic days! There will be no murder, rape, theft, mugging, or any of the social crimes and vices which now afflict the world. As the Bible beautifully prophesies: "The whole earth is at rest and is quiet; they shall break forth into singing" (Isaiah 14:7).

The Church will be dignified. "Do ye not know that the saints shall judge the world? Know ye not that we shall judge angels?" (1 Corinthians 6:2,3). "We shall also reign with Him" (2 Timothy 2:12). Someone has preceptively pointed out that "the Church has her long list of saints, but has never inserted one name in any catalogue of the damned". There are reputed saints in the Church calendar, to many of whom widespread publicity has been given throughout the centuries. Nevertheless the rarest saints have been anonymous, those humble, quiet souls who have at the command of Christ "done their deed and scorned to blot it with a name". Yet a time is coming when the Church will be the Queen of Christ's millennial court. He Himself will reign in Jerusalem; His viceroy will be King David; His cabinet will be the twelve apostles, His royal consort the Church. She is indeed, to borrow a phrase from Paul Billheimer, "destined for the throne".

God will be glorified. "He shall come to be glorified in His saints, and to be admired in all them that believe in that day" (2 Thessalonians 1:10). "I, saith the Lord, will be the glory in the midst of Jerusalem" (Zechariah 2:5). "The glory of the Lord shall be revealed, and all flesh shall see it together" (Isaiah 40:5). "I believe," said Albert Einstein, "that world government is certain to come in time." "The time for world government has come," declared Arnold Toynbee. The glory of world empires – Babylonian, Egyptian, Medo-Persian, Greek, Roman, British – has tarnished with time, but the glory of the Lord shall shine undimmed not only in the Millennial Age but throughout all ages, world without end. Then the Majesty on High will be a majesty most nigh when "the kingdoms of this world become the Kingdom of our God and of His Christ" (Revelation 11:15).

REVOLT

In the study of biblical prophecy nothing strikes us as more strange than that the Millennium is to end in a revolt. Such insurrection following the thousand beneficent years of Christ's reign is utterly unexpected and indeed hardly believable. It seems a startling anticlimax. Yet the Bible plainly predicts it. "At the expiry of one thousand years it is expressly declared that Satan will be 'loosed for a little season' " (Revelation 20:7,) writes J. Stuart Holden. "Do you know why? Probably, it will be easy in the preceding Millennial days for people to believe in Christ. They will not have to overcome the difficulties we all experience in the present age; and there will certainly be widespread profession of allegiance and all such professed faith in Him will have to be tested. Its reality will have to be put to the touch-stone of temptation, and for a little season Satan will be unbound therefore. But his time then, as now, is short."

However that may be, the revealed truth is that the Millennium will terminate in rebellion. "When the thousand years are expired, Satan shall be loosed out of his prison, and he shall go out to deceive the nations which are in the four quarters of the earth, Gog and Magog, to gather them together to battle, the number of whom is as the sand of the sea. And they went up on the breadth of the earth, and compassed the camp of the saints about, and the Beloved City" (Revelation 20:7–9). Geoffrey King concisely comments: "During the Millennium, the Devil will be *chained* but not *changed*. He is the same at the end of his confinement as at the beginning." His imprisonment has led to no improvement. He instigates a great revolt. The uprising is, however, very short-lived. Fire comes down from heaven and consumes his followers and he suffers final defeat.

RESURRECTION

Several resurrections are spoken of in the New Testament. There is, first, Christ's own resurrection and that of those who accompanied Him later into the heavenlies; there is that, too, of the Christian dead at the *parousia*; that, further, of the tribulation saints at the close of that terrible time; that of the Jews at the commencement of Christ's thousand years' reign; and, at its end, what is known as the General Resurrection. This last is referred to in the Apocrypha: "And in those days will the earth also give back those who are treasured upon it, and Sheol also will give back that which it has received, and Hell will give back that which it owes" (Book of Enoch 51:1–5). To the same effect is a passage in the Second Book of Maccabees; where we are told that seven brothers died as martyrs, one of them making this brave confession: 'Thou like a fury takest us out of this present life, but the King of the World shall raise us up, who have died for His laws, unto everlasting life." Another of the brothers, about to have his tongue plucked out and his hands cut off, holding forth his hands courageously, cried: 'These I had from heaven and from God I hope to receive them again.' " But it is to the Scriptures we must turn for authentic information about the General Resurrection. Here are several texts: "Many of them that sleep in the dust shall awake to everlasting shame and contempt" (Daniel 12:2). "The hour is coming in the which all that are in the graves shall hear His voice, they that have done evil unto the resurrection of damnation" (John 5:28,29). "There shall be a resurrection of the unjust" (Acts 24:15). "I saw the dead, small and great, stand before God. The sea gave up the dead which were in it, and death and hell delivered up the dead which were in them" (Revelation 20:12,13).

The word *anastasis,* Greek for resurrection, is one which occurs not infrequently on the pages of the New Testament.

At the beginning of November, 1974, it was intimated in the Press that an American living in Florida had invented a novel "Talking Tombstone". The tombstone was submerged in the earth at the head of a grave, and could be elevated at the touch of a button, so as to display a small screen on which films of the deceased were shown and his voice heard. What a pathetic travesty of the resurrection! Our Lord Himself says that a day is coming when "all that are in the graves shall hear His voice and shall come forth" (John 5:28,29).

RECKONING

"I saw a great white throne and Him that sat upon it, from whose face the earth and the heaven fled away, and there was found no place for them. And I saw the dead, small and great, stand before God, and the books were opened, and another book was opened, which is the Book of Life. And the dead were judged out of those things, which were written in the books, according to their works" (Revelation 20:11,12). "God keeps books," says George Sinclair. He is the Great Auditor. All men are to be "brought to book" at last. Old Bishop Jewel was wont to say that "a judge must walk with feet of lead". That is why God leaves the day of reckoning to the end of human history. He will not finally pass sentence of doom upon the wicked until they have had every possible chance to repent. As Norman B. Harrison puts the awesome truth in tabloid form: "Reserved for the very last is the lot of the lost."

The liberals, of course, do not take those terrifying pictures of the final Great Assize literally. They regard them as mere apocalyptic imagery. "We used to say that we were punished *for* our sins," wrote Harry Emerson

Fosdick, "as though God were a judge on a bench, who passed judgment on the case and meted out the penalty. The truth goes far deeper than that. We are not so much punished *for* our sins as *by* them." "Expressions like 'the Last Judgment' or 'the Great Assize' do not mean that at a chronological end of history there will be legal proceedings on a gigantic scale, consisting of a trial and leading up to a verdict," according to Alec R. Vidler. Well, while there is bound to be an element of imagery in any depictment of the Great White Throne, it is patent beyond all possibility of error that the Bible would not be content with just an ongoing conscientious moral judgment of human acts at the time of their committal. Man's conscience is not the final arbiter. It stands under a judgment infinitely greater and truer and fairer than its own – the judgment of an All-knowing God. Looking at Mont Blanc gleaming, snow-covered, in the sunlight, Frances Ridley Havergal once remarked to friends: "See! The Great White Throne!" One day every unsaved sinner will stand before it. Seated upon it will be "the Judge of all the earth" (Genesis 18:25). "Men shall go into the holes of the rocks for fear of the Lord when He arises to shake terribly the earth" (Isaiah 2;19). "Then shall they begin to say to the mountains, Fall on us, and to the hills, Cover us" (Luke 23:30). Our Lord Himself spoke most solemnly about that terrible tribunal. "Fear not them that kill the body, but are not able to kill the soul," He said, "but rather fear Him, who is able to destroy both soul and body in hell" (Matthew 10:28). In his profound book *The Problem of Pain* C.S. Lewis wrote: "I would pay any price to be able to say truthfully, 'All will be saved'. But my reason retorts: 'With their will or without it?' If I say 'Without their will' I at once perceive a contradiction: How can the supreme voluntary act of self surrender be involuntary? If I say 'With their will', my reason replies: 'How, if they will not give in?'" The Bible makes it poignantly plain that many people will not "give in". It is true, as Carroll E. Simcox argues, that one would think that that is morally obvious, but that perdition will be the fearful plight of multitudes is not open to question; and the most dreadful thing about Hell is not its flame or its darkness, but its separation from God. "Separate the stream from the fountain," writes Charles James, "and there is death; separate the branch from the tree, and there is death; separate the body from the soul, and there is death: separate the soul from God and there is death eternal." The following words of Adolphe Monod tremble on the verge of tears: "I gave in; I bowed my head; I put my hand over my mouth; I made myself believe in eternal suffering."

So far the Devil and his angels are "reserved in everlasting chains under darkness unto the judgment of the Great Day" (Jude 6) and will then be consigned to hell and all those who, by their deliberate rejection of Christ, have chosen to share their frightful fate. "The Lord knoweth how to keep the unrighteous under punishment unto the Day of Judgment" (2 Peter 2:9). And consider the appalling words of the Psalmist: "Thou hast destroyed the wicked; Thou hast put out their name for ever and ever" (9:5). Jonathan Edwards has a terrifying passage in one of his sermons in which he declares that "when the saints in heaven shall look upon the damned in hell, it will serve to give them a greater sense of their own happiness." That is not the sort of reaction to the misery of others which one associates with the saints even in this world. More typical of them is Samuel Johnson as, sobbing, he chanted the *Dies Irae:*

Day of Wrath, O Day of Mourning,
See fulfilled the prophet's warning,
Heaven and earth to ashes turning.

One thing is certain, whatever their emotional response, in the clear light of eternity they will see that "the Judge of all the earth has done right". "There shall be no stain on the Great White Throne." If hell be real at all, it is monstrous folly to minimize it. Thomas Watson, the Puritan writer, has an awesome reflection on it. "Eternity to the godly is a day that has no sunset: eternity to the wicked is a night to which there is no sunrise." "There is a very real danger to our souls," declares Carroll E. Simcox, "in the shocking indifference to hell which prevails in the modern Church." That is true. People nowadays, even Church people, are more afraid of the results of an atomic explosion than of eternal perdition. "I tell you in the name of God," cries A.W. Rainsbury, "that the danger of hell is far more real, far more certain, infinitely more terrible and, for some, far more imminent than the danger of nuclear war."

REMOVAL

The Bible presents us with not a few lurid pictures of the dissolution of the universe. Here are some of them: "Therefore will I shake the heavens, and the earth shall be removed out of her place, in the wrath of the Lord of hosts, and in the day of His fierce anger" (Isaiah 13:13). "The heavens shall vanish away like smoke, and the earth shall wax old like a garment" (Isaiah 51:6). "Heaven and earth shall pass away" (Mark 13:31). "They will perish; they shall all wax old as doth a garment; and as a vesture shalt Thou fold them up, and they shall be changed" (Hebrews 1:11,12). "The heavens shall pass away with a great noise, and the elements shall melt with fervent heat; the earth also and the works that are therein shall be burned up. The heavens, being on fire, shall be dissolved, and the elements shall melt with fervent heat" (2 Peter 3:10,12). "From whose face the earth and the heavens fled away, and there was found no place for them" (Revelation 20:11). The world's greatest poet borrowed imagery from that titanic paragraph in a great passage of *The Tempest:*

The cloud-capped towers, the gorgeous palaces,
The solemn temples, the great globe itself,
Yea, all which it inherit, shall dissolve
And, like this insubstantial pageant faded,
Leave not a rack behind.

Ultimately, the Lord Jesus, "without whom was not anything made that was made" (John 1:2) and by whom God "made the worlds" (Hebrews 1:2), will one day write *Finis* to the history of the world.

Think on the day, when this vast earth shall be
In bursting flames dissolved, those skies so broad
Shrunk like a shrivelled scroll – prepare to meet thy God!

RENEWAL
Many people nowadays are more taken up with establishing the so-called Welfare State than with anticipating the Eternal State, but a million years from now which will matter more? And even now belief in the reality of the Eternal State can give purpose and goal to human living. For unless we can be sure of the final well-being of the universe, the Welfare State will only minister to our extension pending extinction. Because the Bible assures us that, despite all appearances to the contrary, this is God's world and that, when it is done away, He will provide for us a fairer and a better, life now is worthwhile. The ultimate determines the value and even the desirability of the proximate. The Word of God declares in no uncertain terms that all will be well for ever with the saints. "Then cometh the End, when He shall have delivered up the kingdom to God, even the Father, and when all things shall have been subdued unto Him, then shall the Son also Himself be subject unto Him that put all things under Him, that God may be all in all" (1 Corinthians 15:24,28). Or, as James Moffatt trimly puts it: "God will be everything to everybody," or again as John Bengel paraphrases it: "Then all creatures will be able to say: 'God is every-

thing to me.' "

"One day," says Billy Graham, "we shall live in a brand new world." To be sure, we shall. "Behold, I create new heavens and a new earth" (Isaiah 67:17). "We look for new heavens and a new earth, wherein righteousness is at home" (2 Peter 3:13). "He that sat upon the throne, said: 'Behold, I make all things new'" (Revelation 21:5). "I saw a new heaven and a new earth; for the first heaven and the first earth were passed away" (Revelation 21:11).

What sort of world will it be?

With the Word of God open in our hands, we can confidently say six things about it.

(1) *It will be a world of perfection*, a sinless world, a world from which evil is for ever banished, a world of spotless purity. "Sin has no place in heaven," writes Albert Turner. "Then in very truth 'that which is perfect' will have come" (1 Corinthians 13:10). The Holy of Holies, the inner shrine of the Hebrew temple, took the form of a cube. Such is the geometrical symbol of perfection, length, breadth and height being equal; and the Book of Revelation informs us that the New Jerusalem is to be built on the same symmetrical plan. It will be a beautiful place full of beautiful people. Perfection of form will be matched by perfection of character. Someone has dipped his pen in liquid gold and inscribed the following choice sentence: "As they enter the next world, the saints will be like the waters of the sea – pure white when they reach the eternal shore." "Then shall the righteous shine forth as the Sun in the kingdom of their Father" (Matthew 13:43).

(2) *It will be a world of population*. We read of "much people in heaven" (Rev. 19:1). Heaven knows nothing of the hermit. Paradise was not made for solitaries. "After this I beheld, and, lo, a great multitude which no man could number, of all nations, and kindreds, and peoples, and tongues, stood before the throne and before the Lamb, clothed with white robes, and palms in their hands" (Revelation 7:9). "God made the country: man

made the city," affirmed William Cowper. That is true of this world, but, in the next, God is going to build a city. The fall of Babylon, the City of Man, is recorded in Revelation 18, the descent from heaven of the New Jerusalem, the City of God, is related in Revelation 21. Heaven has no room for the recluse. It is a sublime society.

(3) *It will be a world of progression.* "His servants shall serve Him" (Revelation 22:3). There is nothing static or stagnant about the bliss of heaven. "My Father worketh" (John 5:17) is our Lord's description of the Deity. God is not in retirement. He is not unemployed. He is not sitting aloft on a throne, as Carlyle pictured Him, "doing nothing". He is a Worker, and, if they are to be like Him, they also must be active and constructive.

Walking once with Lyman Beecher in Greenwood Cemetery, New York, not long before he died, Henry Ward Beecher remarked: "I suppose they'll bring me out here and leave me before long, but I won't stay here." "Where will you be?" asked Lyman. "I don't know," was the slow, emphatic reply, "but somewhere in the thick of things at work for God." As F.M. Knollis has lyrically expressed it:

In that blessed world above
Work never can bring weariness,
For work itself is love.

(4) *It will be a world of pleasure.* Revelation 21 has been aptly characterized as "the Chapter of the 'No Mores' ". It is a succession of glorious negatives. "No more sea; no more death, no more sorrow, no more crying, no more pain; no more night" (vv.3,4,25). As someone has well said: "Five moments' experience of it will be better than five thousand years' meditation on it." Isaac Watts wrote of it with waking wonder:

Then we shall see His face
And never, never sin;
There from the rivers of His grace
Drink endless pleasures in.

(5) *It will be a world of praise.* The Bible pictures heaven in terms of a cosmic concerto. It portrays it as a sphere in which everything is vocal in adoration to God. All eyes in heaven are on the throne, and the eternal rafters ring with everlasting anthems that roll and reverberate like thunder. "I beheld, and I heard the voice of many angels round about the throne, and the living creatures, and the elders; and the number of them was ten thousand times ten thousand, and thousands of thousands, saying with a loud voice, Worthy is the Lamb that was slain, to receive power, and riches, and wisdom, and strength, and honour, and glory, and blessing. And every creature which is in heaven, and on the earth, and under the earth, and such as are in the sea, and all that are in them, heard I saying, Blessing, and honour, and glory, and power, be unto Him that sitteth upon the throne, and unto the Lamb for ever and ever" (Revelation 5:11–13).

"Suppose," says Spurgeon in that dramatic way of his, "someone entering heaven were to say to the redeemed: 'Suspend your songs for a moment. You have been praising Christ for two thousand years. Many of you have without cessation praised Him now for many centuries. Stop your songs for a moment. Give your songs for a moment to someone else.' What would they reply? 'Stop praising Him! No! Never! Time may stop, for it shall be no more. The world may stop, for its revolutions must cease. The universe may stop its cycles and the moving of its worlds. But for us to stop our songs – never, *never*!' "

(6) *It will be a world of permanence.* "Then cometh the End, when He shall have delivered up the Kingdom to God, even the Father; then shall the Son also Himself be subject unto Him that put all things under Him, that God may be all in all" (1 Corinthians 15:28). "That which is last lasts for

ever." "The whole Creation moves," comments Carroll E. Simcox, "and it moves toward the End, not because there is some wonderful magic of 'inevitable progress', or in evolutionary forces, but because God is drawing and directing His world toward that End."

Some reputable and highly respected writers on religious subjects surprise us at times by making flagrantly unscriptural statements. At the close of one of the best compendiums of Christian doctrine to appear this century, John S. Whale comes out with this curious assertion: "Christian doctrine will have nothing to do with an earthly eternity for the human race, as though the City of God were the goal of secular evolution here on this planet, where men will live happily ever afterwards. The only true evaluation of the world is one which recognizes the impermanence of this world. Here we have no abiding city: we seek one that is beyond history and beyond death. We are always strangers and foreigners. Our citizenship is in heaven."

While there is obvious truth in that declaration, since man is indeed a spiritual being whose deepest needs can only be met in the spiritual world, nevertheless the Scriptures envisage as the scenario of man's ultimate future not only a new *heaven* but also a new *earth*. There is, as we have seen, to be a mundane Millennium, but there is also to be a mundane element in the Eternal State, in contrast to which the Millennium will be briefer than a wink. As J. Dwight Pentecost pertinently points out: "While Christ's earthly theocratic rule is limited to one thousand years, which is sufficient time to manifest God's perfect theocracy on the earth, His reign is eternal." "He shall reign for ever and ever" (Revelation 11:15) over the mundane and the supramundane parts of His eternal empire.

The paradox is that the Wonderful End will be endless.

Where saints are clothed in spotless white
And evening's shadows never fall;
And God, the eternal Light of Light,
Is Lord of all.

BOOKS BY IAN MACPHERSON

BAKER BOOK HOUSE

Live Sermon Outlines
Usable Outlines and Illustrations
Illustrated Sermon Outlines
1001 Sermon Outlines

GRENEHURST PRESS

The Lord Gave the Word

PROPHETIC WITNESS PUBLISHING HOUSE

News of the World to Come
Dial the Future
Bright Tomorrow

FLEMING H. REVELL

God's Middleman